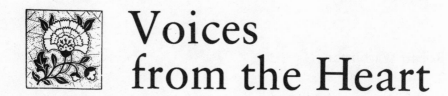

Voices
from the Heart

FOUR CENTURIES OF AMERICAN PIETY

EDITED BY

Roger Lundin
and
Mark A. Noll

WILLIAM B. EERDMANS PUBLISHING COMPANY
GRAND RAPIDS, MICHIGAN

To
Robert Warburton

Library of Congress Cataloging-in-Publication Data:

Voices from the heart.

Includes bibliographical references.
1. Christian literature, American. 2. Piety.
I. Lundin, Roger. II. Noll, Mark A., 1946-
III. Title: Four centuries of American piety.
BR53.V58   1987   242'.0973   87-441

ISBN   0-8028-3633-X

Acknowledgments

The editors would like to thank Mr. Ronald Frank, Mr. Patrick Gallo, and Mrs. Beatrice Horne for their skill and cheerfulness while helping with typing, copying, and other services in the preparation of this book. Roger Lundin would also like to thank the Wheaton College Alumni Association; its grant assisted him in his work on this book.

The editors and publisher gratefully acknowledge permission to reprint the following:

Excerpts from *Of Plymouth Plantation* by William Bradford. Ed. Samuel Eliot Morison. Copyright © 1952 by Samuel Eliot Morison; copyright © renewed 1980 by Emily M. Beck. Reprinted by permission of Alfred A. Knopf, Inc.

Selected letters by Marie of the Incarnation as found in *Women and Religion in America: A Documentary History*, vol. 2: *The Colonial and Revolutionary Periods*. Ed. Rosemary R. Ruether and Rosemary S. Keller. Copyright © 1983 by Rosemary R. Ruether and Rosemary S. Keller. Reprinted by permission of Harper & Row Publishers, Inc.

Excerpt from *God's Plot: The Paradoxes of Puritan Piety, Being the Autobiography and Journal of Thomas Shepard*. Ed. Michael McGiffert. Copyright © 1972 by the University of Massachusetts Press. Reprinted by permission.

Selected poems of Edward Taylor from *The Poems of Edward Taylor*. Ed. Donald E. Stanford. Copyright © 1960 by Yale University Press. Reprinted by permission of Donald E. Stanford.

Excerpt from "The Spiritual Travels of Nathan Cole" by Michael J. Crawford. In *William and Mary Quarterly* 33 (1976): 92-98. Reprinted by permission of the Connecticut Historical Society.

Excerpts from *The Journal and Major Essays of John Woolman*. Ed. Phillips P. Moulton. Copyright © 1971 by Phillips P. Moulton. Reprinted by permission.

Excerpts from *The Journal of Esther Edwards Burr*. Ed. Carol F. Karlsen and Laurie Crumpacker. Copyright © 1984 by Yale University Press. Reprinted by permission.

Excerpts from *The Journal and Letters of Francis Asbury*. 3 vols. Ed. Elmer T. Clark et al. Copyright © 1958 by Elmer T. Clark. Reprinted by permission of Abingdon Press.

Excerpts from *The Journal of Henry Alline*. Ed. James Beverley and Barry Moody. Copyright © 1982 by Acadia Divinity College. Reprinted by permission.

Excerpts from *The Collected Works of Abraham Lincoln*. 9 vols. Ed. Roy P. Basler. Copyright © 1953 by the Abraham Lincoln Association. Reprinted by permission of Rutgers University Press.

Excerpts from *Selected Letters*, trans. Roy A. Suelflow, in the series *Selected Writings of C. F. W. Walther*, ed. August R. Suelflow. Copyright © 1981 by Concordia Publishing House. Reprinted by permission.

Contents

Introduction

In contemporary America, the word "piety" is as likely to be met with scorn as with approval. We might expect such a reaction from the general populace of a secular culture, but it is surprising to find the same reaction among Christians. To many outside the faith, "piety" is a pejorative label describing any experience of spiritual devotion. To many Christians, the term points to complacent attitudes and moralizing practices—to an ethereal, bogus "spirituality" that is to be shunned at all costs.

Voices from the Heart is a protest against such views. In both cases, secular and Christian, the vision is too small. Piety at its best is public as well as private. It embraces the lived world as well as the secret realm of the heart. And it can inspire a broad range of service to God and humankind as well as encourage a deeper personal religion.

To gain perspective on the kind of piety featured in this book, we need the resources of history. A long view back into the Christian past as well as into the world of the noble Romans helps us recover a fuller sense of piety. It also uncovers some of the reasons why the term has recently fallen on hard times.

CHRISTIAN AND CLASSICAL ROOTS OF PIETY

For centuries prior to the modern era, the word "piety" was held in the highest regard. Figures as varied as the Roman author Virgil, the great medieval theologian Saint Augustine, the Protestant Reformer John Calvin, and America's most significant early religious thinker, Jonathan Edwards, looked upon piety as almost the sum of the good life. In the mid-sixteenth century Calvin wrote in his *Institutes of the Christian Religion* that "the first step to piety is to know that God is our Father, to protect, govern, and support us till he gathers us into the eternal inheritance of his kingdom."[1] For Calvin the practice of piety was anything but a matter of being "holier than thou" or adhering to a legalistic code of behavior. For him the term defined the essence of the Christian faith. To act in a pious manner meant to return to God through praise and obedience that which was due him. "By

1. Calvin, *Institutes of the Christian Religion*, 2.7.4.

piety," Calvin said, "I mean a reverence and love of God arising from a knowledge of his benefits."[2] According to Calvin, the pious acknowledge with reverence the glorious deeds of God the Father, God the Son, and God the Holy Spirit. Such people pattern their behavior after the divine example of redemptive concern. "Now, it may also be understood what are the fruits of repentance. They are, the duties of piety towards God, and of charity towards men, with sanctity and purity in our whole life."[3]

This conception of piety has roots in both the Roman world and the Bible. In the *Aeneid*, written only decades before the birth of Christ, the epic poet Virgil celebrated the piety of his hero, Aeneas. One of the main virtues Aeneas repeatedly demonstrates is *pietas*, an attitude of humble devotion before the gods and a humble commitment to his family, to his people, and to the mission the gods have entrusted to him. Virgil's conception of piety differs from our modern one: he is less concerned with inner states of the spirit than with outward acts. Indeed, Aeneas finds his inner desires and outward duties in almost constant conflict. He must counter a hunger for personal fulfillment with obedience to the gods, who have set before him a task ensuring the good of his people.

As important as these classical sources have been in shaping Christian ideals of piety, the Bible remains the single most important source for its definition. Many of the great figures of Scripture—Noah, Abraham and Sarah, Moses, Joseph, Ruth, David, Jeremiah, and Paul—show that genuine spirituality involves both meditation and action, both devotion and practice. Clearly, the piety of Jesus stands as the supreme example of the balance among prayer, reflection, and action. On the night before his death, he defined for his disciples the link between devotion and deeds: "If you love me, you will obey my commands" (John 14:15). In his last hours Jesus demonstrated the very "piety" he was describing to his disciples. He spent much of his final night in prayer and contemplation. Yet when the soldiers came for him, he went forth to do what his Father had willed.

Saint Augustine, writing in the fifth century as the Roman Empire was crumbling around him, paid tribute to these scriptural and Roman ideals. In his masterwork, *The City of God*, Augustine spoke with profound admiration of the example set by the early Romans. "The pagans," he explained, "subordinated their private property to the common welfare, that is to the republic and the public treasury. They resisted the temptation to avarice. They gave their counsel freely in the councils of the state. They indulged in neither public crime nor private passion."[4] Later in the same work, Au-

2. Calvin, *Institutes*, 1.2.1.

3. Calvin, *Institutes*, 3.3.16.

4. Augustine, *The City of God*, trans. Gerald G. Walsh, S.J., ed. Vernon J. Bourke et al. (Garden City, N.Y.: Image Books, 1958), p. 112.

gustine sought to correct a narrow misconception: "The word 'piety' (in Greek, *eusebia*), in its strict sense . . . ordinarily means the worship of God. However, it is also used to express a dutiful respect for parents. Moreover, in everyday speech, the word *pietas* means pity or mercy. . . . God commands us especially to practice mercy, declaring that it pleases Him as much as or even more than sacrifices. Hence God himself is spoken of as pious, in the sense of merciful."[5]

Augustine's conception of piety does not slight intense personal experience. It was, after all, this same Augustine who wrote the *Confessions,* perhaps the most probing account of personal spirituality ever written by a Christian. Yet in spite of his deep commitment to personal holiness, Augustine never viewed piety simply as a transaction between God and the individual soul. Instead, it also entailed a series of attitudes and actions toward others.

WHAT WE MEAN BY "AMERICAN PIETY"

A broad ideal of piety has served as the framework for this book. In other words, we include under "piety" the meanings offered by the Oxford English Dictionary: "habitual reverence and obedience to God (or the gods); devotion to religious duties and observances; godliness, devoutness, religiousness."

We have limited the selections that follow to expressions of Christian piety. To do this does not deny that other religions contain powerful and moving expressions of piety, nor does it deny the sometimes striking parallels between expressions of piety from different religions. Many of the book's readings, for example, illustrate attitudes with which the virtuous Romans would have been pleased. The restriction to Christian piety grows rather from an attempt to give the book conceptual coherence. It also expresses the editors' stance: as Christians, we are eager to promote a fuller understanding of Christian piety in the late twentieth century.

Similarly, the book is limited to *American* piety, not because Americans have been more pious than other people, and certainly not because America is, in a religious sense, a new Promised Land. This restriction is instead a convenience, something that provides a necessary focus. Our anthology features Christians who happened to live in North America, where they recorded the expressions of their faith. In only a few of the selections does "America" take on a different meaning with specific reference to the political ideals that have developed on these shores.

5. Augustine, *The City of God*, p. 188.

In fact, it has been a relatively easy task to assemble accounts of noteworthy, moving, challenging, or otherwise intriguing piety within our broader
definition of the term. As we use it, it pertains to religious conversion and to
ecstatic mystical experience. But it also includes the struggles of faith against
adversity, doubt, illness, and death. It often has very much to do with domestic relationships, parents and children, husbands and wives. It is sometimes
formally ecclesiastic, and sometimes not. It arises both from the activism of
evangelism and the sincerity of social service. Occasionally it speaks for the
affairs of the nation at large.

In addition, we have tried to collect examples of piety from both the well-
known and the obscure, from individuals standing outside the churches as
well as those who have been pillars of their denominations. We do not
endorse every religious conviction or practice found in this book. But we do
think that each one contributes to a fuller understanding of the many dimensions of piety. Moreover, each one possesses some intrinsic human interest
to recommend its reading and re-reading in our day, a day very different
from the times in which most of these selections were written.

Given the broad conception of piety that we employ, it is fitting that our
selections come from many different genres. There are at least eleven represented, including diaries, letters, sermons, lyric poems, short stories, novels,
journals, histories, political treatises, anecdotes, and autobiographies.
American men and women have employed myriad means of expressing their
"habitual reverence and obedience to God; [their] devotion, . . . godliness,
devoutness, religiousness." We have tried to suggest the breadth of these
expressions, the richness of the voices raised, in the variety of genres chosen.

At the same time, however, it is necessary to account for the conventional
assumption that piety involves only the inner life, that it is irrelevant to the
real concerns of the real world. To see how this attitude developed, we must
return to the age of the Puritans and to the changes that time has wrought
with their legacy.

THE PURITAN HERITAGE

The classical tradition, which viewed piety as both private and public, inspired the American Puritans. To be sure, the American practice of piety has
not by any means been limited to the forms of Puritan religion. This anthology celebrates the diversity of that devotion by presenting many more selections from Catholics and other varieties of Protestants than it does from the
Puritans and their Congregationalist descendants. It offers more from Cana-
dians and from citizens of the Midwest, the South, and the West than of New
England.

Nevertheless, the Puritan experience remains central in the American imagination, and the Puritans illustrate most clearly the links to the piety of Augustine and Virgil. The history of Puritan piety, moreover, helps show how a comprehensive ideal—love to God flowing out to faithfulness in the world—took on the more limited scope of our modern conception of the term.

America's most important twentieth-century historian, Perry Miller, recognized that "the Augustinian strain of piety" dominated the Puritan experience. It "was the inspiration for Puritan heroism and the impetus in the charge of Puritan Ironsides [during the English Civil War]. . . . It was foolishness and fanaticism to their opponents, but to themselves it was life eternal."[6] The Puritan counterpart to this intense, introspective experience of the Christian faith was a strong sense of historical destiny and public duty. Our selections from John Winthrop, William Bradford, Mary Rowlandson, and Jonathan Edwards give a sense of this commitment. Winthrop's "Model of Christian Charity" perhaps shows the two sides of Puritan piety at its finest. Winthrop preached this sermon in 1630 aboard the *Arbella,* the ship carrying the first large group of Puritans to the Massachusetts Bay Colony. The sermon speaks eloquently of the experience in which "Christ comes and takes possession of the soul and infuseth another principle, love to God and our brother."[7] In sober language, Winthrop tells his fellow Puritans about their need to remain bound to Christ as devoted individuals. At the same time, he warns them that they dare not forget their covenantal duties and communal loyalties. If they are faithless in their relationship with God, he tells them, they will face the certain destruction of their great enterprise:

> Now the only way to avoid this shipwreck, and to provide for our posterity, is to follow the counsel of Micah, to do justly, to love mercy, to walk humbly with our God. For this end, we must be knit together in this work as one man. . . . We must delight in each other, make other's conditions our own, rejoice together, mourn together, labour and suffer together, always having before our eyes our commission and community in the work, our community as members of the same body.[8]

As noble as this vision of piety may have been, it did not retain its hold upon the American spirit for long. Sydney Ahlstrom, the Yale historian of religion, is most certainly correct when he claims that to understand Puritan-

6. Miller, *The New England Mind,* vol. 1: *The Seventeenth Century* (New York: Macmillan, 1939), pp. 3-5.

7. Winthrop, "A Model of Christian Charity." A convenient modern edition of this work is found in *The Puritans in America: A Narrative Anthology,* ed. Alan Heimert and Nicholas Delbanco (Cambridge: Harvard University Press, 1985); the quotation here is from p. 87.

8. Winthrop, "A Model of Christian Charity," p. 91.

ism we must do away with "the sharp distinction moderns make between the sacred and the secular."[9] Yet this distinction emerged very early in the Puritan experience. The destiny of America was to experience this split between inward religion and outward duty, and to experience it early in our history. The very freedom that brought Winthrop's Puritans to Massachusetts Bay and a closely related group of "Pilgrims" to Plymouth nourished a spirit of individualism that gravely weakened their communities.

This disruptive process was clearly at work among the Puritans in their early years. A plaintive passage from William Bradford's *Of Plymouth Plantation* describes the breakup of the original church at Plymouth in 1632. Only twelve years after Bradford and his companions had arrived in the New World and only two years after Winthrop had preached his sermon celebrating the "city upon a hill," a number of the Puritans at Plymouth were losing the older sense of piety as outward duty: "No man thought he could live except he had cattle and a great deal of ground to keep them, all striving to increase their stocks. By which means they were scattered all over the Bay quickly. . . . And if this had been all, it had been less, though too much; but the church must also be divided, and those that had lived so long together in Christian and comfortable fellowship must now part and suffer many divisions."[10]

This split between the inner life and outer duty in America became increasingly evident during the century that followed. In a letter he wrote several weeks before his death in 1790, Benjamin Franklin told Ezra Stiles, the president of Yale College at that time, that he had "some doubts as to" the divinity of Jesus. Yet this uncertainty did not trouble Franklin: "I do not perceive that the Supreme takes it amiss, by distinguishing the unbelievers in His government of the world with any peculiar marks of his displeasure."[11] It matters not what a person believes, Franklin seemed to say, so long as his public demeanor is one of sobriety, industry, and decency. "I have ever let others enjoy their religious sentiments," Franklin told Stiles, "without reflecting on them for those that appeared to me unsupportable and even absurd."[12]

St. Jean de Crèvecoeur, a Frenchman who settled in America in the late eighteenth century, wrote glowingly of how, in America, the "various Chris-

---

9. Ahlstrom, *A Religious History of the American People* (New Haven: Yale University Press, 1972), p. 21.

10. Bradford, *Of Plymouth Plantation*, conveniently available in the Modern Library College Edition, ed. Francis Murphy (New York: Modern Library, 1981); the quot. here is from pp. 281-82.

11. Franklin, "Letter to Ezra Stiles," in *The Norton Anthology of American Literature*, vol. 1, 2nd ed., ed. Nina Baym et al. (New York: W. W. Norton, 1985), pp. 388-89.

12. Franklin, "Letter to Ezra Stiles," p. 389.

tian sects introduced wear out, and how religious indifference becomes prevalent." When a number of like-minded zealots gather together, they erect a temple and "there worship the Divinity agreeably to their own peculiar ideas. Nobody disturbs them." Nobody disturbed them because religious beliefs and practices, if not publicly offensive, were becoming less consequential: "If they are peaceable subjects, and are industrious, what is it to their religious neighbors how and in what manner they think fit to address their prayers to the Supreme Being?"[13]

The comments from Franklin and Crèvecoeur spoke for a trend. The early Puritans thought that reality was defined by a covenant between God, both terrifying and loving, and his people, both individuals and communities. By contrast, in a more modern America, the most important relationship was between the land, or the national spirit, and the striving individual. The life that individuals led "on the inside" became less and less relevant to the arena in which the public "persona" functioned. Religion as such certainly remained alive in the age of Franklin and thereafter. And many people would live out lives of full-orbed piety in the nineteenth and twentieth centuries. But the process of separating the inner self from the public self—piety of heart from piety in action—had begun. This division was one of the characteristics that anticipated the later secularization of American life.

PIETY IN THE SECULAR CONTEXT

Incipient in the earliest Puritan experiences and increasingly pervasive over the last two hundred years, this process of secularization has had a dramatic impact upon the practice of piety. Most importantly, it has obscured the model envisioned by Virgil, Augustine, and the early Puritans. Even when Christians have sought to bring public and private piety together, they have met, at best, with mixed success. In many instances they have found their Christian distinctives absorbed by a bland civil religion. On other occasions a piety offering a distinct public alternative to the civil faith has been dismissed as the raving of religious fanaticism.

Thus piety in America has been subject to striking ambiguities. What is intensely experienced as inward devotion may appear irrelevant to public life. What affects public existence may seem to lack the root of real religion. Yet this is far from the whole story. Piety reflecting the earlier ideal has never died out. To be sure, most of the selections in this volume are writings of a private nature, be they letters, diaries, or spiritual autobiographies. At the

---

13. Crèvecoeur, "Letter III: What Is an American?" in *Letters from an American Farmer and Sketches of Eighteenth-Century America* (New York: Penguin Books, 1981), p. 68.

same time, however, these records of private devotion invariably have a social consequence, a moral outcome, a public echo, something that keeps them from being merely private. Sometimes—as with the Puritans and an occasional later figure of great stature such as Abraham Lincoln, Reinhold Niebuhr, or Martin Luther King, Jr.—piety finds a convincing and directly public voice. Through the selections we intend to highlight the authenticity of private devotion, but never as a category separated from public faithfulness.

The creation of separate spheres—an outer secular one and an inner sacred one—has led to an impoverishment of public dialogue in American history. On the brighter side, it has also contributed to the development of extraordinarily diverse individual practices. Disparate traditions have grown heartily in the free soil of America. As people who till a parched public ground, we eagerly turn to cultivate our gardens of religious experience. Some of these experiences are rooted in the rich heritage of medieval Catholic mysticism and early Protestant Pietism; others have grown, remarkably, in the stony ground of slavery; still others are offshoots from European ethnic or ecclesiastical vines.

Our anthology seeks to document and celebrate this diversity. It would be easier, perhaps, to lament the loss of a consensus of belief and practice among Christians on the North American continent, and indeed, many are painfully aware of the vexing problems created by the teeming diversity of Christian experience in the New World. But mere lamentation will not lead to genuine reconciliation. In the providence of God, we have been brought to a point in history at which we must acknowledge the prolific complexity of spiritual experience, even within the Christian church. To do less than that is to be dishonest. It is also to lose a unique opportunity to hear those other voices that are part of a great chorus of adoration, service, and wonder.

On the surface it may appear that nothing but the principle of sheer diversity unifies the separate plants that have sprung from the North American spiritual soil. It is hard to imagine what genetic code could be common to these myriad offshoots. And yet that is the mystery of faith that blooms so luxuriantly in a barren terrain. The sensitive ear may be able to hear, however faintly at times, a harmony in the rustling of so many different plantings. The sensitive eye may be able to see, through a glass darkly, how each of these branches runs from a vine sustained in the soil of sacrificial love.

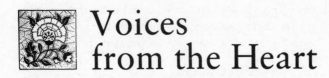

Voices
from the Heart

JOHN WINTHROP (1588-1649)

According to the eminent historian Edmund S. Morgan, John Winthrop stands as a noble illustration of "the central Puritan dilemma, the problem of doing right in a world that does wrong." The "question of what responsibility a righteous man owes to society" troubled Winthrop and other Puritan leaders as they sought a balance between the demands of personal and practical public duty.

In 1629, while still in England, Winthrop was elected the first governor of the Massachusetts Bay Colony. He remained in that post for the better part of the next twenty years. As governor, Winthrop became the advocate of what we might call a public piety, a view of Christianity that was not content merely to consign religious concerns to the inner life of the spirit. He took responsibility both for the daily direction of the colony and, to a significant extent, for the creation of its self-image.

Winthrop developed the concept of public piety in a powerful sermon he preached on board the ship carrying the first large contingent of Puritans to the New World in 1630. In that sermon Winthrop told his fellow colonists that because "Adam rent himself from his creator," now "every man is born with this principle in him, to love and seek himself only." Moreover, selfishness of this sort will be a constant enemy "'til Christ comes and takes possession of the soul and infuseth another principle, love to God and our brother."

To his fellow colonists, Winthrop offered a vision of community "knit together" by a bond of love. Admonishing his fellow Puritans to "follow the counsel of Micah, to do justly, to love mercy, to walk humbly with our God," Winthrop held out the covenantal promise of blessing and the threat of ruin. "For we must consider that we shall be as a city upon a hill," he told them. "The eyes of all people are upon us." (For evidence of the durability of this message, we need look no further than the 1984 presidential election, during which Ronald Reagan and Walter Mondale argued for several weeks over who had correctly interpreted Winthrop's vision of "a city upon a hill.") For two decades Winthrop labored to make New England a community of the covenant in which public and private piety were one. Although the reality of life in the New World was forever to fall short of this grand vision, Winthrop's images have served as benchmarks by which to measure the quality of community life in later America.

The selections that follow include Winthrop's sermon from 1630, first published by the Massachusetts Historical Society in 1838, as well as an address that

Winthrop delivered to the Massachusetts General Court, or legislature, in 1645. That speech attempted to call Massachusetts citizens away from the unchecked pursuit of liberty even as it reminded the legislators of how community good always involves a certain degree of self-sacrifice. The speech is taken from an 1826 edition of Winthrop's journal, in which he regularly referred to himself in the third person.

Sermon and Speech

FROM "A MODEL OF CHRISTIAN CHARITY"

It rests now to make some application of this discourse by the present design, which gave the occasion of writing of it. Herein are four things to be propounded: first the persons, secondly the work, third the end, fourth the means.

I. For the persons. We are a company professing ourselves fellow members of Christ, in which respect only though we were absent from each other many miles, and had our employments as far distant, yet we ought to account ourselves knit together by the bond of love, and live in the exercise of it, if we would have comfort of our being in Christ. This was notorious in the practise of the Christians in former times; as is testified of the Waldenses, from the mouth of one of the adversaries *Aeneas Sylvius* "mutuo [ament] penè antequam norunt," they used to love any of their own religion even before they were acquainted with them.

Secondly, for the work we have in hand. It is by a mutual consent, through a special overvaluing providence and a more than an ordinary approbation of the Churches of Christ, to seek out a place of cohabitation and consortship under a due form of government both civil and ecclesiastical. In such cases as this, the care of the public must oversway all private respects, by which, not only conscience, but mere civil policy, doth bind us. For it is a true rule that particular estates cannot subsist in the ruin of the public.

Third. The end is to improve our lives to do more service to the Lord; the comfort and increase of the body of Christ whereof we are members; that ourselves and posterity may be the better preserved from the common corruptions of this evil world, to serve the Lord and work out our salvation under the power and purity of His holy ordinances.

Fourth, for the means whereby this must be effected. They are twofold, a conformity with the work and end we aim at. These we see are extraordinary, therefore we must not content ourselves with usual ordinary means. Whatsoever we did or ought to have done when we lived in England, the same must we do, and more also, where we go. That which the most in their churches maintain as a truth in profession only, we must bring into familiar and constant practice, as in this duty of love. We must love brotherly without dissimulation; we must love one another with a pure heart fervently. We must bear one another's burthens. We must not look only on our own things, but also on the things of our brethren, neither must we think that the Lord will bear with such failings at our hands as he doth from those among whom we have lived; and that for three reasons.

I. In regard of the more near bond of marriage between Him and us, wherein He hath taken us to be His after a most strict and peculiar manner, which will make Him the more jealous of our love and obedience. So He tells the people of Israel, you only have I known of all the families of the earth, therefore will I punish you for your transgressions. Secondly, because the Lord will be sanctified in them that come near Him. We know that there were many that corrupted the service of the Lord, some setting up altars before His own, others offering both strange fire and strange sacrifices also; yet there came no fire from heaven or other sudden judgment upon them, as did upon Nadab and Abihu, who yet we may think did not sin presumptuously. Third. When God gives a special commission He looks to have it strictly observed in every article. When He gave Saul a commission to destroy Amaleck, He indented with him upon certain articles, and because he failed in one of the least, and that upon a fair pretense, it lost him the kingdom which should have been his reward if he had observed his commission.

Thus stands the cause between God and us. We are entered into covenant with Him for this work. We have taken out a commission, the Lord hath given us leave to draw our own articles. We have professed to enterprise these actions, upon these and those ends, we have hereupon besought Him of favour and blessing. Now if the Lord shall please to hear us, and bring us in peace to the place we desire, then hath He ratified this covenant and sealed our commission, [and] will expect a strict performance of the articles contained in it; but if we shall neglect the observation of these articles which are the ends we have propounded, and, dissembling with our God, shall fall to embrace this present world and prosecute our carnal intentions, seeking great things for ourselves and our posterity, the Lord will surely break out in wrath against us; be revenged of such a perjured people and make us know the price of the breach of such a covenant.

Now the only way to avoid this shipwreck, and to provide for our posterity, is to follow the counsel of Micah, to do justly, to love mercy, to walk humbly with our God. For this end, we must be knit together in this work as one man. We must entertain each other in brotherly affection, we must be willing to abridge ourselves of our superfluities, for the supply of other's necessities. We must uphold a familiar commerce together in all meekness, gentleness, patience and liberality. We must delight in each other, make other's conditions our own, rejoice together, mourn together, labour and suffer together, always having before our eyes our commission and community in the work, our community as members of the same body. So shall we keep the unity of the spirit in the bond of peace. The Lord will be our God, and delight to dwell among us as His own people, and will command a blessing upon us in all our ways, so that we shall see much more of His wisdom, power, goodness and truth, than formerly we have been acquainted with. We shall find that the God of Israel is among us, when ten of us shall be able to resist a thousand of our enemies; when He shall make us a praise and glory that men shall say of succeeding plantations, "the lord make it like that of NEW ENGLAND." For we must consider that we shall be as a city upon a hill. The eyes of all people are upon us, so that if we shall deal falsely with our God in this work we have undertaken, and so cause Him to withdraw His present help from us, we shall be made a story and a by-word through the world. We shall open the mouths of enemies to speak evil of the ways of God, and all professors for God's sake. We shall shame the faces of many of God's worthy servants, and cause their prayers to be turned into curses upon us 'til we be consumed out of the good land whither we are agoing.

And to shut up this discourse with that exhortation of Moses, that faithful servant of the Lord, in his last farewell to Israel, Deuteronomy 30. Beloved, there is now set before us life and good, death and evil, in that we are commanded this day to love the Lord our God, and to love one another, to walk in His ways and to keep His commandments and His ordinance and His laws, and the articles of our covenant with Him, that we may live and be multiplied, and that the Lord our God may bless us in the land whither we go to possess it. But if our hearts shall turn away, so that we will not obey, but shall be seduced, and worship other gods, our pleasures and profits, and serve them; it is propounded unto us this day, we shall surely perish out of the good land whither we pass over this vast sea to possess it.

Therefore let us choose life,
that we and our seed
may live by obeying His
voice and cleaving to Him,
for He is our life and
our prosperity.

SPEECH BEFORE THE GENERAL COURT

Then was the deputy governor [Winthrop] desired by the court to go up and take his place again upon the bench, which he did accordingly, and the court being about to arise, he desired leave for a little speech, which was to this effect.

I suppose something may be expected from me, upon this charge that is befallen me, which moves me to speak now to you; yet I intend not to intermeddle in the proceedings of the court, or with any of the persons concerned therein. Only I bless God, that I see an issue of this troublesome business. I also acknowledge the justice of the court, and, for mine own part, I am well satisfied, I was publicly charged, and I am publicly and legally acquitted, which is all I did expect or desire. And though this be sufficient for my justification before men, yet not so before the God, who hath seen so much amiss in my dispensations (and even in this affair) as calls me to be humble. For to be publicly and criminally charged in this court, is matter of humiliation, (and I desire to make a right use of it,) notwithstanding I be thus acquitted. If her father had spit in her face, (saith the Lord concerning Miriam,) should she not have been ashamed seven days? Shame had lien upon her, whatever the occasion had been. I am unwilling to stay you from your urgent affairs, yet give me leave (upon this special occasion) to speak a little more to this assembly. It may be of some good use, to inform and rectify the judgments of some of the people, and may prevent such distempers as have arisen amongst us. The great questions that have troubled the country, are about the authority of the magistrates and the liberty of the people. It is yourselves who have called us to this office, and being called by you, we have our authority from God, in way of an ordinance, such as hath the image of God eminently stamped upon it, the contempt and violation whereof hath been vindicated with examples of divine vengeance. I entreat you to consider, that when you choose magistrates, you take them from among yourselves, men subject to like passions as you are. Therefore when you see infirmities in us, you should reflect on your own, and that would make you bear the more with us, and not be severe censures of the failings of your magistrates, when you have continual experience of the like infirmities in yourselves and others. We account him a good servant, who breaks not his covenant. The covenant between you and us is the oath you have taken of us, which is to this purpose, that we shall govern you and judge your causes by the rules of God's laws and our own, according to our best skill. When you agree with a workman to build you a ship or house, etc., he undertakes as well for his skill as for his faithfulness, for it is his profession, and you pay him for both. But when you call one to be a magistrate, he doth not profess nor undertake to have sufficient skill for that office, nor can you furnish him with gifts, etc., therefore you must run the hazard of his skill and ability. But if he fail in faithfulness, which by his oath he is bound unto, that he must answer for. If it fall out that the case be clear to common apprehension, and the rule clear also, if he transgress here, the error is not in the skill, but in the evil of the will: it must be required of him. But if the case be doubtful, or the rule doubtful, to men of such understanding and parts as your magistrates are, if your magistrates should err here, yourselves must bear it.

For the other point concerning liberty, I observe a great mistake in the country about that. There is a twofold liberty, natural (I mean as our nature is now corrupt) and civil or federal. The first is common to man with beasts and other creatures. By this, man, as he stands in relation to man simply, hath liberty to do what he lists; it is a liberty to evil as well as to good. This liberty is incompatible and inconsistent with authority, and cannot endure the least restraint of the most just authority. The exercise and maintaining of this liberty makes men grow more evil and in time to be worse than brute beasts. . . . This is that great enemy of truth and peace, that wild beast, which all the ordinances of God are bent against, to restrain and subdue it. The other kind of liberty I call civil or federal, it may also be termed moral, in reference to the covenant between God and man, in the moral law, and the politic covenants and constitutions, amongst men themselves. This liberty is the proper end and object of authority, and cannot subsist without it; and it is a liberty to that only which is good, just, and honest. This liberty you are to stand for, with the hazard (not only of your goods, but) of your lives, if need be. Whatsoever crosseth this is not authority, but a distemper thereof. This liberty is maintained and exercised in a way of subjection to authority; it is of the same kind of liberty wherewith Christ hath made us free. The woman's own choice makes such a man her husband; yet being so chosen, he is her lord, and she is to be subject to him; yet in a way of liberty, not of bondage; and a true wife accounts her subjection her honor and freedom, and would not think her condition safe and free, but in her subjection to her husband's authority. Such is the liberty of the church under the authority of Christ, her king and husband; his yoke is so easy and sweet to her as a bride's ornaments; and if through forwardness or wantonness, etc., she shake it off, at any time, she is at no rest in her spirit, until she take it up again; and whether her lord smiles upon her, and embraceth her in his arms, or whether he frowns, or rebukes, or smites her, she apprehends the sweetness of his life in all, and is refreshed, supported, and instructed by every such dispensation of his authority over her. On the other side, ye know who they are that complain of this yoke and say, let us break their bands, etc., we will not have this man to rule over us. Even so, brethren, it will be between you and your magistrates. If you stand for your natural corrupt liberties, and will do what is good in your own eyes, you will not endure the least weight of authority, but will murmur, and oppose, and be always striving to shake off that yoke; but if you will be satisfied to enjoy such civil and lawful liberties, such as Christ allows you, then will you quietly and cheerfully submit unto that authority which is set over you, in all the administrations of it, for your good. Wherein, if we fail at any time, we hope we shall be willing (by God's assistance) to hearken to good advice from any of you, or in any other way of God; so shall your liberties be preserved, in upholding the honor and power of authority amongst you.

The deputy governor having ended his speech, the court arose, and the magistrates and deputies retired to attend their other affairs.

WILLIAM BRADFORD (1590-1657)

William Bradford, who began his life as a child of respectable but unexceptional parents in Yorkshire, England, lived to become the longtime governor of the first permanent English colony in New England and the most distinguished historian of early America. He wrote his narrative, *Of Plymouth Plantation,* for purposes of personal meditation and as a sign for future generations. Bradford wanted his descendants to learn what it cost their forefathers to settle in the New World, but even more how God had sustained a humble band of "pilgrims" who dared to brave the wilderness in pursuit of a holy life. Bradford's manuscript passed through the hands of several private owners and was even misplaced for some years before it was first published in 1856. It has become a classic of American history both because of its careful depiction of what the Plymouth settlers experienced and because of its thoughtful reflection on the ways of God.

Bradford himself was early attracted to the more extreme forms of Puritan religion and aligned himself with a group at Scrooby that had separated from the Church of England. In 1608, members of the Scrooby congregation departed England for Holland with the hope that conditions in that foreign land would be more favorable for worshiping God in purity and truth. When this hope was disappointed, Bradford and about one hundred other Separatists set off for the New World. They intended to land somewhere near the Hudson River, but their ship was blown north to Cape Cod in Massachusetts. Because they arrived at the beginning of winter in November 1620, they were not able to correct their navigational mistake, and so they settled where they were.

Bradford's group of "pilgrims" shared many of the characteristics of England's larger Puritan movement. His band of Separatists lacked some of the worldly position and wealth of other Puritans and also some of the patience to work for reform within the Anglican Church. Yet their desire to live a holy life, dedicated in every particular to the will of God, was identical to the motive that drove the larger Puritan movement. It was thus not a wrenching change when Plymouth's larger neighbor, the Massachusetts Bay Colony (itself first settled in 1630), eventually absorbed the smaller settlement of Pilgrims in 1691.

The piety of the Pilgrims as exemplified in Bradford's history was quiet yet compelling. Bradford believed that God had commissioned them to establish true worship and a just community. Piety meant acting responsibly toward God and others. "Private faith" was a contradiction in terms. God did indeed deal with individuals, both those who sought his ways and those who despised him, but always for the edification of the community. Heart religion was a necessity, but so also its manifestation in love and concern for others. Before Bradford's own pilgrimage was ended, he had ample opportunity to witness and practice these two intimately related aspects of Puritan piety.

In the selections that follow, we pick up the narrative as Bradford describes the Pilgrims' efforts to leave England for Holland.

From *Of Plymouth Plantation*

Being thus constrained to leave their native soil and country, their lands and livings, and all their friends and familiar acquaintance, it was much; and thought marvelous by many. But to go into a country they knew not but by hearsay, where they must learn a new language and get their livings they knew not how, it being a dear place and subject to the miseries of war, it was by many thought an adventure almost desperate; a case intolerable and a misery worse than death. Especially seeing they were not acquainted with trades nor traffic (by which that country doth subsist) but had only been used to a plain country life and the innocent trade of husbandry. But these did not dismay them, though they did sometimes trouble them; for their desires were set on the ways of God and to enjoy His ordinances; but they rested on His providence, and knew Whom they had believed. Yet this was not all, for though they could not stay, yet were they not suffered to go; but the ports and havens were shut against them, so as they were fain to seek secret means of conveyance, and to bribe and fee the mariners, and give extraordinary rates for their passages. And yet were they often times betrayed, many of them; and both they and their goods intercepted and surprised, and thereby put to great trouble and charge, of which I will give an instance or two and omit the rest.

There was a large company of them purposed to get passage at Boston in Lincolnshire, and for that end had hired a ship wholly to themselves and made agreement with the master to be ready at a certain day, and take them and their goods in at a convenient place, where they accordingly would all attend in readiness. So after long waiting and large expenses, though he kept not a day with them, yet he came at length and took them in, in the night. But

Source: *Of Plymouth Plantation*, ed. Samuel Eliot Morison (New York: Knopf, 1952), pp. 11–12, 66–71, 85–87, 94–95, 364–66.

when he had them and their goods aboard, he betrayed them, having beforehand complotted with the searchers and other officers to do; who took them, and put them into open boats, and there rifled and ransacked them, searching to their shirts for money, yea even the women further than became modesty; and then carried them back into the town and made them a spectacle and wonder to the multitude which came flocking on all sides to behold them. Being thus first, by these catchpoll officers rifled and stripped of their money, books and much other goods, they were presented to the magistrates, and messengers sent to inform the Lords of the Council of them; and so they were committed to ward. Indeed the magistrates used them courteously and showed them what favour they could; but could not deliver them till order came from the Council table. But the issue was that after a month's imprisonment the greatest part were dismissed and sent to the places from whence they came; but seven of the principal were still kept in prison and bound over to the assizes. . . .

[Life in Holland proved unsatisfactory for a number of reasons. The culture was foreign, the language strange, and the religion practiced by the Dutchmen unfamiliar. And so the majority of Bradford's company resolved to go to the New World, a journey that they began on September 6, 1620.]

These troubles being blown over, and now all being compact together in one ship, they put to sea again with a prosperous wind, which continued divers days together, which was some encouragement unto them; yet, according to the usual manner, many were afflicted with seasickness. And I may not omit here a special work of God's providence. There was a proud and very profane young man, one of the seamen, of a lusty, able body, which made him the more haughty; he would alway be contemning the poor people in their sickness and cursing them daily with grievous execrations; and did not let to tell them that he hoped to help to cast half of them overboard before they came to their journey's end, and to make merry with what they had; and if he were by any gently reproved, he would curse and swear most bitterly. But it pleased God before they came half seas over, to smite this young man with a grievous disease, of which he died in a desperate manner, and so was himself the first that was thrown overboard. Thus his curses light on his own head, and it was an astonishment to all his fellows for they noted it to be the just hand of God upon him.

After they had enjoyed fair winds and weather for a season, they were encountered many times with cross winds and met with many fierce storms with which the ship was shroudly shaken, and her upper works made very leaky; and one of the main beams in the midships was bowed and cracked, which put them in some fear that the ship could not be able to perform the voyage. So some of the chief of the company, perceiving the mariners to fear the sufficiency of the ship as appeared by their mutterings, they entered into serious consultation with the master and other officers of the ship, to consider in time of the danger, and rather to return than to cast themselves into a desperate and inevitable peril. And truly there was great distraction and difference of opinion amongst the mariners themselves; fain would they do what could be done for their wages' sake (being now near half the seas over) and on the other hand they were loath to hazard their lives too desperately. But in examining of all opinions, the master and others affirmed they knew the ship to be strong and firm under water; and for the buckling of the main beam, there was a great iron screw the passengers brought out of Holland, which would raise the beam into his place; the which being done, the carpenter and master affirmed that with a post put under it, set firm in the lower deck and otherways bound, he would make it sufficient. And as for the decks and upper works, they would caulk them as well as they could, and though with the working of the ship they would not long keep staunch, yet there would otherwise be no great danger, if they did not overpress her with sails. So they committed themselves to the will of God and resolved to proceed.

In sundry of these storms the winds were so fierce and the seas so high, as they could not bear a knot of sail, but were forced to hull for divers days together. And in one of them, as they thus lay at hull in a mighty storm, a lusty young man called John Howland, coming upon some occasion above the gratings was, with a seele [i.e., roll] of the ship, thrown into the sea; but it pleased God that he caught hold of the topsail halyards which hung overboard and ran out at length. Yet he held his hold (though he was sundry fathoms under water) till he was hauled up by the same rope to the brim of the water, and then with a boat hook and other means got into the ship again and his life saved. And though he was something ill with it, yet he lived many years after and became a profitable member both in church and commonwealth. In all this voyage there died but one of the passengers, which was William Butten, a youth, servant to Samuel Fuller, when they drew near the coast.

But to omit other things (that I may be brief) after long beating at sea they fell with that land which is called Cape Cod; the which being made and certainly known to be it, they were not a little joyful. After some deliberation had amongst themselves and with the master of the ship, they tacked about and resolved to stand for the southward (the wind and weather being fair) to find some place about Hudson's River for their habitation. But after they had sailed that course about half the day, they fell among dangerous shoals and roaring breakers, and they were so far entangled therewith as they conceived themselves in great danger; and the wind shrinking upon them withal, they resolved to bear up again for the Cape and thought themselves happy to get out of those dangers before night overtook them, as by God's good providence they did. And the next day they got into the Cape Harbor where they rid in safety. . . .

Being thus arrived in a good harbor, and brought safe to land, they fell upon their knees and blessed the God of Heaven who had brought them over the vast and furious ocean, and delivered them from all the perils and miseries thereof, again to set their feet on the firm and stable earth, their proper element. And no marvel if they were thus joyful, seeing wise Seneca was so affected with sailing a few miles on the coast of his own Italy, as he affirmed, that he had rather remain twenty years on his way by land than pass by sea to any place in a short time, so tedious and dreadful was the same unto him.

But here I cannot but stay and make a pause, and stand half amazed at this poor people's present condition; and so I think will the reader, too, when he well considers the same. Being thus passed the vast ocean, and a sea of troubles before in their preparation (as may be remembered by that which went before), they had now no friends to welcome them nor inns to entertain or refresh their weatherbeaten bodies; no houses or much less town to repair to, to seek for succour. It is recorded in Scripture as a mercy to the Apostle and his shipwrecked company, that the barbarians showed them no small kindness in refreshing them, but these savage barbarians, when they met with them (as after will appear) were readier to fill their sides full of arrows than otherwise. And for the season it was winter, and they that know the winters of that country know them to be sharp and violent, and subject to cruel and fierce storms, dangerous to travel to known places, much more to search an unknown coast. Besides, what could they see but a hideous and desolate wilderness, full of wild beasts and wild men—and what multitudes there might be of them they knew not. Neither could they, as it were, go up to the top of Pisgah to view from this wilderness a more goodly country to feed their hopes; for which way soever they turned their eyes (save upward to the heavens) they could have little solace or content in respect of any outward objects. For summer being done, all things stand upon them with a weatherbeaten face, and the whole country, full of woods and thickets, represented a wild and savage hue. If they looked behind them, there was the mighty ocean which they had passed and was now as a main bar and gulf to separate them from all the civil parts of the world. If it be said they had a ship to succour them, it is true; but what heard they daily from the master and company? But that with speed they should look out a place (with their shallop) where they would be, at some near distance; for the season was such as he would not stir from thence till a safe harbor was discovered by them, where they would be, and he might go without danger; and that victuals consumed apace but he must and would keep sufficient for themselves and their return. Yea, it was muttered by some that if they got not a place in time, they would turn them and their goods ashore and leave them. Let it also be considered what weak hopes of supply and succour they left behind them, that might bear up their minds in this sad condition and trials they were under; and they could not but be very small. It is true, indeed, the affections and love of their brethren at Leyden was cordial and entire towards them, but they had little power to help them of themselves; and how the case stood between them and the merchants at their coming away hath already been declared.

What could now sustain them but the Spirit of God and His grace? May not and ought not the children of these fathers rightly say: "Our fathers were Englishmen which came over this great ocean, and were ready to perish in this wilderness; but they cried unto the Lord and He heard their voice and looked on their adversity," etc. [Deut. 26:5, 7]. "Let them therefore praise the Lord, because He is good: and His mercies endure forever." "Yea, let them which have been redeemed of the Lord, shew how He hath delivered them from the hand of the oppressor. When they wandered in the desert wilderness out of the way, and found no city to dwell in, both hungry and thirsty, their soul was overwhelmed in them. Let them confess before the Lord His lovingkindness and His wonderful works before the sons of men" [Ps. 107:1-5, 8]. . . .

[Bradford next relates how the new residents swore to uphold the ways of God, the laws of the King of England, and each other's health. This was the famous Mayflower Compact. Bradford then provides further details, including a description of a first winter of nearly unendurable harshness.]

But that which was most sad and lamentable was, that in two or three months' time half of their company died, especially in January and February, being the depth of winter, and wanting houses and other comforts; being infected with the scurvy and other diseases which this long voyage and their inaccommodate condition had brought upon them. So as there died some times two or three of a day in the foresaid time, that of 100 and odd persons, scarce fifty remained. And of these, in the time of the most distress, there was but six or seven sound persons who to their great commendations, be it spoken, spared no pains night nor day, but with abundance of toil and hazard of their own health, fetched them wood, made them fires, dressed them meat, made their beds, washed their loathsome clothes, clothed and unclothed them. In a word, did all the homely and necessary offices for them which dainty and queasy stomachs cannot endure to hear named; and all this willingly and cheerfully, without any grudging in the least, showing herein their true love unto their friends and brethren; a rare example and worthy to be remembered. Two of these seven were Mr. William Brewster, their reverend Elder, and Myles Standish, their Captain and military commander, unto whom myself and many others were much beholden in our low and sick condition. And yet the Lord so upheld these persons as in this general calamity they were not at all infected either with sickness or lameness. And what I have said of these I may say of many others who died in this general visitation, and others yet living; that whilst they had health, yea, or any strength continuing, they were not wanting to any that had need of them. And I doubt not but their recompense is with the Lord.

But I may not here pass by another remarkable passage not to be forgotten. As this calamity fell among the passengers that were to be left here to plant, and were hasted ashore and made to drink water that the seamen might have the more beer, and one in his sickness desiring but a small can of beer, it was answered that if he were their own father he should have none. The disease began to fall amongst them also, so as almost half of their company died before they went away, and many of their officers and lustiest men, as the boatswain, gunner, three quartermasters, the cook and others. At which the Master was something strucken and sent to the sick ashore and told the Governor he should send for beer for them that had need of it, though he drunk water homeward bound.

But now amongst his company there was far another kind of carriage in this misery than amongst the passengers. For they that before had been boon companions in drinking and jollity in the time of their health and welfare, began now to desert one another in this calamity, saying they would not hazard their lives for them, they should be infected by coming to help them in their cabins; and so, after they came to lie by it, would do little or nothing for them but, "if they died, let them die." But such of the passengers as were yet aboard showed them what mercy they could, which made some of their hearts relent, as the boatswain (and some others) who was a proud young man and would often curse and scoff at the passengers. But when he grew weak, they had compassion on him and helped him; then he confessed he did not deserve it at their hands, he had abused them in word and deed. "Oh!" (saith he) "you, I now see, show your love like Christians indeed one to another, but we let one another lie and die like dogs." Another lay cursing his wife, saying if it had not been for her he had never come this unlucky voyage, and anon cursing his fellows, saying he had done this and that for some of them; he had spent so much and so much amongst them, and they were now weary of him and did not help him, having need. Another gave his companion all he had, if he died, to help him in weakness; he went and got a little spice and made him a mess of meat once or twice. And because he died not so soon as he expected, he went amongst his fellows and swore the rogue would cozen him, he would see him choked before he made him any more meat; and yet the poor fellow died before morning. . . .

[Bradford goes on to record that those Pilgrims who survived that first winter bid a fearful farewell to the *Mayflower* in the spring of 1621. He also makes a laconic note of his appointment as the company's governor.]

They now began to dispatch the ship away which brought them over, which lay till about this time, or the beginning of April. The reason on their part why she stayed so long, was the necessity and danger that lay upon them; for it was well towards the end of December before she could land anything here, or they able to receive anything ashore. Afterwards, the 14th of January, the house which they had made for a general rendezvous by casualty fell afire, and some were fain to retire aboard for shelter; then the sickness began to fall sore amongst them, and the weather so bad as they could not make much sooner any dispatch. Again, the Governor and chief of them, seeing so many die and fall down sick daily, thought it no wisdom to send away the ship, their condition considered and the danger they stood in from the Indians, till they could procure some shelter; and therefore thought it better to draw some more charge upon themselves and friends than hazard all. The master and seamen likewise, though before they hasted the passengers ashore to be gone, now many of their men being dead, and of the ablest of them (as is before noted), and of the rest many lay sick and weak; the master durst not put to sea till he saw his men begin to recover, and the heart of winter over.

Afterwards they (as many as were able) began to plant their corn, in which service Squanto stood them in great stead, showing them both the manner how to set it, and after how to dress and tend it. Also he told them, except they got fish and set with it in these old grounds it would come to nothing. And he showed them that in the middle of April they should have store enough to come up the brook by which they began to build, and taught them how to take it, and where to get other provisions necessary for them. All which they found true by trial and experience. Some English seed they sowed, as wheat and pease, but it came not to good, either by the badness of the seed or lateness of the season or both, or some other defect.

In this month of April, whilst they were busy about their seed, their Governor (Mr. John Carver) came out of the field very sick, it being a hot day. He complained greatly of his head and lay down, and within a few hours his senses failed, so as he never spake more till he died, which was within a few days after. Whose death was much lamented and caused great heaviness amongst them, as there was cause. He was buried in the best manner they could, with some volleys of shot by all that bore arms. And his wife, being a weak woman, died within five or six weeks after him.

Shortly after, William Bradford was chosen Governor in his stead, and being not recovered of his illness, in which he had been near the point of

death, Isaac Allerton was chosen to be an assistant unto him who, by renewed election every year, continued sundry years together. Which I here
note once for all. . . .

[Bradford's narrative then traces the life and times of the humble yet
persevering settlers at Plymouth. Toward the end of his own life, he paused
to memorialize the death of the Reverend William Brewster, who had minis-
tered to the Pilgrims "above 36 years in England, Holland and in this wilderness." This memorial led Bradford to reflect on the long life enjoyed by the
Pilgrims who had survived the brutal early days of the settlement in
America.]

I cannot but here take occasion not only to mention but greatly to admire
the marvelous providence of God! That notwithstanding the many changes
and hardships that these people went through, and the many enemies they
had and difficulties they met withal, that so many of them should live to very
old age! It was not only this reverend man's condition (for one swallow
makes no summer as they say) but many more of them did the like, some
dying about and before this time and many still living, who attained to sixty
years of age, and to sixty-five, divers to seventy and above, and some near
eighty as he did. It must needs be more than ordinary and above natural
reason, that so it should be. For it is found in experience that change of air,
famine or unwholesome food, much drinking of water, sorrows and troubles, etc., all of them are enemies to health, causes of many diseases, consum-
ers of natural vigour and the bodies of men, and shorteners of life. And yet of
all these things they had a large part and suffered deeply in the same. They
went from England to Holland, where they found both worse air and diet
than that they came from; from thence, enduring a long imprisonment as it
were in the ships at sea, into New England; and how it hath been with them
here hath already been shown, and what crosses, troubles, fears, wants and
sorrows they had been liable unto is easy to conjecture. So as in some sort
they may say with the Apostle, 2 Corinthians xi.26, 27, they were "in jour-
neyings often, in perils of waters, in perils of robbers, in perils of their own
nation, in perils among the heathen, in perils in the wilderness, in perils in the
sea, in perils among false brethren; in weariness and painfulness, in watching
often, in hunger and thirst, in fasting often, in cold and nakedness."
    What was it then that upheld them? It was God's visitation that preserved
their spirits. Job x.12: "Thou hast given me life and grace, and thy visitation
hath preserved my spirit." He that upheld the Apostle upheld them. "They
were persecuted, but not forsaken, cast down, but perished not." "As unknown, and yet known; as dying, and behold we live; as chastened, and yet
not killed"; 2 Corinthians vi.9.

God, it seems, would have all men to behold and observe such mercies and works of His providence as these are towards His people, that they in like cases might be encouraged to depend upon God in their trials, and also to bless His name when they see His goodness towards others. Man lives not by bread only, Deuteronomy viii.3. It is not by good and dainty fare, by peace and rest and heart's ease in enjoying the contentments and good things of this world only that preserves health and prolongs life; God in such examples would have the world see and behold that He can do it without them; and if the world will shut their eyes and take no notice thereof, yet He would have His people to see and consider it. Daniel could be better liking with pulse than others were with the king's dainties. Jacob, though he went from one nation to another people and passed through famine, fears and many afflictions, yet he lived till old age and died sweetly and rested in the Lord, as infinite others of God's servants have done and still shall do, through God's goodness, notwithstanding all the malice of their enemies, "when the branch of the wicked shall be cut off before his day" (Job xv.32) "and the bloody and deceitful men shall not live [out] half their days"; Psalm lv.23.

JEAN DE BRÉBEUF (1593-1649)

Standard histories of Christianity in America regularly emphasize the important Protestant migrations of the seventeenth and following centuries. Historians are warranted in treating these developments fully in light of how important Protestantism became in the later history of the United States. Yet to neglect other sources of piety in early America impoverishes the story unduly.

Well before the first Protestant settlements in America, Catholic missionaries had proclaimed the gospel story in widely scattered parts of the North American continent. A century before active Protestant settlement, Spanish priests and brothers had accompanied those making colonizing efforts in what would later become Florida, the southwestern United States, and California. In New France (later Canada), French missionaries were already promoting the Christian faith among Native Americans before the *Mayflower* arrived off Cape Cod in 1620.

Early Catholic missionary efforts in the New World were often notable for fervent piety as well as for pioneering evangelization. Especially noteworthy were the efforts to propagate Christianity among the Indians of Canada; there French Jesuits, Ursulines, and members of other religious orders left a record of unusually faithful service.

Prominent among the early missionaries to New France was Father Jean de Brébeuf, a Jesuit. He was thirty-two when he came to Canada in 1626. He helped found the St. Louis and St. Ignatius missions near Georgian Bay, where he enjoyed considerable success in winning the friendly Huron Indians to faith in Christ. In 1930 Brébeuf, along with seven of his fellow Jesuit missionaries, was canonized by Pope Pius XI.

The document that follows is taken from *The Jesuit Relations*, a massive collection of the materials sent back to France by missionaries in the New World. Brébeuf wrote this piece in 1637 to instruct his fellow missionaries on their attitudes toward the Huron Indians. It is a document that reveals an unusual sensitivity toward the cultural integrity of the Native Americans, perhaps because the author himself was so touched by the universal message of the Christian gospel.

Instructions for the Fathers of Our Society Who Shall Be Sent to the Hurons

The Fathers and Brethren whom God shall call to the holy Mission of the Hurons ought to exercise careful foresight in regard to all the hardships, annoyances, and perils that must be encountered in making this journey, in order to be prepared betimes for all emergencies that may arise.

You must have sincere affection for the Savages,—looking upon them as ransomed by the blood of the son of God, and as our Brethren with whom we are to pass the rest of our lives.

To conciliate the Savages, you must be careful never to make them wait for you in embarking.

You must provide yourself with a tinder box or with a burning mirror, or with both, to furnish them fire in the daytime to light their pipes, and in the evening when they have to encamp; these little services win their hearts.

You should try to eat their sagamité or salmagundi in the way they prepare it, although it may be dirty, half-cooked, and very tasteless. As to the other numerous things which may be unpleasant, they must be endured for the love of God, without saying anything or appearing to notice them.

It is well at first to take everything they offer, although you may not be able to eat it all; for, when one becomes somewhat accustomed to it, there is not too much.

You must try and eat at daybreak unless you can take your meal with you in the canoe; for the day is very long, if you have to pass it without eating. The Barbarians eat only at sunrise and sunset, when they are on their journeys.

You must be prompt in embarking and disembarking; and tuck up your gowns so that they will not get wet, and so that you will not carry either water or sand into the canoe. To be properly dressed, you must have your feet and legs bare; while crossing the rapids, you can wear your shoes, and, in the long portages, even your leggings.

You must so conduct yourself as not to be at all troublesome to even one of these Barbarians.

It is not well to ask many questions, nor should you yield to your desire to learn the language and to make observations on the way; this may be carried too far. You must relieve those in your canoe of this annoyance, especially as you cannot profit much by it during the work. Silence is a good equipment at such a time.

Source: *The Jesuit Relations and Allied Documents,* published in English by Burrows Brothers, Cleveland, in 1898 and following years.

You must bear with their imperfections without saying a word, yes, even without seeming to notice them. Even if it be necessary to criticize anything, it must be done modestly, and with words and signs which evince love and not aversion. In short, you must try to be, and to appear, always cheerful.

Each one should be provided with half a gross of awls, two or three dozen little knives called jambettes (pocket-knives), a hundred fish-hooks, with some beads of plain and colored glass, with which to buy fish or other articles when the tribes meet each other, so as to feast the Savages; and it would be well to say to them in the beginning, "Here is something with which to buy fish." Each one will try, at the portages, to carry some little thing, according to his strength; however little one carries, it greatly pleases the savages, if it be only a kettle.

You must not be ceremonious with the Savages, but accept the comforts they offer you, such as a good place in the cabin. The greatest conveniences are attended with very great inconvenience, and these ceremonies offend them.

Be careful not to annoy anyone in the canoe with your hat; it would be better to take your nightcap. There is no impropriety among the Savages.

Do not undertake anything unless you desire to continue it; for example, do not begin to paddle unless you are inclined to continue paddling. Take from the start the place in the canoe that you wish to keep; do not lend them your garments, unless you are willing to surrender them during the whole journey. It is easier to refuse at first than to ask them back, to change, or to desist afterwards.

Finally, understand that the Savages will retain the same opinion of you in their own country that they will have formed on the way; and one who passed for an irritable and troublesome person will have considerable difficulty afterwards in removing this opinion. You have to do not only with those of your own canoe, but also (if it must be so stated) with all those of the country; you meet some today and others tomorrow, who do not fail to inquire, from those who brought you, what sort of man you are. It is almost incredible, how they observe and remember even the slightest fault. When you meet Savages on the way, as you cannot yet greet them with kind words, at least show them a cheerful face, and thus prove that you endure gayly the fatigues of the voyage. You will thus have put to good use the hardships on the way, and have already advanced considerably in gaining the affection of the Savages.

This is a lesson which is easy enough to learn, but very difficult to put into practice; for, leaving a highly civilized community, you fall into the hands of barbarous people who care but little for your Philosophy or your Theology. All the fine qualities which might make you loved and respected in France are like pearls trampled under the feet of swine, or rather mules, which utterly despise you when they see that you are not as good pack animals as they are. If you could go naked, and carry the load of a horse upon your back, as they do, then you would be wise according to their doctrine, and would be recognized as a great man, otherwise not. Jesus Christ is our true greatness; it is He alone and His cross that should be sought in running after these people, for, if you strive for anything else, you will find naught but bodily and spiritual affliction. But having found Jesus Christ in His cross, you have found the roses in the thorns, sweetness in bitterness, all in nothing.

MARIE OF THE INCARNATION
(1599-1672)

Marie Guyart was born in Tours, France, in 1599. She was married at seventeen, bore a son, and then was widowed. After pursuing the life of a merchant for over ten years, she entered the convent. She joined the Ursuline order and became known as Marie of the Incarnation. Eventually she felt called to join the mission to the Indians in New France, and in 1640 she came to Canada as the first French woman missionary to the New World.

From Quebec City, Marie wrote over 13,000 letters back to France about the nature of her work and the state of her soul. Many of these letters were addressed to her son, Claude. He had at first resented his mother's entering the convent, and even more her decision to go to the New World. But eventually he was reconciled to her religious vocation, and he himself became an abbot of a Benedictine monastery in France.

Marie's letters bear out the saying of G. K. Chesterton that "mysticism" is "only a transcendent form of common sense," for she was an individual who combined to an unusual degree concentration on the tasks of this life and contemplation of the unseen world. She was a woman of great energy, and her facility with the Indian languages made her an especially valuable member of the mission, as the list of translating activities mentioned in one of the letters below testifies.

At the same time, however, she did not neglect the inner life. It was especially the person of Christ—his work, his moral beauty, and his all-encompassing perfections—that provided the occasion for her rapturous meditations. On rare occasions she shared these with her son, as in the letter from 1647 reproduced here.

The fervency of Marie's devotion should serve as a reminder that the stream of piety is fed by many tributaries, that its waters are enriched through the lives of women as well as men, and that its central current, in the Old World as well as the New, is the response of the soul in Christ.

Selected Letters

From Quebec, to her son, summer 1647

My very dear and well-beloved Son, the peace of our most lovable and most adorable Jesus be with you.

I received your letter and everything in the package when I was not expecting it anymore. . . . You reproach me for a lack of affection which I can not bear to leave without response, since I am still alive as is God's will. You have some ground to complain about my leaving you. And for myself, I would gladly complain, if I had permission from the one who brought the sword on the earth to make such strange separations. It is true that despite the fact that you were the only thing in the world left for me to which my heart was attached, He still wanted to separate us when you still were at the breast, and I fought almost twelve years more to keep you before it was necessary to part from one another. At last it was necessary to submit to the strength of Divine love and accept this wound of separation, more painful than I can describe to you; this did not stop me from reproaching myself a thousand times for being the cruelest of mothers. I ask your forgiveness my dearest son; you suffered a great deal because of me. However, let us console ourselves in the fact that life is short and that we shall have, thanks to the mercy of Him who separated us in the world, the whole eternity to see each other and to rejoice in Him. . . .

You wish to know how God works in me. I would be happy to tell you so that you can bless this eneffable goodness which so lovingly calls us into its service. However, you know that there is so much danger that these letters might fall into other hands, that the fear that this may happen prevents me. However, I assure you that in the following I will not hide anything of my present state of mind from you: at least I shall describe it so clearly that you will be able to know of it. To tell the truth I feel I owe that to a son who consecrated his life to the service of my divine master and with whom I share the same spirit. Here is a record which will show you in what disposition of mind I was when I recovered from my sickness almost two years ago. Not that I indulge in recording my feelings if it is not necessary; but at that time a sentence of Holy Scripture so drew my mind that, because of my weakness, incapable of sustaining this excitement, I was forced to calm myself by

Source: Christine Allen, "Women in Colonial French America," in *Women and Religion in America: A Documentary History*, vol. 2: *The Colonial and Revolutionary Periods*, ed. Rosemary Radford Ruether and Rosemary Skinner Keller (San Francisco: Harper & Row, 1983), pp. 107-110, 102-3.

taking my pen and writing these few words, which will let you know the path through which this infinite Goodness leads me. . . .

Since my sickness my interior disposition has been characterized by a very particular detachment from all things, so that all exterior things are a cross to me. They do not trouble me, though, for I suffer them by accepting God's orders which put me in a state of obedience in which nothing can happen to me except from Him. I feel in me something which gives me a steady inclination to follow and embrace what I know to be best for the glory of God and what seems most perfect in the maxims of the Gospel, conforming to my situation, everything under the direction of my Superior. I make endless mistakes which extremely humiliate me.

For almost three years I have been thinking of death all of the time; however, I do not want, and can not want, either life or death, but only Him who is the Master of life and death, according to whose adorable judgement I commit myself to doing whatever He in eternity arranged for me. These feelings give my soul and my body a fundamental peace and a spiritual food which helps me to survive and support all kinds of accidents and all the things, general or particular, which happen to others or to me with a balanced mind—in this part of the world, where it is easy to find occasion to practice patience and other virtues that I do not have.

Anyway, do not rejoice, as you say, at the fact that you have a mother who serves God with purity and fidelity; but after having given thanks to this ineffable Goodness for the favours I am filled with, ask Him forgiveness for my infidelities and spiritual impurities; I ask you not to forget that, and to ask for the opposite virtues. Here then is this record I described; I copy it because it is only a rough copy composed without any purpose and only to comfort a weak head. After reading these words of the Prophet: *Speciosus forma proe filiis hominum* (You are the most beautiful of the children of man. Ps. 44,3), a light filled my mind with the double beauty of the Son of God, and I had to clarify my mind with my pen, but without thinking, because the spirit did not allow it. Since it was to the second person of the Holy Trinity that my soul had access, it was to Him that my aspirations were directed, following the ways of the spirit. Everything is ineffable at its foundation, but this is what can be expressed:

You are the most beautiful of all the children of man, O my Beloved! You are beautiful, my dear Love, in both your divine and human beauty.

You are beautiful, my dear Love, and you transport my mind in an interior vision of what you are in your Father and of what your Father is in You. But how could I stand before your splendours, unless you ravished my heart and mind. In this ravishing you brought it to yourself allowing it to be one with you. So even though I see you as God of God, Light of Light and True God of True God, still I kiss you as being my Love and all my goal.

O my Divine Spouse! How is this? I see you belonging to your Father and you belong to me: your Father and you belong to me; your Father also belongs to me and I do not know how this came about.

I see myself in the One in Whom I do that which I desire by the power that this One gives to me, who is my Love and my Life.

O my dear Beloved: In this familiarity which entices my soul I feel I am losing myself in a bottomless abyss. You are this profound abyss, You who hold me with Your power; and then, oh Father, at the same time You inspire me in such a way that I talk to You as if I had power over You.

Forgive my liberty, of which You are Yourself the cause, because in this state you consume me.

This opening you made in my heart, which is continually inhaling, breathing, and sighing, is a mouth which tells you words which would kill the body, if it had to go through the senses, since everything comes to saying that I see You to be essentially Love! Love! Having made me sing this canticle which makes me find myself in You again and again, You render me mute.

I am powerless by a consumption of love in You that I can not express: I can see aspects of your greatness and of your loving actions, O Uncreated Word, they destroy my thoughts in a deep abyss where they become lost.

You know, my dear Spouse, what occurred in my heart at the words my spiritual Father told me after having received my confession: that even if I should die alone and away from him, because of the channel you provide to my soul, I should not be afraid, otherwise I would not treat You like a spouse in whom I must have confidence. My spirit is still touched by these words: to not see you as a Spouse, that is unbearable; that is why, after that, I did not worry about anything anymore.

My beloved, I used to tell You, You know all my affairs; take care of them for me, You know how many souls I am responsible for, presenting them every day to Your Father or Your divine heart; today I am so sick and so weak, that I could not do it any more. I abandon myself to Your will.

After that I felt discharged of all my worries, and my heart aspiring towards You, I spoke with You from time to time, as if abandoned in you: my beloved, you are taking care of my affairs, my dear Love, You took on the responsibility.

I felt annoyed when my Father commanded me to ask You what place You would give me if you called me near You. Because, my dear Love, I so much abandoned myself to Your desires that I barely considered what would become of me.

I asked you, anyway, what obedience wanted me to; but while asking You I felt transported in this abandonment: put me where You want, everywhere You will be my Love. I hope I shall see You in Your double divine beauty—human among the splendour of the saints on the day of Your victory. You, my Beloved, Who, for the love of men became man and visible to make men divine through participation.

I joyfully await your final coming, so that my soul, seeing you triumph over your enemies, may sing Your Victories with You.

What I find incomprehensible to me here, is the degree of possession that your beloved will accept from You.

If my heart follows its bent, only You know the channel it has to Your divine heart.

Ah! I must finish here my dear Love, my pledge, my caution, and my life. You are all to me, and I find I belong to You in spite of my corruption and my weaknesses.

Enough of these matters, my beloved son, for this year. I am so deeply worried by external affairs, that I may only write to you during the brief moments I steal away. I also have to answer more than twenty-six letters and send the other writings to the Community in France. This is how we must spend this life, while waiting for Eternity, which does not pass away. You comforted me by informing me of the news of your holy Congregation and the happy success of its projects. For you finally only know God; remain hidden from all talk except that in which God will be glorified: otherwise remain hidden in our very adorable Jesus, our only Good, our Life, and our Totality.

*　*　*

From Quebec, to her son, 10 August, 1662

My very dear Son . . .

Despite their lovely talks of peace, the Iroquois began murdering again, near Montreal, at the beginning of Fall. Those who kill are Agneronons (Mohawks), and those who ask for peace are the Onnontageronons (Senecas) and the Oiogueronons (Oneidas); but confidence in either one is groundless.

We do not yet know what happened to Father le Moine nor to our French prisoners, nor to Father Mesnard who is staying with the Outaouok (Ottawas), with whom he was supposed to go this year and where he should already have arrived. The Iroquois, who heard about it, hid along the trails to take them prisoner and to steal all their skins. There were about three or four hundred. If they complete the journey successfully, the French merchants who come here to trade will gain a great deal; but if they are destroyed, our merchants will have made the trip for nothing. One of them told me today that he would lose, himself, more than twenty thousand pounds. But alas! All things considered, what is most deplorable is what happens to the souls of these people, most of whom are not yet Christians. If they had been able to come here they would have spent the winter here and we would have had time and opportunity to teach and baptise them. Everyone gravitates to what he likes: the merchants to money, the Fathers and us to souls. This last motive can be a strong spear, to pierce and inspire the heart. Last winter I had three or four young sisters staying near me hoping to learn what I know about the languages of the country. Their strong and fervent desire gave me the ardor and requisite strength to instruct them orally and in writing all that was necessary. From Advent to the end of February I wrote a Huron Catechism, three Algonquin Catechisms, all the Christian prayers in that language, and a big Algonquin dictionary for them. I became extremely tired, I assure you, but it was necessary to satisfy these hearts wishing to serve God in the functions our Institution demands. Pray to the Divine Goodness that all be for His great glory. . . .

ROGER WILLIAMS (1603?-1683)

Roger Williams was a peace-loving man who spent most of his life embroiled in controversy. He was a sincere Calvinist who throughout his adulthood carried on a running battle with the Calvinistic leaders of Massachusetts. He was a Christian of intense conviction who yet offered to others the highest degree of religious liberty to be found in the New World. Altogether he was a remarkable man in a remarkable age.

Roger Williams came to Massachusetts in 1631, only a year after the first major migration of the Puritans under John Winthrop. The seriousness that he had shown in England on behalf of Puritan beliefs and practices set him apart even at that early date. He was offered the pulpit of Boston's only church, but he turned it down because of his uneasiness about the "New England Way." Eventually Williams expressed that uneasiness publicly, and so came into conflict with the leaders of Massachusetts. Williams thought that the form of church establishment in the New World too closely resembled the tyrannical church order in England. He felt strongly that believers must make a clean break, a complete separation from any form of religion that let governments determine the course of Christian faith and practice. Nothing is more abhorrent, he wrote, than "the setting up of civil power and officers to judge the conviction of men's souls." Moreover, he accused the Massachusetts authorities of stealing land from the Indians, and he questioned the legitimacy of their charter.

The result was that Williams was less than welcome in his new home. In October 1635 the Massachusetts authorities banished him, and he spent a long and bitter winter roaming in the wilderness. He finally came to the headwaters of Narragansett Bay, where he purchased land from the Indians. He called the place Providence to memorialize the protection that God had given him through the preceding winter. A new settlement—Providence Plantations—and a new colony—Rhode Island—thus came into existence.

Williams opened this colony to others who, like himself, sought liberty of the soul. Because of this policy of tolerance, Rhode Island became the early American home of Baptists, other Protestant dissenters, and even (eventually) an early congregation of Jews. Williams himself was kept very busy eking out a living, attempting to corral the sometimes unruly souls who settled in Rhode Island, carrying on his controversy—in writing—with Massachusetts authorities, and making several trips to England to secure a proper charter for his colony.

Through it all, no one questioned the sincerity and holiness of Williams's character. Like the biblical Nathaniel, he was one "in whom there was no guile." During one of his trips to London, Williams published a little book containing his thoughts on the nature of spiritual life. The book took the shape of a letter written to his wife shortly after she had recovered from a serious illness. It offers assistance to those seeking spiritual growth by describing various "experiments" to focus the soul on God and to fit it for honorable life in the world. It is a work that shows both Williams's inventive skill at metaphor and his thorough immersion in Scripture. The work's full title was *Experiments of Spiritual Life and Health and Their Preservatives, in which the weakest child of God may get assurance of his spiritual life and blessedness, and the strongest may find proportionable discoveries of his Christian growth and the means of it* (London, 1652). A modern edition with an excellent introduction has been prepared by Winthrop S. Hudson (Philadelphia: Westminster Press, 1951). The book ends with a chapter called "Helps to Preserve Spiritual Health and Cheerfulness," from which the following excerpts are taken. These words of counsel suggest what Williams meant by one of his best-known affirmations: "Having bought truth dear, we must not sell it cheap, not the least grain of it for the whole world."

From "Helps to Preserve Spiritual Health and Cheerfulness"

I am now come, dear love, to the third and last head proposed, which is some few means of recovering and preserving of Christian health and cheerfulness, and the preventing of spiritual sicknesses and diseases. In this I shall desire to be brief, lest by too long a discourse I discourage thy reading and hinder thy use and improvement of it.

THE FIRST HELP: SELF-EXAMINATION [IS] A MEANS OF SPIRITUAL PRESERVATION. First, then, a holy consideration of our estate, a deep and frequent examination of our spiritual condition, is an excellent means of Christian health and temper. Thus teacheth us the Holy Spirit of God by Jeremiah: "'Let us search and try our ways, and turn unto the Lord'" (Lam. 3:40). This searching and examining of our ways in God's presence is (as it were) a casting up of our accounts between God and our souls, wherein we truly verify that true saying that frequent reckoning makes God and our souls true friends. This duty is hard, and therefore we must often cry to God with David, "'Search me, O God, and try my heart, and see if there be any wicked way in me, and lead me in the way everlasting'" (Ps. 139:3, 4).

This holy practice ought to be frequent, but especially so when the hand and rod of the Lord are upon us. For then, as Job saith, God softeneth our hearts; and we are most like then to be as the ground mollified upon a thaw, fit to be broken up, or like the ground moistened with storms and showers from heaven, ready in some hopeful turn for the Lord's most gracious seed and heavenly planting.

A SECOND HELP: PRAYER WITH FASTING IS AN UNDOUBTED MEANS OF CHRISTIAN HEALTH AND CHEERFULNESS. Secondly, maintain an earnest longing and endeavor to enjoy Christ Jesus, who is our soul's life, in every holy ordinance which he hath appointed. If it be possible (with true satisfaction to our consciences and doubts in God's presence), let us never rest from being planted into the holy society of God's children, gathered into the order of Christ Jesus, according to his most holy will and testament. Let us remember that Christian health, growth, and flourishing are promised to the trees planted in Jehovah's house; and that the holy ordinances are the Lord's provisions and soul meals and breasts which he hath graciously appointed for his children of all sorts and ages.

Especially be much in holy prayer and fasting before the Lord. This is an ordinance of which neither pope nor devil could ever deprive a child of God. If it be possible, practice this duty with others, however before the Lord in secret, remembering how frequent the children of God, in Holy Scripture, were in this duty. Daniel is an heavenly pattern, and so is David, who wept and chastised his soul with fasting, although he was reproached for it (Ps. 69). Our holy bridegroom, the Lord Jesus, tells us that the bridegroom shall be taken away, and then his servants fast. It is as if he had expressly named the times of the anti-Christian bondage, wherein the followers of Jesus, like the blessed woman weeping, cry out, "They have taken away my Lord, and I know not where they have laid him" (John 20:13). This holy ordinance is of such admirable use among the saints that even in the first and purest times of Christianity, we read of Christian yokefellows consenting to a separation from each other for a time, that they may give themselves to prayer and fasting (I Cor., ch. 7).

OBJECTION: But some say fasting, as it seems to be more proper to the Old Testament, so seems it not so useful in the new covenant, when more spiritual worship and spiritual joys seem more suitable and seasonable.

I answer: All the former Scriptures declare it to be an ordinance of the New Testament as well as prayer itself. And for the use of it, it is most admirable for the separating and abstracting of the mind and spirit from earthly occasions and comforts, for the devoting of the soul to heavenly consideration and examination of our ways, for the pouring forth of prayers and cries to God in the many great and mighty straits which God's people pass through in this vale of tears and lamentation. And indeed it is, as I may say, the taking of a soul sweat or a soul purge for the avoiding and cleansing out of our spiritual humors and corruptions.

A THIRD HELP: AVOID COLD SOCIETIES AND PLACES DESTITUTE OF CHRIST JESUS. Thirdly, as ever we would preserve our spiritual health, let us carefully take heed of spiritual colds and obstructions. For, as it is in the natural man, a cold itself is a great distemper and the ground and beginning of others when the warm streams of blood and spirits are stopped up and obstructed. So it is (and much more) in the spiritual man when our heavenly spirits are stopped by damp colds and obstructions of unnecessary frequenting of cold societies and places destitute of the life of the Sun of Righteousness, Christ Jesus. The Lord Jesus is a Christian's garment. O let us keep that blessed garment always close about us; and in all places and in all companies and upon all occasions express the life and power of Christ Jesus, longing to know and to follow his blessed words and examples in life and death!

A FOURTH HELP: GOD'S CHILDREN MUST WATCH AGAINST FEEDING TOO MUCH ON WORLDLY COMFORTS. Fourthly, take heed of spiritual surfeits, that the feeding too much upon the comforts of yokefellows, children, credit, profit (though sweet and wholesome as honey) turn not to bitterness and loathing. God's children—as travelers on the land, as passengers in a ship— must use this world and all comforts of it with dead and weaned and mortified affections, as if they used them not. If riches, if children, if cattle, if friends, if whatsoever increase, let us watch that the heart fly not loose upon them. As we use salt with raw and fresh meats, let us use no worldly comfort without a savory remembrance that these worldly goods and comforts are the common portion of the men of this perishing world, who must perish together with them. Let us muse upon their insufficiency to content and fill our hearts; upon their uncertainty and perplexity, full of thorns and vexations; upon their uncertainty of departing, how soon we know not. O let us, therefore, beg grace from heaven that we may use earthly comforts, profits, pleasures, which are only true and lasting—even eternal—in God himself when then these heavens and earth are gone!

A FIFTH HELP: MEDITATE UPON THE JOYS THAT ARE TO COME. Fifthly, to maintain a spiritual health and cheerfulness, it is of no small use sometimes (as Paul writes to Timothy) to help our cold stomachs with a little wine or strong drink of the hope of joys to come. " 'Lay hold,' " saith Paul to Timothy, " 'of eternal life' " (I Tim. 6:12). As the soldier meditates upon the glory of his victories; the sick passenger at sea upon his sweet refreshings on shore; the traveler upon his journey's end and comforts at his home; the laborer and hireling on his wages; the husbandman on his harvest; the merchant on his gain; the woman in travail on her fruit, so let us sometimes warm and revive our cold hearts and fainting spirits with the assured hope of those victories, those crowns, those harvests, those refreshings and fruits, which never eye hath seen, nor ear hath heard, nor never entered into man's heart the things which God hath prepared for them that love him. Of which, however, it pleaseth God to give his servants a taste in this life, yet the harvest and the vintage are to come when they that suffer with Christ Jesus shall reign with him, when they that have sown in tears shall reap the never-ending harvest of inconceivable joys.

A SIXTH HELP: BITTER AND UNTOOTHSOME THINGS MAY BE OF A BLESSED AND WHOLESOME USE. Sixthly, as it is in the restoring of the body to health or in the preserving of it in an healthful condition, it is often necessary to use the help of sharp and bitter things—bitter pills, bitter potions, bitter medicines, sweatings, purgings, vomitings, bloodlettings, etc.—so is it with our souls and spirits and preservation of the health and cheerfulness of the spiritual and the inner man.

The sharp and bitter things which it pleaseth God to make use of in these cases are of two sorts. First, such as he is pleased to use towards us in the way of his fatherly afflictions of all sorts (on our yokefellows, children, servants, cattle, goods, etc.), out of which—yea, also out of the injurious and slanderous and persecuting dealing of others; yea, and out of our own sins and failings—his most holy and infinite wisdom fetcheth all sorts of cleansing and purging; yea, and sometimes a cordial and healing physic. The second sort of sharp and bitter means are such as we voluntarily use and apply unto ourselves for the slaying and the purging out of the filthy humors and corruptions of pride, security, uncleanness, self-love, covetousness, and whatever else remains behind of the body of death in us.

It is true that the Word of God and all his holy ordinances are not only a feeding and nourishing of the inner man, but also possess a purging and cleansing nature, and a preserving and restoring quality. And, therefore, out of these we must take direction for all our spiritual remedies against those soul distempers unto which our spiritual and inner man are subject.

1. *The Remembrance of Our Sins Is a Bitter Yet an Wholesome Pill.* First, then, it is an wholesome though bitter pill often to call to mind our many, our great, our known, our unknown transgressions against the Lord as a creator, against the Lord as a father, against the Lord as a redeemer, against Christ Jesus, against his Holy Spirit, against his ordinances, against his saints, against ourselves, etc.; yea, the sins and several corruptions of our natures, callings, conditions, to which we are subject and lie open, and into which, without supply of grace and strength from heaven, we shall fall and tumble, as well as the strongest of God's servants of whose woeful falls we read in Holy Scripture.

OBJECTION: It is a part of the Lord's new covenant that he will forgive our sins and remember our iniquities no more.

I answer: Unto all the promises of all sorts, as in Ezek., ch. 36, it pleaseth the Lord to add this gospel proviso, according to that most holy direction of the Lord Jesus, to pray daily not only for daily bread but also for daily forgiveness.

OBJECTION: The Lord hath forgiven them already in Christ. What need to pray for forgiveness of them again?

I answer: We must mark the Lord's ordinance: Prayer and other spiritual ordinances hath the Lord appointed for our soul's good, as well as corporeal means for our bodily comfort. Hence the many examples of the servants of God throughout the whole Scripture, both before Jesus Christ and since—David, Peter, Mary Magdalene—breaking forth into heavenly showers of godly tears. Hence the Paschal Lamb (the figure of Christ Jesus) was appointed by the Lord to be eaten with bitter herbs, implying and teaching that Jesus Christ himself, his blood, pardon of sin, life and salvation, and all the spiritual and eternal sweets that here below we find in Christ Jesus, have not their native and proper relish without the help of such sharp and bitter herbs.

What if, in God's counsel before the world was, all his works of creation and redemption, vocation, justification, and glorification are known to him and acted by him? What if, I say, they are known in the most inconceivable deep counsels of his will, according to which he worketh all things (Eph., ch. 1)? Yet were it presumptuous madness in us and a tempting of the jealous eyes of the Most High to neglect the ways and means and paths of mercy for soul or body which his most holy wisdom, out of infinite grace and goodness, hath appointed to us.

2. *The Due Consideration of God's Justice Is an Heavenly Though Bitter Pill.* A second sharp and bitter pill to purge out spiritual corruption is a due and serious pondering of the nature of the justice of the Most High, notwithstanding all the infinite sweetness of the ocean of mercy and notwithstanding all the colors and pretenses which we poor sinners invent to ourselves to hide from our eyes the greatness and dreadfulness and terrors of it. Well, therefore, might Job say, "'Therefore, am I troubled at his presence; and when I consider, I am afraid of him'" (Job 23:15). And well might David say, "'My flesh trembleth for fear of thee, and I am afraid of thy judgments'" (Ps. 119:120).

OBJECTION: But John saith, "'Perfect love casteth out fear'" (I John 4:18).

I answer: The true love of God never casteth out the true fear of God but only that which is false and counterfeit, that which is the fear of a beast, of slaves, and of devils. Hence it is that the spirit of the fear of the Lord was poured upon the Lord Jesus himself. This fear is an holy awe or reverence proper to a true and heavenly ingenious child of God, even (first and chiefly) to Christ Jesus, the elder brother (in a sense) of all the children of God.

* * *

A SEVENTH AND LAST HELP: THE MEDITATION OF DEATH. In the last place, my dear love, let us go down together by the steps of holy meditation into the valley of the shadow of death. It is of excellent use to walk often into Golgotha, and to view the rotten skulls of so many innumerable thousands of millions of men and women like ourselves, gone, gone forever from this life, and being, as if they never had life or being, as the swift ships, as the weaver's shuttle, as an arrow, as the lightning through the air, etc.

It is not unprofitable to remember the faces of such whom we knew, with whom we had sweet acquaintance and sweet society, with whom we have familiarly eaten and lodged, but who are now grown loathsome, ugly, terrible, even to their dearest, since they fell into the jaws of death, the king of terrors. And yet they are but gone before us in the path all flesh must tread. How, then, should we make sure (and infinitely much) of a Savior who delivers us from the power and bitterness of death and the grave and hell; who is a resurrection and a life unto us and will raise up and make our bodies glorious, like his glorious body, when he shall shortly appear in glory?

It is further of great and sweet use against the bitterness of death and against the bittersweet delusions of this world, daily to think that each day is our last, the day of our last farewell, the day of the splitting of this vessel, the breaking of this bubble, the quenching of this candle, and of our passage into the land of darkness, never more to behold a spark of light until the heavens be no more. Those three uncertainties of that most certain blow, death—to wit, of the *time* when, of the *place* where, of the *manner* how it shall come upon us and dash our earthen pitcher all to pieces—should, I say (that is, the consideration of them), be a threefold cord to bind us fast to an holy watchfulness for our departures, and a spur to quicken us to abundant faithfulness in doing and suffering for the Lord and his Christ. It should draw up our minds unto heavenly objects and loosen us from the vexing vanities of this vain puff of this present sinful life.

Oh, how weaned, how sober, how temperate, how mortified should our spirits, our affections, our desires be, when we remember that we are but strangers—converse with strange companies, dwell in strange houses, lodge in strange beds—and know not whether this day or this night shall be our final change of this strange place for one far stranger, dark, and doleful, except it be enlightened by the death and life of the Son of God! How contented should we be with any pittance, any allowance of bread, of clothes, of friendship, of respect, etc.! How thankful unto God and unto man should we poor strangers be for the least crumb or drop or rag vouchsafed unto us, when we remember that we are but strangers in an inn or passengers in a ship, and though we dream of long summer days, yet our very life and being is but a swift, short passage from the bank of time to the other side or bank of a doleful eternity!

How patient should our minds and bodies be under the crossing, disappointing hand of our all-powerful Maker, of our most gracious Father, when we remember that this is the short span of our purging and fitting for an eternal glory, and that when we are judged we are chastened of the Lord that we should not be condemned with the world! How quietly, without the swellings of revenge and wrath, should we bear the daily injuries, reproaches, persecutings, etc., from the hands of men who pass away and wither (it may be before night) like grass, or as the smoke on the chimney's top, and their love and hatred shall quickly perish! Yea, how busy, how diligent, how solicitous should we be (like strangers upon a strange coast waiting for a wind or passage) to get despatched what we have to do before we hear that final call: "Away, away, let us be gone from hence," etc.! How should we ply to get aboard that which will pass and turn to blessed account in our own country! How should we overlook and despise this world's trash which, as the holy woman going to be burned said of money, will not pass in heaven! How zealous for the true God, the true Christ, his praise, his truth, his worship; how faithful in an humble witness against the lies and cozening delusions of the father of lies, though gilded over with truth by the hands of the highest and holiest upon the earth!

How frequent, how constant ought we to be, like Christ Jesus our founder and example, in doing good, especially to the souls of all men and especially to the household of faith (yea, even to our enemies), when we remember that this is our seedtime, of which every minute is precious, and that as our sowing is, so shall be our eternal harvest. For, so saith the Spirit by Paul to the Galatians, "'He that soweth to the flesh, shall of the flesh reap corruption or rottenness; and he that soweth to the spirit, shall of the spirit reap life everlasting'" (Gal. 6:8).

THOMAS SHEPARD (1605-1649)

The earlier selections from William Bradford and John Winthrop reveal the public side of Puritan piety. Thomas Shepard's autobiography takes us to the inside, to the realm of the spirit where Puritanism took shape. The wrestling with God, the search for the divine meaning of daily events, the struggle against sin, the constant meditation upon the Scriptures—these lay behind efforts to create "a city upon a hill" in the New World. Nowhere is the inward character of Puritan piety revealed more clearly than in the personal records left by Shepard, one of the most beloved ministers of the first Massachusetts Puritans.

Thomas Shepard, like so many of the early Puritan leaders, received his education at Cambridge University. As the following narrative shows, Cambridge was the scene of Shepard's conversion and the place where he received a call to preach. Pressure from the established Anglican Church made his life difficult after he left Emmanuel College at Cambridge, but he doggedly stuck to the Calvinistic convictions that the authorities opposed. In addition, he sought a public worship energized by the longings of the heart rather than the formalities of the establishment. And so he became a target for the agents of Archbishop William Laud, who harried Shepard and his family from place to place. Finally, in 1635, Shepard resolved to follow the lead of associates like Winthrop who had abandoned England for the prospects—and perils—of New England.

Shepard's reputation preceded him. After arriving in Massachusetts, he was made the minister of the Congregational church in Cambridge near Boston, where he immediately won a large and devoted following. It was largely through his influence that the colony's assembly located its new college, named in honor of the Reverend John Harvard, in Cambridge. Shepard served as the unofficial chaplain to the undergraduates at Harvard for the first decade of its existence. For many of them he was a model of winsome piety, very much like Laurence Chaderton and John Preston had been for him at "the other Cambridge" across the ocean.

Shepard soon settled into life in the New World. He grieved at the death of his first wife, and he suffered the deprivations that fell upon most of those who came to the New World in that day. Yet his outward situation was far more secure than it had been in England. Still, he continued to wrestle with the Lord. The entries in his journal reveal a man who never took his spiritual ease. He knew that his sins were great and that the justice of God was severe. But he also knew that God's mercy was ever-present to solace the longings of his heart. This perspective made Shepard one of the most effective preachers of his generation, a man who could terrify his listeners with recitals of God's wrath, but who more characteristically brought comfort through a message of divine mercy.

The effectiveness of Shepard's autobiography, written as a private legacy for his son and namesake, lies in its combination of striving and contentment. Its first section, which describes the effort to get to New England, is a parable of Shepard's life. The boat sets out, it is confronted with storms, it returns to England, Shepard's pregnant wife suffers harrowing misfortunes, a son is safely born, further hiding is necessary, and at last a ship is found to carry them to New England. That journey is filled with peril, but the migrants survive. In the new land, disease first threatens the baby, but it is the mother who eventually succumbs. Through it all Shepard sees the hand of God—chastening and disciplining, but also soothing and consoling. It was this same divine hand that had guided his undergraduate conversion, the conversion he describes in the following excerpt.

Autobiographical Excerpt

In the year of Christ 1604 upon the fifth day of November, called the powder treason day, and that very hour of the day wherein the Parliament should have been blown up by Popish priests, I was then born, which occasioned my father to give me this name Thomas, because he said I would hardly believe that ever any such wickedness should be attempted by men against so religious and good Parliament. My father's name was William Shepard, born in a little poor town in Northamptonshire called Fossecut near Towcester, and being a prentice to one Mr. Bland, a grocer, he married one of his daughters of whom he begat many children—three sons: John, William, and Thomas; and six daughters: An[na], Margaret, Mary, Elizabeth, Hester, Sarah—of all which only John, Thomas, Anna, and Margaret are still living in the town where I was born, viz., Towcester in Northamptonshire, six miles distant from the town of Northampton in old England. I do well remember my father and have some little remembrance of my mother. My father was a wise, prudent man, the peacemaker of the place, and toward his

Source: The excellent edition of Shepard's work prepared by Michael McGiffert, *God's Plot: The Paradoxes of Puritan Piety, Being the Autobiography & Journal of Thomas Shepard* (Amherst: University of Massachusetts Press, 1972), pp. 37-46.

latter end much blessed of God in his estate and in his soul, for there being no good ministry in the town he was resolved to go and live at Banbury in Oxfordshire under a stirring ministry, having bought a house there for that end. My mother was a woman much afflicted in conscience, sometimes even unto to distraction of mind, yet was sweetly recovered again before she died, and I being the youngest she did bear exceeding great love to me and made many prayers for me. But she died when I was about four years old, and my father lived and married a second wife not dwelling in the same town, of whom he begat two children, Samuel and Elizabeth, and died when I was about ten years of age. But while my father and mother lived, when I was about three year old, there was a great plague in the town of Towcester which swept away many in my father's family, both sisters and servants. I being the youngest and best beloved of my mother was sent away the day the plague brake out to live with my aged grandfather and grandmother in Fossecut, a most blind town and corner, and those I lived with also being very well to live yet very ignorant. And there was I put to keep geese and other such country work all that time, much neglected of them, and afterward sent from them unto Adthrop, a little blind town adjoining, to my uncle, where I had more content but did learn to sing and sport as children do in those parts and dance at their Whitsun Ales, until the plague was removed and my dear mother dead who died not of the plague but of some other disease after it. And being come home, my sister An[na] married to one Mr. Farmer, and my sister Margaret loved me much, who afterward married to my father's prentice, viz., Mr. Waples. And my father married again—to another woman who did let me see the difference between my own mother and a stepmother: she did seem not to love me but incensed my father often against me; it may be that it was justly also for my childishness. And having lived thus for a time, my father sent me to school to a Welshman, one Mr. Rice, who kept the Free School in the town of Towcester, but he was exceeding curst and cruel and would deal roughly with me and so discouraged me wholly from desire of learning that I remember I wished oftentimes myself in any condition to keep hogs or beasts rather that to go to school and learn. But my father at last was visited with sickness, having taken some cold upon some pills he took, and so had the hickets [i.e., hiccoughs] with his sickness a week together, in which time I do remember I did pray very strongly and heartily for the life of my father and made some covenant, if God would do it, to serve him the better as knowing I should be left alone if he was gone. Yet the Lord took him away by death, and so I was left fatherless and motherless when I was about ten years old, and was committed to my stepmother to be educated who therefore had my portion which was £100 which my father left me. But she neglecting my education very much, my brother John, who

was my only brother alive, desired to have me out of her hands and to have
me with him, and he would bring me up for the use of my portion. And so at
last it was granted, and so I lived with this my eldest brother who showed
much love unto me and unto whom I owe much, for him God made to be
both father and mother unto me. And it happened that the cruel schoolmas-
ter died and another came into his room to be a preacher also in the town,
who was an eminent preacher in those days and accounted holy but afterward turned a great apostate and enemy to all righteousness and I fear did
commit the impardonable sin. Yet it so fell out by God's good providence
that this man stirred up in my heart a love and desire of the honor of learning,
and therefore I told my friends I would be a scholar. And so the Lord blessed
me in my studies and gave me some knowledge of the Latin and Greek
tongues, but much ungrounded in both. But I was studious because I was
ambitious of learning and being a scholar, and hence when I could not take
notes of the sermon I remember I was troubled at it and prayed the Lord
earnestly that he would help me to note sermons. And I see cause of wondering at the Lord's providence therein, for as soon as ever I had prayed (after
my best fashion) then for it, I presently the next Sabbath was able to take
notes who the precedent Sabbath could do nothing at all that way. So I
continued till I was about fifteen years of age and then was conceived to be
ripe for the University, and it pleased the Lord to put it into my brother's
heart to provide and to seek to prepare a place for me there, which was done
in this manner: one Mr. [Daniel] Cockerell, Fellow of Emmanuel College in
Cambridge, being a Northamptonshire man, came down into the country to
Northampton and so sent for me, who upon examination of me gave my
brother encouragement to send me up to Cambridge. And so I came up, and
though I was very raw and young, yet it pleased God to open the hearts of
others to admit me into this College a pensioner, and so Mr. Cockerell
became my tutor. But I do here wonder and I hope shall bless the Lord
forever in heaven that the Lord did so graciously provide for me, for I have
oft thought what a woeful estate I had been left in if the Lord had left me in
the profane, ignorant town of Towcester where I was born, that the Lord
should pluck me out of that sink and Sodom, who was the least in my father's
house, forsaken of father and mother, yet that the Lord should fetch me out
from thence by such a sweet hand.

The first two years I spent in Cambridge was in studying and in much
neglect of God and private prayer which I had sometime used, and I did not
regard the Lord at all unless it were at some fits. The third year, wherein I
was Sophister, I began to be foolish and proud and to show myself in the
public schools, and there to be a disputer about things which now I see I did
not know then at all but only prated about them. And toward the end of this

year when I was most vile (after I had been next unto the gates of death by the smallpox the year before), the Lord began to call me home to the fellowship of his grace, which was in this manner:

(1) I do remember that I had many good affections (but blind and inconstant) oft cast into me since my father's sickness by the spirit of God wrastling with me, and hence I would pray in secret. And hence when I was at Cambridge I heard old Doctor [Laurence] Chaderton, the Master of the College, when I came, and the first year I was there to hear him upon a Sacrament day my heart was much affected, but I did break loose from the Lord again. And half a year after I heard Mr. Dickinson common-place in the chapel upon those words—I will not destroy it for ten's sake (Genesis 19)—and then again was much affected, but I shook this off also and fell from God to loose and lewd company, to lust and pride and gaming and bowling and drinking. And yet the Lord left me not, but a godly scholar, walking with me, fell to discourse about the misery of every man out of Christ, viz., that whatever they did was sin, and this did much affect me. And at another time when I did light in godly company I heard them discourse about the wrath of God and the terror of it and how intolerable it was, which they did present by fire: how intolerable the torment of that was for a time—what then would eternity be! And this did much awaken me, and I began to pray again. But then by loose company I came to dispute in the schools and there to join to loose scholars of other colleges and was fearfully left of God and fell to drink with them. And I drank so much one day that I was dead drunk, and that upon a Saturday night, and so was carried from the place I had drink at and did feast at unto a scholar's chamber, one Basset of Christ's College, and knew not where I was until I awakened late on that Sabbath and sick with my beastly carriage. And when I awakened I went from him in shame and confusion, and went out into the fields and there spent that Sabbath lying hid in the cornfields where the Lord, who might justly have cut me off in the midst of my sin, did meet me with much sadness of heart and troubled my soul for this and other my sins which then I had cause and leisure to think of. And now when I was worst he began to be best unto me and made me resolve to set upon a course of daily meditation about the evil of sin and my own ways. Yet although I was troubled for this sin, I did not know my sinful nature all this while.

(2) The Lord therefore sent Doctor [John] Preston to be Master of the College, and, Mr. [Samuel] Stone and others commending his preaching to be most spiritual and excellent, I began to listen unto what he said, and the first sermon he preached was Romans 12—be renewed in the spirit of your mind—in opening which point, viz., the change of heart in a Christian, the Lord so bored my ears as that I understood what he spake and the secrets of my soul were laid upon [i.e., open] before me—the hypocrisy of all my good

things I thought I had in me—as if one had told him of all that ever I did, of all the turnings and deceits of my heart, insomuch as that I thought he was the most searching preacher in the world. And I began to love him much and to bless God I did see my frame and my hypocrisy and self and secret sins, although I found a hard heart and could not be affected with them.

(3) I did therefore set more constantly (viz., 1624, May 3) upon the work of daily meditation, sometimes every morning but constantly every evening before supper, and my chief meditation was about the evil of sin, the terror of God's wrath, day of death, beauty of Christ, the deceitfulness of the heart, etc., but principally I found this misery: sin was not my greatest evil, did lie light upon me as yet, yet I was much afraid of death and the flames of God's wrath. And this I remember: I never went out to meditate in the fields but I did find the Lord teaching me somewhat of myself or himself or the vanity of the world I never saw before. And hence I took out a little book I have every day into the fields and writ down what God taught me lest I should forget them, and so the Lord encouraged me and I grew much. But in my observation of myself I did see my atheism, I questioned whether there were a God, and my unbelief, whether Christ was the Messiah, whether the Scriptures were God's word or no. I felt all manner of temptations to all kind of religions, not knowing which I should choose, whether education might not make me believe what I had believed, and whether if I had been educated up among the Papists I should not have been as verily persuaded that Popery is the truth or Turkism is the truth, and at last I heard of Grindleton [a sect of perfectionists], and I did question whether that glorious estate of perfection might not be the truth and whether old Mr. [Richard] Rogers' *Seven Treatises* and the *Practice of Christianity,* the book which did first work upon my heart, whether these men were not all legal men and their books so, but the Lord delivered me at last from them. And in the conclusion after many prayers, meditations, duties, the Lord let me see three main wounds in my soul: (1) I could not feel sin as my greatest evil; (2) I could do nothing but I did seek myself in it and was imprisoned there, and though I desired to be a preacher, yet it was honor I did look to like a vile wretch in the use of God's gifts I desired to have; (3) I felt a depth of atheism and unbelief in the main matters of salvation and whether the Scriptures were God's word. These things did much trouble me and in the conclusion did so far trouble me that I could not read the Scriptures or hear them read without secret and hellish blasphemy, calling all into question and all Christ's miracles, and hereupon I fell to doubt whether I had not committed the impardonable sin. And because I did question whether Christ did not cast out devils from Beelzebub, etc., I did think and fear I had, and now the terrors of God began to break in like floods of fire into my soul. For three quarters of a year this temptation did last, and I had some strong temptations to run my head against walls and

brain and kill myself. And so I did see, as I thought, God's eternal reprobation of me, a fruit of which was this dereliction to these doubts and darkness,
and I did see God like a consuming fire and an everlasting burning, and
myself like a poor prisoner leading to that fire, and the thought of eternal
reprobation and torment did amaze my spirits, especially at one time upon a
Sabbath day at evening, and when I knew not what to do (for I went to no
Christian and was ashamed to speak of these things), it came to my mind that
I should do as Christ: when he was in an agony he prayed earnestly. And so I
fell down to prayer, and being in prayer I saw myself so unholy and God so
holy that my spirits began to sink, yet the Lord recovered me and poured out
a spirit of prayer upon me for free mercy and pity, and in the conclusion of
the prayer I found the Lord helping me to see my unworthiness of any mercy
and that I was worthy to be cast out of his sight and to leave myself with him
to do with me what he would, and there and never until then I found rest.
And so my heart was humbled and cast down, and I went with a stayed heart
unto supper late that night and so rested here, and the terrors of the Lord
began to assuage sweetly. Yet when these were gone I felt my senselessness of
sin and bondage to self and unconstancy and losing what the Lord had
wrought and my heartlessness to any good and loathing of God's ways.
Whereupon walking in the fields the Lord dropped this meditation into me:
Be not discouraged therefore because thou art so vile, but make this double
use of it: (1) loathe thyself the more; (2) feel a greater need and put a greater
price upon Jesus Christ who only can redeem thee from all sin—and this I
found of wonderful use to me in all my course whereby I was kept from
sinkings of heart and did beat Satan as it were with his own weapons. And I
saw Christ teaching me this before any man preached any such thing unto
me. And so the Lord did help me to loathe myself in some measure and to say
oft: Why shall I seek the glory and good of myself who am the greatest
enemy, worse than the Devil can be, against myself, which self ruins me and
blinds me, etc.? And thus God kept my heart exercised, and here I began to
forsake my loose company wholly and to do what I could to work upon the
hearts of other scholars and to humble them and to come into a way of holy
walking in our speeches and otherwise. But yet I had no assurance Christ was
mine.

(4) The Lord therefore brought Dr. Preston to preach upon that text,
I Corinthians 1:30: Christ is made unto us wisdom, righteousness, sanctification, and redemption. And when he had opened how all the good I had,
all the redemption I had, it was from Jesus Christ, I did then begin to prize
him and he became very sweet unto me, although I had heard many a time
Christ freely offered by his ministry if I would come in and receive him as
Lord and Savior and Husband. But I found my heart ever unwilling to accept
of Christ upon these terms; I found them impossible for me to keep that

condition, and Christ was not so sweet as my lust. But now the Lord made himself sweet to me and to embrace him and to give up myself unto him. But yet after this I had many fears and doubts.

(5) I found therefore the Lord revealing free mercy and that all my help was in that to give me Christ and to enable me to believe in Christ and accept of him, and here I did rest.

(6) The Lord also letting me see my own constant vileness in everything put me to this question: Why did the Lord Jesus keep the Law, had no guile in his heart, had no unbrokenness but holiness there? Was it not for them that did want it? And here I saw Christ Jesus righteousness for a poor sinner's ungodliness, but yet questioning whether ever the Lord would apply this and give this unto me.

(7) The Lord made me see that so many as receive him, he gives power to be the sons of God (John 1:12), and I saw the Lord gave me a heart to receive Christ with a naked hand, even naked Christ, and so the Lord gave me peace.

OBADIAH HOLMES (1607?-1682)

Obadiah Holmes was not one of the great men of his age. Rather, he was a hardworking farmer who took his place among the unsung ranks of common people who made the perilous journey from Old England to the New World. Holmes was born near Manchester, England, sometime around 1607, and married Catherine Hyde in 1630. In 1638 he and his family left for New England, where they eventually settled in Salem, Massachusetts; thirteen years later they moved from the Bay Colony to Newport, Rhode Island, where Holmes lived until his death. Holmes's journey through life was much like that of his contemporaries. He was constantly busy clearing and working the land. He served on local juries, lent his signature as witness to legal transactions, and with his wife brought numerous children into the world.

Two things, however, set Obadiah Holmes apart. The first was his dedication to Baptist principles during an age dominated by the Church of England (in the Old Country) and by the Congregationalists (in Massachusetts). Holmes had experienced a religious quickening as a teenager, an experience that eventually left him dissatisfied with the restrictions on religious expression in England. One of the reasons he traveled to the New World was to worship God as he had come to believe he should. Once in Massachusetts, however, Holmes found that even in the New World religious freedom was a scarce commodity. Soon he was attracted to the teaching of the Baptists, who felt that the colony's church-state establishment violated God-given principles of Christian liberty. So dissatisfied did he become that he moved his family to Rhode Island, where, under the leadership of Roger Williams, extraordinary religious liberty could be found. There he joined the Baptist church in Newport and participated in over thirty years of Baptist history in that colony.

Holmes's one entrance into a larger historical sphere came shortly after his move to Rhode Island. With two other Baptists he returned to Lynn, Massachusetts, in order to visit a disabled friend who inclined toward Baptist principles. The three also hoped to be able to persuade other Massachusetts residents to accept the practices of their faith. But local officials would have none of this. They regarded the effort to spread Baptist convictions as a breach of the peace. So Holmes and his friends were taken to Boston, put on trial, convicted, and fined. When Holmes refused to let friends pay his fine, he was publicly whipped. Reflecting on this experience many years later, he wrote, "It is therefore the love of liberty that must free the soul."

The second thing that set Holmes apart in his day was his desire, as an old man, to set down on paper the essence of his faith. In 1675, as he sensed the end approaching, Holmes wrote a last will and testimony. He did not so much address the affairs of this world as consider the realities of the life to come. He used brief testimonies, or exhortations, to tell the story of his life and faith and to provide specific encouragement to his wife, his children, his church, and the world. For the times it was an unusual record because it showed so clearly the convictions of a "common person." Although he had not been formally educated, Holmes knew his letters. And even though he was not a minister, he also had long studied the Scriptures and pondered the essence of faith. The record he left therefore offers modern readers a great deal. It is from the pen of a simple man, but it reveals a piety of unexpected depth.

Selections from His Last Will and Testimony

A LETTER TO HIS WIFE

MY MOST DEAR WIFE,

My heart has ever cleaved to thee, ever since we came together, and is knit to thee in death which is the cause of these lines as a remembrance of God's goodness to us in continuing us together almost forty years (not diminishing us in our offspring since the first day until now, only our first born). God has made all our conditions comfortable to us, whether in fullness or emptiness, lifted up or thrown down, in honor or disgrace, sickness or health, by giving us contentment and love one with and to another. But more in a special manner [God has blessed us] in causing His fear to fall upon us and His love to be placed in our hearts and to know His will and to conform up to the obedience of the same—as to be willing to take up the cross and follow the Lord, not fearing what man can do unto us. For the Lord being on our side, who can be against us? For with His rod and His staff he has comforted us. Yea, He has been our present help in a needful time, and we have cause while we live to praise His holy name while we are together. And when death does separate us, may the only one still living praise Him while breath remains.

Wherefore, having some thought that I may go away before thee, having signs or token that my day is but short and it may fall out that I cannot or may not speak to thee at the last, I shall give thee some considerations for thy

Source: *Baptist Piety: The Last Will and Testimony of Obadiah Holmes,* superbly edited by Edwin S. Gaustad (Grand Rapids: Eerdmans, 1978), pp. 95-98, 101-4.

meditations in a time of trouble or affliction—that they may speak when I
cannot (if the Lord is pleased to speak in them and by them).

Consider how the Lord carried thee along ever since thou had a being in
this world, as by tender parents and since thou came from them, the Lord has
provided for thee and preserved thee in many dangers both by sea and land,
and has given thee food and raiment with contentment. He has increased our
store, sometimes to our admiration, also continuing our health in very great
measure. He has given us a great posterity who have increased to a great
number and has provided for them in a comfortable manner. And the Lord
has kept them from such evils as might have befallen them to our grief, but
we have had comfort in them. Also, consider the peace we have enjoyed and
love we have obtained from our friends and our neighbors and strangers.

Yet, my dear wife, those things are but common favors that many may
have their part in. But consider that the choice particular favor that many
receive not which God has given to thee in choosing and calling thee to the
knowledge of Himself and His dear Son which is eternal. [So, do] order thy
heart to cleave to Him alone, esteeming Him as the chief good, as a pearl of
great price, as worthy and causing thy heart to part with all for Him. His love
has continued [to help] thee to hearken to His voice, inquiring about His
will, so that thou might obey His holy will and commandments, so as to
serve Him in thy generation. Oh, consider that great love of the Lord, to
cause thy soul to cleave to Him alone and so He to be thy only protection!
Having given thee His Son, He has with Him given thee all things thou dost
enjoy, and so to be to thee—both in life and in death—thy advantage.

The consideration of this causes me to put thee now in mind, when I am
removed, to consider Him as thy husband, as thy father, as thy Lord and
Savior who has said that whom He loveth, He loveth to the end. And He will
not leave them, nor forsake them, either in the six or seven troubles, but
carry thee through all, until he bring thee to glory. Wherefore, lift up thy
head and be not discouraged. Say to thy soul, "Why are thou disquieted
within me? Hope in God and trust in His name," and thou shall not be
disappointed. Let thy love to me end in this: that it is better for me to be out
of the body and to be with the Lord at rest with Him and to be freed from
that body of sin and death which I was in while I was in this present evil
world. [That body] caused much sorrow of heart to me in secret; for, when I
would do good, evil was present with me. And consider the fears you had
concerning me every day both for pains and weakness and dangers, of the
many troubles that might befall me. But now let thy soul say, He is out of all
dangers, freed from sin and Satan and all enemies and doubts; and death is
past and he is at rest in a bed of quietness (as to the body) and with the Lord
in spirit. And at the resurrection, that weak corrupt mortal body shall be
raised immortal and glorious and shall see and know as he is known. There-

fore, say, Why shall I mourn as one without hope? Rather, rejoice in hope of the glorious resurrection of the just.

And now, my dear wife, do thou live by the faith of the son of God, exercise patience, and let patience have its perfect work in thee. It will be a little while before thy day will end and thy time come to sleep with me in rest. He that will come *will come* and will not tarry. Keep close to the Lord in secret, be much with God in prayer, and improve every season for thy soul's advantage, especially in holy meditations. Be cheerful and rejoice in God continually. Care not for the things of this world: say not, What shall I eat or wherewith shall I be clothed, for thy Father knoweth what thou hast need of. And He has given thee much more of these things than ever thou and I could expect or have deserved, and thou hast enough and to spare if His good pleasure be to let thee enjoy the same. If not, He alone is a sufficient portion. Yet, I question not but that He will preserve what thou hast, and bless it to thee. Wherefore, make use of that which He is pleased to let thee enjoy—I say, make use of it for thy present comfort.

Now that thou art weak and aged, cease from thy labor and great trial, and take a little rest and ease in thy old age. Live on what thou hast, for what the Lord has given us, I freely have given thee for thy life, to make thy life comfortable. Wherefore, see that thou dost [enjoy?] it so long as house, land, or cattle remain. Make much of thyself. At thy death, then, what remains may be disposed of according to my will.

And now, my dear wife whom I love as my own soul, I commit thee to the Lord who has been a gracious, merciful God to us all our days, not once doubting but He will be gracious to thee in life—or death. He will carry thee through the valley of tears with His own supporting hand. Sorrow not at my departure, but rejoice in the Lord, and again I say rejoice in the God of our salvation. In nothing be careful [anxious], but make thy request to Him who only is able to supply thy necessities and to help thee in time of need. Unto Whom I commit thee for counsel, wisdom and strength, and to keep thee blameless to the coming of the Lord Jesus Christ, to Whom be all glory, honor and praise forever and ever, Amen. Fare thee well.

A LETTER TO ALL MY CHILDREN

MY DEAR CHILDREN,

A word or two unto you who are near and dear unto me, and much on my heart as I draw near to my end and am not likely to see you nor speak to you at my departure. Wherefore I am moved to leave these lines for your consideration when I am gone and you shall see me no more. Take it as the real truth of my heart in love to you all. For as I have been a means to bring you into the world as corrupted and sinful creatures as you were when conceived and brought forth into the world (as so I was), even so are you by nature children of wrath as others are. And yet the Lord had mercy on me, and I trust He will show mercy on you, in and through the Lord Jesus Christ. As He has begun with some of you to cause them to know Him and to serve Him, to love and obey Him, so I trust He will show mercy to you all. Wherefore, my dear children, above all things in this world let it be your care to seek the Kingdom of Heaven and His righteousness first and above all things, and to consider what you are by nature—even enemies of God. Be you thoroughly convinced of that and, by actual trangressions, that you are sinners. Yet, know that such great love as cannot be expressed by man nor angels has the Lord sent and held forth: even his Son, his only Son, to save and deliver you from wrath. [By such great love you are] not to perish but to have eternal life, even to all and every one that believes in His only Son, for in Him is life.

And now my son, Joseph: Remember that Joseph of Arimathea was a good man and a disciple of Jesus; he was bold and went in boldly and asked for the body of Jesus, and buried it.

My son, John: Remember what a loving and beloved disciple he was.

My daughter, Hope: Consider what a grace of God hope is, and covet after that hope that will never be ashamed but has hope of eternal life and salvation of Jesus Christ.

My son, Obadiah: Consider that Obadiah was a servant of the Lord and tender in spirit, and in a troublesome time hid the prophets by fifty in a cave.

My son, Samuel: Remember Samuel was a chief prophet of the Lord, ready to hear his voice saying, "Speak, Lord, for thy servant heareth."

My daughter, Martha: Remember Martha, although she was encumbered with many things, yet she loved the Lord and was beloved of Him, for He loved Mary and Martha.

My daughter, Mary: Remember Mary who chose the better part that shall not be taken away and did hearken to the Lord's instructions.

My son, Jonathan: Remember how faithful and loving he was to David, that servant of the Lord.

My daughter, Lydia: Remember how Lydia's heart was open, her care borne, her spirit made to be willing to receive and obey the apostle in what the Lord required, and was baptized; and entertained and refreshed the servants of the Lord.

Now, my dear children, consider the great love the Lord has held forth in His Son, and [turn?] to Him for life and for cleansing and pardoning that you may be delivered from that great bondage and slavery that by nature you are in. Know you that it is the Lord only that must draw you by His own power unto His Son. The Son came to seek and save that which was lost, even to the sick—the whole need Him not. Therefore, be careful that you reject Him not. Defer not the present tender of grace, but while it is called day harden not your hearts; turn to the Lord in true repentance. Give credit to the Lord's own testimony concerning His Son, that is, to believe on Him and so shall you be saved.

My soul has been in great trouble for you, to see Christ formed in you by a thorough work of the Holy Spirit of the Lord that it may appear you are born again and ingrafted in the true vine; so you, being true branches, may bring forth fruit unto God and serve Him in your generation. Although my care and counsel has been extended to you, as you well know, yet it is the Lord who must work both to will and to do of His good pleasure. Wherefore, wait on Him with care and diligence; carefully read the Scriptures and mind well what is therein contained for they testify of Him. Let your hearty desires be to Him that He would effectually be your Teacher by His Holy Spirit. Beware that you hearken to any that shall speak contrary to the Scripture, for if they do speak otherways it is because they have no might in them. Let your conversation and life be squared by the same, and they will direct you how to behave yourselves toward God and man.

Next to loving and fearing the Lord, have you a most dear and tender respect to your faithful, careful, tender-hearted, loving and aged Mother. Show your duty in all things; honor her with high and cheerful love and respect, and then make sure you love one another. It has been my joy to see your love, one to another. Let it continue and increase, so may you be good examples to others. Visit one another as often as you can, and put one another in mind of the uncertainty of life and what need there is to prepare for death. Take counsel one of another and, if one see cause to advise or reprove, hearken to it and take it well.

Be you content with your present condition and portion God has given you. Make a good use of what you have by making use of it for your comfort. For meat, drink or apparel, it is the gift of God. Take care to live honestly, justly, quietly with love and peace among yourselves, your neighbors and, if possible, be at peace with all men. In what you can, do good to all men, especially to such as fear the Lord. Forget not to entertain strangers, according to your ability; if it be done in sincerity, it will be accepted, especially if to a disciple in the name of a disciple. Do to all men as you would have them do to you. Seek not honor or praise from men, but the honor that is of God by the truth: that is, part with all for truth's sake. If you would be Christ's disciples, you must know and consider that you must take up your cross and follow Him, through evil report and losses. But yet know, he that will lose his life for Him shall save it. If you put your hand to the plough, you must not turn or look back—remember Lot's wife; but, be constant to death, and you shall receive the crown of life.

Thus, my dear children, have I according to my measure, as is my duty, counselled you. May the good Lord give you understanding in all things and by His Holy Spirit convince, reprove and instruct and lead you into all truth as it is in Jesus. So that when you have done your work here, He may receive you to glory. Now the God of truth and peace be with you, unto Whom I commit this and you, even to Him be glory forever and ever, Amen. (the 17th day, 10th month [December], 1675)

ANNE BRADSTREET (1612?-1672)

One of early America's most accomplished poets, Anne Bradstreet was also one of the first settlers of the Massachusetts Bay Colony. When she was eighteen, she and her husband sailed to the New World with John Winthrop's group. Anne later wrote of the shock of finding "a new world and new manners," and told of how her "heart rose" in resistance to this rude experience. "But after I was convinced it was the way of God, I submitted to it and joined the church at Boston."

In the wilderness, Anne, her husband Simon, and their fellow colonists were faced with many challenges. They were forced to contend with a harsh climate, a strange and forbidding landscape, and the threat of Indian attack. In addition, Anne had her own special difficulties. Having suffered rheumatic fever as a child, she was subject to repeated periods of exhaustion throughout her life, and she risked death each time she gave birth to a child. (She and Simon had eight children.)

In spite of the hardships, the life of the Bradstreets was a joyous one, and Anne writes with warmth about her home and domestic duties. Simon was a leader in Puritan Massachusetts, at one point serving as the colony's governor, and Anne's poems to him show loving respect and genuine fondness. She wrote both long, meditative poems on the nature of God and his dealings with humanity, and short lyrics that celebrate her love of her family and God's nature.

Some of her early poems were published in 1650 without her knowledge through the efforts of her brother-in-law. These were the first poems to be published by a resident of the English colonies. In many ways they are representative of much later American verse. They celebrate the splendor and sheer abundance of the natural world. They are more likely to search for proof for the existence of God in natural wonder than in complicated theological argument. "The eyes and ears are the inlets or doors of the soul," Bradstreet wrote in one meditation. Although she was quick to acknowledge that nothing could fill the soul save the one "in whom all fullness dwells," she never slighted God's tangible bounty. Her poetry shows an early American piety deeply rooted in a sense of natural wonder.

The following poems appeared together in an edition published posthumously in Boston in 1678. (The spelling, capitalization, and punctuation have been normalized here.)

The Flesh and the Spirit

In secret place where I once stood
Close by the banks of lacrim flood,
I heard two sisters reason on
Things that are past and things to come.
One Flesh was called, who had her eye
On worldly wealth and vanity;
The other Spirit, who did rear
Her thoughts unto a higher sphere.
"Sister," quoth Flesh, "what liv'st thou on—
Nothing but meditation?
Doth contemplation feed thee, so
Regardlessly to let earth go?
Can speculation satisfy
Notion without Reality?
Dost dream of things beyond the moon,
And dost thou hope to dwell there soon?
Hast treasures there laid up in store,
That all in th' world thou count'st but poor?
Art fancy sick, or turned a sot,
To catch at shadows which are not?
Come, come, I'll show unto thy sense
Industry hath its recompense.
What canst desire but thou mayst see
True substance in variety?
Dost honor like? Acquire the same,
As some of their immortal fame,
And trophies to thy name erect
Which wearing time shall ne'er deject.
For riches dost thou long full sore?
Behold enough of precious store;
Earth hath more silver, pearls, and gold
Than eyes can see or hands can hold.
Affect'st thou pleasure? Take thy fill;
Earth hath enough of what you will.
Then let not go, what thou mayst find
For things unknown, only in mind."
Spirit: "Be still, thou unregenerate part;
Disturb no more my settled heart,
For I have vowed (and so will do)

Thee as a foe, still to pursue,
And combat with thee will and must
Until I see thee laid in th' dust.
Sisters we are, yea, twins we be,
Yet deadly feud 'twixt thee and me;
For from one father we are not:
Thou by old Adam wast begot,
But my arise is from above,
Whence my dear Father I do love.
Thou speak'st me fair but hat'st me sore;
Thy flattering shows I'll trust no more.
How oft thy slave hast thou me made
When I believed what thou hast said,
And never had more cause of woe
Than when I did what thou bad'st do.
I'll stop mine ears at these thy charms
And count them for my deadly harms.
Thy sinful pleasures I do hate,
Thy riches are to me no bait,
Thine honors do nor will I love,
For my ambition lies above.
My greatest honor it shall be
When I am victor over thee
And triumph shall, with laurel head,
When thou my captive shalt be led.
How I do live thou need'st not scoff,
For I have meat thou know'st not of;
The hidden manna I do eat,
The world of life it is my meat.
My thoughts do yield me more content
Than can thy hours in pleasure spent.
Nor are they shadows which I catch,
Nor fancies vain at which I snatch;
But reach at things that are so high,
Beyond thy dull capacity,
Eternal substance I do see,
With which enriched I would be;
Mine eye doth pierce the heavens, and see
What is invisible to thee.
My garments are not silk nor gold
Nor such like trash which earth doth hold,
But royal robes I shall have on

More glorious than the glist'ring sun.
My crown not diamonds, pearls, and gold,
But such as angels' heads infold.
The City where I hope to dwell
There's none on earth can parallel;
The stately walls both high and strong
Are made of precious jasper stone;
The gates of pearl both rich and clear;
And angels are for porters there;
The streets thereof transparent gold,
Such as no eye did e'er behold;
A crystal river there doth run,
Which doth proceed from the Lamb's throne;
Of life there are the waters sure,
Which shall remain forever pure;
Nor sun nor moon they have no need,
For glory doth from God proceed;
No candle there, nor yet torchlight,
For there shall be no darksome night.
From sickness and infirmity
For evermore they shall be free,
Nor withering age shall e'er come there,
But beauty shall be bright and clear.
This city pure is not for thee,
For things unclean there shall not be.
If I of heaven may have my fill,
Take thou the world, and all that will."

Verses upon the Burning of Our House, July 10th, 1666

In silent night, when rest I took,
For sorrow near I did not look.
I wakened was with thundering noise
And piteous shrieks of dreadful voice.
That fearful sound of "Fire!" and "Fire!"
Let no man know, is my desire.

I, starting up, the light did spy,
And to my God my heart did cry
To strengthen me in my distress,
And not to leave me succorless;

Then coming out, beheld apace
The flame consume my dwelling-place.

And when I could no longer look
I blest His name that gave and took,
That laid my goods now in the dust;
Yea, so it was, and so 'twas just—
It was His own; it was not mine.
Far be it that I should repine.

He might of all justly bereft,
But yet sufficient for us left.
When by the ruins oft I passed
My sorrowing eyes aside did cast,
And here and there the places spy
Where oft I sat, and long did lie.

Here stood that trunk, and there that chest;
There lay that store I counted best;
My pleasant things in ashes lie,
And them behold no more shall I.
Under thy roof no guest shall sit,
Nor at thy table eat a bit;

No pleasant tale shall e'er be told,
Nor things recounted done of old;
No candle e'er shall shine in thee,
Nor bridegroom's voice heard shall be.
In silence ever shall thou lie.
Adieu, adieu; all's vanity.

Then straight I 'gan my heart to chide:
And did thy wealth on earth abide?
Didst fix thy hope on mouldering dust
The arm of flesh didst make thy trust?
Raise up thy thoughts above the sky,
That dunghill mists away may fly.

Thou hast an house on high erect;
Framed by that mighty Architect,
With glory richly furnished,
Stands permanent though this be fled.
It's purchaséd, and paid for, too,
By Him who hath enough to do—

A price so vast as is unknown,
Yet, by His gift, is made thine own.
There's wealth enough; I need no more.

Farewell, my pelf; farewell, my store;
The world no longer let me love.
My hope and treasure lie above.

As Weary Pilgrim, Now at Rest

As weary pilgrim, now at rest,
   Hugs with delight his silent nest;
His wasted limbs now lie full soft
   That miry steps have trodden oft;
Blesses himself to think upon
   His dangers past and travails done;
The burning sun no more shall heat,
   Nor stormy rains on him shall beat;
The briars and thorns no more shall scratch,
   Nor hungry wolves at him shall catch;
He erring paths no more shall tread
   Nor wild fruits eat instead of bread;
For waters cold he doth not long,
   For thirst no more shall parch his tongue;
No rugged stones his feet shall gall,
   Nor stumps nor rocks cause him to fall;
All cares and fears he bids farewell
   And means in safety now to dwell:
A pilgrim I on earth, perplexed
   With sins, with cares and sorrows vexed,
By age and pains brought to decay,
   And my clay house mould'ring away.
Oh! how I long to be at rest
   And soar on high among the blest!
This body shall in silence sleep;
   Mine eyes no more shall ever weep;
No fainting fits shall me assail,
   Nor grinding pains, my body frail;
With cares and fears ne'er cumbered be,
   Nor losses know, nor sorrows see.
What though my flesh shall there consume?
   It is the bed Christ did perfume;
And when a few years shall be gone,
   This mortal shall be clothed upon;
A corrupt carcass down it lies,

A glorious body it shall rise;
In weakness and dishonor sown,
    In power 'tis raised by Christ alone.
Then soul and body shall unite
    And of their maker have the sight.
Such lasting joys shall there behold
    As ear ne'er heard nor tongue e'er told.
Lord, make me ready for that day!
    Then come, dear bridegroom, come away.

MARY ROWLANDSON (1636?-1678?)

Mary Rowlandson lived at a time of troubling uncertainty in Puritan New England. During the decades that separate her captivity narrative from John Winthrop's earlier sermon of hopeful expectation, significant causes for anxiety had arisen within Massachusetts. Troubled by poor crops, disobedient children, impiety in the community, and the animosity of the Indians whose land they were taking, the people of the Massachusetts Bay Colony struggled to account for such difficulties. What had happened to the great promise of the Puritan enterprise?

The Narrative of the Captivity and Restoration of Mrs. Mary Rowlandson was one attempt to account for these spiritual and communal difficulties. Mary Rowlandson, about whom little is known except what we glean from her narrative, was a victim of an Indian raid in the conflict later known as King Philip's War (1675-1676). In that war the Wampanoag Indians made a desperate attempt to regain the territory that the English colonists were appropriating. In little more than a year of actual fighting, more than a thousand settlers' homes were destroyed, three thousand Indians were killed, and some six hundred colonists died. Rowlandson was abducted during an attack on her village, Lancaster, on February 10, 1676.

Rowlandson's narrative provides evidence of the enduring faith of the common Puritan in the face of great adversity. It also demonstrates how fervently the Puritan community strove to find satisfying reasons for their suffering. Rowlandson repeatedly attributes her present affliction to her past improprieties, like her failure to observe the Sabbath properly or her failure to appreciate the simple mercies of God that she had enjoyed with great complacency. She sees her pain and the colony's suffering as a sign of God's judgment. And she reads her deliverance as fulfillment of God's promise to make special provision for his people.

Beyond doubt, Mary Rowlandson thought of herself and her fellow colonists as the chosen people of God. In her narrative she relates how she constantly turned to the Scriptures for comfort during her confinement among the Indians. But she does more than appropriate an occasional verse of comfort to calm herself when afflicted. When she quotes the Bible in her narrative, the passage is almost always from the Old Testament rather than the New. Moreover, it is likely to concern God's special protection for his Old Testament people. Like many seventeenth-century Puritans, Rowlandson all but abandoned any distinctions between the ancient Israelities and those New England sojourners in a strange land.

The first edition of Rowlandson's narrative was published posthumously in 1682, and the book became one of the most popular prose works in the last years of the seventeenth century. Its intriguing delineation of character, its suspense, its narrative skill, and its deep sincerity all made it a treasured work of the time. We pick up the narrative with an account of the tension between Mary Rowlandson and her Indian "mistress."

Captivity Narrative

As I was sitting once in the wigwam here, Philip's maid came in with the child in her arms, and asked me to give her a piece of my apron, to make a flap for it. I told her I would not. Then my mistress bade me give it, but still I said no. The maid told her if I would not give her a piece, she would tear a piece off it. I told her I would tear her coat then. With that my mistress rises up, and takes up a stick big enough to have killed me, and struck at me with it. But I stepped out, and she struck the stick into the mat of the wigwam. But while she was pulling of it out I ran to the maid and gave her all my apron, and so that storm was over.

Hearing that my son was come to this place, I went to see him, and told him his father was well, but very melancholy. He told me he was as much grieved for his father as for himself. I wondered at his speech, for I thought I had enough upon my spirit in reference to myself, to make me mindless of my husband and everyone else; they being safe among their friends. He told me also, that awhile before, his master (together with other Indians) were going to the French for powder; but by the way the Mohawks met with them, and killed four of their company, which made the rest turn back again, for which I desire that myself and he may bless the Lord; for it might have been worse with him, had he been sold to the French, than it proved to be in his remaining with the Indians.

I went to see an English youth in this place, one John Gilbert of Springfield. I found him lying without doors, upon the ground. I asked him how he did? He told me he was very sick of a flux, with eating so much blood. They had turned him out of the wigwam, and with him an Indian papoose, almost dead (whose parents had been killed), in a bitter cold day, without fire or clothes. The young man himself had nothing on but his shirt and waistcoat.

This sight was enough to melt a heart of flint. There they lay quivering in the cold, the youth round like a dog, the papoose stretched out with his eyes and nose and mouth full of dirt, and yet alive, and groaning. I advised John to go and get some fire. He told me he could not stand, but I persuaded him still, lest he should lie there and die. And with much ado I got him to a fire, and went myself home. As soon as I was got home his master's daughter came after me, to know what I had done with the Englishman. I told her I had got him to a fire in such a place. Now had I need to pray Paul's Prayer "That we may be delivered from unreasonable and wicked men" (2 Thessalonians 3.2). For her satisfaction I went along with her, and brought her to him; but before I got home again it was noised about that I was running away and getting the English youth, along with me; that as soon as I came in they began to rant and domineer, asking me where I had been, and what I had been doing? and saying they would knock him on the head. I told them I had been seeing the English youth, and that I would not run away. They told me I lied, and taking up a hatchet, they came to me, and said they would knock me down if I stirred out again, and so confined me to the wigwam. Now may I say with David, "I am in great strait" (2 Samuel 24.14). If I keep in, I must die with hunger, and if I go out, I must be knocked in head. This distressed condition held that day, and half the next. And then the Lord remembered me, whose mercies are great. Then came an Indian to me with a pair of stockings that were too big for him, and he would have me ravel them out, and knit them fit for him. I showed my self willing, and bid him ask my mistress if I might go along with him a little way; she said yes, I might, but I was not a little refreshed with that news, that I had my liberty again. Then I went along with him, and he gave me some roasted ground-nuts, which did again revive my feeble stomach.

Being got out of her sight, I had time and liberty again to look into my Bible; which was my guide by day, and my pillow by night. Now that comfortable scripture presented itself to me, "For a small moment have I forsaken thee, but with great mercies will I gather thee" (Isaiah 54.7). Thus the Lord carried me along from one time to another, and made good to me this precious promise, and many others. Then my son came to see me, and I asked his master to let him stay awhile with me, that I might comb his head, and look over him, for he was almost overcome with lice. He told me, when I had done, that he was very hungry, but I had nothing to relieve him, but bid him go into the wigwams as he went along, and see if he could get any thing among them. Which he did, and it seems tarried a little too long; for his master was angry with him, and beat him, and then sold him. Then he came running to tell me he had a new master, and that he had given him some ground-nuts already. Then I went along with him to his new master who told me he loved him, and he should not want. So his master carried him away, and I never saw him afterward, till I saw him at Piscataqua in Portsmouth.

That night they bade me go out of the wigwam again. My mistress's papoose was sick, and it died that night, and there was one benefit in it—that there was more room. I went to a wigwam, and they bade me come in, and gave me a skin to lie upon, and a mess of venison and ground-nuts, which was a choice dish among them. On the morrow they buried the papoose, and afterward, both morning and evening, there came a company to mourn and howl with her; though I confess I could not much condole with them. Many sorrowful days I had in this place, often getting alone. "Like a crane, or a swallow, so did I chatter; I did mourn as a dove, mine eyes ail with looking upward. Oh, Lord, I am oppressed; undertake for me" (Isaiah 38.14). I could tell the Lord, as Hezekiah, "Remember now O Lord, I beseech thee, how I have walked before thee in truth." Now had I time to examine all my ways: my conscience did not accuse me of unrighteousness toward one or other; yet I saw how in my walk with God, I had been a careless creature. As David said, "Against thee, thee only have I sinned": and I might say with the poor publican, "God be merciful unto me a sinner." On the sabbath-days, I could look upon the sun and think how people were going to the house of God, to have their souls refreshed; and then home, and their bodies also; but I was destitute of both; and might say as the poor prodigal, "He would fain have filled his belly with the husks that the swine did eat, and no man gave unto him" (Luke 15.16). For I must say with him, "Father, I have sinned against Heaven and in thy sight." I remembered how on the night before and after the sabbath, when my family was about me, and relations and neighbors with us, we could pray and sing, and then refresh our bodies with the good creatures of God; and then have a comfortable bed to lie down on; but instead of all this, I had only a little swill for the body and then, like a swine, must lie down on the ground. I cannot express to man the sorrow that lay upon my spirit; the Lord knows it. Yet that comfortable scripture would often come to my mind, "For a small moment have I forsaken thee, but with great mercies will I gather thee."

* * *

I can remember the time when I used to sleep quietly without workings in my thoughts, whole nights together, but now it is other ways with me. When all are fast about me, and no eye open, but His who ever waketh, my thoughts are upon things past, upon the awful dispensation of the Lord towards us, upon His wonderful power and might, in carrying of us through so many difficulties, in returning us in safety, and suffering none to hurt us. I remember in the night season, how the other day I was in the midst of thousands of enemies, and nothing but death before me. It is then hard work to persuade myself, that ever I should be satisfied with bread again. But now we are fed with the finest of the wheat, and, as I may say, with honey out of the rock. Instead of the husk, we have the fatted calf. The thoughts of these things in the particulars of them, and of the love and goodness of God

towards us, make it true of me, what David said of himself, "I watered my
Couch with my tears" (Psalm 6.6). Oh! the wonderful power of God that
mine eyes have seen, affording matter enough for my thoughts to run in, that
when others are sleeping mine eyes are weeping.

I have seen the extreme vanity of this world: One hour I have been in
health, and wealth, wanting nothing. But the next hour in sickness and
wounds, and death, having nothing but sorrow and affliction.

Before I knew what affliction meant, I was ready sometimes to wish for it.
When I lived in prosperity, having the comforts of the world about me, my
relations by me, my heart cheerful, and taking little care for anything, and
yet seeing many, whom I preferred before myself, under many trials and
afflictions, in sickness, weakness, poverty, losses, crosses, and cares of the
world, I should be sometimes jealous least I should have my portion in this
life, and that scripture would come to my mind, "For whom the Lord loveth
he chasteneth, and scourgeth every Son whom he receiveth" (Hebrews 12.6).
But now I see the Lord had His time to scourge and chasten me. The portion
of some is to have their afflictions by drops, now one drop and then another;
but the dregs of the cup, the wine of astonishment, like a sweeping rain that
leaveth no food, did the Lord prepare to be my portion. Affliction I wanted,
and affliction I had, full measure (I thought), pressed down and running
over. Yet I see, when God calls a person to anything, and through never so
many difficulties, yet He is fully able to carry them through and make them
see, and say they have been gainers thereby. And I hope I can say in some
measure, as David did, "It is good for me that I have been afflicted." The
Lord hath showed me the vanity of these outward things. That they are the
vanity of vanities, and vexation of spirit, that they are but a shadow, a blast,
a bubble, and things of no continuance. That we must rely on God Himself,
and our whole dependance must be upon Him. If trouble from smaller
matters begin to arise in me, I have something at hand to check myself with,
and say, why am I troubled? It was but the other day that if I had had the
world, I would have given it for my freedom, or to have been a servant to a
Christian. I have learned to look beyond present and smaller troubles, and to
be quieted under them. As Moses said, "Stand still and see the salvation of
the Lord" (Exodus 14.13).

EDWARD TAYLOR (1645?-1729)

Though Edward Taylor was the most accomplished American poet before Walt Whitman, his poems lay unpublished in the Yale University library for more than two hundred years after his death. They had been deposited there some sixty years after Taylor's death by Ezra Stiles, a grandson of the poet who at that time was president of Yale College. What an American literary historian found when he came upon these poems in the late 1930s were the works of a devout and highly intelligent Puritan pastor.

Edward Taylor served for more than five decades as the minister of a church in the frontier town of Westfield, Massachusetts. He was a staunch defender of the "old" New England way. That is, he required a personal confession of the experience of "saving grace" before he would admit an individual to full church membership and grant him or her the right to participate in the Lord's Supper. In taking this stand Taylor opposed Solomon Stoddard, the highly influential pastor of a church in Northampton, Massachusetts. Stoddard, the grandfather of Jonathan Edwards and Edwards's predecessor in the Northampton pulpit, offered communion as a "converting ordinance" to those who gave assent to Christian doctrine but could not necessarily testify to a certain experience of the work of the Spirit in their lives.

In addition to its obvious importance as a theological and social issue, this controversy over communion had great significance for Taylor's poetry. Portions of only a few of his poems were published in his lifetime. Most were private meditations intended only to express himself to God.

The three poems reproduced below are from Taylor's "Preparatory Meditations." He wrote them as exercises in spiritual devotion in preparation for the monthly administration of communion. Because he held such a high view of the Lord's Supper, he valued all means of preparing the soul for participation in it. Writing poetry was one of the most important of those means.

Although scant information survives about Taylor's education in England, his poems show the influence of English Metaphysical poets such as John Donne and George Herbert. Taylor's works often display a twisted syntax and startling diction. They employ metaphysical conceits, arresting metaphors elaborated at great length (like the image of Jesus as "Heavens Sugar Cake" in "Meditation 8"). Taylor's convoluted syntax and earthy diction offer us a view of God as the covenantal healer of life's brokenness. The famished soul of "Meditation 8" finds at the communion table the God of promise, "the Bread of Life in't at my doore." In "Meditation 22," the poet whose "quaintest metaphors are ragged Stuff, / Making the Sun seem like a Mullipuff," must cry out to God for the power to praise:

> That I thy glorious Praise may Trumpet right,
> Be thou my Song, and make Lord, me thy Pipe.

Meditation 8, on John 6:51:
I Am the Living Bread

I kening through Astronomy Divine
    The Worlds bright Battlement, wherein I spy
A Golden Path my Pensill cannot line,
    From that bright Throne unto my Threshold ly.
    And while my puzzled thoughts about it pore
    I finde the Bread of Life in't at my doore.

When that this Bird of Paradise put in
    This Wicker Cage (my Corps) to tweedle praise
Had peckt the Fruite forbad: and so did fling
    Away its Food; and lost its golden dayes;
    It fell into Celestiall Famine sore:
    And never could attain a morsell more.

Alas! alas! Poore Bird, what wilt thou doe?
    The Creatures field no food for Souls e're gave.
And if thou knock at Angells dores they show
    An Empty Barrell: they no soul bread have.
    Alas! Poore Bird, the Worlds White Loafe is done.
    And cannot yield thee here the smallest Crumb.

In this sad state, Gods Tender Bowells run
    Out streams of Grace: And he to end all strife
The Purest Wheate in Heaven, his deare-dear Son
    Grinds, and kneads up into this Bread of Life.
    Which Bread of Life from Heaven down came and stands
    Disht on thy Table up by Angells Hands.

Did God mould up this Bread in Heaven, and bake,

Source: *The Poems of Edward Taylor*, ed. Donald E. Stanford (New Haven: Yale University Press, 1960).

Which from his Table came, and to thine goeth?
Doth he bespeake thee thus, This Soule Bread take.
    Come Eate thy fill of this thy Gods White Loafe?
    Its Food too fine for Angells, yet come, take
    And Eate thy fill. Its Heavens Sugar Cake.
What Grace is this knead in this Loafe? This thing
    Souls are but petty things it to admire.
Yee Angells, help: This fill would to the brim
    Heav'ns whelm'd-down Chrystall meele Bowle, yea and higher.
    This Bread of Life dropt in thy mouth, doth Cry.
    Eate, Eate me, Soul, and thou shalt never dy.

The Preface*

Infinity, when all things it beheld
In Nothing, and of Nothing all did build,
Upon what Base was fixt the Lath, wherein
He turn'd the Globe, and riggalld it so trim?
Who blew the Bellows of his Furnace Vast?
Or held the Mould wherein the world was Cast?
Who laid its Corner Stone? Or whose Command?
Where stand the Pillars upon which it stands?
Who Lac'de and Fillitted the earth so fine,
With Rivers like green Ribbons Smaragdine?
Who made the Sea's its Selvedge, and it locks
Like a Quilt Ball within a Silver Box?
Who Spread its Canopy? Or Curtains Spun?
Who in this Bowling Alley bowld the Sun?
Who made it always when it rises set
To go at once both down, and up to get?
Who th' Curtain rods made for this Tapistry?
Who hung the twinckling Lanthorns in the Sky?
Who? who did this? or who is he? Why, know
Its Onely Might Almighty this did doe.
His hand hath made this noble worke which Stands
His Glorious Handywork not made by hands.
Who spake all things from nothing; and with ease
Can speake all things to nothing, if he please.
Whose Little finger at his pleasure Can
Out mete ten thousand worlds with halfe a Span:

*From "God's Determinations Touching His Elect"

Whose Might Almighty can by half a looks
Root up the rocks and rock the hills by th' roots.
Can take this mighty World up in his hande,
And shake it like a Squitchen or a Wand.
Whose single Frown will make the Heavens shake
Like as an aspen leafe the Winde makes quake.
Oh! what a might is this Whose single frown
Doth shake the world as it would shake it down?
Which All from Nothing fet, from Nothing, All:
Hath All on Nothing set, lets Nothing fall.
Gave All to nothing Man indeed, whereby
Through nothing man all might him Glorify.
In Nothing then imbosst the brightest Gem
More pretious than all pretiousness in them.
But Nothing man did throw down all by Sin:
And darkened that lightsom Gem in him.
    That now his Brightest Diamond is grown
    Darker by far than any Coalpit Stone.

Huswifery

Make me, O Lord, thy Spining Wheele compleate.
    Thy Holy Worde my Distaff make for mee.
Make mine Affections thy Swift Flyers neate
    And make my Soule thy holy Spoole to be.
    My Conversation make to be thy Reele
    And reele the yarn thereon spun of thy Wheele.

Make me thy Loome then, knit therein this Twine:
    And make thy Holy Spirit, Lord, winde quills:
Then weave the Web thyselfe. The yarn is fine.
    Thine Ordinances make my Fulling Mills.
    Then dy the same in Heavenly Colours Choice,
    All pinkt with Varnisht Flowers of Paradise.

Then cloath therewith mine Understanding, Will,
    Affections, Judgment, Conscience, Memory
My Words, and Actions, that their shine may fill
    My wayes with glory and thee glorify.
    Then mine apparell shall display before yee
    That I am Cloathd in Holy robes for glory.

JONATHAN EDWARDS (1703-1758)

Jonathan Edwards deserves a preeminent place in any account of American piety. He was the editor of David Brainerd's journal, a work with far-reaching influence on evangelical conceptions of the spiritual life. Edwards and George Whitefield were the two most prominent figures in the colonial Great Awakening, a general revival sparked to considerable degree by Edwards's account of spiritual renewal in his own congregation at Northampton, Massachusetts. Edwards also preached perhaps the most famous sermon in all of American history on July 8, 1741, at Enfield, Connecticut. That sermon, "Sinners in the Hands of an Angry God," provided the definitive statement for later generations who preached hellfire and brimstone. Those familiar with more of Edwards's accomplishments know that Edwards also wrote *A Treatise Concerning Religious Affections* (1746), one of the most sensitive analyses of the religious life. In this book, Edwards—showing remarkable insight into spiritual experience and solid grounding in both the Bible and other forms of learning—attempted to discriminate between those human manifestations that indicated the presence of genuine faith and those that did not. In addition, scholars know Edwards as the author of carefully argued works in philosophy and theology.

Edwards's concern for the spiritual life is especially remarkable in light of his great intellect. Unlike many others in history for whom thought replaced faith, Edwards was a man whose mental reflection seemed always to push him further in his search for God.

Edwards was the only son in the large family of a Congregationalist minister. After going to Yale when that college was still in its infancy, he spent some time in independent study, served briefly as a minister to a new Presbyterian church in New York City, and put in a stint as a Yale tutor. Then he became the assistant to his grandfather, Solomon Stoddard, at Stoddard's church in Northampton. In 1729 Edwards succeeded his grandfather and remained in that station for over twenty years. In 1750 his congregation dismissed him after a controversy over standards for admission to the church. He then worked in a frontier mission at Stockbridge, Massachusetts, preaching to both Native Americans and whites. Edwards died on March 22, 1758, from an inoculation for smallpox that he received shortly after arriving in Princeton to take up duties as the president of the College of New Jersey (later Princeton University).

Throughout his life Edwards devoted himself to diligent study but also to exacting spiritual discipline. He became a notable defender of Calvinist theology, bringing older arguments up to date in works like *Freedom of the Will* (1754) and *Original Sin* (1758). These books were dominated by Edwards's sense of the glory and grandeur of God, themes that he worked out with regard to all of world history in a series of sermons called *A History of the Work of Redemption* (1744) and in a meditative reflection entitled *A Dissertation Concerning the End for Which God Created the World* (published posthumously in 1765).

Above all else, Edwards was an analyst of the heart. His sermons probed the spiritual lives of his parishioners, urging them to flee self-reliance and turn wholeheartedly to Christ. His larger works examined the religious consequences of doctrinal propositions. These public pronouncements were not the fruit of abstract thought alone; they grew out of Edwards's own experience. Before he attempted to offer the balm of the gospel to others, he looked first to his own need. Sometime after the first wave of revival had passed over Northampton, he set down an account of his own journey to faith. While this personal narrative is the record of a conversion, it is also much more. Primarily it contains a key to understanding Edwards's exalted sense of God, a sense that drove, comforted, inspired, and humbled him throughout his life.

Personal Narrative

I had a variety of concerns and exercises about my soul from my childhood, but had two more remarkable seasons of awakening, before I met with that change by which I was brought to those new dispositions, and that new sense of things, that I have since had. The first time was when I was a boy, some years before I went to college, at a time of remarkable awakening in my father's congregation, I was then very much affected for many months, and concerned about the things of religion, and my soul's salvation; and was abundant in duties. I used to pray five times a day in secret, and to spend much time in religious talk with other boys; and used to meet with them to pray together. I experienced I know not what kind of delight in religion. My mind was much engaged in it, and had much selfrighteous pleasure; and it was my delight to abound in religious duties. I with some of my schoolmates joined together, and built a booth in a swamp, in a very retired spot, for a place of prayer. And besides, I had particular secret places of my own in the

Source: This excerpt was printed in the 1808 Austin edition of Edwards's *Works*, volume one.

woods, where I used to retire by myself; and was from time to time much affected. My affections seemed to be lively and easily moved, and I seemed to be in my element when engaged in religious duties. And I am ready to think, many are deceived with such affections, and such a kind of delight as I then had in religion, and mistake it for grace.

But in process of time, my convictions and affections wore off; and I entirely lost all those affections and delights and left off secret prayer, at least as to any constant performance of it; and returned like a dog to his vomit, and went on in the ways of sin. Indeed I was at times very uneasy, especially towards the latter part of my time at college; when it pleased God, to seize me with a pleurisy; in which he brought me nigh to the grave, and shook me over the pit of hell. And yet, it was not long after my recovery, before I fell again into my old ways of sin. But God would not suffer me to go on with any quietness; I had great and violent inward struggles, till, after many conflicts with wicked inclinations, repeated resolutions, and bonds that I laid myself under by a kind of vows to God, I was brought wholly to break off all former wicked ways, and all ways of known outward sin; and to apply myself to seek salvation, and practice many religious duties; but without that kind of affection and delight which I had formerly experienced. My concern now wrought more by inward struggles and conflicts, and selfreflections. I made seeking my salvation the main business of my life. But yet, it seems to me, I sought after a miserable manner; which has made me sometimes since to question, whether ever it issued in that which was saving; being ready to doubt, whether such miserable seeking ever succeeded. I was indeed brought to seek salvation in a manner that I never was before; I felt a spirit to part with all things in the world, for an interest in Christ. My concern continued and prevailed, with many exercising thoughts and inward struggles; but yet it never seemed to be proper to express that concern by the name of terror.

From my childhood up, my mind had been full of objections against the doctrine of God's sovereignty, in choosing whom he would to eternal life, and rejecting whom he pleased; leaving them eternally to perish, and be everlastingly tormented in hell. It used to appear like a horrible doctrine to me. But I remember the time very well, when I seemed to be convinced, and fully satisfied, as to this sovereignty of God, and his justice in thus eternally disposing of men, according to his sovereign pleasure. But never could give an account, how, or by what means, I was thus convinced, not in the least imagining at the time, nor a long time after, that there was any extraordinary influence of God's Spirit in it; but only that now I saw further, and my reason apprehended the justice and reasonableness of it. However, my mind rested in it; and it put an end to all those cavils and objections. And there has been a wonderful alteration in my mind, in respect to the doctrine of God's sovereignty, from that day to this; so that I scarce ever have found so much as the rising of an objection against it, in the most absolute sense, in God's shewing mercy to whom he will shew mercy, and hardening whom he will. God's absolute sovereignty and justice, with respect to salvation and damnation, is what my mind seems to rest assured of, as much as of any thing that I see with my eyes; at least it is so at times. But I have often, since that first conviction, had quite another kind of sense of God's sovereignty than I had then. I have often since had not only a conviction, but a delightful conviction. The doctrine has very often appeared exceeding pleasant, bright, and sweet. Absolute sovereignty is what I love to ascribe to God. But my first conviction was not so.

The first instance that I remember of that sort of inward, sweet delight in God and divine things that I have lived much in since, was on reading those words, I Tim. i.17. *Now unto the King eternal, immortal, invisible, the only wise God, be honor and glory for ever and ever, Amen.* As I read the words, there came into my soul, and was as it were diffused through it, a sense of the glory of the Divine Being; a new sense, quite different from any thing I ever experienced before. Never any words of scripture seemed to me as these words did. I thought with myself, how excellent a Being that was, and how happy I should be, if I might enjoy that God, and be rapt up to him in heaven, and be as it were swallowed up in him for ever! I kept saying, and as it were singing over these words of scripture to myself; and went to pray to God that I might enjoy him, and prayed in a manner quite different from what I used to do; with a new sort of affection. But it never came into my thought, that there was any thing spiritual, or of a saving nature in this.

From about that time, I began to have a new kind of apprehensions and ideas of Christ, and the work of redemption, and the glorious way of salvation by him. An inward, sweet sense of these things, at times, came into my heart; and my soul was led away in pleasant views and contemplations of them. And my mind was greatly engaged to spend my time in reading and meditating on Christ, on the beauty and excellency of his person, and the lovely way of salvation by free grace in him. I found no books so delightful to me, as those that treated of these subjects. Those words Cant. ii.1, used to be abundantly with me, *I am the Rose of Sharon, and the Lilly of the valleys.* The words seemed to me, sweetly to represent the loveliness and beauty of Jesus Christ. The whole book of Canticles used to be pleasant to me, and I used to be much in reading it, about that time; and found, from time to time, an inward sweetness, that would carry me away, in my contemplations. This I know not how to express otherwise, than by a calm, sweet abstraction of soul from all the concerns of this world; and sometimes a kind of vision, or fixed ideas and imaginations, of being alone in the mountains, or some solitary wilderness, far from all mankind, sweetly conversing with Christ, and wrapt and swallowed up in God. The sense I had of divine things, would often of a sudden kindle up, as it were, a sweet burning in my heart; an ardor of soul, that I know not how to express.

Not long after I first began to experience these things, I gave an account to my father of some things that had passed in my mind. I was pretty much affected by the discourse we had together; and when the discourse was ended, I walked abroad alone, in a solitary place in my father's pasture, for contemplation. And as I was walking there, and looking up on the sky and clouds, there came into my mind so sweet a sense of the glorious *majesty* and *grace* of God, that I know not how to express. I seemed to see them both in a sweet conjunction; majesty and meekness joined together; it was a sweet, and gentle, and holy majesty; and also a majestic meekness; an awful sweetness; a high, and great, and holy gentleness.

After this my sense of divine things gradually increased, and became more and more lively, and had more of that inward sweetness. The appearance of every thing was altered; there seemed to be, as it were, a calm, sweet cast, of appearance of divine glory, in almost every thing. God's excellency, his wisdom, his purity and love, seemed to appear in every thing; in the sun, moon, and stars; in the clouds, and blue sky; in the grass, flowers, trees; in the water, and all nature; which used greatly to fix my mind. I often used to sit and view the moon for continuance; and in the day, spent much time in viewing the clouds and sky, to behold the sweet glory of God in these things; in the mean time, singing forth, with a low voice my contemplations of the Creator and Redeemer. And scarce any thing, among all the works of nature, was so sweet to me as thunder and lightning; formerly, nothing had been so terrible to me. Before, I used to be uncommonly terrified with thunder, and to be struck with terror when I saw a thunder storm rising; but now, on the contrary, it rejoiced me. I felt God, so to speak, at the first appearance of a thunder storm; and used to take the opportunity, at such times, to fix myself in order to view the clouds, and see the lightnings play, and hear the majestic and awful voice of God's thunder, which oftentimes was exceedingly entertaining, leading me to sweet contemplations of my great and glorious God. While thus engaged, it always seemed natural to me to sing, or chant for my meditations; or, to speak my thoughts in soliloquies with a singing voice.

* * *

My sense of divine things seemed gradually to increase, until I went to preach at Newyork, which was about a year and a half after they began; and while I was there, I felt them, very sensibly, in a much higher degree than I had done before. My longings after God and holiness, were much increased. Pure and humble, holy and heavenly Christianity, appeared exceeding amiable to me. I felt a burning desire to be in every thing a complete Christian; and conformed to the blessed image of Christ; and that I might live, in all things, according to the pure, sweet and blessed rules of the gospel. I had an eager thirsting after progress in these things; which put me upon pursuing and pressing after them. It was my continual strife day and night, and constant inquiry, how I should *be* more holy, and *live* more holily, and more becoming a child of God, and a disciple of Christ. I now sought an increase of grace and holiness, and a holy life, with much more earnestness, than ever I sought grace before I had it. I used to be continually examining myself, and studying and contriving for likely ways and means, how I should live holily, with far greater diligence and earnestness, than ever I pursued any thing in my life; but yet with too great a dependence on my own strength; which afterwards proved a great damage to me. My experience had not then taught me, as it has some since, my extreme feebleness and impotence, every manner of way; and the bottomless depths of secret corruption and deceit there was in my heart. However, I went on with my eager pursuit after more holiness, and conformity to Christ.

The heaven I desired was a heaven of holiness; to be with God, and to spend my eternity in divine love, and holy communion with Christ. My mind was very much taken up with contemplations on heaven, and the enjoyments there; and living there in perfect holiness, humility and love: And it used at time to appear a great part of the happiness of heaven, that there the saints could express their love to Christ. It appeared to me a great clog and burden, that what I felt within, I could not express as I desired. The inward ardor of my soul, seemed to be hindered and pent up, and could not freely flame out as it would. I used often to think, how in heaven this principle should freely and fully vent and express itself. Heaven appeared exceedingly delightful, as a world of love; and that all happiness consisted in living in pure, humble, heavenly, divine love.

I remember the thoughts I used then to have of holiness; and said sometimes to myself, "I do certainly know that I love holiness, such as the gospel prescribes." It appeared to me, that there was nothing in it but what was ravishingly lovely; the highest beauty and amiableness . . . a *divine* beauty; far purer than any thing here upon earth; and that every thing else was like mire and defilement, in comparison of it.

Holiness, as I then wrote down some of my contemplations on it, appeared to me to be of a sweet, pleasant, charming, serene, calm nature; which brought an inexpressible purity, brightness, peacefulness and ravishment to the soul. In other words, that it made the soul like a field or garden of God, with all manner of pleasant flowers; all pleasant, delightful, and undisturbed; enjoying a sweet calm, and the gently vivifying beams of the sun. The soul of a true Christian, as I then wrote my meditations, appeared like such a little white flower as we see in the spring of the year; low and humble on the ground, opening its bosom to receive the pleasant beams of the sun's glory; rejoicing as it were in a calm rapture; diffusing around a sweet fragrancy; standing peacefully and lovingly, in the midst of other flowers round about; all in like manner opening their bosoms, to drink in the light of the sun. There was no part of creature holiness, that I had so great a sense of its loveliness, as humility, brokenness of heart and poverty of spirit; and there was nothing that I so earnestly longed for. My heart panted after this, to lie low before God, as in the dust; that I might be nothing, and that God might be ALL, that I might become as a little child.

While at Newyork, I was sometimes much affected with reflections of my past life, considering how late it was before I began to be truly religious; and how wickedly I had lived till then; and once so as to weep abundantly, and for a considerable time together.

On *January* 12, 1723. I made a solemn dedication of myself to God, and wrote it down; giving up myself, and all that I had to God; to be for the future, in no respect, my own; to act as one that had no right to himself, in any respect. And solemnly vowed, to take God for my whole portion and felicity; looking on nothing else, as any part of my obedience: engaging to fight, with all my might, against the world, the flesh, and the devil, to the end of my life. But I have reason to be infinitely humbled, when I consider, how much I have failed, of answering my obligation.

I had, then, abundance of sweet, religious conversation, in the family where I lived, with Mr. John Smith, and his pious mother. My heart was knit in affection, to those, in whom were appearances of true piety; and I could bear the thoughts of no other companions, but such as were holy, and the disciples of the blessed Jesus. I had great longings, for the advancement of Christ's kingdom in the world; and my sweet prayer used to be, in great part, taken up in praying for it. If I heard the least hint, of any thing that happened, in any part of the world, that appeared, in some respect or other, to have a favourable aspect, on the interests of Christ's kingdom, my soul eagerly catched at it; and it would much animate and refresh me. I used to be eager to read public news-letters, mainly for that end; to see if I could not find some news, favourable to the interest of religion in the world.

I very frequently used to retire into a solitary place, on the banks of Hudson's River, at some distance from the city, for contemplation on divine things and secret converse with God; and had many sweet hours there. Sometimes Mr. Smith and I walked there together, to converse on the things of God; and our conversation used to turn much on the advancement of Christ's kingdom in the world, and the glorious things that God would accomplish for his church in the latter days. I had then, and at other times, the greatest delight in the holy scriptures, of any book whatsoever. Often-times in reading it, every word seemed to touch my heart. I felt a harmony between something in my heart, and those sweet and powerful words. I seemed often to see so much light exhibited by every sentence, and such a refreshing food communicated, that I could not get along in reading; often dwelling long on one sentence, to see the wonders contained in it; and yet almost every sentence seemed to be full of wonders.

I came away from Newyork in the month of April, 1723, and had a most bitter parting with Madam Smith and her son. My heart seemed to sink within me, at leaving the family and city, where I had enjoyed so many sweet and pleasant days. I went from New York to Wethersfield, by water; and as I sailed away, I kept sight of the city as long as I could. However, that night after this sorrowful parting, I was greatly comforted in God at Westchester, where we went ashore to lodge. . . .

. . . I continued much in the same frame, in the general, as when at New-york, till I went to Newhaven, as Tutor of the College: particularly, once at Bolton, on a journey from Boston, while walking out alone in the fields. After I went to Newhaven, I sunk in religion; my mind being diverted from my eager pursuits after holiness, by some affairs, that greatly perplexed and distracted my thoughts.

* * *

Since I came to this town [Northampton], I have often had sweet complacency in God, in views of his glorious perfections and the excellency of Jesus Christ. God has appeared to me a glorious and lovely Being, chiefly on account of his holiness. The holiness of God has always appeared to me the most lovely of all his attributes. The doctrines of God's absolute sovereignty, and free grace, in shewing mercy to whom he would shew mercy; and man's absolute dependence on the operations of God's Holy Spirit, have very often appeared to me as sweet and glorious doctrines. These doctrines have been much my delight. God's sovereignty has ever appeared to me, great part of his glory. It has often been my delight to approach God, and adore him as a sovereign God, and ask sovereign mercy of him.

I have loved the doctrines of the gospel; they have been to my soul like green pastures. The gospel has seemed to me the richest treasure; the treasure that I have most desired, and longed that it might dwell richly in me. The way of salvation by Christ has appeared, in a general way, glorious and excellent, most pleasant and most beautiful. It has often seemed to me, that it would in a great measure spoil heaven, to receive it in any other way. That text has often been affecting and delightful to me, Isa. xxxii.2. *A man shall be an hiding place from the wind, and a covert from the tempest, &c.*

* * *

Once, as I rode out into the woods for my health, in 1737, having alighted from my horse in a retired place, as my manner commonly has been, to walk for divine contemplation and prayer, I had a view that for me was extraordinary, of the glory of the Son of God, as Mediator between God and man, and his wonderful, great, full, pure and sweet grace and love, and meek and gentle condescension. This grace that appeared so calm and sweet, appeared also great above the heavens. The person of Christ appeared ineffably excellent with an excellency great enough to swallow up all thought and conception . . . which continued as near as I can judge, about an hour; which kept me the greater part of the time in a flood of tears, and weeping aloud. I felt an ardency of soul to be, what I know not otherwise how to express, emptied and annihilated; to lie in the dust, and to be full of Christ alone; to love him with a holy and pure love; to trust in him; to live upon him; to serve and follow him; and to be perfectly sanctified and made pure, with a divine and heavenly purity. I have, several other times, had views very much of the same nature, and which have had the same effects.

I have many times had a sense of the glory of the third person in the Trinity, in his office of Sanctifier; in his holy operations, communicating divine light and life to the soul. God, in the communications of his Holy Spirit, has appeared as an infinite fountain of divine glory and sweetness; being full, and sufficient to fill and satisfy the soul; pouring forth itself in sweet communications; like the sun in its glory, sweetly and pleasantly diffusing light and life. And I have sometimes had an affecting sense of the excellency of the word of God, as a word of life; as the light of life; a sweet, excellent lifegiving word; accompanied with a thirsting after that word, that it might dwell richly in my heart.

Often, since I lived in this town, I have had very affecting views of my own sinfulness and vileness; very frequently to such a degree as to hold me in a kind of loud weeping, sometimes for a considerable time together; so that I have often been forced to shut myself up. I have had a vastly greater sense of my own wickedness, and the badness of my heart, than ever I had before my conversion. It has often appeared to me, that if God should mark iniquity against me, I should appear the very worst of all mankind; of all that have been, since the beginning of the world to this time; and that I should have by far the lowest place in hell. When others, that have come to talk with me about their soul concerns, have expressed the sense they have had of their own wickedness, by saying that it seemed to them, that they were as bad as the devil himself; I thought their expressions seemed exceeding faint and feeble, to represent my wickedness.

* * *

I have a much greater sense of my universal, exceeding dependence on God's grace and strength, and mere good pleasure, of late, than I used formerly to have; and have experienced more of an abhorrence of my own righteousness. The very thought of any joy arising in me, on any consideration of my own amiableness, performances, or experiences, or any goodness of heart or life, is nauseous and detestable to me. And yet I am greatly afflicted with a proud and selfrighteous spirit, much more sensibly than I

used to be formerly. I see that serpent rising and putting forth its head
continually, every where, all around me.

Though it seems to me, that, in some respects, I was a far better Christian,
for two or three years after my first conversion, than I am now; and lived in a
more constant delight and pleasure; yet, of late years, I have had a more full
and constant sense of the absolute sovereignty of God, and a delight in that
sovereignty; and have had more of a sense of the glory of Christ, as a
Mediator revealed in the gospel. On one Saturday night, in particular, I had
such a discovery of the excellency of the gospel above all other doctrines,
that I could not but say to myself, "This is my chosen light, my chosen
doctrine;" and of Christ, "This is my chosen Prophet." It appeared sweet,
beyond all expression, to follow Christ, and to be taught, and enlightened,
and instructed by him; to learn of him, and live to him. Another Saturday
night, (*January* 1739) I had such a sense, how sweet and blessed a thing it
was to walk in the way of duty; to do that which was right and meet to be
done, and agreeable to the holy mind of God; that it caused me to break forth
into a kind of loud weeping, which held me some time, so that I was forced to
shut myself up, and fasten the doors. I could not but, as it were, cry out,
"How happy are they which do that which is right in the sight of God! They
are blessed indeed, they are the happy ones!" I had, at the same time, a very
affecting sense, how meet and suitable it was that God should govern the
world, and order all things according to his own pleasure; and I rejoiced in it,
that God reigned, and that his will was done.

NATHAN COLE (1711-1783)

Nathan Cole was a carpenter and farmer who lived in Kensington, Connecticut, during the time of the colonial Great Awakening. His account of going to hear George Whitefield, the celebrated evangelist, and of the lengthy spiritual struggle that followed is most striking. It comes from the pen of a common person about whom not too much more is known. Nathan Cole was not a member of the spiritual elite. He was not a well-trained minister. Yet his "spiritual travels" represent what a number of his contemporaries also experienced during the Great Awakening. And his account is important for understanding one of the most visible kinds of piety in America.

Cole's spiritual autobiography shows us, first, the great importance of the itinerant preacher in America. He had an extraordinary experience in response to hearing Whitefield preach, but it is an experience that has been repeated countless times in later history. Whether the speaker has been Charles Finney, Dwight L. Moody, Billy Sunday, Sam Jones, Oral Roberts, Jimmy Swaggert, Billy Graham, or some other widely recognized evangelist, Americans have consistently drawn inspiration from the forceful preaching of traveling revivalists. George Whitefield set the mold. His preaching in the colonial South, in Philadelphia and New York, and in the towns and villages of New England made him the first truly American religious phenomenon. When he came to Middletown, Connecticut, in 1740, he was already a sensation. Nathan Cole's reaction to his preaching was itself a model for how others—in different times and other places—would respond to similar appeals.

A second reason why Cole's spiritual pilgrimage is so interesting has to do with its detailed record of a conversion. The history of Christianity in America is, to an unusual extent, the history of dramatic conversions. The Puritans had been among the first to develop a theology for the conversion experience. The long line of revivalists who followed in their train sharpened both techniques and expectations for conversions. Of course, many other things besides conversions enter into American piety. But the passage from a sense of sin to a sense of grace, from darkness to light, from alienation to reconciliation, looms very large in any history of faith in America. In some ways Nathan Cole's conversion was not typical. It took longer than most others, it involved a Calvinistic understanding of the Christian message that soon passed from favor, and it occurred under unusual and extended psychological strain. Yet the life-changing effect on Cole very much resembled the effects of other conversions—of both the humble and the well-known—that would follow.

In his later years Cole broke with the established Congregationalist Church to worship with a "separate" body. Such groups sprang up in the wake of the colonial revival as some Congregationalist converts grew dissatisfied with the more formal worship of that church. The members of these groups sought ongoing spiritual experiences that could match in fervor and insight the ardor of their conversions. In this way too, Nathan Cole anticipated a path that later converts in American history would also pursue.

Cole wrote his spiritual autobiography in 1765, a quarter of a century after George Whitefield burst into his world.

Spiritual Travels

I was born Feb 15th 1711 and born again octo 1741—

When I was young I had very early Convictions; but after I grew up I was an Arminian untill I was *near* 30 years of age; I intended to be saved by my own works such as prayers and good deeds.

Now it pleased God to send Mr Whitefield into this land; and my hearing of his preaching at Philadelphia, like one of the Old apostles, and many thousands flocked to hear him preach the Gospel; and great numbers were converted to Christ; I felt the Spirit of God drawing me by conviction; I longed to see and hear him, and wished he would come this way. I heard he was come to New York and the Jerseys and great multitudes flocking after him under great concern for their Souls which brought on my Concern more and more hoping soon to see him but next I heard he was at long Island; then at Boston and next at Northampton.

Then on a Sudden, in the morning about 8 or 9 of the Clock there came a messenger and said Mr Whitfield preached at Hartford and Weathersfield yesterday and is to preach at Middletown this morning at ten of the Clock, I was in my field at Work, I dropt my tool that I had in my hand and ran home to my wife telling her to make ready quickly to go and hear Mr Whitfield preach at Middletown, then run to my pasture for my horse with all my might; fearing that I should be too late; having my horse I with my wife soon mounted the horse and went forward as fast as I thought the horse could

Source: Michael J. Crawford, "The Spiritual Travels of Nathan Cole," *William and Mary Quarterly* 33 (1976): 92-98.

bear, and when my horse got *much* out of breath I would get down and put my wife on the Saddle and bid her ride as fast as she could and not Stop or Slack for me except I bad her and so I would run untill I was *much* out of breath; and then mount my horse again, and so I did several times to favour my horse; we improved every moment to get along as if we were fleeing for our lives; all the while fearing we should be too late to hear the Sermon, for we had twelve miles to ride double in little more than an hour and we went round by the upper housen parish.

And when we came within about half a mile or a mile of the Road that comes down from Hartford weathersfield and Stepney to Middletown; on high land I saw before me a Cloud or fogg rising; I first thought it came from the great River, but as I came nearer the Road, I heard a noise something like a low rumbling thunder and presently found it was the noise of Horses feet coming down the Road and this Cloud was a Cloud of dust made by the Horses feet; it arose some Rods into the air over the tops of Hills and trees and when I came within about 20 *rods* of the Road, I could see men and horses Sliping along in the Cloud like shadows and as I drew nearer it seemed like a steady Stream of horses and their riders, scarcely a horse more than his length behind another, all of a Lather and foam with sweat, their breath rolling out of their nostrils every Jump; every horse seemed to go with all his might to carry his rider to hear news from heaven for the saving of Souls, it made me tremble to see the Sight, how the world was in a Struggle; I found a Vacance between two horses to Slip in mine and my Wife said law our Cloaths will be all spoiled see how they look, for they were so Covered with dust, that they looked almost all of a Colour Coats, hats, Shirts, and horses.

We went down in the Stream but heard no man speak a word all the way for 3 miles but every one pressing forward in great haste and when we got to Middletown old meeting house there was a great Multitude *it was said to be 3 or 4000* of people Assembled together; we dismounted and shook of[f] our Dust; and the ministers were then Coming to the meeting house; I turned and looked towards the Great River and saw the ferry boats Running swift backward and forward bringing over loads of people and the Oars Rowed nimble and quick; every thing men horses and boats seemed to be Struggling for life; *The land and banks over the river looked black with people and horses* all along the 12 miles I saw no man at work in his field, but all seemed to be gone.

When I saw Mr Whitfield come upon the Scaffold he Lookt almost angelical; a young, Slim, slender, youth before some thousands of people with a bold undaunted Countenance, and my hearing how God was with him every where as he came along it Solemnized my mind; and put me into a trembling fear before he began to preach; for he looked as if he was Clothed with authority from the Great God; *and a sweet sollome solemnity sat upon his*

brow And my hearing him preach, gave me a heart wound; By Gods blessing: my old Foundation was broken up, and I saw that my righteousness
would not save me; then I was convinced of the doctrine of Election: and
went right to quarrelling with God about it; because that all I could do
would not save me; and he had decreed from Eternity who should be saved
and who not.

I began to think I was not Elected, and that God made some for heaven and
me for hell. And I thought God was not Just in so doing, I thought I did not
stand on even Ground with others, if as I thought; I was made to be damned;
My heart then rose against God exceedingly, for his making me for hell;
Now this distress lasted Almost two years:—Poor—Me—Miserable me.—It
pleased God to bring on my Convictions more and more, and I was loaded
with the guilt of Sin, I saw I was undone for ever; I carried Such a weight of
Sin in my breast or mind, that it seemed to me as if I should sink into the
ground every step; and I kept all to my self as much as I could; I went month
after month mourning and begging for mercy, I tryed every way I could think
to help my self but all ways failed:—Poor me it took away *most* all my
Comfort of eating, drinking, Sleeping, or working. Hell fire was most always
in my mind; and I have hundreds of times put my fingers into my pipe when I
have been smoaking to feel how fire felt: And to see how my body could bear
to lye in Hell fire for ever and ever. Now my countenance was sad so that
others took notice of it.

   Sometimes I had some secret hope in the mercy of God; that some time or
other he would have mercy on me; And so I took some hopes, and thought I
would do all that I could do, and remove all things out of the way that might
possibly be an hindrance; and I thought I must go to my Honoured Father
and Mother and ask their forgiveness for every thing I had done amiss
toward them in all my life; if they had any thing against me; I went and when
I came near the house one of my Brothers was there, and asked me what was
the matter with me: I told him I did not feel well, and passed by; But he
followed and asked again what was the matter. I gave him the same answer,
but said he something is the matter more than Ordinary for I see it in your
Countenance: I refused to tell at present—Poor me—I went to my Father and
Mother and told them what I came for: and asked them to forgive me every
thing they had against me concerning my disobedience or whatsoever else it
might be; they said they had not any thing against me, and both fell aweeping
like Children for Joy to see me so concerned for my Soul.

   Now when I went away I made great Resolutions that I would forsake
every thing that was Sinfull; And do to my uttermost every thing that was
good; And at once I felt a calm in my mind, and I had no desire to any thing
that was sin as I thought; But here the Devil thought to Catch me on a false

hope, for I began to think that I was converted, for I thought I felt a real Change in me. But God in his mercy did not leave me here to perish; but in the space of ten days I was made to see that I was yet in the Gall of bitterness; my Convictions came on again more smart than ever—poor me—Oh then I long'd to be in the Condition of some good Man.

There was then a very Mortal disease in the land, the fever and bloody flux; and I was possest with a notion that if I had it I should die and goe right to hell, but I presently had it and very hard too: then my heart rose against God again for making me for hell, when he might as well have made me for heaven; or not made me at all:—Poor me—Oh that I could be a Dog or a toad or any Creature but Man: I thought that would be a happy change for they had no Souls and I had. Oh what will become of me was the language of my mind; for now I was worse than ever, my heart was as hard as a Stone; my Eyes were dry, once I could weep for my Self but now cannot shed one tear; I was as it were in the very mouth of hell. The very flashes of hell fire were in my Mind; Eternity before me, and my time short here. Now when all ways failed me then I longed to be annihilated; or to have my Soul die with my body; but that way failed too. Hell fire hell fire ran Swift in my mind and my distemper grew harder and harder upon me, and my nature was just wore out—Poor me—poor Soul.

One night my brother Elisha came to see me, and I spake to him and said I should certainly die within two or three days at the out Side for my Nature cannot possibly hold it any longer; and I shall certainly goe right to hell: And do you always remember that your poor brother is in hell; don't you never think that I am in heaven but take care of yourself and always remember every day that your poor brother is in hell fire.—Misery—Miserable me; my brother got out of his Chair and went to speak to me, but he could not for weeping and went out of the house; and went away home and told my Father and Mother what I had said to him, and they were greatly distressed for me, and thought in the morning they would come and see me; but their distress grew so great for me that they could not stay but Came in the night.

And when they came into the house Mother seem'd to bring heaven into the house; but there was no heaven for me: She said Oh Nathan will you despair of the mercy of God, do not for a thousand of worlds, don't despair of the mercy of God, for he can have mercy at the very last gasp; I told her there was no mercy for me, I was going right down to hell, for I cannot feel grieved for my self, I can't relent, I can't weep for my self, I cannot shed one tear for my Sins; I am a gone Creature: Oh Nathan says she I have been so my self that I could not shed one tear if I might have had all the world for it; And the next moment I could cry as freely for Joy as ever I could for any thing in the world: Oh said she I know how you feel now. O if God should Shine into your Soul now it would almost take away your life, it would almost part soul and body; I beg of you not to despair of the mercy of God. I told her I could not bear to hear her talk so; for I cannot pray, my heart is as hard as a stone, do be gone, let me alone: do go home; you cannot do me any good, I am past all help of men or means, either for soul or Body, and after some time I perswaded them to go away; and there I lay all night in such a condition untill sometime the next day with pining thoughts in my mind that my Soul might die with my Body.

And there came some body in with a great Arm full of dry wood and laid it on the fire, *and went out* and it burnt up very briskly as I lay on my Bed with my face toward the fire looking on, with these thoughts in my mind, Oh that I might creep into that fire and lye there and burn to death and die for ever Soul and Body; Oh that God would suffer it—Oh that God would suffer it.—Poor Soul.

And while these thoughts were in my mind God appeared unto me and made me Skringe: before whose face the heavens and the earth fled away; and I was Shrinked into nothing; I knew not whether I was in the body or out, I seemed to hang in open Air before God, and he seemed to Speak to me in an angry and Sovereign way what won't you trust your Soul with God; My heart answered O yes, yes, yes; before I could stir my tongue or lips, And then He seemed to speak again, and say, may not God make one Vessel to honour and an other to dishonour and not let you know it; My heart answered again O yes yes before I cou'd stir my tongue or lips. Now while my Soul was viewing God, my fleshly part was working imaginations and saw many things which I will omitt to tell at this time.

When God appeared to me every thing vanished and was gone in the twinkling of an Eye, as quick as A flash of lightning; But when God disappeared or in some measure withdrew, every thing was in its place again and I was on my Bed. My heart was broken; my burden was fallen of[f] my mind; I was set free, my distress was gone, and I was filled with a pineing desire to see Christs own words in the bible; and I got up off my bed being alone; And by the help of Chairs I got along to the window where my bible was and I opened it and the first place I saw was the 15th Chap: John—on Christs own words and they spake to my very heart and every doubt and scruple that rose in my heart about the truth of Gods word was took right off; and I saw the whole train of Scriptures all in a Connection, and I believe I felt just as the Apostles felt the truth of the word when they writ it, every leaf line and letter smiled in my face; I got the bible up under my Chin and hugged it; it was sweet and lovely; the word was nigh me in my hand, then I began to pray and to praise God.

I could say Oh my God, and then I could think of no expression good enough to speak to Him, *he was altogether—lovely* and then I wou'd fall down into a muse and look back into my past life to see how I had lived and it seemed as if my very heart strings would break with sorrow and grief, to see how I had lived in abuse to this God I saw; then I began to pray and to praise God again, and I could say Oh my God and then I could not find words good enough to speak to his praise; then I fell into a muse and look'd back on my past life; and saw what an abominable unbeliever I had been, O now I could weep for joy and Sorrow, now I had true mourning for sin and never before now I saw sin to be right against God; now my heart and Soul were filled as full as they Could hold with Joy and sorrow; now I perfectly felt truth: now my heart talked with God; now every thing praised God; the trees, the stone, the walls of the house and every thing I could set my eyes on, they all praised God.

And while I was weeping, Sobing and Sighing, as if my heart wou'd break; there came somebody and opened the Door and spake to me, but I made no answer nor turned to see who it was: but I remember I knew the voice but soon forgat who it was: presently my Wife came into the room and asked me what I cryed for; I gave her little or no answer, she stood a while and went out again; for I was swallowed up in God.

Now I had for some years a bitter prejudice against three scornfull men that had wronged me, but now all that was gone away Clear, and my Soul longed for them and loved them; there was nothing that was sinfull that could any wise abide the presence of God; And all the Air was love, now I saw that every thing that was sin fled from the presence of God: As far as darkness is gone from light or beams of the sun for where ever the Sun can be seen clear there is no Darkness. I saw that Darkness could as well be in the Clear light of the Sun, as well as Sin in the presence of God; who is so holy and Sovereign.

Now I saw that I must Suffer as well as do for Christ, now I saw that I must forsake all and follow Christ; now I saw with new eyes; all things became new, A new God; new thoughts and new heart; Now I began to hope I should be converted some time or other, for I was sure that God had done some great thing for my soul; I knew that God had subdued my stubborn heart; I knew my heart would never rise so against God as it had done; here I saw in the aforesaid 15 Chap: of John where I opened the bible first that Christ says to his disciples if ye love me keep my Commandments and then says he this is my Commandment that ye love one another. Oh I thought I could die A thousand deaths for Christ, I thought I could have been trodden under foot of man, be mocked or any thing for Christ—Glory be to God.

> Jesus and I shall never part
> For God is greater than my heart

Now I had in my mind the form of A Gospel Church, and the place where it was settled, and Angels hovering over it, saying, the Glory of the town, the Glory of the town, and strangers that came pressing by had the same to say.

DAVID BRAINERD (1718-1747)

A standard picture of American piety features the serious-minded "Puritan" driven to ever-deeper inwardness in the struggle for godliness. This picture combines otherworldliness and devotion, a heart given over to God and a life barely touching the world. The durability of this picture in America owes a very great deal to the diary of a young Congregationalist missionary of the eighteenth century, David Brainerd.

Brainerd, born in Haddam, Connecticut, in 1718, came to maturity in a New England convulsed by the spiritual dynamism of the colonial Great Awakening. He experienced an earthshaking conversion in 1739 and three years later was expelled from Yale College for displaying too much enthusiasm for religion. After his appointment by the Scottish Society for the Propagation of Christian Knowledge, he worked for four years as a missionary to the Indians in western Massachusetts, eastern New York, New Jersey, and Pennsylvania. Only in his last station at the forks of the Delaware did he find significant response to his message.

Brainerd's importance for American piety lies more in the record he left of his religious strivings than in the actual results of his missionary work. He was an intense, determined, and thoroughly persistent individual who could not be content with a conventional faith. His heart was consumed with spiritual struggle, with a battle against the inertia that kept him from apprehending the blinding vision of God's glory.

Brainerd's religious convictions matched those of the leading defender of the Awakening's "New Light" religion, Jonathan Edwards. Edwards had early become acquainted with Brainerd and acted as something of a spiritual mentor. Brainerd even became engaged to Edwards's daughter Jerusha before his premature death. Shortly before the young missionary died of tuberculosis in 1747, he handed over to Edwards (in whose home he passed away) a journal-diary covering most of his adult life. Edwards immediately set other writing projects aside to prepare an edition of these documents for publication. His concern was not so much to describe missionary work among the Indians as to reveal a heart aflame for God. Brainerd was an exacting taskmaster of the soul who put into practice the Calvinistic piety that Edwards advocated in his own preaching and writing. The result was a book of painful self-scrutiny but also of challenging spiritual dedication. It consisted of Brainerd's own jottings as edited, introduced, and augmented by Edwards.

No other work associated with Edwards has been published so often as this diary. It has had an immense impact on Protestant missionary aspirations to this day. Francis Asbury, the pioneering Methodist evangelist, spoke of Brainerd as "that model of meekness, moderation, temptation and labor, and self-denial." In Brainerd, Jonathan Edwards—and, over the years, many others—found a stellar example of a life devoted entirely to God. At Brainerd's funeral Edwards prayed words that many other readers of Brainerd's diary have echoed:

> Oh, that the things that were seen and heard in this extraordinary person, his holiness, heavenliness, labor and self-denial in life, his so remarkable devoting himself and his all, in heart and practice, to the glory of God, and the wonderful frame of mind manifested, in so steadfast a manner, under the expectation of death, and the pains and agonies that brought it on, may excite in us all, both ministers and people, a due sense of the greatness of the work we have to do in the world, the excellency and amiableness of thorough religion in experience and practice, and the blessedness of the end of such whose death finishes such a life, and the infinite value of their eternal reward, when absent from the body and present with the Lord; and effectually stir us up to endeavors that in the way of such an holy life we may at last come to so blessed an end. Amen.

The following entries from Brainerd's journal, with Jonathan Edwards's editorial comments in brackets, were made early in the young missionary's career, 1744-1745. They were first published in 1749 as *An Account of the Life of the Late Reverend Mr. David Brainerd, Minister of the Gospel, Missionary to the Indians . . . Who died at Northampton in New-England, Octob. 9th. 1747. in the 30th year of his age: chiefly taken from his own diary, and other private writings written for his own use; and now published. By Jonathan Edwards, A.M.* The best modern edition is volume 7 of the Yale edition of *The Works of Jonathan Edwards,* superbly edited by Norman Pettit (New Haven: Yale University Press, 1985).

Journal Entries

Lord's Day, December 30. Discoursed, both parts of the day, from Mark 8:34, "Whosoever will come after me," etc. God gave me very great freedom and clearness, and (in the afternoon especially) considerable warmth and fervency. In the evening also, had very great clearness while conversing with friends on divine things: I don't remember ever to have had more clear apprehensions of religion in my life: But found a struggle, in the evening, with spiritual pride.

[On Monday, he preached again in the same place with freedom and fervency; and rode home to his lodging and arrived in the evening under a considerable degree of bodily illness, which continued the two next days. And he complains much of spiritual emptiness and barrenness on those days.]

Thursday, January 3, 1744-5. Being sensible of the great want of divine influences, and the outpouring of God's Spirit; I spent this day in fasting and prayer to seek so great a mercy for myself, and my poor people in particular, and for the Church of God in general. In the morning, was very lifeless in prayer, and could get scarce any sense of God. Near noon, enjoyed some sweet freedom to pray that the will of God might in every respect become mine: And I am persuaded it was so at that time in some good degree. In the afternoon I was exceeding weak and could not enjoy much fervency in prayer; but felt a great degree of dejection; which, I believe, was very much owing to my bodily weakness and disorder.

Friday, January 4. Rode up to the Indians, near noon; spent some time there under great disorder: My soul was "sunk down into deep waters" [Ps. 69:2], and I was almost overwhelmed with melancholy.

Saturday, January 5. Was able to do something at writing; but was much disordered with pain in my head. At night, was distressed with a sense of my spiritual pollution, and ten thousand youthful, yea, and childish follies, that nobody but myself had any thought about; all which appeared to me now fresh, and in a lively view, as if committed yesterday, and made my soul ashamed before God, and caused me to hate myself.

Lord's Day, January 6. Was still distressed with vapory disorders. Preached to my poor Indians; but had little heart or life. Towards night, my soul was pressed under a sense of my unfaithfulness. Oh, the joy and peace that arises from a sense of "having obtained mercy of God to be faithful" [I Cor. 7:25]! And oh, the misery and anguish that spring from an apprehension of the contrary!

[His dejection continued the two next days; but not to so great a degree on Tuesday, when he enjoyed some freedom and fervency in preaching to the Indians.]

Wednesday, January 9. In the morning, God was pleased to remove that gloom which has of late oppressed my mind, and gave me freedom and sweetness in prayer. I was encouraged and strengthened, and enabled to plead for grace for myself and mercy for my poor Indians; and was sweetly assisted in my intercessions with God for others. Blessed be his holy Name forever and ever; Amen, and Amen. Those things that of late have appeared most difficult and almost impossible, now appeared not only possible, but easy. My soul so much delighted to continue instant in prayer, at this blessed season, that I had no desire for my "necessary food" [Job 23:12]: even dreaded leaving off praying at all, lest I should lose this spirituality and this blessed thankfulness to God which I then felt. I felt now quite willing to live and undergo all trials that might remain for me in a world of sorrow; but still longed for heaven, that I might glorify God in a perfect manner. Oh, "come, Lord Jesus, come quickly" [Rev. 22:20]! Spent the day in reading a little; and in some diversions which I was necessitated to take by reason of much weakness and disorder. In the evening, enjoyed some freedom and intenseness in prayer.

[The three remaining days of the week he was very low and feeble in body; but nevertheless continued constantly in the same comfortable sweet frame of mind as is expressed on Wednesday. On the Sabbath this sweetness and spiritual alacrity began to abate: But still he enjoyed some degree of comfort, and had assistance in preaching to the Indians.]

Monday, January 14. Spent this day under a great degree of bodily weakness and disorder; and had very little freedom, either in my studies or devotions: And in the evening I was much dejected and melancholy. It pains and distresses me that I live so much of my time for nothing. I long to do much in a little time, and if it might be the Lord's will, to "finish my work" [I Chron. 28:20] speedily in this tiresome world. I'm sure I don't desire to live for anything in this world; and through grace I am not afraid to look the "king of terrors" [Job 18:14] in the face: I know I shall be afraid if God leaves me; and therefore I think it always duty to lay in for that solemn hour. But for a very considerable time past, my soul has rejoiced to think of death in its nearest approaches; and even when I have been very weak and seemed nearest eternity. "Not unto me, not unto me, but to God be the glory" [Ps. 115:1]. I feel that which convinces me, that if God don't enable me to maintain a holy dependence upon him, death will easily be a terror to me; but at present, I must say, "I long to depart and to be with Christ" [Phil. 1:23], which is best of all. When I am in a sweet resigned frame of soul, I am willing to tarry a while in a world of sorrow, I am willing to be from home as long as God sees fit it should be so: But when I want the influence of this temper, I am then apt to be impatient to be gone. Oh, when will the day appear that I shall be perfect in holiness, and in the enjoyment of God?

[The next day was spent under a great degree of dejection and melancholy; which (as he himself says he was persuaded) was owing partly to bodily weakness and vapory disorders.]

Wednesday and Thursday, January 16 and 17. I spent most of the time in writing on a sweet divine subject, and enjoyed some freedom and assistance. Was likewise enabled to pray more frequently and fervently than usual: and my soul, I think, rejoiced in God; especially on the evening of the last of these days: "Praise" then seemed "comely" [Ps. 147:1], and I delighted to bless the Lord. Oh, what reason have I to be thankful that God ever helps me to labor and study for him! He does but "receive his own" [I Cor. 3:8], when I am enabled in any measure to praise him, labor for him, and live to him. Oh, how comfortable and sweet it is to feel the assistance of divine grace in the performance of the duties God has enjoined us! "Bless the Lord, O my soul" [Ps. 103:1,2].

[The same enlargement of heart and joyful frame of soul continued through the next day. But on the day following it began to decline; which decay seems to have continued the whole of the next week: Yet he enjoyed some seasons of special and sweet assistance.]

Lord's Day, January 27. Had the greatest degree of inward anguish that almost ever I endured: I was perfectly overwhelmed, and so confused, that after I began to discourse to the Indians, before I could finish a sentence, sometimes I forgot entirely what I was aiming at; or if, with much difficulty, I had recollected what I had before designed, still it appeared strange and like something I had long forgotten and had now but an imperfect remembrance of. I know it was a degree of distraction occasioned by vapory disorders, melancholy, spiritual desertion, and some other things that particularly pressed upon me this morning with an uncommon weight, the principal of which respected my Indians. This distressing gloom never went off the whole day; but was so far removed that I was enabled to speak with some freedom and concern to the Indians at two of their settlements; and I think there was some appearance of the presence of God with us, some seriousness and seeming concern among the Indians, at least a few of them. In the evening this gloom continued still till family prayer, about nine o'clock, and almost through this until I came near the close, when I was praying (as I usually do) for the illumination and conversion of my poor people; and then the cloud was scattered so that I enjoyed sweetness and freedom, and conceived hopes that God designed mercy for some of them. The same I enjoyed afterwards in secret prayer; in which precious duty I had for a considerable time sweetness and freedom, and (I hope) faith, in praying for myself, my poor Indians, and dear friends and acquaintance in New England and elsewhere, and for the dear interest of Zion in general. "Bless the Lord, O my soul, and forget not all his benefits" [Ps. 103:2].

[He spent the rest of this week, or at least the most of it, under dejection and melancholy: which on Friday rose to an extreme height; he being then, as he himself observes, much exercised with vapory disorders. This exceeding gloominess continued on Saturday, till the evening, when he was again relieved in family prayer; and after it, was refreshed in secret and felt willing to live and endure hardships in the cause of God; and found his hopes of the advancement of Christ's kingdom, as also his hopes to "see the power of God" [John 11:40] among the poor Indians, considerably raised.]

Lord's Day, February 3. In the morning I was somewhat relieved of that gloom and confusion that my mind has of late been greatly exercised with: Was enabled to pray with some composure and comfort. But however, went to my Indians trembling; for my soul remembered "the wormwood and the gall" [Lam. 3:19] (I might almost say the hell) of Friday last; and I was greatly afraid I should be obliged again to drink of that "cup of trembling" [Is. 51:17], which was inconceivably more bitter than death, and made me long for the grave more, unspeakably more, than for hid treasures; yea, inconceivably more than the men of this world long for such treasures. But God was pleased to hear my cries, and to afford me great assistance; so that I felt peace in my own soul; and was satisfied that if not one of the Indians should be profited by my preaching, but should all be damned, yet I should be accepted and rewarded as faithful; for I am persuaded God enabled me to be so. Had some good degree of help afterwards, at another place; and much longed for the conversion of the poor Indians. Was somewhat refreshed, and comfortable towards night, and in the evening. Oh, that my soul might praise the Lord for his goodness! Enjoyed some freedom in the evening, in meditation on Luke 13:24.

[In the three next days he was the subject of much dejection: But the three remaining days of the week seem to have been spent with much composure and comfort. On the next Sabbath he preached at Greenwich in New Jersey. In the evening he rode eight miles to visit a sick man at the point of death, and found him speechless and senseless.]

Monday, February 11. About break of day, the sick man died. I was affected at the sight: Spent the morning with the mourners; and after prayer and some discourse with them, I returned to Greenwich and preached again from Ps. 89:15. And the Lord gave me assistance: I felt a sweet love to souls and to the kingdom of Christ; and longed that poor sinners might "know the joyful sound." Several persons were much affected. And after meeting, I was enabled to discourse, with freedom and concern, to some persons that applied to me under spiritual trouble. Left the place, sweetly composed, and rode home to my house about eight miles distant. Discoursed to friends and inculcated divine truths upon some. In the evening, was in the most solemn frame that almost ever I remember to have experienced: I know not that ever death appeared more real to me, or that ever I saw myself in the condition of a dead corpse, laid out and dressed for a lodging in the silent grave, so evidently as at this time. And yet I felt exceeding comfortably: My mind was composed and calm, and "death" appeared without a "sting" [I Cor. 15:55]. I think I never felt such an universal mortification to all created objects as now. Oh, how great and solemn it appeared to die! Oh, how it lays the greatest honor in the dust! And oh, how vain and trifling did the riches, honors, and pleasures of the world appear! I could not, I dare not, so much as think of any of them: for death, death, solemn (though not frightful) death appeared at the door. Oh, I could see myself dead, and laid out, and enclosed in my coffin, and put down into the cold grave, with greatest solemnity, but without terror! I spent most of the evening in conversation with a dear Christian friend: And blessed be God, it was a comfortable evening to us both. What are friends? What are comforts? What are sorrows? What are distresses? "The time is short: It remains, that they which weep, be as though they wept not; and they which rejoice, as though they rejoiced not: for the fashion of this world passeth away" [I Cor. 7:29-31]. Oh, "come, Lord Jesus, come quickly; Amen" [Rev. 22:20]! Blessed be God for the comforts of the past day.

JOHN WOOLMAN (1720-1772)

John Woolman was a Quaker who more than any other individual was responsible for the stand that his denomination took against slavery in the eighteenth century. During his lifetime most Christian bodies in America either tolerated the slave trade and slavery itself, or showed little concern for these injustices. By contrast, Woolman and a few associates in the Society of Friends grew ever clearer in their belief that slavery was an offense against God and a perverse attack on humanity. For Woolman this belief was not simply a moral proposition. It was grounded in a larger vision of spiritual reality.

Woolman was born on October 19, 1720, in Burlington County, New Jersey. As a youth he was troubled by spiritual conflicts, but eventually these were resolved, and he sensed a clear call to a religious life. Although Woolman earned his living as a tailor, his life's consuming passion was to spread the message of God's love. In 1743, as a young man of twenty-three, he made a two-week journey to various locations in New Jersey, visiting groups of Friends and urging them to follow the spiritual disciplines of their heritage. His message was in most ways the traditional one of the Friends—seek the "Inner Light of Christ," avoid evil entanglements with the world, let the Scriptures shape attitudes toward life in general. To these common themes of eighteenth-century Quakerism Woolman soon added specific words of practical morality. He called upon his hearers to reaffirm the traditional Quaker stand against warfare. And increasingly he attacked the institution of slavery.

Woolman's journeys grew in length and frequency. He traveled within New Jersey and paid special attention to the influential body of Quakers in Philadelphia. But he also traveled to New York and New England and on several occasions to the South. He was not a rabble-rousing orator, nor did he denounce slaveholders with flamboyant rhetoric. His testimony was quiet in words but forceful in deeds. When he traveled in the South, for instance, he insisted upon paying the slaves who served him his meals. And he resolved not to wear clothing made by slaves and sold for another's profit. His tracts, like the two-part *Considerations on the Keeping of Negroes* (1754, 1762), spelled out his conviction that the slave system violated the God-given humanity of both slave and slaveholder. His persuasion had much to do with the movement by Quakers in both Rhode Island and Philadelphia to oppose slavery.

Sometime in the mid-1750s Woolman began keeping a journal in which he recorded his travels, his protests against slavery, and his impressions of God's presence. Among the most memorable sections of the journal are the entries that he made during a journey to Great Britain in May and June of 1772. His purpose on this trip was the same as it had been for earlier ones: to persuade English Quakers to deepen their spiritual commitment and oppose slavery. These entries reveal the subtle combination of mystical piety and moral earnestness that made Woolman's testimony so effective. The journey to Britain, however, turned out to be his last: he died of smallpox in York, England, on October 7, 1772.

Journal Entries

7th day, 5th month [1772]. Have had rough weather mostly since I came on board, and the passengers James Reynolds, John Till Adams, Sarah Logan and hired maid, and John Bispham all seasick more or less at times, from which sickness through the tender mercies of my Heavenly Father I have been preserved, my afflictions now being of another kind.

There appeared an openness in the minds of the master of the ship and in the cabin passengers toward me. We were often together on the deck and sometimes in the cabin.

My mind through the merciful help of the Lord hath been preserved in a good degree watchful and inward, and have this day great cause to be thankful in that I remain to feel quietness of mind.

As my lodgings in the steerage, now near a week, hath afforded me sundry opportunities of seeing, hearing, and feeling with respect to the life and spirit of many poor sailors, an inward exercise of soul hath attended me in regard to placing out children and youth where they may be likely to be exampled and instructed in the pure fear of the Lord. And I, being much amongst the seamen, have from a motion of love sundry times taken opportunities with one alone and in a free conversation laboured to turn their minds toward the fear of the Lord; and this day we had a meeting in the cabin, where my heart was contrite under a feeling of divine love.

Now concerning lads being trained up as seamen: I believe a comunication from one part of the world to some other parts of it by sea is at times consistent with the will of our Heavenly Father, and to educate some youth

Source: *The Journal and Major Essays of John Woolman*, ed. Phillips P. Moulton (New York: Oxford University Press, 1971), pp. 166-68, 169-72, 173-74, 178-80.

in the practice of sailing I believe may be right; but how lamentable is the present corruption of the world! How impure are the channels through which trade hath a conveyance! How great is that danger to which poor lads are now exposed when placed on shipboard to learn the art of sailing?

Five lads training up for the seas were now on board this ship, two of them brought up amongst our Society, one of which hath a right amongst Friends, by name James Nayler, to whom James Nayler mentioned in Sewel's history appears to have been uncle to his father. I often feel a tenderness of heart toward these poor lads and at times look at them as though they were my children according to the flesh.

Oh, that all may take heed and beware of covetousness! Oh, that all may learn of Christ who is meek and low of heart! Then in faithfully following him, he will teach us to be content with food and raiment without respect to the customs or honours of this world. Men thus redeemed will feel a tender concern for their fellow creatures and a desire that those in the lowest stations may be encouraged. And where owners of ships attain to the perfect law of liberty and are doers of the word, these will be blessed in their deeds.

A ship at sea commonly sails all night, and the seamen take their watches four hours at a time. Rising to work in the night is not commonly pleasant in any case, but in dark rainy nights it is very disagreeable, even though each man were furnished with all convenience; but if men must go out at midnight to help manage the ship in the rain, and having small room to sleep and lay their garments in, are often beset to furnish themselves for the watch, their garments or something relating to their business being wanting and not easily found, when from the urgency occasioned by high winds they are hastened and called up suddenly, here is a trial of patience on the poor sailors and the poor lads their companions.

If after they have been on deck several hours in the night and come down into the steerage soaking wet, and are so close stowed that proper convenience for change of garments is not easily come at, but for want of proper room their wet garments thrown in heaps, and sometimes through much crowding are trodden under foot in going to their lodgings and getting out of them, and great difficulties at times each one to find his own—here are trials on the poor sailors.

Now as I have been with them in my lodge, my heart hath often yearned for them and tender desires been raised in me that all owners and masters of vessels may dwell in the love of God and therein act uprightly, and by seeking less for gain and looking carefully to their ways may earnestly labour to remove all cause of provocation from the poor seamen either to fret or use excess of strong drink; for indeed the poor creatures at times in the wet and cold seem to apply to strong drink to supply the want of other convenience.

Great reformation in the world is wanting! and the necessity of it amongst these who do business in great waters hath at this time been abundantly opened before me.

* * *

13th day, 5th month. As I continue to lodge in the steerage, I feel an openness this morning to express some further the state of my mind in respect to poor lads bound apprentice to learn the art of sailing. As I believe sailing is of some use in the world, a labour of soul attends me that the pure counsel of Truth may be humbly waited for in this case by all concerned in the business of the seas.

A pious father whose mind is exercised for the everlasting welfare of his child may not with a peaceful mind place him out to an employment amongst a people whose common course of life is manifestly corrupt and profane. So great is the present defect amongst seafaring men in regard to piety and virtue, and through an abundant traffic and many ships of war, so many people are employed on the sea, that this subject of placing lads to the employment appears very weighty.

Profane examples are very corrupting and very forcible. And as my mind, day after day and night after night, hath been affected with a sympathizing tenderness toward poor children put to the employment of sailors, I have sometimes had weighty conversation with the sailors in the steerage, who were mostly respectful to me, and more and more so the longer I was with them. They mostly appeared to take kindly what I said to them, but their minds have appeared to be so deeply impressed with that almost universal depravity amongst sailors that the poor creatures, in their answers to me on this subject, have revived in my remembrance that of the degenerate Jews a little before the captivity, as repeated by Jeremiah the prophet, "There is no hope" [Jer. 18:12].

Now under this exercise a sense of the desire of outward gain prevailing amongst us hath felt grievous, and a strong call to the professed followers of Christ *hath* been raised in me that all may take heed, lest through loving this present world they be found in a continued neglect of duty with respect to a faithful labour for a reformation.

Silence as to every motion proceeding from the love of money, and an humble waiting upon God to know his will concerning us, hath now appeared necessary. He alone is able to strengthen us to dig deep, to remove all which lies between us and the safe foundation, and so direct us in our outward employments that pure universal love may shine forth in our proceedings.

Desires arising from the spirit of Truth are pure desires; and when a mind divinely opened toward a young generation is made sensible of corrupting examples powerfully working and extensively spreading amongst them, how moving is the prospect.

A great trade to the coast of Africa for slaves, of which I now heard frequent conversation amongst the sailors!

A great trade in that which is raised and prepared through grievous oppression!

A great trade in superfluity of workmanship, formed to please the pride and vanity of peoples' mind!

Great and extensive is that depravity which prevails amongst the poor sailors!

When I remember that saying of the Most High through his prophet, "This people have I formed for myself: they shall show forth my praise" [Is. 43:21], and think of placing children amongst them to learn the practice of sailing joined with a pious education, as to me, my condition hath been like that mentioned by the prophet, "There is no answer from God" [Mic. 3:7].

In a world of dangers and difficulties like a thorny, desolate wilderness, how precious! how comfortable! how safe! are the leadings of Christ the good Shepherd, who said, "I know my sheep and am known of mine" [Jn. 10:14].

16th day, 5th month, 1772. Wind for several days past often high, what the sailors call squally, rough sea and frequent rains. This last night a very trying night to the poor seamen, the water chief part of the night running over the main deck, and sometimes breaking waves come on the quarter deck. The latter part of the night as I lay in bed, my mind was humbled under the power of divine love, and resignedness to the great Creator of the earth and the seas renewedly wrought in me, whose fatherly care over his children felt precious to my soul; and desires were now renewed in me to embrace every opportunity of being inwardly acquainted with the hardships and difficulties of my fellow creatures and to labour in his love for the spreading of pure universal righteousness in the earth.

The frequent opportunities of hearing conversation amongst the sailors in respect to the voyages to Africa and the manner of bringing the deeply oppressed slaves into our islands, the thoughts of their condition, frequently in chains and fetters, on board the vessels, with hearts loaded with grief under the apprehension of miserable slavery—as my mind was frequently opened to meditate on these things, my own lodging, now in the steerage, with the advantage of walking the deck when I would, appeared a commodious situation compared with theirs.

* * *

24th day, 5th month, and first of the week. A clear, pleasant morning, and as I sat on deck I felt a reviving in my nature, which through much rainy weather and high winds, being shut up in a close, unhealthy air, was weakened. Several nights of late I felt breathing difficult, that a little after the rising of the second watch (which is about midnight) I got up and stood, I believe, near an hour with my face near the hatchway, to get the fresh air at the small vacancy under the hatch door, which was commonly shut down, partly to keep out rain and sometimes to keep the breaking waves from dashing into the steerage.

I may with thankfulness to the Father of Mercies acknowledge that in my present weak state my mind hath been supported to bear the affliction with patience, and have looked at the present dispensation as a kindness from the great Father of mankind, who in this my floating pilgrimage is in some degree bringing me to feel that which many thousands of my fellow creatures often suffer.

My appetite failing, the trial hath been the heavier, and I have felt tender breathing in my soul after God, the fountain of comfort, whose inward help hath supplied at times the want of outward convenience; and strong desires have attended me that his family, who are acquainted with the movings of his Holy Spirit, may be so redeemed from the love of money and from that spirit in which men seek honour one of another that in all business by sea or land we may constantly keep in view the coming of this kingdom on earth as it is in heaven, and by faithfully following this safe guide, may show forth examples tending to lead out of that under which the creation groans! This day we had a meeting in the cabin, in which I was favoured in some degree to experience the fulfilling of that saying of the prophet, "The Lord hath been a strength to the poor, a strength to the needy in their distress" [Is. 25:4], for which my heart is bowed in thankfulness before Him.

* * *

31st, 5th month, and first of the week. Had a meeting in the cabin with near all the ship's company, the whole being near thirty. In this meeting the Lord in mercy favoured us with the extendings of his love.

2nd day, 6th month, 1772. Last evening the seamen found bottom at about seventy fathom. This morning fair wind and pleasant, and as I sat on deck, my heart was overcome with the love of Christ and melted into contrition before him. And in this state the prospect of that work to which I have felt my mind drawn when in my native land being in some degree opened before me, I felt like a little child; and my cries were put up to my Heavenly Father for preservation, that in a humble dependence on him my soul may be strengthened in his love and kept inwardly waiting for his counsel.

This afternoon, saw that part of England called the Lizard. Some dunghill fowls yet remained of those the passengers took for eating. I believe about fourteen perished in the storms at sea by the waves breaking over the quarter deck, and a considerable number with sickness at different times. I observed the cocks crew coming down [the] Delaware and while we were near the land, but afterward I think I did not hear one of them crow till we came near the land in England, when they again crowed a few times.

In observing their dull appearance at sea and the pining sickness of some of them, I often remembered the Fountain of Goodness, who gave being to all creatures, and whose love extends to that of caring for the sparrows; and [I] believe where the love of God is verily perfected and the true spirit of government watchfully attended to, a tenderness toward all creatures made subject to us will be experienced, and a care felt in us that we do not lessen that sweetness of life in the animal creation which that great Creator intends for them under our government, and believe a less number carried off to eat at sea may be more agreeable to this pure wisdom.

* * *

7th day, 6th month, and first day of the week. Clear morning. Lay at anchor for the tide and had a parting meeting with the ship's company, in which my heart was enlarged in a fervent concern for them, that they may come to experience salvation through Christ. Had a head wind up the Thames; lay sometimes at anchor; saw many ships passing and some at anchor near; and had large opportunity of feeling the spirit in which the poor bewildered sailors too generally live. That lamentable degeneracy which so much prevails in the people employed on the seas so affected my heart that I may not easily convey the feeling I have had to another.

The present state of the seafaring life in general appears so opposite to that of a pious education, so full of corruption and extreme alienation from God, so full of examples the most dangerous to *young people* that in looking toward a young generation I feel a care for them, that they may have an education different from the present education of lads at sea, and that all of us who are acquainted with the pure gospel spirit may lay this case to heart, may remember the lamentable corruptions which attends the conveyance of merchandise across the seas, and so abide in the love of Christ that being delivered from the love of money, from the entangling expenses of a curious, delicate, and luxurious life—that we may learn contentment with a little and promote the seafaring life no further than that spirit which leads into all Truth attends us in our proceedings.

ESTHER EDWARDS BURR (1732-1758)

One of the reasons that the word "piety" often conjures up images of the ethereal is that we are used to reading about the religious life in works by men—often men who have set aside the domestic concerns of this world. Yet piety can look very different, and no less attractive, when it appears *in* the normal daily round instead of extracted from it.

The journal of Esther Edwards Burr testifies eloquently to that fact. She was the third child of Jonathan and Sarah Pierrepont Edwards, and so a daughter of a family well-experienced in the disciplines of spiritual life. In 1750 Esther married the Reverend Aaron Burr, a Presbyterian minister from Newark, New Jersey. She was eighteen at the time; he was thirty-four. Soon Esther moved with her husband to Princeton, where the Reverend Burr gave his full attention to superintending the College of New Jersey (later Princeton University). For her part, Esther entered into the cycle of entertaining, child nurturing, and domestic management that would be her calling for the rest of her short life. During the brief time allotted to this family, Esther bore two children, the second of whom became famous as vice president of the United States and as the duelist who killed Alexander Hamilton. However, by the time Aaron Burr, Jr., was an adult, Esther had long since departed the earth. Death carried her off in 1758, shortly after the passing of her husband, and in the same year both of her parents died.

From October 1, 1754, to September 2, 1757, Esther Burr kept a diary that is one of the fullest records of a woman's experience in colonial America. It took the form of a serial letter to Sarah Prince, daughter of a Congregational minister in Boston and longtime friend of the Edwards family. The diary shows us a very busy young mother who yet took time, amid her pressing duties, to reflect on her relationship with God. The life that shines forth in the diary is one of sincere religion, hard work, family joys and sorrows, nearly overwhelming domestic responsibility, and faithful friendship. The selections that follow, entries from December 1756 to May 1757, provide insight into another intriguing spiritual event. During those months the College of New Jersey experienced a religious awakening, an event that warmed Esther Burr's heart but that also made for a great deal more work for her as visitors streamed to the president's house in order to witness the event.

Shortly after Esther Burr's death, her friend Sarah Prince tried to take the measure of this unusual woman in a moving, private meditation of her own. Sarah wrote,

> The God of Nature had furnished her with all that I desir'd in a Friend—her Natural Powers were superior to most Women, her knowledge was extensive of Men and Things, her Accomplishments fine—her Prudence forethought and sagacity wonderfull—her Modesty rare—In Friendly Quallity none Exceeded her—she was made for a Refin'd Friend. How Faithfull? how sincere? how Open hearted? how Tender how careful how disinterested—And *she was mine!* O the tenderness which tied our hearts.

The following entries, as previously noted, are from December 1756 to May 1757. Esther wrote something in her journal nearly every day, so many entries have been omitted in order to present this record of several months of her life. Spelling is not always conventional (as is often the case in eighteenth-century writing), but Esther Burr's meaning is rarely in doubt.

Journal Entries

[December 24, 1756]
Decmbr 24.

After a long silence I have time and strength to write—since I wrote last, much has passed, Company come and gone from all quarters. Had received many vissits and begun to return em—but last Week on Thursday was taken Ill and have been confined ever since to my Room with the Canker in my Throat and violent fever, tho' throu mercy am better. Hope soon to recover.

The Weather is very fine but everybody is taken up with the slaying [i.e., sleighing]. Mr Burr and Miss Abby gone from home so I am alone with my Children—I hant spirits and Life enough to write altho' tis to one that would give new Life as soon as any absent friend I have—I am greatly troubled with lowness of spirits and feel at times as if I should be meloncholy which will be a new thing with me—I can add no more at present but that I am Your Burissa

---

Source: *The Journal of Esther Edwards Burr*, ed. Carol F. Karlsen and Laurie Crumpacker (New Haven: Yale University Press, 1984), pp. 236-63.

[January 2, 1757]
Sabbath Jan—2 day.

I long to begin this year with God—O for Gods presence throu this year!
When I look back on the year past and take a view of the Numberless
Mercies I have been the subject off, I stand amazed at Gods goodness to such
an Ill deserving Hell deserving Creature *[as]* I am—Why am I thus distinguished from the greater part of the World—What obligations am I under
to spend the remainder of my time for God—I dont want to live unless I can
live more to the glory of God and do more good—Eve Mr Symons and Wife
dined, drank Tea and spent the Eve here.

[January 19, 1757]
Jan—19. Wednsday

God is threttening us but as yet the stroke is withheld—there has not one
day passed in my famaly since I came from Stockbri[dge] but one or more of
us [. . .] have bee[n] so Ill as to want attendance—My Wentch has been in a
poor way ever since our remooval—but now is so bad as to keep her Bed. She
has been under the Doctrs hands for six Weeks past but to no purpose—she
is in a very uncommon way I fear poisoned, and if that is the case I dont
expect she will live. The loss o[f] her will be very great. She is uncommonly
good for her Colour, and I cant expect to have her place filled, but God does
all Wisely and knows what is best—I desire to submit and say the Will of the
Lord be done.

[February 8, 1757]
Teusday A.M.

Company come and go—come and go—continually it is Rap, Rap—is the
President at home all this day.

Eve. We have had people from all parts of the country to day, this eve a
Room full.

There is a considerable awakening in College more general then has ever
been since Mr Burr has had the care of it—the sickness of Loyer Smiths Son
and his concern (I think I mentioned i*[t]* my last that he had been at the point
of Death with the Bloody flux and was under great concern for his soul
which still continues.) I hope has been sanctified to the good of several very
rude young fellows.

[February 10, 1757]
Thursday A.M.

Heard that the Governor is at the point of death which will be such a loss
to this Province that we cant expect to have it made up in a Governor—

things look dark—Good men one after another die, and I see none ariseng to fill their place—but this is and shall be my hope and comfort—That our God is the same Mercyfull, Wise, Powerfull, Good God that he was from Eternity, and so will continue to Eternity—altho all things Change, yet our God is what he always was.

[February 11, 1757]
Fryday fine Weather—11.

Farther incuragement—Mr Burr tells me that yesterday a Young Man from Danbury in New England, one of his schollars, came to talk with him twice under very pressing concern for his soul—this morn came again—O me dear who knows what God may do for the poor youth of this College if we pray ernestly for them! O it would be a Heaven upon Erth if he should shower down plentifully of his holy spirit upon them—God is as able and willing as ever he was, if we were prepard for so great a mercy.

P.M. and eve. Thronged with company—you know tis common for people under great afflictions to apply to some good Minnister for advise and comfort. This is the case of the people we have had to day—poor unhappy Cretures! As they were calmly and pleasantly sailing (or slaying) for their diversion, there arose a sudden storm of Violent Wind and Warm Rain, that in six hours carried off all the snow not a patch as big as one of your hands left, and they cast into the Mudd, and there left to stick to their unspeakable Mortifycation! However, we found they were better able to comfort themselves then we were, and in a way that I should not have thought off—that is that there are a great many others in as bad a Box as they are—this is a sordid sort of a comfort methinks—tis not becoming the Man—nay I really think it beneath the Beasts—there is somthing of the Old Scratchum in this, ant there?

(The governor is recovered.)

[February 19, 1757]
Saturday Morn

The young Man from Danbury (Gregory by Name) we have reason to hope has found God—the temper of his mind is very Christian like. He seems to have a great sense of God and himself, and the sufficency of Christ and the safty of venturing his soul upon him, and wonders he could ever be affraid to trust his all upon him—the Concern is now become general in College— none of it in Town and several under very great distress of soul—O Help me to bless the Lord! Mr Burr is almost over joyed—for my part I am affraid that (as the Lord in Samaria) I am affraid I shall only behold it with mine eyes and not tast of these heavenly blessings.

[February 20, 1757]
Sabbath Eve.

Mr Spencer preached all day (he is much inlivened) from He that cometh to me hath life, etc. I never saw the scholars so attentive in my life. They really seemed as if they heard for their lives.

9 o'Clock—Mr Burr returnd from College, Mr Spencer with him, and glorious things they relate—Mr Burr was sent for to the College about dark, and when he came their he found above 20 young Men in one room Crying and begging to know what they should do to be saved, 4 of them under the deepest sense of thier wicked Hearts and need of Christ, Faniuel amongst the rest, and how it will rejoice his good Mothers Heart—Mr Burr praied and talked in the best Manner he could and left them and comes home greatly affected—we sat and talked till late and knew not how to lay by the glorious subject. (Mr Spencer wont lodge with us but returns to Colleg to see the salvation of the Lord.)

[February 21, 1757]
Monday Morn.

Good News my dear I have to tell you this morn—A Minnisters Son near Philadelphia hopfully received Comfort last Night in the Night. There was little sleep amongst them, some up all Night. Mr Spencer sat up till 1 o'Clock then left these poor young cretures seeking God—the Conversion of this young Treat, for that is his name, is a very dear and remarkable one. The peteculars I hant heard but Mr Burr says he thinks evidently a Work of Grace—he has been under some impressions for more then a year, but his concern has increased lately—10. o'Clock—a pious young Man comes from the College, for Mr Burr. He tells me that great part of the schollars are gathered into one Room Crying in great distress, and that another has received comfort—O my Heart Exults at the thought that God is about to revive Relegion in general—May we not hope for it—My soul doth magnify the Lord for what he has done.

Eve—The Lords work goes on gloriously in the College—Mr Burr sent for Mr Tennent of Freehold to come and assist in drawing the Net ashore for it is ready to Break with the aboundance of the Fish that are Caught in it—just now he came and is gone up to the College greatly rejoiced. (This Mr Tennent is not attal like Gilbert but as prudent a Man in Conducting affairs of religion as ever I saw in my life. He hates noise—and hates [. . .] anything that looks like judging persons safe in a hurry but says time must descover what they are.)

9 o'Clock. No work carried on here, but only to get somthing to Eat, and a little of that will suffice two—for my part I hant any creature to say one word two, and when I am ready to burst I have recourse to my pen and you—Mr

Tennent is astonished, and amazed, between joy, sorrow, hope, and fear and says he dont know what passion is uppermost, but he must call it an Awfull joy that he feels, which is the case with us all—My Brother is under a great deal of concern amongst the rest—O what shall I render to the Lord for his goodness in powering *[pouring]* out his spirit in such an wonderfull degree.

[February 22, 1757]
Teusday P.M. 2 o'Clock

I am ready to set up my Tabernacle and say Lord it is good to be here—indeed my dear the thoughts of living hant been so comfortable to me not for years past as now—The Lord is indeed here—Mr Tennent said just now at Table (that is all the time I have with him and Mr Burr, and they begrudge one minnit from College) that he thought there was not above three or 4 in all the College but what were deeply affected—and it is not a Noisy distress but a deep concern, not a flight of fancy but their judgments are thorougly convinced, and they are deeply wounded at Heart with a sense of their sin and need of Christ. No need now of Mr Burrs sending to rooms to see if the schollars keep good hours and mind their studdies. Never was there so much studdying in College since it has had a being as now.

This wonderfull pouring out of the spirit at this time just as the College is finnished and things a little settled looks to me exactly like Gods descending into the Temple in a Cloud of Glory, there by signifying that he did except of the House for his dwelling place and would Bless it—but I fear and tremble, for fear that Sattan will get an advantage and obstruct by sowing Tares amongst the Wheat—Mr Tennent says that some will turn out for God, and some for the Divel with a Vengance—this is likely, but it looks awfull—but stay, why do I distrust God, he is as able to Carry on this work as to begin it—I will hope and pray that it may become universal—O that this might be the dawn of the glorious day! O I am transported at the thought? Come Lord Jesus come quickly! Make no tarry but come now!

Eve—Doct Shippen came in very unexpectedly—and seems rejoiced to see his son Jackey under such concern for his soul—10 o'Clock a person comes to call Mr Burr and Tennent, says that Loyer Smiths Son is in great Horror, so Mr Tennent is gone—My dear Brother is deeply distressed.

[March 1, 1757]

Teusday Eve March the first—whiles the company is at College.

This is the first vacant moment I have had since Saturday last—yes every moment has been taken up with company or some nesesary duty—When I left off last Saturday I told you I was about writing to Stockbridge, but before I could write came Mr Gilbert Tennent and Daughter in Law, so with great regret missed the oppertunity. This Lady I love because she looks and walks and Talks and is like our dear and ever to be remembered Sister Mercy—a very pious woman tho' not equil to our departed Sister—Mr Burr has had a difficult task of it to mannage Mr Gilbert and not affront him, for he is mighty forward to preach and pray, and would fain preach em to death if he could—however Mr Burr let him preach 3 times on the Sabbath for no one thinks amiss of Preaching on the Sabbath—as there has been no er-ragularities heithertwo it would be very desireable that there might be none so long as this glorious work lasts, [so] that Satan might have no handle—but he'll work, handle or none, and does work—Yesterday Loyer Ogden of Newark sent for 3 Sons of his that were at the College. He had heard that the schollars were all Run Mad and desired his Sons might be sent home imme-diately, and to Day another is sent for that belongs to Brunswick—these poor young Cretures have begun well, but alass! I doubt here it will end, tho there is reason to hope that one of the Loyers Sons is savingly rought upon but he is very young and one cant be so sertain—this Morn Mr Tennent and Daughter left us to go to Freehold but will return this Week—We have now 4 Minnisters here and expect more—they are coming, so good night.

[March 4, 1757]
Fryday—P.M.

This day Dined with us Mr Loyd who brought your dear kind large paquit, long looked for, come at last—Altho' our House was crouded with Company, the two Mr Tennents etc, I slyly stole away and read all—O what a friend have I in my Fidelia—O! for a thankfull heart for such a favour—I am heartily greived to here of Secretary Willard['s] Death. It looks awfull that one good Man and Woman after another dies, and none arrising to fill their Place—I am affraid I shant have time to write much more before Mr Loyd calls for my Letter but will do what I can.

[March 9, 1757]
March 9 1757
Wednsday A.M. 11 o'Clock.

Last eve 3 schollars were sent for that belong to Newyork, this by the Instigation of Loyer Ogden of Newark. He has been to Newyork on pur-pose—O how busy is Satan. He was drove out of College, and now stands at a distance and Barks at it like a surly Dog at the full Moon in its Glory because 'tis out of his reach—about a dzn people coming in—so lay down your pen or they will wonder what this Woman does a writing forever, for these same people have seen me at it last Night.

P.M. I had as good conclude my schralls, for perhaps Mr Loyd will call to night, and tis impossible for me to get time to say any thing. I am really drove—I dont contrive what will become of us if people drive this stroke. For my part I have been very dilligent, but for a month past hant done a shillings worth of Work, not seting work, but tis Trot, Trot, around the House, day after day, waiting upon Tom Tinker and Tom Tite.

My kindest regards to the Sisters, Duty to your honored parents and Deal out Complements as you think proper. My love to Julia in all which Mr Burr joins as also in kindest Love to you—from your most affectionate Friend—

E. Burr

[April 11, 1757]
Monday A.M. 11. o'Clock—fine wea[ther]
This morn feel affected with Gods goodness to a sinf[ul] Worm of the dust. I arose erly with a violent sick Headach, kept up about an hour and was obliged to betake my self to Bed again not expecting to [be] able to rise again this day and not to recover for several days—Whiles on the bed got a little sleep and it has in a surpriszing manner almost intirely carried it off—Helth God knows I need at this time in my Famaly—I am ready to think that we loose much of the comforts of relegion, and G[od] looses much prais, by not remarking small mercies—as we are apt to call 'em—I dare not add now for fear it may return the pain. . . .

[April 12, 1757]
Teusday A.M. 10. o'Clock
I have had a smart Combat with Mr Ewing about our sex—he is a man of good parts and Lerning but has mean thoughts of Women—he began the dispute in this Manner. Speaking of Miss Boudanot I said she was a sociable friendly creture. A Gentleman seting by joined with me, but Mr Ewing says—*she and the Stocktons are full of talk about Friendship and society and such stuff—and made up a Mouth as if much disgusted*—I asked what he would have 'em talk about—whether he chose they should talk about fashions and dress—*he said things that they understood. He did not think women knew what Friendship was. They were hardly capable of anything so cool and rational as friendship*—(My Tongue, you know, hangs pretty loose, thoughts Crouded in—so I sputtered away for dear life.) You may Guss what a large field this speach opened for me—I retorted several severe things upon him before he had time to speak again. He Blushed and seemed confused. The Gentleman seting by said little but when did speak it was to my purpose and we carried on the dispute for an hour—I talked him quite silent. He got up and said your servant and went off—I dont know that ever I meet with one that was so openly and fully in Mr Pop[e's] sordid scheam—One of the last things that he said was that he never in all his life knew or hear[d] of a woman that had a little more lerning then [common?] but it made her proud to such a degree that she was disgusfull [to] all her acquaintance. P.M. Made

two vissits—came home and found my Aaron very unwell and a bad purging. The Bloudy-Flux is in Town which gives me concern. Two Children
have died of it and several more sick of it.

[April 18, 1757]
Monday

A day of much confusion and hurry, more company to dine, comers and
goers constantly, and Lies by the Bushels and Cart Loads about our College—they think to overset it but the House is two large and strong for
them—Mr Brainerd I hear has got a Son. These Boys are mighty things with
the Men—I am Weaning Aaron and he makes a great Noise about it so cant
add.

[May 1, 1757]
Sabbath Eve, May the first

Tis almost a Fortnight sinc I have conversed with *[you]* but you have been
the subject of many of my thoughts and remembred in my praiers—It would
be two tedious for me to relate the reasons that you have been so neglected,
but this you may always be sure of, that I cant pass you by one day no more
then I can pass by my Food but when nesesity obliges.

The students are generally returnd from their several Homes and I was
highly delighted to observe the same solemn attention to the word, the same
grave decent behaviour that appeared in them before the vacancy. It looks as
if it would prove abiding—O! what a joyfull prospect does it afford. A large
Class goes out into the World and almost all of them we have reason to hope
truely Pious. Poor Peter Fanueil I fear will be ruined. *[Half line deleted.]* He
was near the Kingdome of Heaven, *[two lines deleted.]* (This about Mr
Brown Mr Burr says must not go for fear the Letter should be opened—tis
the first that ever he made me scratch out—they dont stick a tall at opening
private Letters.)

The College has meet with a great deal of trouble from the Enemies of jo[y]
but it will turn out for the temporal as well as spirittual good of the society.
This is already evident. We have lost but three and have got Ten for 'em,
good exchange ant it. Some of 'em the Top of Philadelphia too.

[May 2, 1757]
Monday May 2

Gods judgments thretten on all hands. The oldest people we have amongst
us cant remember such a changable Winter and cold backward spring—the
Wheat in these parts is much hurt, some intirely ruined by the frequent
heavings of the frost the Winter past. Things look dark all around but

Blessed be god that any Light appears in the Middest of so great darkness—
Last Week I saw a Consert for prayer published by our Reverend Fathers in
Scotland, a proposal to spend an hour every Sabbath and Wednsday Morn
from 7 to 8 o'Clock—It did me good to see it, and I am determined to comply
as far as tis consistant with duty. I have heithertwo found assistance—I
conclude you have seen the proposals—It gives great incouragement to see
Gods people stired up to extreordinary prayer—Eve. A Gentleman from
Philadelphia.

[*May 3, 1757*]
Teusday.

Fine Weather for the first day this spring—Company all the Morn and
expecting more every minute.

[*May 19, 1757*]
Thursday

An Army to Breakfast—I am quite sick with a pain in my Breast Cold and
bad Cough—10 O'Clock 4 Ladies and 4 Gentlemen, top of Philadelphia call
and want Mr Burr and me to go up to College so we went and I am tired
down and sick two—Mr Burr is sick with a Cold, Sally with Worms and
Lucy with the Headach so you see what a poor pack of Crew we are as *the*
Negro said.

[*May 22, 1757*]
Sabbath Eve.

This Morn my Sister broke out very full with the small-pox—We have
removed her to a House of Mr Burrs about a mile off—it has done her no
hurt as we have reason to think. I just now heard she was very comfortable—
I fear I have taken the infection. Yesterday she took a Vomit and I attended
her which is said to be daingerous—O my dear, dear Friend pray for us, in
petecular that Mr Burr may be preserved—I am almost sunk to the depths of
Meloncholy at the possibility of Mr Burrs geting of it.

I have read all your dear kind friendly Letters but am so confused cant
write anything upon them. Mr Olivers vissit is very short. They set out
tomorrow morn—You need not be concernd about your Love to a sertain
person for if you dont know that you Love, I know it and if he was to leve
you, you would soon know it too.

Marry and be happy—God be with you and ever Bless you—perhaps this
may be the last Letter you ever receive from me—But pray—pray ernestly
that I may be fitted for Gods holy will and pleasure conserning me and mine
and my dear Sister. I cant Write.

[*May 25, 1757*]
Wednsday P.M.

Lucy yet in a fine way—Blessed be God I found More freedom at the hour of prayer then usual, and in petecular for you my dear—Your Circumstances lay heavy upon me, but this Morn found freedom to leve you with God—O my dear how able and willing is he to assist and comfort the afflicted—I must go this A.M. to vissit a Minnisters Wife that is in Town—You will wonder why she ant here but she has a Mother in Town or you may be sure she would be at our house.

[*May 28, 1757*]
Saturday.

My Sister is like to do better than we expected. Her Pock begins to turn— My Little Son very Ill.

FRANCIS ASBURY (1745-1816)

Francis Asbury, the father of American Methodism, was born near Birmingham, England. When he was still a boy, his family came under the influence of the growing Methodist movement, and soon Francis began to preach. In 1771, when John Wesley asked for volunteers to go to America as missionaries, Asbury responded eagerly.

He came to this country at an opportune time for the proclamation of his message. The growing population was spreading over greater and greater distances, and Methodist forms of organization that Wesley had perfected in England would soon work very well in America. First, however, came the crisis of the American Revolution. Because the missionaries were British, and because Wesley's own opposition to the Revolution was well known, patriots were often suspicious of the Methodists. Due to these circumstances, most of Asbury's colleagues returned to their homeland, but Asbury stayed on. He was sequestered during part of the war, and even fired upon once, but still he kept working as he could. After the peace was signed, his persistence paid off. He quickly regained the confidence of officials in the new United States, even as he organized a new crop of missionaries for energetic service.

Asbury once urged his associates to "go into every kitchen and shop; address all, aged and young, on the salvation of their souls." And he followed his own advice. He remained on the move for the rest of his life, traveling nearly 300,000 miles (mostly on horseback), crossing the Appalachians more than sixty times, preaching many times a week, and conducting countless prayer sessions. Through this incessant activity he became perhaps the best-known person in North America.

Growth for the Methodists was slow at first, but soon accelerated. Their message was a traditional Protestant one with a special concern for the doctrines that John Wesley emphasized: God's free grace, the human ability to accept or reject that grace, and the necessity of striving to abolish every known sin. Asbury's organization of circuit riders provided for both first-time evangelization and systematic follow-through. Asbury was also an effective preacher at camp meetings and other revival gatherings. When he came to America in 1771, there were four Methodist ministers caring for about 300 lay people. When he died in 1816, there were 2,000 ministers and over 200,000 Methodists.

Asbury's piety was bracing. It tolerated no nonsense, no time-wasting, no frivolity. It was a spirituality for action. Asbury's diary and his many letters testify boldly to the qualities that made this Methodist faith so potent in the early history of the United States. The selections from the diary that follow—entries from November and December of 1779—show something of the energy that Asbury poured into his spiritual service. The letters, written late in his life, are elegant testimony to a faith active in love.

Diary and Letters

DIARY ENTRIES

Wednesday, [November] 17, [1779]. I rode to Stradley's: had about sixty people to hear: met the society of about twenty-two members, all serious, and under good impressions. I was surprised to find them so clear in their ideas of religion, and was blest among them: returned to Thomas White's, met the people, gave a warm, searching exhortation. I am troubled about our separating brethren, in Virginia; I have read through the Book of Genesis; and again have read the Confessions of Faith, the Assembly's Catechism, Directory of Church Government, and Form for the Public Worship: now I understand it better than I like it. I purposed to rise at four o'clock, as often as I can, and spend two hours in prayer and meditation; two hours in reading, and one in recreating and conversation; and in the evening, to take my room at eight, pray and meditate an hour, and go to bed at nine o'clock: all this I purpose to do, when not travelling; but to rise at four o'clock every morning.

Thursday, 18. Spent the day in reading and prayer, but was sorely tempted; wrote letters to William Lynch, William Watters, and the venerable Otterbein.

Friday, 19. I kept a day of fasting and humiliation.

Saturday, 20. Ended the reading of Salmon's Grammar, more than six hundred pages.

Sunday, 21. Preached on John v, 44, to the end of the chapter, and was clear and pointed: the people are stirred up, but there are disorders among them, occasioned by their unfaithfulness. Met the society, and afterward the Africans.

Source: *The Journal and Letters of Francis Asbury,* 3 vols., ed. Elmer T. Clark et al. (Nashville: Abingdon Press, 1958), I: 323-25; III: 474, 493, 507-9.

Monday, 22. Rose between four and five, spent an hour in prayer and meditation, read a few chapters in the Bible before it was day-light: I want to be all devoted to God; every moment given up to Christ. Rode to Maxfield's, and preached to about three hundred people; spoke on "Lord, are there few that be saved?" First, showed, What we are to be saved from. 2. How we are saved. 3. Why there are few. No open sinner can be in a state of salvation; no formalist, violent sectarian, having only opinions and modes of religion; no hypocrites or backsliders; no, nor those who are only seekers. I came back, was much tried, prayed to the Lord for peace, and opened my Bible on these words: "So the service was prepared, and the priests stood in their places, and the Levites in their courses, according to the king's commandment."

Tuesday, 23. Rode to Robert Layton's, and preached to about thirty people, from "Through much tribulation we must enter into the kingdom of God." Spoke as my own experience led me; then returned to Edward White's, and lectured on Moses meeting his father-in-law. (Exodus xviii.) There were not many people, but they were happy.

Wednesday, 24. Rode to the widow Jump's, and preached to about thirty souls, on "Why sayest thou, O Jacob, and speakest thou, O Israel," &c. There is a declension here; but I follow my own feelings. A great sweetness has attended me this day, although I drank of the wormwood and the gall in the morning. When I get out into the work, I am always happy.

Thursday, 25. Rose at four o'clock, and had a sweet time in meditation and prayer, from four to six; purpose to spend two hours in the morning, and one at night, in these blessed exercises. Began this morning to read books on the practice of physic: I want to help the bodies and souls of men.

Friday, 26. Preached at William Laws's to about a hundred people; spoke on Numbers x, 29. While meeting the class, some appeared greatly affected: this evening I read in the Bible, and some books on physic: also exhorted; for the people press upon us to hear the word.

Saturday, 27. Was kept in a calm after the devil had been tearing my soul like a lion; but he hath left me for a season. I looked into Rutherford's Letters, and they were blest to me: also looked into Doddridge's Rise and Progress of Religion, and that was also blessed to me. My soul is waiting on the Lord for full Christian perfection. I poured out my soul to the Lord for this, and for my brethren in all parts of the world, that the power of religion may continue with us, as a people. I tremble to think of the cloud of the Divine presence departing from us; if this should be, I hope not to live to see it; and with Mr. Wesley, desire that God may rather scatter the people to the ends of the earth; I had rather they should not be, than to be a dead society:—Amen, says poor William Spencer.

Sunday, 28. Preached at the widow Brady's before church, on Hebrews x, 12, and following verses; had some liberty in speaking: afterward went to church, received the sacrament, and returned to Brady's, and heard Joseph Cromwell, an original indeed—no man's copy. Spent a day with Mr. Thorne.

Tuesday, 30. I intended to go to Choptank, but Mr. Magaw was coming down to preach a funeral sermon, and desired me to stay. We spent an evening at the widow Brady's together, and had some talk about erecting a Kingswood school in America.

Wednesday, December 1, 1779. Rode twelve miles to Cardeen's, and preached to about one hundred serious people, and I hope there will be good done: met Mr. Airey, from Dorchester county, who was convinced by read-ing the writings of old Mr. Perkins. Mr. Airey solicits preaching in that county. I have taken cold by some means, it has brought on an inflammation in my throat.

Thursday, 2. There fell a very heavy rain, that prevented my going to Johnny-cake Landing.

Sunday, 26. Preached at Andrew Purden's to a large congregation: spoke with great power from "His name shall be called Jesus." Afterward preached at Jonathan Sipple's, on John ii, 8; there was some moving among the people.

Monday, 27. Visited the sick, Cranmer, a faithful soul, and Ruth Smith, wearing away fast with a consumption, but praising God, and continually preaching Christ.

Tuesday, 28. A stormy, rainy day: went to Lewis's, but none came. I must spend the whole night in prayer, after the example of my Lord; for tempta-tion is to try me; perhaps for my good, as I have many things to lift me up. Brother Hartley is now married, and begins to care for his wife. I have spent but little time to-day in reading or writing. There is a prospect of a work of religion in this State, if the preachers are faithful; but I fear none more than myself; yet, sure I am that I want to be the Lord's. The hard, cold weather is broke at last. People suffer much more in winter by cold, and in summer by heat, here than in England. I find the care of a wife begins to humble my young friend, and makes him very teachable: I have thought he always carried great sail; but he will have ballast now.

Wednesday, 29. Preached at D. Dehadway's to about two hundred peo-ple, and spoke livingly from 2 Cor. vi, 17, 18. I was led out greatly. Preached at night at Joseph Purden's, from 1 Cor. xv, 58, and had much liberty. One of the devil's camps, a tavern, is broken up here; for most of their neighbours have forsaken them.

Thursday, 30. Rode to Stradley's, and preached on Luke iv, 17, 18. I had life, and there were more people than I expected. I came to Thomas White's, and went to see James Patterson, very ill; he appears to decline swiftly.

Friday, 31. I went to Cardeen's; a dreadful road, eight miles through the woods, and very cold. I spoke with great warmth on 1 John iii, 4, 5. Always, when most tried I have the greatest liberty.

SELECTED LETTERS

[To Jonathan Lyons]

July 3, 1813

My dear Jonathan:

Great grace attend us, for indeed to bear one another's burdens and so fulfil the law of Christ, given twice in the 13th and 15th of John's Gospel. Ah what changes, in health, in life and friends. Brother Garrettson informed me of the change between you and Brother Ward. I wish it may be for the best and I am satisfied. The general union in the New England and Genesee is great. Now the world is at war, the church is at peace. You will watch and pray, believe and love, preach and meet the classes and societies, instruct the children and visit from house to house. We have had to ride 700 miles since New York, steady and shall [carry] on our work in sickness and heat and pain, but in faith and prayer we must out preach and pray and live our former selves and all others.

Let them build houses, we must build churches and build up souls in holiness whilst others are contenting their minds with 4 hours work once in 7 days. Let us preach every day, from morning to evening, every day in the week, let us have souls for our hire, God for our portion, heaven for our home. We live upon God and feel answers to the prayers of God's people and we are invulnerable, Immortal till our master's work is done. With respect to thee and thine.

In our Saviour, as ever
F. Asbury

[To Joseph Frye]

August 21, 1813

My very dear Joseph:

Great grace attend thee. We are kept alive with death so near. I doubt if you are like St. Paul, that was it possible, or proper could wish himself accursed or insipid. Yea after they had hunted him like a deer, and beaten almost to death like a dog and still his Lord had to forbid him and tell him to depart and then Paul humbly disputed the cause with his Lord! Oh the Jews! What continual sorrow, what inexpressible grief! Oh Winchester help them! You will be called for greater services and suffering in the ministry, prepare, be faithful, keep thyself pure, make great sacrifices for God! I am never afraid to trust young men. The same measure that has been meeted to me, I meet back, Great confidence was put in me, a boy!

Young men are strong in body, and mind, not skilled in craft, not the same temptation to ease and indulgence as aged. I have never repented of the confidence I have put in you and thousands. Increase this year not ascertained. No returns from Upper and Lower Canadas. Some circuits dismantled and the people scattered, upon the lines. Great peace in conferences, serious afflictions and deaths among preachers and people. I have a few appointments for the west, the brethren will wish to see me. Editors left out the Mississippi conferences thinking we shall not go, but the work suffers and dies. We are growing old every year perhaps serious times, more and more serious coming.

I am
F. Asbury

[To Nelson Reed]

August 26, 1814

My dear Nelson:

Here we have Perry Hall, as also Bazaleel Wells, Stubenville, [Ohio]. Perry Hall continued. Oh my dear, I can truly say with Fletcher; that the uncommon attention of my friends; the unwillingness they have showed, to let me go to glory; (of which I have had the fullest confidence; the brightest views; is my greatest trial.) Well I pant! I cough! I speak hoarsely! I pray, I speak, sitting. I am slowly gaining strength. I love my own, the church: I hope to love them to the end of life, to love forever! I am willing to move in the line of duty, little in state, like the great. Our travelling is expensive in 600 miles, we have found by the founder of one, of the purchase of another horse and road expenses, a call to appropriate near 100 dollars; but hope to save the lame horse. Could I be an hewer of wood, or drawer of water, a beggar for the camp of Israel, here I am a moving skeleton.

Oh my soul feels for our bleeding country, bad times! worse to come! Oh what a desire I have to preach, Oh what bodily debility! What am I spared for and that I shall not leave this new world in distress; be taken from the evil to come like hundreds of the people of God that have died with the prevailing fever. Am I given back to the prayers of the Church of God? Am I spared to mourn over the judicial blindness! Egyptian darkness! that hath taken riveted hold, of the rulers of the united kingdoms, and United States, and provinces? Am I spared to see the spirit of heresy the spirit of schism rise up in the Church of God? Am I spared to see a laxity in discipline among the ministry and members in the Church of God? Am I spared to see numeration decreasing 1,000 in a year? the work of God drooping, and dying generally. Newspapers read with such attention, Bibles shamefully neglected, conversation that ought to turn upon God, religion, and his work, all about the world. Shall I be spared to see two men God hath shewed me ought to be appointed in unity, and trinity, in our Episcopacy, one high in merit, long in labours every where. Oh Daniel highly favoured of God, Oh Saul, man of mind.

It is not proper, after 40 years friendship we should tell our friends, could we tell how we love them. Dear brother you for age stand as such, and an equal, you always sat like a son at my side. It will be mercy, yea miracle, if ever I see Baltimore, again, or if Baltimore seeth another conference in peace. I rejoice to hear, (but not *officially*, that the work revives) in Baltimore. I presume your term will expire in the District next March. You will think (should it rest with me in part), a district, a circuit, a station. For this cause sometimes it seems the case, shall man leave in some degree his spiritual father, and his mother, the *Church* and cleave to his wife. Philip Bruce either to save himself, or the Church; said he would quit the district; because if he rested, those under his charge would do the same, without considering the difference of age, or strength and that he had borne the burden for near 40 years. I have feebly spoken in almost every place, feeble enough! I have taken the holy Book into my hands but twice to preach or expound. I have friends in fellowship, and only congregational Methodists.

I need not be a burden to city societies, that collect and expend annually 2,000, 3,000 or perhaps 4,000 dollars per year church expenses, *poor preachers*, and collections. Select friends, seeing my ease have housed me in a conveyance, if possibly they may restore my health. My whole affliction (unlike my last sickness was epidemical) I lay it wholly to unseasonable exposedness in travelling, and damp weather.

Senator Worthington will bear this letter, should you see him treat him with respect, he is a worthy friend of mine; but not joined with any society of religious people. John Wesley Bond without exception is the best aid I ever had, of a young man, only too attentive to me. I shall be highly indebted to Baltimore Conference for my present aid. Oh, when brought by affliction as low as dribbling infancy, and even now a boy 6 years of age would excell me in strength, and motion. My mouth has failed. I cannot even eat without difficulty, food to supply; the late physick or age or affliction, thank God for eyes. I have read Saurin, Oh he makes me feel little. When I review my life, and labours, I say *purity of intention, diligence* no more. My justifying, sanctifying, practical righteousness all in and from *Christ,* heaven opens *Glory Glory Glory.* I cannot give any account of Bishop McKendree. I am waiting his arrival in the neighbourhood of Chillicothe. Present me to dear Nancy and all my male and female friends. We will pray on, suffer on, we shall rest, and reign with Jesus, there all our family, national, and personal, and church troubles shall end, I am thine,

Still, in the Saviour,
F. Asbury

HENRY ALLINE (1748-1784)

Henry Alline (pronounced "Allen") was the George Whitefield of the Canadian Maritime Provinces. Just as Whitefield had been a catalyst for a "New Light" revival in New England during the 1740s, so Alline three decades later became the chief promoter of an influential revival of Christian faith in Nova Scotia and neighboring provinces.

In many ways Alline's spirituality resembled that which Whitefield had earlier promoted in the colonies farther to the South. It was marked by a burning drive to preach to the unconverted, the exaltation of the New Birth, the cultivation of a distinct language of religious emotion, and an expectation that holiness of life would flow from the experience of conversion. Like Whitefield, Alline played down the importance of denominational differences and gladly worked with whoever could assist in the propagation of the revival message. Only in his insistence upon the powers of human free will, which was a departure from Calvinism, did Alline move significantly beyond his colonial model.

Alline was born on June 14, 1748, in Newport, Rhode Island, where he also received his early education. When he was twelve, he moved with his family to Falmouth in the Minas Basin region of Nova Scotia. There he learned and practiced the trade of a tanner. The combination of political stress occasioned by the American Revolution and a deeply ingrained fear of death led Alline to a personal crisis in 1775 that culminated in a liberating conversion. So profound was this experience that Alline felt he had actually tasted the spiritual fruits of Paradise. (Early in the twentieth century William James in his *Varieties of Religious Experience* described Alline's conversion as a classic example of the "curing of a 'sicksoul.'") After further personal turmoil, Alline felt a definite call to preach. Almost immediately he became a sensation with his message of instantaneous conversion, his ecstatic sense of union with Christ, and his promotion of a purified church.

Like Whitefield, Alline was a preacher who could move his listeners. His active ministry did not last much more than a decade, but he left centers of revivalistic piety scattered throughout the region he traveled, the influence of which can be felt to this day. The norms for public religion that he established still shape the Baptist churches and related bodies of the Maritime Provinces.

Besides being an itinerant preacher, Alline was also an indefatigable hymn-writer. The more than 500 "hymns and spiritual songs" that gave life to his

revival message also constituted the bulk of what he published in his lifetime.
Shortly before his death in 1784, Alline wrote a hymn that reasserted many of
the important emphases of his piety:

> Soon I shall end this rapid race,
> And tread your mortal climes no more;
> But through Jehovah's boundless grace,
> Safe shall I reach the Heav'nly shore. . . .
>
> I drink, I soar, I gaze, I rove,
> O'er the transparent scenes of bliss,
> Still lost with wonder in his love,
> My soul! and what a God as this!
>
> Ten thousand blazing realms of light
> Proclaim their God, and say, Amen!
> My soul still soaring in her flight,
> My God is all, I drop my pen.

The following passages from Alline's journal relate to his call to preach and
describe the effects that his ministry had on his hometown. They provide a flavor
of his fervid devotion.

Journal Entries

CHRIST is the fountain of life, the source of happiness, the glory of angelic
realms, and the triumph of Saints, and I trust is the life of my soul, the joy of
my life, my present and everlasting portion. I therefore desire, and intend by
his grace that his name should be my theme, until the last period of my days.
And O may his blessed Spirit be breathed into all my endeavours, may his
love sweeten all my trials, invigorate all my labours; may his name fill up
every period of my life, when in private, and every sentence, when in public:
and hoping that he will cause me to write and leave amongst the rest of my
writings this short account of my life. And as that is my design, I shall not
overburden the reader with a relation of many passages that would be of no
benefit, but shall only relate that, which may be worth the readers perusal.

Source: *The Journal of Henry Alline*, ed. James Beverley and Barry Moody (Hantsport,
Nova Scotia: Lancelot Press for Acadia Divinity College and Baptist Historical Commit-
tee, 1982), pp. 29, 73-76, 89-91. Another volume from this same series, Baptist Heritage
in Atlantic Canada, entitled *New Light Letters and Songs*, ed. George A. Rawlyk, is the
source for the hymn; it provides a fine general introduction to Alline and his age.

* * *

ABOUT the 13th or 14th day of April, 1776, I began to see that I had all this time been led astray by labouring so much after human learning and wisdom, and had held back from the call of God. One day in my meditation I had such a discovery of Christ's having every thing I needed, and that it was all mine, that I saw I needed nothing to qualify me but Christ; and that if I had all the wisdom that could ever be obtained by mortals, without having the spirit of Christ with me, I should never have any success in preaching; and if Christ went with me I should have all in all. And O what a willingness I felt in my soul to go in his name and strength, depending on him alone. I found I had nothing more to inquire into, but whether God had called me: for he knew what learning I had, and could have in the course of his providence brought me through all the seats of learning, that ever man went through, together with all the orders of men; but he had not; therefore I had nothing else to observe, but the call of God: and when I got near to him and enjoyed a sense of divine things, I was fully convinced (though in the dark I would often doubt) and was now determined to come forward the first opportunity I could get. The 18th April, being a day set apart for fasting and prayer, I came out and spoke by way of exhortation, had some liberty, but was under great trials, the night following, when I was watching with a young man, that appeared to be near his end. The devil was all night against me, telling me that I had gone astray, and had no business to speak, and *that I had wounded* (-wound) the cause of Christ *in so doing:* and so powerful and great was the temptation (-& trialls) that I was about to make a promise, that I never would speak again in public while I lived; for I had certainly gone astray; for if I had not, I should not be under such trials. But when I was about to make a vow, never to speak again in public, a thought came into my mind, that it was now not a proper time, for I intended to make such a promise, I ought to take a time when I had nothing to encumber my mind, and when I should get near to God, with nothing to interrupt me: I then put off the vow until morning, intending to seek a convenient opportunity for it. Accordingly I went early in the morning in the woods, and endeavoured to lay my case before God, and the Lord gave me a nearness to him: and O what a change of mind I found; for I was willing then to make ten vows that I would speak, and that the first opportunity, which accordingly I did the next sabbath. I spoke a few words the Saturday before to my parents to know their minds, and although they did not dissuade me, yet I saw it was not agreeable to them. This was a great trial to me; and the devil made a great use of it for my discouragement, telling me, that I held them to be christians, and I saw they were against it, which was an evidence, that it was not the will of God. But the Lord carried me through it all; and I found I must go and speak before them; although I saw at the same time that it was disagreeable to them. They discoursed as if they were jealous that I was under a delusion; but two or three of my christian friends were exceeding solicitous for me to proceed: which by the Grace of God I did, and it immediately spread abroad over the whole place, and caused many to come out of curiosity; but the Lord gave me boldness to speak. I spoke from the following words: If thou art wise, thou art wise for thyself, but if thou scornest, thou alone shalt bear it. [Prov. 9:12] There seemed to be a great attention paid by some; although others made a scoff, but some seemed to be taken hold of, and some christians took me by the hand, and bid me God speed: but all the trials I met from without were not equal to those within. I still continued improving every Sabbath-day, being sometimes in the dark and sometimes in the light; and when I was in darkness, and did not find the spirit of God with me, when speaking, I would be ready to sink, and thought I would preach no more; and when I got life and liberty again, my strength and my resolutions were renewed; and thus God dealt with me, and carried me through various scenes.

IT being reported at this time that Henry *Alline* (-Allein) was turned New-Light preacher, many would come from other towns, even whole boat-loads. Some came to hear what the babler had to say; some came with gladness of heart that God had raised up one to speak in his name; and some come to make a scoff, but it did not seem to trouble me much; for I trust God was with me and supported and enabled me to face a frowning world. The greatest trials I met with *were from* (-was my friends, together with) my parents, who were so much against my improving, as sometimes to leave the house as I was speaking. O how it would cut me sometimes: but, blessed be God, he not only carried me through these trials; but likewise so opened their eyes, that they were as much engaged for me to preach the Gospel, as I was, and would have plucked out even their eyes for my encouragement. Thus God was kind to me in every respect, and ever worked for my good. He blessed my soul, supported my body, blessed my labours in some degree, increased my desires and my resolutions, lifted me above the fears and trials of the world, *weaned* (-& shook) me in a great degree from the flattering charms of this world of sense, and increased my faith.

*   *   *

JANUARY 1st, 1778. I went to Falmouth, where it was enough to make a christian's heart rejoice to see the alteration of things. A little time ago they were going on in all manner of wickedness, frolicking, sin and vanity; and now meeting to praise the Lord, the great Redeemer of mankind, and thirsting after the word of life. Some, who a few years ago were the ringleaders *to* (-of) vice, now singing Hosannas to the son of David, [Mt. 21:9, 15] and live so exemplary, that they are an ornament to the gospel they profess. O may the blessed Jesus have all the praise. O what great things has God done for this desert land! The wilderness is become a fruitful field, and the desert blossoms as a rose. [Isa. 32:15; 35:1] When I had been in town about three weeks I returned to Cornwallis, where I had likewise blessed days and hours: for God was there of a truth; and I spent some blessed moments with them. *One* (-But in the) evening after I was in bed, I was very much troubled in my mind, which seemed to forbode no good. I got up in the morning under gloomy apprehensions of some disagreeable turn, and remained so almost all the day; in the evening I preached, after which I invited two of my christian friends to my lodging, one of them told me, he had had dark and distressing hours for some time, occasioned by a certain text that bore upon his mind. I asked him what text it was. He answered the words are these: Sleep on now and take thy rest: [Mt. 26:45] and he asked my mind about them. I immediately told him that it appeared to me, the interpretation at that time carried a very gloomy aspect. He asked me what I learned from them to us in these days. I answered him thus, while I was striving with my spirit and labouring among you for the salvation of souls, intreating you to be up and doing, while the waters were troubled, by watching and praying, which you have too much neglected, while I was with you and now sleep if you can; for be assured there is a dying hour a coming. He said it expressed much the same to him. I then told him what I had passed through in my own mind the night before, and how it bore on my mind. We went to my lodging and about eleven o'clock at night, had as I may say very suddenly such horror of darkness, as was said Abraham was once in. [Gen. 15:12] My whole soul was benighted, and a storm of temptation rose up against me so that I was obliged to say with David, The strong bulls of Bashan have beset me around. [Ps. 22:12] O the darkness and distress of my mind. This was the first distress, darkness or doubt of my standing that ever I had known since my conversion: for now I gave way to the enemy (it being new to me) so that I wholly doubted my standing, that I tried to invalidate all the evidences I had since my conversion of having enjoyed the presence of God, and to throw it all away: yet I found something like an anchor of hope within the veil, [Heb. 6:19] which I could not get rid of; though I tried much, and prayed to God to take if way. O the unspeakable distress I was under! I could neither eat, drink nor sleep with any satisfaction; for it was wholly new to me, so that I knew not what to do, what to say, where I had been, where I now was, nor where I was going. O my soul cried out to some unknown God. Help, help, O my God; if thou art mine; if not, O my God undeceive me. My darkness and distress was without any relief more than a minute at a time, for three days and three nights (as Jonah was) [Jonah 1:17] and I could say with him, that I was in the belly of hell; I went down to the bottom of the mountains, and the earth with her bars were about me. [Jonah 2:2, 6] But my God remembered me, and brought me again to rejoice in the wonders of his love, and to triumph over the powers of darkness. O the unspeakable happiness my soul enjoyed when God delivered me. I am convinced it was all in great love, yea, of unspeakable benefit to fit me for the work I had before me, which God knew, though I did not. O let me remember, and forever adore his love.

TIMOTHY DWIGHT (1752-1817)

Timothy Dwight was a grandson of Jonathan Edwards, a noted author and public spokesman, and one of the most distinguished presidents in the early history of Yale College. After graduating from Yale at the age of seventeen, Dwight spent more than two decades farming, teaching, preaching, and establishing a co-educational academy before he assumed the Yale presidency in 1795.

Under Dwight's leadership, Yale increased in stature dramatically. In the eyes of many it became the model of what a "New England college" should be. Dwight strove against spiritual indifference and unbelief and became one of the leaders in the great revival known as the Second Great Awakening. In addition to having significant abilities as a persuasive spiritual advisor, he was an illustrious teacher and a leading political spokesman of the day. In the wake of the French Revolution and its excesses, he defended the conservative programs of the Federalists.

In his early years Dwight had been a member of the "Hartford Wits," a group of writers that included John Trumbull and Joel Barlow. This small band attempted to establish a distinct American literary tradition. Among Dwight's poetic productions were *The Conquest of Canaan* (1785), an epic about the battle for political independence; *The Triumph of Infidelity* (1788), a satire against the atheism of the European enlightenment; and *Greenfield Hill* (1794), a poem proposing a course of moral improvement.

As the themes and emphases of these works might indicate, the America of Timothy Dwight was a far different land from that of William Bradford, Mary Rowlandson, John Winthrop, or even that of his grandfather, Jonathan Edwards. Though Dwight's Christian commitment is genuine, his tone is more subdued and dispassionate than that employed by his spiritual ancestors. The following passages constitute the main themes from one of his sermons, "Joy in the Holy Spirit," and are taken from an 1843 edition of his five-volume work, *Theology, Explained and Defended.*

From "Joy in the Holy Spirit"

Romans 14:17.—For the kingdom of God is not meat and drink, but righteousness, peace, and joy in the Holy Ghost.

On the last Sabbath, I considered the nature and importance of Spiritual Peace. I shall proceed to examine another consequence of Regeneration: viz. Joy in the Holy Ghost.

In the text, the Apostle declares, that the Kingdom of God is formed of Righteousness, Peace, and Joy in the Holy Ghost. By this kingdom he intends, plainly, not the kingdom of Creation, nor the kingdom of Providence, nor, in a strict sense, what is usually called the kingdom of Grace. The word kingdom is here used in a figurative manner; and denotes the Effects of that secret, invisible, incomprehensible influence over the hearts of mankind, which is exerted by the Spirit of Grace in the work of Sanctification. This influence is the great engine of the divine government over the hearts of Intelligent beings; and is often with the utmost propriety termed in the Gospel the kingdom of God. Of this influence, righteousness, peace, and joy in the Holy Ghost are effects, primarily important; and in the text are, figuratively, called by a name, which, in simple language, would properly belong to the Cause of their existence. In a similar manner is the term used by Christ, Luke 17:20, "The kingdom of God cometh not with observation; neither shall they say concerning it, Lo here, or lo there: for the kingdom of God is within you."

Of these three great effects of the energy of the divine Spirit, the first, viz. Righteousness, here used for holiness or Evangelical virtue, is, in the soul, the cause of the two last. From Righteousness, in this sense, spring, of course, the Peace and Joy of the Spiritual character. Joy in the Holy Ghost, therefore, is obviously a consequence of Regeneration. In the text, as well as in the order of nature, it is subjoined to Peace; although we are ever to remember, that they always exist together in the same mind, and at the same time.

In examining this subject, the following considerations have occurred to me as particularly deserving the attention of a religious assembly.

I. The Joy, spoken of in the text, is not a mere Natural joy.

By natural joy, I intend the pleasure which is found by the mind in natural or physical good, whether possessed, or expected. Such is the pleasure, which we experience in property, health, friends, food, and other gratifications of a similar nature. Such is the pleasure, found in the contemplation of beauty, novelty, and greatness; in the multitude, variety, and sublimity, of the works of Creation and Providence; or in the skill, power, and wisdom displayed by their Author. Such, also, is the satisfaction, experienced in the mere belief, that God is reconciled to us, and become our friend and benefactor.

All these I acknowledge to be innocent and lawful enjoyments. I acknowledge them to be enjoyments which we are not merely permitted, but required, to experience; and to be enjoyments also, in greater or less degrees, experienced by every sanctified mind. Still they may be possessed in a manner, merely natural; and by a mind, utterly destitute of the Evangelical character. When the Christian rejoices in these things, he rejoices virtuously; because he regards them with just views. But when a sinner rejoices in them, he regards them with erroneous views, and with emotions destitute of virtue. Evangelical joy in these things is one of the fruits of the Spirit. But nothing, experienced by a sinner, can be a peculiar characteristic of a Christian. Nor is any genuine fruit of the Spirit ever found in an unsanctified mind.

II. Joy in the Holy Ghost is, however, joy in God.

God is the only solid foundation of joy to the universe; and is seen and acknowledged, in this character, by every virtuous being. In this most pleasing and magnificent manner, he is every where exhibited in the Scriptures. "Rejoice in the Lord, O ye righteous!" says the Psalmist. Ps. xxxiii.1. "Thou shalt rejoice in the Lord," saith the Prophet Isaiah, "and shalt glory in the Holy One of Israel." Is. xli.16. "I will greatly rejoice in the Lord; my soul shall be joyful in my God;" saith our Saviour; Is. xli.10. "Be glad then, ye children of Zion, and rejoice in the Lord your God;" saith Joel ii.23. "Although the fig-tree shall not blossom, neither shall fruit be in the vine; the labour of the olive shall fail, and the fields shall yield no meat; the flocks shall be cut off from the fold, and there shall be no herd in the stall: yet I will rejoice in the Lord; I will joy in the God of my salvation." Hab. iii.17, 18. The same language is adopted by the Virgin Mary, and by St. Paul, in the New Testament; and is applied by Christ to the Apostles; and to the whole body of Christians; either as an account of facts; or as a precept, directing their duty.

To Revelation, Reason joins her fullest testimony; and easily discerns, when informed of the true character of God by Revelation, that in him the proper, rational, supreme, and eternal joy of his Intelligent creatures must ultimately centre; and that he is the object, to be thus enjoyed, as well as the source whence this enjoyment flows. The eternal, unchangeable, almighty, all-knowing, the infinitely just, faithful, true, benevolent, and merciful Mind is, in an infinite degree, a more beautiful, lovely, and glorious object in itself, than any, or than all, others. Of such a Mind all the conduct, all the manifestations, are accordant with its true and essential nature; are beautiful, glorious, and lovely, like itself. These amazing considerations are also enhanced, in a manner literally boundless, by the great fact, that from this

Mind sprang all the objects of admiration, and delight, which are found in the Universe.

In the Power of God, we are presented with an everlasting and unlimited source of joy; when it is considered as perfect Sufficiency for every great and good purpose; for the accomplishment of whatever wisdom can approve, or virtue delight in; and for the accomplishment of this in the manner, which is perfectly desirable.

In the Knowledge of God, there is an endless source of delight; as the original spring, whence have flowed the innumerable beings, and events, of the Universe; together with their attributes, operations, and effects. In the perpetually diversified structure, the wonderful purposes, and the no less wonderful uses, of these, is the state of the infinite Mind, as the Origin of whatever is great and good, presented to us in a manner, perfect in itself, and endlessly delightful to every virtuous beholder. The mineral, vegetable, and animal, kingdoms, even of this world, are full of these displays; and the structure, powers, and operations of a single being, furnish a field of investigation, altogether too wide for the comprehension of any human understanding.

In the Bounty of God, we behold an amazing source of gratitude, and of the pleasure, always found in that most amiable and delightful emotion. We here discern ample provision made for our continuance in being; for our daily wants; and for all our reasonable wishes. Our food and raiment are most liberally supplied; our innocent desires most richly gratified; our taste delighted with the beauty, novelty, and grandeur, of the world around us; our eyes charmed with the glorious prospects of the earth and the heavens; and our ears feasted with melody and harmony.

In the Mercy of God, the soul is assured, that its sins may be forgiven, and its nature renewed; is presented with the most illustrious proofs of divine Love, and the overflowings of infinite tenderness towards a world of apostates. It is here furnished with the greatest and best gift of God; Evangelical Virtue; and beyond the grave, is secured in the endless possession of unmingled and unfading happiness. From sin, its own most debased character, and from misery, its proper reward, it is here presented with a final deliverance; is instamped with the image of God, and admitted to the kingdom of the blessed.

In the Truth and Faithfulness of this perfect Being, the soul is furnished with entire security, that His declarations are steadfast and immoveable; and that his promises endure for ever. The encouragement, given to it, therefore, of both present and future good, is encouragement, on which perfect reliance may be placed, and with regard to which disappointment can never arise, either here or hereafter. When we remember, that one of these promises to Christians is, that all things shall be theirs; and another, that all things shall work together for their good; the importance of this consideration appears to be literally infinite. On these declarations the virtuous Universe reposes with absolute safety, and with reliance which will strengthen for ever.

The Justice of God is seen to be the immensely grand and awful, yet the immensely beneficial, administration of the vast kingdom of Jehovah. In the exercise of this glorious attribute are secured all the rights of intelligent creatures, and their infallible and complete protection from every ultimate wrong. The least right, and the least wrong, of the least individual, are as firmly assured, as the greatest interests of Angels and Archangels. By this amazing Mind nothing is forgotten, or unregarded. Lazarus, at the gate, is as effectually remembered, as David, on the throne; or Gabriel, standing before God in the highest heavens.

Alone, and to a world of sinners, the Justice of God would be only great and terrible; but, harmonizing with Mercy and all its dictates, it renders, even to our view, the character of the great Possessor transcendently excellent and amiable. What would become of the universe, were God to be unjust? What creature would for a moment be safe; what interest uninvaded?

Of these glorious attributes, we need not, in order to find displays, cast our eyes abroad into incomprehensible systems of worlds and beings. At home, by our firesides, in our friends, in our families, in our bodies, and in our minds, they are seen with high advantage and supreme endearment. Are we fed? The hand which feeds us is that of our heavenly Father. Are we clothed? He made the flax to grow; he formed the fleece; he gave the silkworm skill, to spin her mysterious thread; and brought to us the necessary, and beautiful materials, to form our attire. Are we in health? He preserves in their pristine strength the numerous powers of our bodies; sends the stream of life through our veins; and animates our hearts with wonderful and unceasing energy. Do we see? He contrived the eye. Do we hear? He fashioned the ear. Do we think, and choose, and feel? He lighted up the lamp of Reason in our minds. Are we, and ours, virtuous? He poured out the Spirit of sanctification upon our minds. Have we enjoyments? He provided them. Have we hopes? They all sprang from his bounty, and are secured by his unchangeable promise.

* * *

To the Christian, in all these respects, is God the source of supreme and unceasing joy. As a Christian, he has become a new creature; entered into a new creation; and enrolled himself as a subject of a new and immortal kingdom. This kingdom is a kingdom in which will be progressively accomplished, universal, entire, and everlasting good. For this end it was created. To this end it is uniformly conducted by the all-pervading, all-ruling, hand of JEHOVAH. The subjects of it are universally children of light. Their intercourse is an endless succession of diversified virtue and loveliness. Purity, dignity, and excellence, are their inherent characteristics; and everlasting happiness, and glory, their final destination. In all that they are, in all that they do, and in all that is done to them, God himself rejoices with intense and eternal joy.

With this new kingdom the Christian has begun an everlasting connexion. His union to the members of it, and his intercourse with them, instead of terminating, will unceasingly become more intimate, more endearing, more exalted. The views of their minds and his are destined to become perpetually more and more just and comprehensive; their affections and his to be more pure, intense, and noble; their mutual friendship to be more sweet and serene; and their conduct to be, in unceasing gradation, such as is proper to be exhibited in the house, and presence, of God.

In accordance with this state of things, therefore, will the whole scheme of the Christian's future being be formed. His plans will, of course, be concerted in such a manner, as to embrace, and promote eternal purposes. They will be the plans of an immortal being, destined to act with immortal beings in a boundless field of existence: the plans of a dutiful and faithful subject of the infinite Ruler; of a child, warmed with perpetual and filial piety to his divine Parent; of a brother, finally united to the household which is named after Christ; of a redeemed, sanctified, returning prodigal, brought back with infinite compassion, and infinite expense, to the house of his father, and welcomed with exquisite joy by the family of the first-born. To glorify God, to bless his fellow-creatures, and to be blessed by both, will be the combined and perfect end for which he lives. This end he will pursue in a world where no obstructions ever arise; where no toil ever wearies; where no disappointments ever intrude; where his affections cannot be too intense, nor his pursuits too ardent; and where his only professional business will be to be virtuous and happy. As a citizen of this new and heavenly kingdom, the Christian begins his course of spiritual life. All these things are already become his. God is his Father; Christ his Redeemer; the Spirit of Grace his Sanctifier; and all the children of virtue are his brethren. In the present world he is only a stranger and a sojourner: he regards it, therefore, as a mere lodging; and fixes his eye on heaven as his home.

With this new character, all things, with which he here converses, assume, to his eye, a new aspect; and are filled with the presence and agency of God. The heavens declare his glory, and the firmament sheweth his handy work. Day unto day uttereth speech, and night unto night sheweth knowledge. The year, in all its revolutions, is crowned with his goodness. The Spring is his beauty, blooming in endless varieties of elegance and splendour. Summer and Autumn are manifestations of his bounty; filling his creatures with good. The Winter is a solemn display of his majesty. Then the Lord hath his way in the whirlwind, and in the storm; and the clouds are the dust of his feet.

In his own blessings the Christian sees God in a manner still more delightful. His blessings are not mere enjoyments: they are gifts; unspeakably endeared by the Hand from which they flow. When he is in prosperity; The Lord is his Shepherd, who maketh him to lie down in green pastures, and leadeth him beside the still waters; who prepareth a table before him in the presence of his enemies, who anointeth his head with oil; who causeth his cup to run over, and goodness and mercy to follow him all the days of his life. Is he in adversity? The rod and staff of the same Shepherd support and comfort him. Is he in doubt and darkness, where he is scarcely able to trace the path of life? He hears a voice behind him saying, This is the way: walk thou therein. Is he mourning in Zion? God appoints to him beauty for ashes, and the oil of joy for mourning. Is he sick? God is his physician; and has already taught him to say, "Why are thou cast down, O my soul? and why art thou disquieted within me? Hope thou in God: for I shall yet praise Him, who is the health of my countenance, and my God." Has he come to a dying bed? Christ has vanquished death and the grave; and has taught him to sing at their approach, "O death! where is thy sting? O grave! where is thy victory?" Has he friends? God has raised them up. Has he children? They are an heritage from the Lord. Is the land of his nativity safe? God is a wall of fire round about it. Does Religion flourish? God is the glory in the midst of it. The Church, to which he is united, is a garden, which the Lord hath planted. Is it enlightened, quickened, and edified? It is not by might, nor by power, but by my Spirit, saith the Lord of Hosts. Is it comforted? The consolations have come down from the heavenly Comforter. Is it protected? The Lord hath created upon Mount Zion, and upon all her assemblies, a cloud and a smoke by day, and a light of a flaming fire by night.

Thus to the christian all things in heaven and earth are full of God. Wherever he walks, wherever he is, he is surrounded with His presence; and in that presence there is abundance of joy. To Him, in his meditations, and in his worship, he instinctively turns, as the supreme Object of his affections, and of his obedience. In loving, fearing, and serving Him, with all the heart, he finds his chief delight; and becomes continually able, with more and more propriety and truth, to say, "Whom have I in heaven but Thee? and there is none upon the earth, whom I desire, beside thee?"

* * *

V. The Joy of the Christian, in this world, is the beginning of Everlasting Joy.

To be spiritually minded is both life and peace. This mind is the mind of every Christian. Of course, life and peace eternal are begun in him, while he resides in this evil and melancholy world.

There are, indeed, many interruptions, diminutions, and preventions, of this glorious possession, accomplished by remaining sin, and its inseparable companion, sorrow of heart. But in the midst of all these he finds consolation, often abundant, almost unceasing, and always sufficient for his wants. The promises of the Gospel, are continually before him. God he knows, will never leave him, nor forsake him. Christ, he knows, will always be with him unto the end. He may, indeed, be cast down, but he will not be destroyed: he may be afflicted, but he will not be forsaken. The Father of the spirit may, indeed, smite him in his wrath for a small moment, yet with everlasting kindness will he have mercy on him. In every gloomy and distressing day there will be gleams of sunshine, and openings of a serene, unclouded heaven. In the dry and thirsty ground, where there is apparently no water, and in the midst of a desolation visibly without limits, the wilderness will suddenly rejoice and blossom as the rose.

His piety is a seed, sown here in an unkind, barren soil, indeed, and under a wintry climate; but it will live, and grow, until it shall be transplanted to a happier region beneath a more friendly sky: where it will shoot forth in its native strength and beauty. The flame of divine love, kindled feebly in his heart, will never cease to burn, until it shall rise, and glow, with unextinguishable ardour, beyond the grave. The light, which here dawns in darkness, and feebly illumines the surrounding gloom, will perpetually shine brighter and brighter, unto the perfect day. All his sins and sorrows will continually lessen, and recede, and fade: all his graces, consolations, and hopes, will expand, and improve: until the imperfect good, which he finds in this vale of tears, shall be lost in the everlasting beauty, happiness, and glory, of heaven.

CHARLES G. FINNEY (1792-1875)

Charles Finney was born in Connecticut and raised in upstate New York, where his family moved when he was still a boy. As a young man he entered into an apprenticeship to train for a lawyer's career. But Finney received, as he later said, an unexpected "retainer from the Lord," and so abandoned the law for the ministry.

After a period of training under a local minister, Finney began preaching in Jefferson County, New York, under the sponsorship of the Female Missionary Society of the Western District of New York State. Although he was largely self-taught, Finney sought ordination as a Presbyterian. During his career he maintained loose ties with this body, with the Congregational Church, and with other mainline Protestant groups. He made his first efforts at preaching in New York villages like Evan Mills, LeRayville, and Antwerp. Soon he went to larger towns like Rome, Utica, and Rochester. From 1824 to 1832 Finney enjoyed great success in these ventures. Upstate New York came to be known as "the Burned-Over District" because of the revival fires that swept across it so regularly.

But Finney's work, though successful, also led to much controversy, which centered on two issues. First was the question of technique. Finney's "New Measures," as they came to be called, were innovative, reflecting Finney's straightforward determination. He prayed for individuals by name, he held protracted meetings that went on night after night, he called people to gather at "anxious benches" and persevere until they were converted, he allowed women to pray in public meetings, he often came into a town for meetings without bothering to request permission from local pastors, and so on. These methods upset traditional conservatives, who worried about the faith being made too familiar. And they bothered religious liberals like the Unitarians, who felt that Finney was too crude.

The second point of controversy had to do with the philosophy of revival. Early American evangelists had made great efforts but had always spoken of revival as being under the sole direction of the Holy Spirit. God worked renewal when and where he willed. Finney, on the other hand, felt that God had given people the innate capacity to understand the gospel, commit themselves to God, and get to work for the Kingdom. What was needed was action, willpower exerted toward conversion and the holy life, not passive waiting around for something to happen. Eventually Finney came to the conclusion that a higher form of spiritual life, which he sometimes called "Christian perfection," was possible. Christians should turn their wills to attain this higher life just as unbelievers were obligated to turn their wills to faith in Christ. To defenders of the older, more Calvinistic view of revival, these proposals were frightening. But due in large part to Finney's own energy, they carried the day and set the standard for most later revivalism in the United States.

Finney eventually left full-time evangelistic work for more permanent, settled work, first as a minister in New York City, and then, for forty years, as a professor of theology and president at Oberlin College in Ohio. From these locations he did some itinerant preaching, but he had an even greater impact through his published works. As an old man he looked back over his life in an extensive memoir that was published shortly after his death. From that document comes the following record of his conversion. The indelible memory of that dramatic experience gave a definite shape to his own ministry, which in turn shaped much of religious life in America.

Selections from His Memoirs

On a Sabbath evening in the autumn of 1821, I made up my mind that I would settle the question of my soul's salvation at once, that if it were possible I would make my peace with God. But as I was very busy in the affairs of the office, I knew that without great firmness of purpose, I should never effectually attend to the subject. I therefore, then and there resolved, as far as possible, to avoid all business, and everything that would divert my attention, and to give myself wholly to the work of securing the salvation of my soul. I carried this resolution into execution as sternly and thoroughly as I could. I was, however, obliged to be a good deal in the office. But as the providence of God would have it, I was not much occupied either on Monday or Tuesday; and had opportunity to read my Bible and engage in prayer most of the time.

*   *   *

During Monday and Tuesday my convictions increased; but still it seemed as if my heart grew harder. I could not shed a tear; I could not pray. I had no opportunity to pray above my breath; and frequently I felt, that if I could be alone where I could use my voice and let myself out, I should find relief in prayer. I was shy, and avoided, as much as I could, speaking to anybody on

---

Source: "Conversion to Christ," chap. 2 in *Memoirs of Charles G. Finney, Written by Himself,* published in 1876 by the trustees of Oberlin College.

any subject. I endeavored, however, to do this in a way that would excite no suspicion, in any mind, that I was seeking the salvation of my soul.

Tuesday night I had become very nervous; and in the night a strange feeling came over me as if I was about to die. I knew that if I did I should sink down to hell; but I quieted myself as best I could until morning.

At an early hour I started for the office. But just before I arrived at the office, something seemed to confront me with questions like these: indeed, it seemed as if the inquiry was within myself, as if an inward voice said to me, "What are you waiting for? Did you not promise to give your heart to God? And what are you trying to do? Are you endeavoring to work out a righteousness of your own?

Just at this point the whole question of Gospel salvation opened to my mind in a manner most marvellous to me at the time. I think I then saw, as clearly as I ever have in my life, the reality and fulness of the atonement of Christ. I saw that his work was a finished work; and that instead of having, or needing, any righteousness of my own to recommend me to God, I had to submit myself to the righteousness of God through Christ. Gospel salvation seemed to me to be an offer of something to be accepted; and that it was full and complete; and that all that was necessary on my part, was to get my own consent to give up my sins, and accept Christ. Salvation, it seemed to me, instead of being a thing to be wrought out, by my own works, was a thing to be found entirely in the Lord Jesus Christ, who presented himself before me as my God and my Saviour.

Without being distinctly aware of it, I had stopped in the street right where the inward voice seemed to arrest me. How long I remained in that position I cannot say. But after this distinct revelation had stood for some little time before my mind, the question seemed to be put, "Will you accept it now, to-day?" I replied, "Yes; I will accept it to-day, or I will die in the attempt."

North of the village, and over a hill, lay a piece of woods, in which I was in the almost daily habit of walking, more or less, when it was pleasant weather. It was now October, and the time was past for my frequent walks there. Nevertheless, instead of going to the office, I turned and bent my course toward the woods, feeling that I must be alone, and away from all human eyes and ears, so that I could pour out my prayer to God.

But still my pride must show itself. As I went over the hill, it occurred to me that some one might see me and suppose that I was going away to pray. Yet probably there was not a person on earth that would have suspected such a thing, had he seen me going. But so great was my pride, and so much was I possessed with the fear of man, that I recollect that I sulked along under the fence, till I got so far out of sight that no one from the village could see me. I then penetrated into the woods, I should think, a quarter of a mile, went over on the other side of the hill, and found a place where some large trees had fallen across each other, leaving an open place between. There I saw I could make a kind of closet. I crept into this place and knelt down for prayer. As I turned to go up into the woods, I recollect to have said, "I will give my heart to God, or I never will come down from there." I recollect repeating this as I went up—"I will give my heart to God before I ever come down again."

But when I attempted to pray I found that my heart would not pray. I had supposed that if I could only be where I could speak aloud, without being overheard, I could pray freely. But lo! when I came to try, I was dumb; that is, I had nothing to say to God; or at least I could say but a few words, and those without heart. In attempting to pray I would hear a rustling in the leaves, as I thought, and would stop and look up to see if somebody were not coming. This I did several times.

Finally I found myself verging fast to despair. I said to myself, "I cannot pray. My heart is dead to God, and will not pray." I then reproached myself for having promised to give my heart to God before I left the woods. When I came to try, I found I could not give my heart to God. My inward soul hung back, and there was no going out of my heart to God. I began to feel deeply that it was too late; that it must be that I was given up of God and was past hope.

The thought was pressing me of the rashness of my promise, that I would give my heart to God that day or die in the attempt. It seemed to me as if that was binding upon my soul; and yet I was going to break my vow. A great sinking and discouragement came over me, and I felt almost too weak to stand upon my knees.

Just at this moment I again thought I heard some one approach me, and I opened my eyes to see whether it were so. But right there the revelation of my pride of heart, as the great difficulty that stood in the way, was distinctly shown to me. An overwhelming sense of my wickedness in being ashamed to have a human being see me on my knees before God, took such powerful possession of me, that I cried at the top of my voice, and exclaimed that I would not leave that place if all the men on earth and all the devils in hell surrounded me. "What!" I said, "such a degraded sinner as I am, on my knees confessing my sins to the great and holy God; and ashamed to have any human being, and a sinner like myself, find me on my knees endeavoring to make my peace with my offended God!" The sin appeared awful, infinite. It broke me down before the Lord.

Just at that point this passage of Scripture seemed to drop into my mind with a flood of light: "Then shall ye go and pray unto me, and I will hearken unto you. Then shall ye seek me and find me, when ye shall search for me with all your heart." I instantly seized hold of this with my heart. I had intellectually believed the Bible before; but never had the truth been in my mind that faith was a voluntary trust instead of an intellectual state. I was as conscious as I was of my existence, of trusting at that moment in God's veracity. Somehow I knew that that was a passage of Scripture, though I do not think I had ever read it. I knew that it was God's word, and God's voice, as it were, that spoke to me. I cried to Him, "Lord, I take thee at thy word. Now thou knowest that I do search for thee with all my heart, and that I have come here to pray to thee; and thou hast promised to hear me."

That seemed to settle the question that I could then, that day, perform my vow. The Spirit seemed to lay stress upon that idea in the text, "When you search for me with all your heart." The question of when, that is of the present time, seemed to fall heavily into my heart. I told the Lord that I should take him at his word; that he could not lie, and that therefore I was sure that he heard my prayer, and that he would be found of me.

He then gave me many other promises, both from the Old and the New Testament, especially some most precious promises respecting our Lord Jesus Christ. I never can, in words, make any human being understand how precious and true those promises appeared to me. I took them one after the other as infallible truth, the assertions of God who could not lie. They did not seem so much to fall into my intellect as into my heart, to be put within the grasp of the voluntary powers of my mind; and I seized hold of them, appropriated them, and fastened upon them with the grasp of a drowning man.

I continued thus to pray, and to receive and appropriate promises for a long time, I know not how long. I prayed till my mind became so full that, before I was aware of it, I was on my feet and tripping up the ascent toward the road. The question of my being converted, had not so much as arisen to my thought; but as I went up, brushing through the leaves and bushes, I recollect saying with great emphasis, "If I am ever converted, I will preach the Gospel."

I soon reached the road that led to the village, and began to reflect upon what had passed; and I found that my mind had become most wonderfully quiet and peaceful. I said to myself. "What is this? I must have grieved the Holy Ghost entirely away. I have lost all my conviction. I have not a particle of concern about my soul; and it must be that the Spirit has left me." "Why!" thought I, "I never was so far from being concerned about my own salvation in my life."

Then I remembered what I had said to God while I was on my knees—that I had said I would take him at his word; and indeed I recollected a good many things that I had said, and concluded that it was no wonder that the Spirit had left me; that for such a sinner as I was to take hold of God's word in that way, was presumption if not blasphemy. I concluded that in my excitement I had grieved the Holy Spirit, and perhaps committed the unpardonable sin.

I walked quietly toward the village; and so perfectly quiet was my mind that it seemed as if all nature listened. It was on the 10th of October, and a very pleasant day. I had gone into the woods immediately after an early breakfast; and when I returned to the village I found it was dinner time. Yet I had been wholly unconscious of the time that had passed; it appeared to me that I had been gone from the village but a short time.

But how was I to account for the quiet of my mind? I tried to recall my convictions, to get back again the load of sin under which I had been laboring. But all sense of sin, all consciousness of present sin of guilt, had departed from me. I said to myself, "What is this, that I cannot arouse any sense of guilt in my soul, as great a sinner as I am?" I tried in vain to make myself anxious about my present state. I was so quiet and peaceful that I tried to feel concerned about that, lest it should be a result of my having grieved the Spirit away. But take any view of it I would, I could not be anxious at all about my soul, and about my spiritual state. The repose of my mind was unspeakably great. I never can describe it in words. The thought of God was sweet to my mind, and the most profound spiritual tranquility had taken full possession of me. This was a great mystery; but it did not distress or perplex me.

I went to my dinner, and found I had no appetite to eat. I then went to the office, and found that Squire W—— had gone to dinner. I took down my bass-viol, and, as I was accustomed to do, began to play and sing some pieces of sacred music. But as soon as I began to sing those sacred words, I began to weep. It seemed as if my heart was all liquid; and my feelings were in such a state that I could not hear my own voice in singing without causing my sensibility to overflow. I wondered at this, and tried to suppress my tears, but could not. After trying in vain to suppress my tears, I put up my instrument and stopped singing.

After dinner we were engaged in removing our books and furniture to another office. We were very busy in this, and had but little conversation all the afternoon. My mind, however, remained in that profoundly tranquil state. There was a great sweetness and tenderness in my thoughts and feelings. Everything appeared to be going right, and nothing seemed to ruffle or disturb me in the least.

Just before evening the thought took possession of my mind, that as soon as I was left alone in the new office, I would try to pray again—that I was not going to abandon the subject of religion and give it up, at any rate; and therefore, although I no longer had any concern about my soul, still I would continue to pray.

By evening we got the books and furniture adjusted; and I made up, in an open fire-place, a good fire, hoping to spend the evening alone. Just at dark Squire W——, seeing that everything was adjusted, bade me good-night and went to his home. I had accompanied him to the door; and as I closed the door and turned around, my heart seemed to be liquid within me. All my feelings seemed to rise and flow out; and the utterance of my heart was, "I want to pour my whole soul out to God." The rising of my soul was so great that I rushed into the room back of the front office, to pray.

There was no fire, and no light, in the room; nevertheless it appeared to me as if it were perfectly light. As I went in and shut the door after me, it seemed as if I met the Lord Jesus Christ face to face. It did not occur to me then, nor did it for some time afterward, that it was wholly a mental state. On the contrary it seemed to me that I saw him as I would see any other man. He said nothing, but looked at me in such a manner as to break me right down at his feet. I have always since regarded this as a most remarkable state of mind; for it seemed to me a reality, that he stood before me, and I fell down at his feet and poured out my soul to him. I wept aloud like a child, and made such confessions as I could with my choked utterance. It seemed to me that I bathed his feet with my tears; and yet I had no distinct impression that I touched him, that I recollect.

I must have continued in this state for a good while; but my mind was too much absorbed with the interview to recollect anything that I said. But I know, as soon as my mind became calm enough to break off from the interview, I returned to the front office, and found that the fire that I had made of large wood was nearly burned out. But as I turned and was about to take a seat by the fire, I received a mighty baptism of the Holy Ghost. Without any expectation of it, without ever having the thought in my mind that there was any such thing for me, without any recollection that I had ever heard the thing mentioned by any person in the world, the Holy Spirit descended upon me in a manner that seemed to go through me, body and soul. I could feel the impression, like a wave of electricity, going through and through me. Indeed it seemed to come in waves and waves of liquid love; for I could not express it in any other way. It seemed like the very breath of God. I can recollect distinctly that it seemed to fan me, like immense wings.

No words can express the wonderful love that was shed abroad in my heart. I wept aloud with joy and love; and I do not know but I should say, I literally bellowed out the unutterable gushings of my heart. These waves came over me, and over me, one after the other, until I recollect I cried out, "I shall die if these waves continue to pass over me." I said, "Lord, I cannot bear any more;" yet I had no fear of death.

How long I continued in this state, with this baptism continuing to roll over me and go through me, I do not know. But I know it was late in the evening when a member of my choir—for I was the leader of the choir—came into the office to see me. He was a member of the church. He found me in this state of loud weeping, and said to me, "Mr. Finney, what ails you?" I could make him no answer for some time. He then said, "Are you in pain?" I gathered myself up as best I could, and replied, "No, but so happy that I cannot live."

He turned and left the office, and in a few minutes returned with one of the elders of the church, whose shop was nearly across the way from our office. This elder was a very serious man; and in my presence had been very watchful, and I had scarcely ever seen him laugh. When he came in, I was very much in the state in which I was when the young man went out to call him. He asked me how I felt, and I began to tell him. Instead of saying anything, he fell into a most spasmodic laughter. It seemed as if it was impossible for him to keep from laughing from the very bottom of his heart.

There was a young man in the neighborhood who was preparing for college, with whom I had been very intimate. Our minister, as I afterward learned, had repeatedly talked with him on the subject of religion, and warned him against being misled by me. He informed him that I was a very careless young man about religion; and he thought that if he associated much with me his mind would be diverted, and he would not be converted.

After I was converted, and this young man was converted, he told me that he had said to Mr. Gale several times, when he had admonished him about associating so much with me, that my conversations had often affected him more, religiously, than his preaching. I had, indeed, let out my feelings a good deal to this young man.

But just at the time when I was giving an account of my feelings to this elder of the church, and to the other member who was with him, this young man came into the office. I was sitting with my back toward the door, and barely observed that he came in. He listened with astonishment to what I was saying, and the first I knew he partly fell upon the floor, and cried out in the greatest agony of mind, "Do pray for me!" The elder of the church and the other member knelt down and began to pray for him; and when they had prayed, I prayed for him myself. Soon after this they all retired and left me alone.

The question then arose in my mind, "Why did Elder B—— laugh so? Did he not think that I was under a delusion, or crazy?" This suggestion brought a kind of darkness over my mind; and I began to query with myself whether it was proper for me—such a sinner as I had been—to pray for that young man. A cloud seemed to shut in over me; I had no hold upon anything in which I could rest; and after a little while I retired to bed, not distressed in mind, but still at a loss to know what to make of my present state. Notwithstanding the baptism I had received, this temptation so obscured my view that I went to bed without feeling sure that my peace was made with God.

I soon fell asleep, but almost as soon awoke again on account of the great flow of the love of God that was in my heart. I was so filled with love that I could not sleep. Soon I fell asleep again, and awoke in the same manner. When I awoke, this temptation would return upon me, and the love that seemed to be in my heart would abate; but as soon as I was asleep, it was so warm within me that I would immediately awake. Thus I continued till, late at night, I obtained some sound repose.

When I awoke in the morning the sun had risen, and was pouring a clear light into my room. Words cannot express the impression that this sunlight made upon me. Instantly the baptism that I had received the night before, returned upon me in the same manner. I arose upon my knees in the bed and wept aloud with joy, and remained for some time too much overwhelmed with the baptism of the Spirit to do anything but pour out my soul to God. It seemed as if this morning's baptism was accompanied with a gentle reproof, and the Spirit seemed to say to me, "Will you doubt?" "Will you doubt?" I cried, "No! I will not doubt; I cannot doubt." He then cleared the subject up so much to my mind that it was in fact impossible for me to doubt that the Spirit of God had taken possession of my soul.

In this state I was taught the doctrine of justification by faith, as a present experience. That doctrine had never taken any such possession of my mind, that I had ever viewed it distinctly as a fundamental doctrine of the Gospel. Indeed, I did not know at all what it meant in the proper sense. But I could now see and understand what was meant by the passage, "Being justified by faith, we have peace with God through our Lord Jesus Christ." I could see that the moment I believed, while up in the woods all sense of condemnation had entirely dropped out of my mind; and that from that moment I could not feel a sense of guilt or condemnation by any effort that I could make. My sense of guilt was gone; my sins were gone; and I do not think I felt any more sense of guilt than if I never had sinned.

This was just the revelation that I needed. I felt myself justified by faith; and, so far as I could see, I was in a state in which I did not sin. Instead of feeling that I was sinning all the time, my heart was so full of love that it overflowed. My cup ran over with blessing and with love; and I could not feel that I was sinning against God. Nor could I recover the least sense of guilt for my past sins. Of this experience I said nothing that I recollect, at the time, to anybody; that is, of this experience of justification.

CHARLES HODGE (1797-1878)

Charles Hodge was one of the most influential American theologians of the nineteenth century. A professor of theology at Princeton Theological Seminary in New Jersey, he made a strong impact on religious life in America through his students, his activities in the Presbyterian Church, and his many writings.

During his career at Princeton Seminary, Hodge taught over 3,000 students, many of whom became leaders in the Presbyterian Church. He himself had been raised in Philadelphia and had attended Princeton College and Princeton Seminary. His own instructor at the seminary, Archibald Alexander, continued as his colleague for more than a quarter of a century. Alexander, who as a young man had participated in revivals in Virginia, passed on to Hodge a concern for living religion as well as formal doctrine. The work of these two men shaped a religious tradition that still exercises considerable influence in American religious life.

Hodge was a doctrinal conservative, what was then called an "Old School" Calvinist. For such believers the strictness of Christian truth was a most important matter. Hodge himself was an experienced polemicist who often used the pages of his journal, the *Biblical Repertory and Princeton Review,* to chastise other theologians or denominations for deviating from the theological norm. Near the end of his life he published a three-volume work entitled *Systematic Theology* (1871-73), whose 2,000 pages offered a full exposition of confessional Calvinism. Hodge was also an earnest student of the Scriptures and published commentaries on many biblical books.

At the same time that he defended orthodoxy, however, Hodge was also aware of the need for vital Christian life. During an extended study tour in Germany during the 1820s, he was greatly impressed with the piety displayed by his German mentors, even some whose theological opinions he suspected. And for as long as he taught at Princeton Seminary, Hodge regularly participated in the Sunday afternoon services held for the seminarians. These were occasions for the seminary's professors to remind the would-be ministers that all the formal learning in the world could not remove the need for an active, devoted spiritual life.

Hodge's fullest treatment of the spiritual side of Christian experience came in a book published in 1841 at the request of the American Sunday School Union. It was called *The Way of Life.* In its pages Hodge attempted to show how a thorough grounding in the doctrines of Scripture led to genuine spirituality. Predictably, he defined that necessary dogmatic foundation in Protestant terms inherited from the Reformation. But his interest was not in the doctrines as such but in their effect. They were a door to fellowship with God, not merely abstractions important for their own sake.

The following excerpt is from the last part of "Holy Living," the last chapter in *The Way of Life,* as published in Philadelphia by the American Sunday School Union in 1841.

From "Holy Living"

The attainment of holiness is often treated, by Christian writers, as a mere question of morals, or at most, of natural religion. Men are directed to control, by the force of reason, their vicious propensities; to set in array before the mind the motives to virtuous living, and to strengthen the will by acts of self-restraint. Conscience is summoned to sanction the dictates of reason, or to warn the sinner of the consequences of transgression. The doctrines of the presence and providence of God, and of future retribution, are more or less relied upon to prevent the indulgence of sin, and to stimulate to the practice of virtue. Special directions are given how to cultivate virtuous habits, or to correct those which are evil.

As we are rational beings, and were meant to be governed by reason in opposition to appetite and passion, there is much that is true and important in such disquisitions on the practice of virtue. But as we are depraved beings, destitute of any recuperative power in ourselves, such rules, and the efforts to which they lead, must, by themselves, be ineffectual. God has endowed the body with a restorative energy, which enables it to throw off what is noxious to the system, and to heal the wounds which accident or malice may have inflicted. But when the system itself is deranged, instead of correcting what is amiss, it aggravates what would otherwise be a mere temporary disorder. And if by external means the evil is checked in one part, it reappears in another. Though you amputate a decaying limb, the remaining portion may soon exhibit symptoms of mortification. So long as the system is deranged, such means are mere palliatives, concealing or diverting the evil, but leaving the source of it untouched. It is no less true, that so long as the heart is unrenewed, all that reason and conscience can do is of little avail. They may obstruct the stream, or divert it into secret channels, but they cannot reach the fountain. As we retain, since the fall, reason, the power of choice, conscience, the social affections, a sense of justice, fear, shame, etc., much may be done, by a skilful management of these principles of action, towards producing propriety of conduct, and even great amiability and worth of character. But it is impossible, by these means, to call into existence right views and feelings towards God and our neighbour, or to eradicate the selfishness, pride, and other forms of evil by which our nature is corrupted. A man may be brought, by reason and conscience, to change his conduct, but not to change his heart. A sense of duty may force him to give alms to a man he hates, but it cannot change hatred into love. The desire of happiness may induce him to engage externally in the service of God, but it cannot make that service a delight. The affections do not obey the dictates of reason, nor the commands of conscience. They may be measurably restrained in their manifestations, but cannot be changed in their nature. They follow their own law. They delight in what is suited to the disposition of him who exercises them. Holding up to them what they ought to delight in, cannot secure their devotion.

*   *   *

The Scriptures teach . . . that believers are so united to Christ, that they are not only partakers of the merit of his death, but also of his Holy Spirit, which dwells in them as a principle of life, bringing them more and more into conformity with the image of God, and working in them both to will and to do, according to his own good pleasure. They teach, that so long as men are under the law—that is, are bound to satisfy its demands as the ground of their acceptance with God, and are governed by a legal spirit, or a mere sense of duty and fear of punishment, they are in the condition of slaves, incapable of right feelings towards God, or of producing the fruits of holiness. But when, by the death of Christ, they are freed from the law, in the sense above stated, their whole relation to God is changed. They are no longer slaves, but children. Being united to Christ in his death, they are partakers of his life, and in virtue of this union they bring forth fruit unto God. They are henceforth led by the Spirit which dwells in them; and this Spirit is a source of life, not only to the soul, but also to the body; for if the Spirit of him that raised Christ from the dead dwell in us, he that raised Christ from the dead shall also quicken our bodies by his Spirit that dwelleth in us [Rom. 8:2]. The doctrine of sanctification, therefore, as taught in the Bible, is, that we are made holy not by the force of conscience, or of moral motives, nor by acts of discipline, but by being united to Christ so as to become reconciled to God, and partakers of the Holy Ghost. Christ is made unto us sanctification as well as justification. He not only frees from the penalty of the law, but he makes holy. There is, therefore, according to the gospel, no such thing as sanctification without or before justification. Those who are out of Christ are under the power, as well as under the condemnation, of sin. And those who are in Christ are not only free from condemnation, but are also delivered from the dominion of sin.

The nature of the union between Christ and his people, on which so much depends, is confessedly mysterious. Paul having said, "We are members of his body, of his flesh, and of his bones," immediately adds, "This is a great mystery" [Eph. 5:30, 32]. It is vain, therefore, to attempt to bring this subject down to the level of our comprehension. The mode in which God is present, and operates throughout the universe, is to us an impenetrable secret. We cannot even understand how our own souls are present and operate in the bodies which they occupy. We need not, then, expect to comprehend the mode in which Christ dwells by his Spirit in the hearts of his people. The fact that such union exists is clearly revealed; its effects are explicitly stated, and its nature is set forth, as far as it can be made known, by the most striking illustrations. In his intercessory prayer, our Savior said, "I pray—that they all may be one; as thou, Father, art in me, and I in thee, that they also may be one in us.—I in them, and thou in me, that they may be made perfect in one" [John 17:21-23]. "He that keepeth his commandments," says the apostle John, "dwelleth in him and he in him. And hereby we know that he abideth in us, by the Spirit which he hath given us" [1 John 3:24]. "If any man have not the Spirit of Christ, he is none of his;" but if Christ be in you, the body, adds the apostle, may die, but the soul shall live [Rom. 8:9-11]. "Know ye not," asks Paul, "that your body is the temple of the Holy Ghost which is in you, which ye have of God, and ye are not your own" [1 Cor. 6:19]. And to the same effect, "Know ye not that ye are the temple of God, and that the Spirit of God dwelleth in you?" [1 Cor. 3:16].

The Scriptures are filled with this doctrine. The great promise of the Old Testament in connexion with the advent of the Messiah was, that the Holy Spirit should then be abundantly communicated to men. Christ is said to have redeemed us in order that we might receive this promised Spirit [Gal. 3:13, 14]. And the only evidence of a participation of the benefits of redemption, recognized by the apostles, was the participation of the Holy Ghost, manifesting itself either in the extraordinary powers which he then communicated, or in those lovely fruits of holiness which never fail to mark his presence.

The effects ascribed to this union, as already stated, are an interest in the merits of Christ, in order to our justification, and the indwelling of his Spirit, in order to our sanctification. Its nature is variously illustrated. It is compared to that union which subsists between a representative and those for whom he acts. In this view Adam is said to be like Christ, and Christ is said to be the second Adam; "for as in Adam all die, even so in Christ shall all be made alive" [1 Cor. 15:22]. This idea is also presented whenever Christ is said to have died for his sheep, or in their place; or when they are said to have died with him, his death being virtually their death, satisfying in their behalf the demands of justice, and redeeming them from the curse of the law. It is compared to the union between the head and members of the same body. The meaning of this illustration is by no means exhausted by saying that Christ governs his people, or that there is a community of feeling and interest between them. The main idea is, that there is a community of life; that the same Spirit dwells in him and in them. As the body is everywhere animated by one soul, which makes it one, and communicates a common life to all its parts, so the Holy Ghost, who dwells in Christ, is by him communicated to all his people, and makes them, in a peculiar sense, one with him, and one among themselves, and imparts to all that life which has its seat and source in him. "As the body is one, and hath many members, and all the members of that one body, being many, are one body: so also is Christ. For by one Spirit are we all baptized into one body;—and have been all made to drink into one Spirit" [1 Cor. 7:12, 13]. Another illustration, but of the same import, is employed by Christ, when he says, "I am the vine, ye are the branches: he that abideth in me, and I in him, the same bringeth forth much fruit: for without me ye can do nothing" [John 15:5]. As the branches are so united to the vine as to partake of its life, and to be absolutely dependent upon it, so believers are so united to Christ as to partake of his life, and to be absolutely dependent on him. The Holy Spirit communicated by him to them, is in them the principle of life and fruitfulness.

Christ and his people are one. He is the Foundation, they are the building. He is the Vine, they are the branches. He is the head, they are the body. Because he lives, they shall live also; for it is not they that live, but Christ that liveth in them. The Holy Spirit, concerning which he said to his disciples, "He dwelleth with you, and shall be in you" [John 14:17], is to them not only the source of spiritual life, but of all its manifestations. They are baptized by the Spirit [Luke 3:16], they are born of the Spirit [John 3:5]; they are called spiritual, because the Spirit of God dwells in them [1 Cor. 3:16]; whereas, the unregenerate are called natural, or sensual, "having not the Spirit" [Jude 19]. Believers are sanctified by the Spirit [1 Cor. 6:11]; they are led by the Spirit [Rom. 8:14]; they live in the Spirit [Gal. 5:25]; they are strengthened by the Spirit [Eph. 3:16]; they are filled with the Spirit [Eph. 5:18]. By the Spirit they mortify sin [Rom. 8:13]; through the Spirit they wait for the hope of righteousness [Gal. 5:5]; they have access to God by the Spirit [Eph. 2:18]; they pray and sing in the Spirit [John 4:24; Jude 20]. The Spirit is to them a source of knowledge [Eph. 1:17], of joy [1 Thess. 1:6], of love, long-suffering, goodness, faith, meekness, temperance [Gal. 5:22]. This doctrine of the indwelling of the Holy Spirit is so wrought into the texture of the gospel as to be absolutely essential to it. It ceases to be the gospel if we abstract from it the great truth, that the Spirit of God, as the purchase and gift of Christ, is ever present with his people, guiding their inward exercises and outward conduct, and bringing them at last, without spot or blemish, to the purity and blessedness of heaven.

The secret of holy living lies in this doctrine of the union of the believer with Christ. This is not only the ground of his hope of pardon, but the source of the strength whereby he dies unto sin and lives unto righteousness. It is by being rooted and grounded in Christ that he is strengthened with might by his Spirit in the inner man, and is enabled to comprehend the breadth, and length, and depth, and height of the mystery of redemption, and to know the love of Christ which passes knowledge, and is filled with all the fulness of God. It is this doctrine which sustains him under all his trials, and enables him to triumph over all his enemies; for it is not he that lives, but Christ that lives in him, giving him grace sufficient for his day, and purifying him unto himself, as one of his peculiar people zealous of good works.

NATHANIEL HAWTHORNE (1804-1864)

The life and works of Nathaniel Hawthorne offer a disturbing portrait of spiritual life in nineteenth-century America. Hawthorne's roots in Puritan culture reached back into the seventeenth century, but he had painfully ambivalent feelings about his heritage. He admired the moral seriousness of his forebears, but because an ancestor named Hathorne had served as a judge at the Salem witch trials, young Nathaniel, in shame, changed the family name to Hawthorne.

A native of Salem and a graduate of Bowdoin College, Hawthorne toiled in relative obscurity for several decades. From his mid-twenties to his mid-forties, he wrote a series of distinguished short stories that gained a small but genuinely appreciative readership. After his marriage in 1842, he settled in Concord, Massachusetts, home to Ralph Waldo Emerson, Henry David Thoreau, and their band of Transcendentalist friends. Hawthorne at last found fame with the publication of *The Scarlet Letter* in 1850.

During the following decade Hawthorne published three more novels: *The House of the Seven Gables* (1851), *The Blithedale Romance* (1852), and *The Marble Faun* (1860). For seven of these ten years he lived with his family in England (serving as American consul at Liverpool) and on the Continent. When he and his family returned to America in 1860, the nation was on the brink of civil war. Disheartened by the conflict and distraught at the loss of his own productive power, Hawthorne rapidly declined and died in 1864.

Hawthorne's writing reveals what we also see in the work of Emily Dickinson: the clash of the powerful and contradictory forces of Romanticism and Calvinism. His fiction dwells upon the theme of Romantic ambition coming into irreconcilable conflict with human limitation. His main characters are men and women who strain against the limits of tradition and the natural world. Seeking to break through the boundaries of what is customary and possible, they often suffer a tragic fate.

One such character is Arthur Dimmesdale in *The Scarlet Letter*. This Puritan minister has committed adultery with a parishioner, Hester Prynne, and has hidden his guilt from his community even as she, in giving birth to the child of their union, has suffered punishment and shame. Living a lie because he is unable to confess his guilt, Dimmesdale struggles to find release from his torment. As the following selection suggests, Hawthorne understood the painful irony of Dimmesdale's plight. "The Reverend Mr. Dimmesdale had achieved a brilliant popularity in his sacred office," Hawthorne wrote in the novel. "He won it, indeed, in great part, by his sorrows." It is Dimmesdale's own sin that gives him sympathetic insight into the hidden agonies of his parishioners; he has, we are told, "the Tongue of Flame," the power to address the whole human brotherhood in the heart's native language. But to confess his guilt would be to risk banishment or death, so the Reverend Dimmesdale must compound the guilt of the deed with the shame of deceit. To gain release, he practices a tortured piety, seeking somehow to placate an angry God and a nagging conscience. Dimmesdale's dilemma is in many ways Hawthorne's also: how does one assume an attitude of devoted adoration in the presence of a God whom one fears and can never hope to love?

The following selection is Chapter Eleven of *The Scarlet Letter*, entitled "The Interior of a Heart." It begins with the revelation that Dimmesdale's rival, Roger Chillingworth, has somehow discerned his secret, and then proceeds to Dimmesdale's own wrestling with the thought of perhaps making a public confession of his sin.

The Interior of a Heart

After the incident last described, the intercourse between the clergyman and the physician, though externally the same, was really of another character than it had previously been. The intellect of Roger Chillingworth had now a sufficiently plain path before it. It was not, indeed, precisely that which he had laid out for himself to tread. Calm, gentle, passionless, as he appeared, there was yet, we fear, a quiet depth of malice, hitherto latent, but active now, in this unfortunate old man, which led him to imagine a more intimate revenge than any mortal had ever wreaked upon an enemy. To make himself the one trusted friend, to whom should be confided all the fear, the remorse, the agony, the ineffectual repentance, the backward rush of sinful thoughts, expelled in vain! All that guilty sorrow, hidden from the world, whose great heart would have pitied and forgiven, to be revealed to him, the Pitiless, to him, the Unforgiving! All that dark treasure to be lavished on the very man, to whom nothing else could so adequately pay the debt of vengeance!

The clergyman's shy and sensitive reserve had balked this scheme. Roger Chillingworth, however, was inclined to be hardly, if at all, less satisfied with the aspect of affairs, which Providence—using the avenger and his victim for its own purposes, and, perchance, pardoning, where it seemed most to punish—had substituted for his black devices. A revelation, he could almost say, had been granted to him. It mattered little, for his object, whether celestial, or from what other region. By its aid, in all the subsequent relations betwixt him and Mr. Dimmesdale, not merely the external presence, but the very inmost soul of the latter seemed to be brought out before his eyes, so that he could see and comprehend its every movement. He became, thenceforth, not a spectator only, but a chief actor, in the poor minister's interior world. He could play upon him as he chose. Would he arouse him with a throb of agony? The victim was for ever on the rack; it needed only to know the spring that controlled the engine;—and the physician knew it well! Would he startle him with sudden fear? As at the waving of a magician's wand, uprose a grisly phantom,—uprose a thousand phantoms,—in many shapes, of death, or more awful shame, all flocking round about the clergyman, and pointing with their fingers at his breast!

All this was accomplished with a subtlety so perfect, that the minister, though he had constantly a dim perception of some evil influence watching over him, could never gain a knowledge of its actual nature. True, he looked doubtfully, fearfully,—even, at times, with horror and the bitterness of hatred,—at the deformed figure of the old physician. His gestures, his gait, his grizzled beard, his slightest and most indifferent acts, the very fashion of his garments, were odious in the clergyman's sight; a token, implicitly to be relied on, of a deeper antipathy in the breast of the latter than he was willing to acknowledge to himself. For, as it was impossible to assign a reason for such distrust and abhorrence, so Mr. Dimmesdale, conscious that the poison of one morbid spot was infecting his heart's entire substance, attributed all his presentiments to no other cause. He took himself to task for his bad sympathies in reference to Roger Chillingworth, disregarded the lesson that he should have drawn from them, and did his best to root them out. Unable to accomplish this, he nevertheless, as a matter of principle, continued his habits of social familiarity with the old man, and thus gave him constant opportunities for perfecting the purpose to which—poor, forlorn creature that he was, and more wretched than his victim—the avenger had devoted himself.

While thus suffering under bodily disease, and gnawed and tortured by some black trouble of the soul, and given over to the machinations of his deadliest enemy, the Reverend Mr. Dimmesdale had achieved a brilliant popularity in his sacred office. He won it, indeed, in great part, by his sorrows. His intellectual gifts, his moral perceptions, his power of experiencing and communicating emotion, were kept in a state of preternatural activity by the prick and anguish of his daily life. His frame, though still on its upward slope, already overshadowed the soberer reputations of his fellow-clergymen, eminent as several of them were. There were scholars among them, who had spent more years in acquiring abstruse lore, connected with the divine profession, than Mr. Dimmesdale had lived; and who might well, therefore, be more profoundly versed in such solid and valuable attainments than their youthful brother. There were men, too, of a sturdier texture of mind than his, and endowed with a far greater share of shrewd, hard, iron or granite understanding: which, duly mingled with a fair proportion of doctrinal ingredient, constitutes a highly respectable, efficacious, and unamiable variety of the clerical species. There were others, again true saintly fathers, whose faculties had been elaborated by weary toil among their books, and by patient thought, and etherealized, moreover, by spiritual communications with the better world, into which their purity of life had almost introduced these holy personages, with their garments of mortality still clinging to them. All that they lacked was the gift that descended upon the chosen disciples, at Pentecost, in tongues of flame; symbolizing, it would seem, not the power of speech in foreign and unknown languages, but that of addressing the whole human brotherhood in the heart's native language. These fathers, otherwise so apostolic, lacked Heaven's last and rarest attestation of their office, the Tongue of Flame. They would have vainly sought—had they ever dreamed of seeking—to express the highest truths through the humblest medium of familiar words and images. Their voices came down, afar and indistinctly, from the upper heights where they habitually dwelt.

Not improbably, it was to this latter class of men that Mr. Dimmesdale, by many of his traits of character, naturally belonged. To their high mountain-peaks of faith and sanctity he would have climbed, had not the tendency been thwarted by the burden, whatever it might be, of crime or anguish, beneath which it was his doom to totter. It kept him down, on a level with the lowest; him, the man of ethereal attributes, whose voice the angels might else have listened to and answered! But this very burden it was, that gave him sympathies so intimate with the sinful brotherhood of mankind; so that his heart vibrated in unison with theirs, and received their pain into itself, and sent its own throb of pain through a thousand other hearts, in gushes of sad, persuasive eloquence. Oftenest persuasive, but sometimes terrible! The people knew not the power that moved them thus. They deemed the young clergyman a miracle of holiness. They fancied him the mouth-piece of Heaven's messages of wisdom, and rebuke, and love. In their eyes, the very ground on which he trod was sanctified. The virgins of his church grew pale around him, victims of a passion so imbued with religious sentiment that they imagined it to be all religion, and brought it openly, in their white bosoms, as their most acceptable sacrifice before the altar. The aged members of his flock, beholding Mr. Dimmesdale's frame so feeble, while they were themselves so rugged in their infirmity, believed that he would go heavenward before them, and enjoined it upon their children, that their old bones should be buried close to their young pastor's holy grave. And, all this time, perchance, when poor Mr. Dimmesdale was thinking of his grave, he questioned with himself whether the grass would ever grow on it, because an accursed thing must there be buried!

It is inconceivable, the agony with which this public veneration tortured him! It was his genuine impulse to adore the truth, and to reckon all things shadow-like, and utterly devoid of weight or value, that had not its divine essence as the life within their life. Then, what was he?—a substance?—or the dimmest of all shadows? He longed to speak out, from his own pulpit, at the full height of his voice, and tell the people what he was. "I, whom you behold in these black garments of the priesthood,—I, who ascend the sacred desk, and turn my pale face heavenward, taking upon myself to hold communion, in your behalf, with the Most High Omniscience,—I, in whose daily life you discern the sanctity of Enoch,—I, whose footsteps, as you suppose, leave a gleam along my earthly track, whereby the pilgrims that shall come after me may be guided to the regions of the blest,—I, who have laid the hand of baptism upon your children,—I, who have breathed the parting prayer over your dying friends, to whom the Amen sounded faintly from a world which they had quitted,—I, your pastor, whom you so reverence and trust, am utterly a pollution and a lie!"

More than once, Mr. Dimmesdale had gone into the pulpit, with a purpose never to come down its steps, until he should have spoken words like the above. More than once, he had cleared his throat, and drawn in the long, deep, and tremulous breath, which, when sent forth again, would come burdened with the black secret of his soul. More than once—nay, more than a hundred times—he had actually spoken! Spoken! But how? He had told his hearers that he was altogether vile, a viler companion of the vilest, the worst of sinners, an abomination, a thing of unimaginable iniquity; and that the only wonder was, that they did not see his wretched body shrivelled up before their eyes, by the burning wrath of the Almighty! Could there be plainer speech than this? Would not the people start up in their seats, by a simultaneous impulse, and tear him down out of the pulpit which he defiled? Not so, indeed! They heard it all, and did but reverence him the more. They little guessed what deadly purport lurked in those self-condemning words. "The godly youth!" said they among themselves. "The saint on earth! Alas, if he discern such sinfulness in his own white soul, what horrid spectacle would he behold in thine or mine!" The minister well knew—subtle, but remorseful hypocrite that he was!—the light in which his vague confession would be viewed. He had striven to put a cheat upon himself by making the avowal of a guilty conscience, but had gained only one other sin, and a self-acknowledged shame, without the momentary relief of being self-deceived.

He had spoken the very truth, and transformed it into the veriest falsehood. And yet, by the constitution of his nature, he loved the truth, and loathed the lie, as few men ever did. Therefore, above all things else, he loathed his miserable self!

His inward trouble drove him to practices, more in accordance with the old, corrupted faith of Rome, than with the better light of the church in which he had been born and bred. In Mr. Dimmesdale's secret closet, under lock and key, there was a bloody scourge. Oftentimes, this Protestant and Puritan divine had plied it on his own shoulders; laughing bitterly at himself the while, and smiting so much the more pitilessly, because of that bitter laugh. It was his custom, too, as it has been that of many other pious Puritans, to fast,—not, however, like them, in order to purify the body and render it the fitter medium of celestial illumination,—but rigorously, and until his knees trembled beneath him, as an act of penance. He kept vigils, likewise, night after night, sometimes in utter darkness; sometimes with a glimmering lamp; and sometimes, viewing his own face in a looking-glass, by the most powerful light which he could throw upon it. He thus typified the constant introspection wherewith he tortured, but could not purify, himself. In these lengthened vigils, his brain often reeled, and visions seemed to flit before him; perhaps seen doubtfully, and by a faint light of their own, in the remote dimness of the chamber, or more vividly, and close beside him, within the looking-glass. Now it was a herd of diabolic shapes, that grinned and mocked at the pale minister, and beckoned him away with them; now a group of shining angels, who flew upward heavily, as sorrow-laden, but grew more ethereal as they rose. Now came the dead friends of his youth, and his white-bearded father, with a saint-like frown, and his mother, turning her face away as she passed by. Ghost of a mother,—thinnest fantasy of a mother,—methinks she might yet have thrown a pitying glance towards her son! And now, through the chamber which these special thoughts had made so ghastly, glided Hester Prynne, leading along little Pearl, in her scarlet garb, and pointing her forefinger, first, at the scarlet letter on her bosom, and then at the clergyman's own breast.

None of these visions ever quite deluded him. At any moment, by an effort of his will, he could discern substances through their misty lack of substance, and convince himself that they were not solid in their nature, like yonder table of carved oak, or that big, square, leathern-bound and brazen-clasped volume of divinity. But, for all that, they were, in one sense, the truest and most substantial things which the poor minister now dealt with. It is the unspeakable misery of a life so false as his, that it steals the pith and substance out of whatever realities there are around us, and which were meant by Heaven to be the spirit's joy and nutriment. To the untrue man, the whole universe is false,—it is impalpable,—it shrinks to nothing within his grasp. And he himself, in so far as he shows himself in a false light, becomes a shadow, or, indeed, ceases to exist. The only truth, that continued to give Mr. Dimmesdale a real existence on this earth, was the anguish in his inmost soul, and the undissembled expression of it in his aspect. Had he once found power to smile, and wear a face of gayety, there would have been no such man!

PHOEBE PALMER (1807-1874)

A persistent theme in Christian piety is the effort to draw nearer to God, to experience more completely the fullness of his gracious gifts. Well-established patterns of Catholic spirituality provide adherents of that communion with several different paths to this goal. Among American Protestants for the last century and a half, the most common aspiration to such a spirituality has been known as "Holiness," "The Higher Life," or something similar. The nineteenth-century revivalist Charles G. Finney played a large role in encouraging interest in such a second stage of spiritual growth. In the twentieth century there have been many examples of its outworking among Pentecostals, in the Holiness denominations, and also among members of most other Protestant bodies. But perhaps the most important influence in establishing the desire for a higher life as a legitimate part of the Christian's calling was the work of a woman evangelist of the nineteenth century, Mrs. Phoebe Palmer.

Phoebe Palmer was reared in New York in a conventionally Christian home. In time she married a wealthy physician, Walter Palmer, with whom she enjoyed a long and happy life. Though active in the early years of her marriage as a Christian worker and instructor of Bible-study groups, Mrs. Palmer still longed for a fuller manifestation of divine love. This was revealed to her on July 26, 1837, which thereafter she always called "the day of days." On that occasion she experienced a special manifestation of the Holy Spirit's closeness and indwelling power. She had been praying and hoping for such an event, and soon after it occurred she began to share the experience, and the life that it opened up, with others. Her principal resolve was to be a simple Christian of the Bible, but not to rest until she had experienced all that the Scriptures held out for the believer. Her experiences and the interpretation of Scripture upon which they were based supplied the material for her early contributions to the religious press.

The first related series of her essays in the *Christian Advocate and Journal* were eventually published in book form under the title *The Way of Holiness*. It was modest in scope and intent, being primarily a description of her own path to the higher spiritual life. But it enjoyed an immediate success and went through innumerable printings at home and abroad. Years later, Mrs. Palmer confessed that when she set to work on the essays making up the book, she was in poor health and expecting to die soon. But her life was spared, and she went on with her husband to develop a wide-ranging ministry of personal counseling, public speaking, and publication.

In an age awakening to the rights of women, Mrs. Palmer was relatively nonassertive; she even published several of her books without putting her name on the title page. At the same time, however, she insisted that God's grace was poured out upon women and men alike, and that all who tasted the heavenly gift should pass it on to others. The following selection, which puts that principle into practice, illustrates her unassuming nature; in it she refers to herself in the third person, calling herself "a sister."

From *The Way of Holiness*

SECTION I.

"Be always ready to give an answer to every man that asketh you a reason of the hope that is within you, with meekness and fear." —*Peter.*

"I HAVE thought," said one of the children of Zion to the other, as in love they journeyed onward in the way cast up for the ransomed of the Lord to walk in; "I have thought," said he, "whether there is not a *shorter way* of getting into this way of holiness than some of our . . . brethren apprehend?"

"Yes," said the sister addressed, who was a member of the denomination alluded to; "Yes, brother, THERE IS A SHORTER WAY! O! I am sure this long waiting and struggling with the powers of darkness is not necessary. There is a shorter way." And then, with a solemn feeling of responsibility, and with a realizing conviction of the truth uttered, she added, "But, brother, there is but one way."

Days and even weeks elapsed, and yet the question, with solemn bearing, rested upon the mind of that sister. She thought of the affirmative given in answer to the inquiry of the brother—examined yet more closely the Scriptural foundation upon which the truth of the affirmation rested—and the result of the investigation tended to add still greater confirmation to the belief, that many sincere disciples of Jesus, by various needless perplexities, consume much time in endeavoring to get into this way, which might, more advantageously to themselves and others, be employed in making progress in it, and testifying, from experimental knowledge, of its blessedness.

How many, whom Infinite Love would long since have brought into this state, instead of seeking to be brought into the possession of the blessing at

---

Source: *The Way of Holiness*, 52nd ed. (New York: Palmer & Hughes, 1867), pp. 17-28.

once, are seeking a preparation for the reception of it! They feel that their *convictions* are not deep enough to warrant an approach to the throne of grace, with the confident expectation of receiving the blessing *now*. Just at this point some may have been lingering months and years. Thus did the sister, who so confidently affirmed "there is a shorter way." And here, dear child of Jesus, permit the writer to tell you just how that sister found the "shorter way."

On looking at the requirements of the word of God, she beheld the command, "Be ye holy." She then began to say in her heart, "Whatever my former deficiencies may have been, God requires that I should *now* be holy. Whether *convicted*, or otherwise, *duty is plain*. God requires *present* holiness." On coming to this point, she at once apprehended a simple truth before unthought of, i.e., *Knowledge is conviction*. She well knew that, for a long time, she had been assured that God required holiness. But she had never deemed this knowledge a sufficient plea to take to God—and because of present need, to ask a present bestowment of the gift.

Convinced that in this respect she had mistaken the path, she now, with renewed energy, began to make use of the knowledge already received, and to discern a "shorter way."

Another difficulty by which her course had been delayed she found to be here. She had been accustomed to look at the blessing of holiness as such a high attainment, that her general habit of soul inclined her to think it almost beyond her reach. This erroneous impression rather influenced her to rest the matter thus:—"I will let every high state of grace, in name, alone, and seek only to be *fully conformed to the will of God, as recorded in his written word*. My chief endeavors shall be centered in the aim to be an humble *Bible Christian*. By the grace of God, all my energies shall be directed to this one point. With this single aim, I will journey onward, even though my faith may be tried to the uttermost by those manifestations being withheld, which have previously been regarded as essential for the establishment of faith."

On arriving at this point, she was enabled to gain yet clearer insight into the simplicity of the way. And it was by this process. After having taken the Bible as the rule of life, instead of the opinions and experience of professors, she found, on taking the blessed word more closely to the companionship of her heart, that no one declaration spoke more appealingly to her understanding than this: "Ye are not your own, ye are bought with a price, therefore glorify God in your body and spirit which are his."

By this she perceived the duty of *entire consecration* in a stronger light, and as more sacredly binding, than ever before. Here she saw God as her Redeemer, claiming, by virtue of the great price paid for the redemption of body, soul, and spirit, the *present and entire service* of all these redeemed powers.

By this she saw that if she lived constantly in the entire surrender of all that had been thus dearly purchased unto God, she was but an unprofitable servant; and that, if less than all was rendered, she was worse than unprofitable, inasmuch as she would be guilty of keeping back part of that price which had been purchased unto God: "Not with corruptible things, such as silver and gold, but by the precious blood of Jesus." And after so clearly discerning the will of God concerning her, she felt that the sin of Ananias and Sapphira would be less culpable in the sight of Heaven than her own, should she not at once resolve on living in the *entire* consecration of all her redeemed powers to God.

Deeply conscious of past unfaithfulness, she now determined that the time past should suffice; and with a humility of spirit, induced by a consciousness of not having lived in the performance of such a "reasonable service," she was enabled, through grace, to resolve, with firmness of purpose, that entire devotion of heart and life to God should be the absorbing subject of the succeeding pilgrimage of life.

SECTION II.

"We by his Spirit prove,
And know the things of God,
The things which freely of his love
He hath on us bestow'd."

AFTER having thus resolved on devoting the entire service of her heart and life to God, the following questions occasioned much serious solicitude:— How shall I know *when* I have consecrated all to God? And how ascertain whether God accepts the sacrifice—and how know the manner of its acceptance? Here again the blessed Bible, which she had now taken as her counselor, said to her heart, "We have received not the spirit of the world, but the Spirit which is of God, that we might know the things freely given to us of God."

It was thus she became assured that it was her privilege to know when she had consecrated all to God, and also to know that the sacrifice was *accepted,* and the resolve was solemnly made that the subject should not cease to be absorbing until this knowledge was obtained.

Feeling it a matter of no small importance to stand thus solemnly pledged to God, conscious that sacred responsibilities were included in these engagements, a *realization* of the fact, that neither body, soul, nor spirit, time, talent, nor influence, were, even for one moment, at her own disposal, began to assume the tangibility of living truth to her mind, in a manner not before apprehended.

From a sense of responsibility thus imposed, she began to be more abundant in labors, "instant in season and out of season."

While thus engaged in active service, another difficulty presented itself. How much of self in these performances? said the accuser. For a moment, almost bewildered at being thus withstood, her heart began to sink. She felt most keenly that she had no certain standard to raise up against this accusation?

It was here again that the blessed word sweetly communed with her heart, presenting the marks of the way, by a reference to the admonition of Paul: "Therefore, my beloved brethren, be ye steadfast and unmovable, always abounding in the work of the Lord, forasmuch as ye know that your labor is not in vain in the Lord."

These blessed communings continued thus. If the primitive Christians had the assurance that their labors were in the Lord; and thus enjoyed the heart-inspiring *confidence* that their labors were *not in vain,* because performed in the might of the Spirit, then it is also your privilege to *know* that your labor is in the Lord. It was at this point in her experience that she first perceived the *necessity,* and also the *attainableness* of the witness of *purity of intention*— which, in her petition to God, as most expressive of her peculiar need, she denominated, "The witness that the spring of every motive is pure."

It was by the word of the Lord she became fully convinced that she needed this heart-encouraging confidence in order to insure success in her labors of love. The next step taken was to resolve, as in the presence of the Lord, not to cease importuning the throne of grace until the witness was given "that the spring of every motive was pure."

On coming to this decision, the blessed Word, most encouragingly, yea, and also assuringly said to her heart, "Stand still, and see the salvation of God."

SECTION III.

> "Here, in thine own appointed way,
>   I wait to learn thy will;
> Silent I stand before thy face,
>   And hear thee say, 'Be still!
> Be still! and know that I am God:'
>   'Tis all I wish to know,
> To feel the virtue of thy blood,
>   And spread its praise below."

THUS admonished, she began to anticipate, with longings unutterable, the fulfillment of the word upon which she had been enabled to rest her hope.

These exercises, though so deep as to assure the heart, most powerfully and permanently, that "the word of the Lord is quick and powerful, and sharper than any two-edged sword, piercing to the dividing asunder of the soul and spirit, and of the joints and marrow, and is a discerner of the thoughts and intents of the heart," were not of that distressing character which, according to her preconceived opinions, were necessary, preparatory to entering into a state of holiness.

So far from having those overwhelming perceptions of guilt, on which she afterward saw she had been too much disposed to place reliance, as somewhat meritorious, she was constantly and *consciously* growing in grace daily—yea, even hourly her heavenward progress seemed marked as by the finger of God.

No gloomy fears that she was *not a child of God* dimmed her spiritual horizon, presenting fearful anticipation of impending wrath. There had been a period in her experience, some time previous to that under present consideration, from which she had not *one lingering doubt of her acceptance with God, as a member of the household of faith.* But, conscious that she had *not the witness of entire consecration to God,* neither the assurance that the great deep of her heart, the fountain from whence action emanates, was pure, which at this time stood before the vision of her mind as two distinct objects, (yet which, as she afterward perceived, most clearly merged in *one,*) and impelled onward also by such an intense desire to be *fruitful in every good work,* the emotions of her spirit could not perhaps be more clearly expressed than in the nervous language of the poet—

> "My heart strings groan with deep complaint.
>   My flesh lies panting, Lord, for thee;
> And every limb, and every joint
>   Stretches for perfect purity"

And yet, to continue poetic language, it was a "sweet distress," for the *word of the Lord* continually said to her heart, "The Spirit helpeth our infirmities;" and conscious that she had submitted herself to the dictations of the Spirit, a sacred conviction took possession of her mind that she was being led into all truth.

"Stand still, and see the salvation of God," was now the listening attitude in which her soul eagerly waited before the Lord, and it was but a few hours after the above encouraging admonition had been spoken to her heart that she set apart a season to wait before the Lord, especially for the bestowment of the object, or rather the two distinct objects previously stated.

On first kneeling, she thought of resolving that she would continue to wait before the Lord until the desire of her heart was granted. But the adversary, who had stood ready to withstand every progressive step, suggested, "Be careful, God may disappoint your expectations; and suppose you should be left to wrestle all night; ay, and all the morrow too?"

She had ever felt it a matter of momentous import to say, either with the language of the heart or lip, "I have lifted my hand to God;" and for a moment she hesitated whether she should really determine to continue in a waiting attitude until the desire of her heart was fulfilled; but afterward concluded to rest the matter thus: One duty can never, in the order of God, interfere with another; and, unless necessarily called away by surrounding circumstances, I will, in the strength of grace, wait till my heart is assured, though it may be all night, and all the morrow too.

And here most emphatically could she say, she was led by a "way she knew not;" so simple, so clearly described, and urged by the word of the Lord, and yet so often overlooked, for want of that child-like simplicity which, without reasoning, takes God at his word. It was just while engaged in the act of preparing the way, as she deemed, to some great and undefinable exercise, that the Lord, through the medium of faith in his *written word,* led her astonished soul directly into the "way of holiness," where, with unutterable delight, she found the comprehensive desires of her soul blended and satisfied in the fulfillment of the command, *"Be ye holy."*

It was thus, waiting child of Jesus, that this traveler in the King's highway was directed onward, through the teachings of the word of God and induced so confidently to affirm, in reply to the brother, *"There is a shorter way."*

G. W. OFFLEY (1808-?)

The fact that black Americans accepted the Christian faith is one of the great miracles of our history. Christianity was employed to justify the slave trade and also to justify the continued bondage of Africans kidnapped and taken to the New World. Despite the way in which supporters of the slave system attempted to use the gospel for their own purposes, however, they could not stifle the Christian faith entirely. By the time of the American Revolution, significant numbers of black Americans, both in the North and in the South, had become believers. By the time of the Civil War, the Christian faith was deeply rooted in the country's black communities.

The stories of black slaves who came to faith in Christ are relatively rare. Slave masters did not usually encourage reading and writing among their human chattel, and some southern legislatures even passed laws against educating the slaves. Yet individual blacks persisted, often heroically, in the effort to read and write. One of the compelling motivations behind that drive was the desire to read the Scriptures for themselves, freed from the restrictions imposed upon the Bible's message by masters.

The Christian faith gave many slaves a sense of self-worth and taught them of a higher law by which God judged the laws of the land. Such teachings became part of a powerful Christian tradition that acted as a counterpoint to the piety of white Christians. This was a Christian faith that stressed the universality of God's grace. It nerved believers to face sometimes inhuman oppression.

The Reverend G. W. Offley, born a slave in Maryland, wrote about both his journey to freedom and the shape of his faith in a short pamphlet published on the eve of the Civil War. The pamphlet was published in Hartford, Connecticut, in 1860, under a lengthy title that began, "A Narrative of the Life and Labors of the Rev. G. W. Offley, A Colored Man, and Local Preacher, Who lived twenty-seven years at the South and twenty-four at the North; who never went to school a day in his life, and only commenced to learn his letters when nineteen years and eight months old; the emancipation of his mother and her three children; how he learned to read while living in a slave state, and supported himself from the time he was nine years old until he was twenty-one. . . ." It is a narrative that reflects the importance of the Bible for the faith of slaves as well as the sustaining courage that faith bestowed upon its adherents. It also provides insight into the importance of family life in the development of black piety.

Narrative Excerpt

My mother was born a slave in the State of Virginia, and sold in the State of Maryland, and there remained until married, and became the mother of three children. She was willed free at the death of her master; her three children were also willed free at the age of twenty-five. But my youngest brother was put on a second will, which was destroyed by the widow and the children, and he was subjected to bondage for life. My father was a free man, and therefore bought him as a slave for life and give him his freedom at the age of twenty years. He also bought my sister for a term of years, say until she was twenty-five years old. He gave her her freedom at the age of sixteen years. He bought my grand-mother, who was too old to set free, that she might be exempted from hard servitude in her old age.

Previous to the sale of this family, my mother was living with her master's children, and they persuaded mother to not consent to father's buying the children, and told father if he attempted to buy one of them they would shoot him dead on the auction ground; that they would buy the children themselves, and they should have their freedom according to their father's will. Mother told them they might buy them and welcome, but you had better throw your money in the fire, for if you buy one of my children I will cut all three of their throats while they are asleep, and your money will do you no good. Her young masters were afraid that she meant what she said, and they concluded that it would bring a disgrace upon the family to prohibit a man from buying his own children, though mother had no intention of doing as she said.

* * *

I was born Dec. 18th, 1808, in the State of Maryland, Queen Ann's County, Centerville. My mother and father were illiterate, and kept no record of their children's births, only refering to circumstances. But when I was seven years old I heard mother say that her young master's daughter Ann was two weeks older than myself, and I got a stick, or piece of wood, and made |||||| notches, and at the end of every year would add another 1 notch until I was twenty-one years old. . . . During my boyhood father hired me to a slaveholder for a term of four years to pay his house rent. From the time I was nine years old I worked and supported myself until I was twenty-one years old, and never received one dollar of my wages. When I was ten

---

An introduction to Offley's life and the kind of writing contained in this pamphlet may be found in *Five Black Lives,* with an introduction by Arna Bontemps (Middletown, Conn.: Wesleyan University Press, 1971).

years old I sat down and taking an old basket to pieces, learned myself to make baskets. After that I learned to make foot mats and horse collars, not of leather but of corn husks; also two kinds of brooms. These articles I used to make nights and sell to get money for myself. When I was sixteen years old I commenced taking contracts of wood-chopping, at fifty cents per cord, and hired slaves to chop for me nights, when the moon shone bright. In the fall and winter we would make our fire and chop until eleven or twelve at night. We used to catch oysters and fish nights, and hire other slaves to peddle them out on Sunday mornings. By this way I have helped some to get their freedom.

EXODUS 20—12: Honor thy father and thy mother, that thy days may be long upon the land which the Lord thy God giveth thee.

When I was twenty-one years old I gave my father one year's work to buy him a horse. One year's wages for an able bodied man $50, or $60, fifty or sixty dollars per year, and two holidays at Easter,—two in June, two in harvest, and six at the end of the year; one pair of shoes, one pair stockings, one pair woolen pants, one coat, two pairs coarse tow linen pants, two shirts, and board, is the law of the State of Maryland allows a man, free or slave, black or white, who hires for one year.

My friends who may read this little work, will make due allowance when they see that I never possessed the advantage of one day's schooling in my life, and only commenced to learn my letters when nineteen years and eight months old.

At one time, when going to my work, I found a piece of a chapter of an old Bible, Genesis 25, concerning Isaac, Jacob, and Esau. At this time there was an old colored man working for my father. He, taking the piece of Bible, and read it to me; I do not remember ever hearing that much of the Bible read before. I told him I would like to learn to read; he told me to get a book and he would learn me, while he stayed with us. I bought a little primer, and Sunday morning he commenced learning me my letters. By Monday morning I could say them all. He would give me lessons nights and Sabbath mornings. He said when he used to take his master's children to school, he would carry his book in his hat and get the children to give him a lesson in the interval of the school. He grew up to be a young man, experienced religion, and joined the M[ethodist] E[piscopal] church, and was authorized to preach among his colored brethren, free and slave, and was set free some time before he worked for my father.

After he left our house I was without a teacher, and there was an old man about seventy-five or eighty years old, a slaveholder, owned a small farm and one slave woman married to a slave belonging to another slaveholder. This woman was the mother of two small children. Her old master had five daughters, one son eighteen years of age, a family of ten in number, to be supported from this little farm,—no one to work except this son and the slave woman, only as I would go and help them occasionally. By this the young man and I became very intimate, and I learned him the art of wrestling, boxing and fighting, and he learned me to read. After that I went to work on a rail road; then I taught boxing school, and learned to write. After that I went to St. George, Del[aware], to work at a hotel. One day a white boy came to me and said that he was hungry; his father gambled away his money, and if I would give him and his little sister something to eat occasionally, he would come three nights in the week and set copies for me to write, and learn me to cypher. The landlady was very glad of the opportunity, and gave me the privilege of giving them as much as I pleased, and I used to take them in the kitchen and give them what they could eat, and fill their little basket to take home. He would stay with me sometimes until 2 or 3 o'clock P.M., and learn me to cypher to the single rule of three.

I arrived at Hartford on the 15th of Nov., 1835. Since that time some of my good white friends have assisted me by refering me to good books, and giving good instruction, of which I have reason to believe some of them are in heaven, and others on earth doing good.

My mother's and father's theology, or the way we children were taught by our parents, neither of them could read; but as mother's master was a member of the M[ethodist] E[piscopal] church, and used to read the Bible to his slaves—not learn nor teach them to read, but read the Bible to them.

First, man is a compound being, possessing two natures, a soul and a body; the body is of the earth, and must die and return to the dust from whence it came; but the soul is immortal; that is, will never die, but will live forever in happiness with God, or exist in hell for ever. This theology teaches of two places for the souls of the human family after death, and the condition by which they must go first. If children were obedient to their parents or their owners, and prayed to the Lord to forgive them of their sins and make them good children, and keep them from telling lies, from stealing, from taking the Lord's name in vain, and to keep the Sabbath holy. But above all, never to be saucy to old people, lest our case should be like the forty-two children destroyed by the two she bears—II KINGS, chap. 2-23: and he went up from thence unto Bethel, and as he was going up by the way there came forth little children out of the city and mocked him, and said unto him, Go up, thou bald head, go up thou bald head. Verse 24: and he turned back and looked on them and cursed them in the name of the Lord; and there came forth two she-bears out of the wood and tore forty and two children of them. And I am glad to know that even from the most oppressed slave to the most refined white family's children at the south, are taught to respect the old, white or black. Their children call old colored people aunt and uncle by way of respect. None use the word "nigger" but the low and vulgar.

Our family theology teaches that God is no respecter of persons, but gave his son to die for all, bond or free, black or white, rich or poor. If we keep his commandments, we will be happy after death. It also teaches that if God calls and sanctifies a person to do some great work, that person is immortal until his work is done; that God is able and will protect him from all danger or accident in life if he is faithful to his calling or charge committed by the Lord. This is a borrowed idea from circumstances too numerous to mention. Here is one man we present as a proof of the immortality of man, while in the flesh: Praying Jacob. This man was a slave in the State of Maryland. His master was very cruel to his slaves. Jacob's rule was to pray three times a day, at just such an hour of the day; no matter what his work was or where he might be, he would stop and go and pray. His master has been to him and pointed his gun at him, and told him if he did not cease praying he would blow out his brains. Jacob would finish his prayer and then tell his master to shoot in [and] welcome—your loss will be my gain—I have two masters, one on earth and one in heaven—master Jesus in heaven, and master Saunders on earth. I have a soul and a body; the body belongs to you, master Saunders, and the soul to master Jesus. Jesus says men ought always to pray, but you will not pray, neither do you want to have me pray. This man said in private conversation that several times he went home and drank an unusual quantity of brandy to harden his heart that he might kill him; but he never had power to strike nor shoot him, and he would freely give the world, if he had it in his possession for what he believed his Jacob to possess. He also thought that Jacob was as sure of Heaven as the apostle Paul or Peter. Sometimes Mr. S. would be in the field about half drunk, raging like a madman, whipping the other slaves; and when Jacob's hour would come for prayer, he would stop his horses and plough and kneel down and pray; but he could not strike the man of God.

The first Methodist minister that ever preached in a certain town in Queen Ann's county, there was a great revival of religion among the rich and poor, black and white, free and slaves. When many of them experienced religion they would disobey their ungodly masters and would go to meetings nights and Sundays. Two rich slaveholders waylaid the minister at night, and taking him off from his horse and beat him until they thought he was dead. But the Lord saved his life to preach his Word, and many were converted in the same town through his preaching, and many masters, when converted, set their slaves free.

My grandmother died at ninety years of age; my mother at seventy, and my father at eighty years of age. These three friends died in the strongest triumph of faith in Jesus, who when on earth said he would be with his people to the end of the world. Amen.

Perhaps some person will ask why did I teach the art of wrestling, boxing and fighting, when desirous to learn to read the Bible? I answer because no one is so contemptible as a coward. With us a coward is looked upon as the most degraded wretch on earth, and is only worthy to be a slave. My brother's master, Governor R. Right, of Maryland, taught his children never to take an insult from one of their equals—that is, from the rich and educated. Their domestic slaves were taught not to take an insult from another rich man's domestic slave under any consideration. By this, you perceive, I was trying to be respectable by doing like the rich. Those who read the lives of our great statesmen, know they were duellists. Then I thought he who could control his antagonist by the art of his physical power was a great man. But I thank the Lord, since the 21st of Feb., 1836, I have been enabled to see things in a different light, and believe the man is greater who can overcome his foes by his Christlike example.

A word to my colored friends. It is often said that we are a degraded people in this country as well as in Africa. Before we consent to the charge, let us look at the word degradation. Walker says it means "deprivation of office or dignity, degeneracy, to lessen, to diminish." I cannot see that his explanation has anything to do with the charge against us in a moral sense of the term. When properly taken into consideration, if we only number one-sixth part of the population of the United States. Because we have six men against one to vote us out of office; that is not degrading us, it is oppressing us. If six colored men should take a white child from its parents, and teach it that its highest obligations belong to us, we six men, that we stand in the place of God—this is the kind of education many of our people have at the south. Now I ask if this child should become a sabbath-breaker, or a liar, a thief, or a drunkard, or an adulterer, not having the advantage to know better, I ask who is the degraded man? Paul says, Romans 4;15: For where there is no law there is no transgression. Then the moral guilt rests on the oppressor and not on the oppressed. We must not feel that we are degraded. The true meaning of the word degrade, is to be low, mean, contemptible, willing to do a mean act that we know is displeasing in the sight of God and man. Therefore we may be oppressed by man, but never morally degraded, only as we are made willng subjects to do sinful acts against what we know or have the power to know is wrong in the sight of God and man.

No difference how poor we are, if we are respectable, honest, and uprght, with God, ourselves, and our fellow man. For St. Peter declares, Acts 10, 34-35, that God is no respecter of persons. But in every nation, he that feareth him, and worketh righteousness, is accepted with him. And if any man is accepted with his God, then oppression, nor prejudice, or prisons, or chains, or whips, or anything formed by man, cannot degrade us. No, we must voluntarily subscribe to some mean act before we can be mean or low in the sight of our dear Lord and Master.

My dear and much beloved friends, allow me to say to one and all, be sure to send your children to the day and sabbath school.

Yours in love,
G. W. OFFLEY.

ABRAHAM LINCOLN (1809-1865)

By conventional standards, Abraham Lincoln was not especially devout. He was never a church member; he had no use for denominations—their creeds or their quarrels; and he made the overtly pious of his day uncomfortable with both his melancholy and his humor. Yet all of this was deceptive. In ways that mattered—in his respect for the sovereignty of God, in his integrity of public life, in his passion for human dignity—Lincoln was, as an older political biography put it, "a man of more intense religiosity than any other President the United States has ever had."

Lincoln's piety reflected the experiences of his own life. He spent his youth on small farms in the upper South and the lower Midwest, where life was hard. He had virtually none of the romantic optimism that marked the character of Ralph Waldo Emerson, who was his contemporary. The intense ecclesiastical partisanship that flourished in the Indiana and Illinois of his childhood soured him on denominations. And the sternest master, death, was a constant companion. The passing of his mother when he was nine, the death of his sister shortly after her marriage, the death of his two sons (in 1850 and 1862), the death of several close friends early in the Civil War, and heart-wrenching list after list of casualties from the battlefield—these left him with no taste for easy belief, no escape from the mysteries of God and the universe.

Lincoln's faith was never inspirational in the conventional meaning of that term. Rather, it was biblical and moral. And it came to fullest expression in the combination of Christian ethics and noble American ideals that marked him and his actions. This combination did lead to a kind of "civil religion." Lincoln felt that the aspirations of documents like the Declaration of Independence and the moral checks and balances of the constitutional system embodied the principles of biblical religion. Unlike other kinds of "civil religions," however, Lincoln's had a strong transcendent dimension. The American way stood under divine judgment precisely because it so nearly captured the divine intent for social order. In other words, Lincoln's faith in American ideals made him less rather than more complacent about the fate of righteousness in public life.

Lincoln, we must remember, was not a plaster saint. His political ambitions sometimes led him to equivocate on moral issues; his dedication to human rights was often immature, at least before the dark days of the Civil War; and his innate caution meant that he progressed at a slower pace than other advocates of reform desired. He shared the follies and foibles of the human condition. Yet it was also given to him to see more clearly than almost any other public American—and with greater moral urgency—the religious character of public life. The documents that follow illustrate Lincoln's faith as it developed over a number of years, from an early response to charges arising in a political campaign that he was an infidel, through the documents of profound spirituality called forth by the War Between the States. That conflict, which tore at his inner being even as it tore the nation in two, both matured and revealed the character of his faith. In particular, Lincoln's Second Inaugural Address shows how thoroughly he had forged together the ethics of Scripture and the ideals of the nation into a piety of singular intensity.

Selected Documents

CLARIFICATION OF RELIGIOUS VIEWS DURING A POLITICAL CAMPAIGN (JULY 31, 1846)

To the Voters of the Seventh Congressional District.

FELLOW CITIZENS:

A charge having got into circulation in some of the neighborhoods of this District, in substance that I am an open scoffer at Christianity, I have by the advice of some friends concluded to notice the subject in this form. That I am not a member of any Christian Church, is true; but I have never denied the truth of the Scriptures; and I have never spoken with intentional disrespect of religion in general, or of any denomination of Christians in particular. It is true that in early life I was inclined to believe in what I understand is called the "Doctrine of Necessity"—that is, that the human mind is impelled to action, or held in rest by some power, over which the mind itself has no control; and I have sometimes (with one, two or three, but never publicly) tried to maintain this opinion in argument. The habit of arguing thus however, I have, entirely left off for more than five years. And I add here, I have always understood this same opinion to be held by several of the

---

Source: *The Collected Works of Abraham Lincoln*, 9 vols., ed. Roy P. Basler (New Brunswick, N.J.: Rutgers University Press, 1953), I, 382; II, 96-97; VI, 155-56; VI, 535-36; VII, 542; VIII, 154-55; VIII, 332-33.

Christian denominations. The foregoing, is the whole truth, briefly stated, in relation to myself, upon this subject.

I do not think I could myself, be brought to support a man for office, whom I knew to be an open enemy of, and scoffer at, religion. Leaving the higher matter of eternal consequences, between him and his Maker, I still do not think any man has the right thus to insult the feelings, and injure the morals, of the community in which he may live. If, then, I was guilty of such conduct, I should blame no man who should condemn me for it; but I do blame those, whoever they may be, who falsely put such a charge in circulation against me.

LETTER TO STEPBROTHER DURING HIS FATHER'S LAST ILLNESS (JANUARY 12, 1851)

Dear Brother:

On the day before yesterday I received a letter form Harriett, written at Greenup. She says she has just returned from your house; and that Father [is very] low, and will hardly recover. She also s[ays] you have written me two letters; and that [although] you do not expect me to come now, yo[u wonder] that I do not write. I received both your [letters, and] although I have not answered them, it is no[t because] I have forgotten them, or been uninterested about them—but because it appeared to me I could write nothing which could do any good. You already know I desire that neither Father or Mother shall be in want of any comfort either in health or sickness while they live; and I feel sure you have not failed to use my name, if necessary, to procure a doctor, or any thing else for Father in his present sickness. My business is such that I could hardly leave home now, if it were not, as it is, that my own wife is sick-abed. (It is a case of baby-sickness, and I suppose is not dangerous.) I sincerely hope Father may yet recover his health; but at all events tell him to remember to call upon, and confide in, our great, and good, and merciful Maker; who will not turn away from him in any extremity. He notes the fall of a sparrow, and numbers the hairs of our heads; and He will not forget the dying man, who puts his trust in Him. Say to him that if we could meet now, it is doubtful whether it would not be more painful than pleasant; but that if it be his lot to go now, he will soon have a joyous [meeting] with many loved ones gone before; and where [the rest] of us, through the help of God, hope ere-long [to join] them.

Write me again when you receive this. Affectionately

A. LINCOLN

PROCLAMATION OF A NATIONAL FAST
(MARCH 30, 1863)

By the President of the United States of America.

A Proclamation.

Whereas, the Senate of the United States, devoutly recognizing the Supreme Authority and just Government of Almighty God, in all the affairs of men and of nations, has, by a resolution, requested the President to designate and set apart a day for National prayer and humiliation:

And whereas it is the duty of nations as well as of men, to own their dependence upon the overruling power of God, to confess their sins and transgressions, in humble sorrow, yet with assured hope that genuine repentance will lead to mercy and pardon; and to recognize the sublime truth, announced in the Holy Scriptures and proven by all history, that those nations only are blessed whose God is the Lord:

And, insomuch as we know that, by His divine law, nations like individuals are subjected to punishments and chastisements in this world, may we not justly fear that the awful calamity of civil war, which now desolates the land, may be but a punishment, inflicted upon us, for our presumptuous sins, to the needful end of our national reformation as a whole People? We have been the recipients of the choicest bounties of Heaven. We have been preserved, these many years, in peace and prosperity. We have grown in numbers, wealth and power, as no other nation has ever grown. But we have forgotten God. We have forgotten the gracious hand which preserved us in peace, and multiplied and enriched and strengthened us; and we have vainly imagined, in the deceitfulness of our hearts, that all these blessings were produced by some superior wisdom and virtue of our own. Intoxicated with unbroken success, we have become too self-sufficient to feel the necessity of redeeming and preserving grace, too proud to pray to the God that made us!

It behooves us then, to humble ourselves before the offended Power, to confess our national sins, and to pray for clemency and forgiveness.

Now, therefore, in compliance with the request, and fully concurring in the views of the Senate, I do, by this my proclamation, designate and set apart Thursday, the 30th. day of April, 1863, as a day of national humiliation, fasting and prayer. And I do hereby request all the People to abstain, on that day, from their ordinary secular pursuits, and to unite, at their several places of public worship and their respective homes, in keeping the day holy to the Lord, and devoted to the humble discharge of the religious duties proper to that solemn occasion.

All this being done, in sincerity and truth, let us then rest humbly in the hope authorized by the Divine teachings, that the united cry of the Nation will be heard on high, and answered with blessings, no less than the pardon of our national sins, and the restoration of our now divided and suffering Country, to its former happy condition of unity and peace.

REMARKS TO BALTIMORE PRESBYTERIANS (OCTOBER 24, 1863)

I can only say in this case, as in so many others, that I am profoundly grateful for the respect given in every variety of form in which it can be given from the religious bodies of the country. I saw, upon taking my position here, that I was going to have an administration, if an administration at all, of extraordinary difficulty. It was, without exception, a time of the greatest difficulty that this country ever saw. I was early brought to a living reflection that nothing in my power whatever, in others to rely upon, would succeed without the direct assistance of the Almighty, but all must fail.

I have often wished that I was a more devout man than I am. Nevertheless, amid the greatest difficulties of my Administration, when I could not see any other resort, I would place my whole reliance in God, knowing that all would go well, and that He would decide for the right.

I thank you, gentlemen, in the name of the religious bodies which you represent, and in the name of the Common Father, for this expression of your respect. I cannot say more.

REMARKS AFTER BEING PRESENTED A BIBLE BY LOYAL BLACKS FROM BALTIMORE (SEPTEMBER 7, 1864)

This occasion would seem fitting for a lengthy response to the address which you have just made. I would make one, if prepared; but I am not. I would promise to respond in writing, had not experience taught me that business will not allow me to do so. I can only now say, as I have often before said, it has always been a sentiment with me that all mankind should be free. So far as able, within my sphere, I have always acted as I believed to be right and just; and I have done all I could for the good of mankind generally. In letters and documents sent from this office I have expressed myself better than I now can. In regard to this Great Book, I have but to say, it is the best gift God has given to man.

All the good the Savior gave to the world was communicated through this book. But for it we could not know right from wrong. All things most desirable for man's welfare, here and hereafter, are to be found portrayed in it. To you I return my most sincere thanks for the very elegant copy of the great Book of God which you present.

RECORD OF AN ACCOUNT OF A PARDON (DECEMBER 6, 1864)

On thursday of last week two ladies from Tennessee came before the President asking the release of their husbands held as prisioners of war at Johnson's Island. They were put off till friday, when they came again; and were again put off to saturday. At each of the interviews one of the ladies urged that her husband was a religious man. On saturday the President ordered the release of the prisoners, and then said to this lady "You say your husband is a religious man; tell him when you meet him, that I say I am not much of a judge of religion, but that, in my opinion, the religion that sets men to rebel and fight against their government, because, as they think, that government does not sufficiently help *some* men to eat their bread on the sweat of *other* men's faces, is not the sort of religion upon which people can get to heaven!"

THE SECOND INAUGURAL ADDRESS (MARCH 4, 1865)

At this second appearing to take the oath of the presidential office, there is less occasion for an extended address than there was at the first. Then a statement, somewhat in detail, of a course to be pursued, seemed fitting and proper. Now, at the expiration of four years, during which public declarations have been constantly called forth on every point and phase of the great contest which still absorbs the attention, and engrosses the eneregies [*sic*] of the nation, little that is new could be presented. The progress of our arms, upon which all else chiefly depends, is as well known to the public as to myself; and it is, I trust, reasonably satisfactory and encouraging to all. With high hope for the future, no prediction in regard to it is ventured.

On the occasion corresponding to this four years ago, all thoughts were anxiously directed to an impending civil-war. All dreaded it—all sought to avert it. While the inaugural address was being delivered from this place, devoted altogether to *saving* the Union without war, insurgent agents were in the city seeking to *destroy* it without war—seeking to disol[v]e the Union, and divide effects, by negotiation. Both parties deprecated war; but one of them would *make* war rather than let the nation survive; and the other would *accept* war rather than let it perish. And the war came.

One eighth of the whole population were colored slaves, not distributed generally over the Union, but localized in the Southern part of it. These slaves constituted a peculiar and powerful interest. All knew that this interest was, somehow, the cause of the war. To strengthen, perpetuate, and extend this interest was the object for which the insurgents would rend the

Union, even by war; while the government claimed no right to do more than to restrict the territorial enlargement of it. Neither party expected for the war, the magnitude, or the duration, which it has already attained. Neither anticipated that the *cause* of the conflict might cease with, or even before, the conflict itself should cease. Each looked for an easier triumph, and a result less fundamental and astounding. Both read the same Bible, and pray to the same God; and each invokes His aid against the other. It may seem strange that any men should dare to ask a just God's assistance in wringing their bread from the sweat of other men's faces; but let us judge not that we be not judged. The prayers of both could not be answered; that of neither has been answered fully. The Almighty has His own purposes. "Woe unto the world because of offences! for it must needs be that offences come; but woe to that man by whom the offence cometh!" If we shall suppose that American Slavery is one of those offences which, in the providence of God, must needs come, but which, having continued through His appointed time, He now wills to remove, and that He gives to both North and South, this terrible war, as the woe due to those by whom the offence came, shall we discern therein any departure from those divine attributes which the believers in a Living God always ascribe to Him? Fondly do we hope—fervently do we pray— that this mighty scourge of war may speedily pass away. Yet, if God wills that it continue, until all the wealth piled by the bond-man's two hundred and fifty years of unrequited toil shall be sunk, and until every drop of blood drawn with the lash, shall be paid by another drawn with the sword, as was said three thousand years ago, so still it must be said "the judgments of the Lord, are true and righteous altogether"

With malice toward none; with charity for all; with firmness in the right, as God gives us to see the right, let us strive on to finish the work we are in; to bind up the nation's wounds; to care for him who shall have borne the battle, and for his widow, and his orphan—to do all which may achieve and cherish a just, and a lasting peace, among ourselves, and with all nations.

C. F. W. WALTHER (1811-1887)

Carl Ferdinand Wilhelm Walther was born at Langenschursdorf in German Saxony and came to the United States in 1838 with a group of about seven hundred Lutheran immigrants. He had trained at the University of Leipzig and had embarked on a pastoral career in Saxony, but he had found the prevailing rationalism of his day uncongenial. Shortly after Walther and the group arrived in America, the leader of this Lutheran migration was expelled from the community, and Walther became its leader. Soon he was active on many fronts. He pastored a church in St. Louis; he helped start a college for would-be ministers that eventually became Concordia Theological Seminary; he founded a publishing house, a newspaper *(Der Lutheraner)*, and a theological journal *(Lehre und Wehre)*; and he worked to unify the many different bodies of Lutherans in the United States. He was the president of the German Evangelical Lutheran Synod of Missouri, Ohio, and Other States for most of its early existence, and he was a leading figure in the Evangelical Lutheran Synodical Conference of North America that came into existence in 1872. He was probably the most influential American Lutheran leader of the nineteenth century.

Walther combined an ability to adjust to circumstances in the New World with an unswerving commitment to the Augsburg Confession and the Formula of Concord, the historic confessions of the German Lutherans. In his views on the church he leaned toward a congregationalism adapted to the free air of America. Regarding salvation, he advocated such a high view of grace that his opponents called him a "crypto-Calvinist." His most significant work, *The Proper Distinction between Law and Gospel,* reaffirmed the relevance of one of Martin Luther's most important doctrinal emphases. Walther was also an unswerving opponent of the theological liberalism that had made such strides in Germany and that began to appear also in the United States shortly before his death.

Walther's sturdy faith grew from solid German roots. Yet as an immigrant he was subject to strains unknown in his native land. The nature of Walther's piety—both its forthright Lutheran character and its reflection of his adjustments to the new environment—shines through in his letters. They reveal an energetic church bureaucrat who yet had time for the most important things. The rush of business on behalf of his denomination could not be allowed to overwhelm gratitude to God for his grace.

Walther wrote in German, and so his works have not been widely used in this country. But now competent translations are at hand to let a wider audience share in the strength of his piety. The letters that follow include a series that Walther wrote to his wife during one of his many trips back to Germany, and a word of practical spiritual counsel to a fellow minister beginning work far to the west in San Francisco.

Selected Letters

TO HIS WIFE

On board the ship *Oder* off Helgoland, May 2, 1860

My precious, heartily beloved Emilie,

Just now we have come to the last port before reaching Germany. Therefore I make haste to record our anticipated safe arrival, so I can mail it off to you immediately upon landing.

As you can see from the above date, we have had a fairly long journey. Today is the 52nd day on board ship. But we have nothing to complain about. Indeed we have reason only to be filled with thanks and praise to our Lord God. He has not only graciously protected us against all danger, but has blessed our trip more than we asked and can comprehend. My throat ailment has completely disappeared, and my whole constitution is strengthened. I have always had the best appetite and was able to endure even the heavy shipboard cuisine, since I never had even a hint of seasickness. Even the crew and passengers congratulated me for looking so much better— people who know me only from the time we boarded. I have even been able to do a little intellectual work now and then. To be able to do this on board *ship* is by itself significant. Even the bitter cold during the storms we often encountered did not hurt me, even though I was daily exposed to it when I would take my walks on the upper deck above the cabin and the stove in the cabin was not lit because of lack of firewood.

For disobeying the doctor's orders not to go over the North Sea but to go to Havre, we have been severely punished, and as you will have seen in my travel account sent to Ferdinand we were whipped by icy winds precisely in

Source: *Selected Letters,* trans. Roy A. Suelflow, in the series *Selected Writings of C. F. W. Walther,* ed. August R. Suelflow (St. Louis: Concordia Publishing House, 1981), pp. 30-34, 69-72.

the North Sea and at the entrance to the English Channel. But as I stated, all this seems only to have strengthened my nerves and tuned my whole system. Without doubt God turned our foolishness into good, for cold weather on land would not have been as kind to me as on the sea, where the coldest wind not only lays hold of one but also hardens a person. After I have this year experienced two winters, between which the New Orleans spring intervened, so I am now also approaching my second spring, which I can now (on May 2) already feel wafting out on the breezes from Germany.

But the ocean trip has not only had a beneficial effect on me, but also on Constantin [his son]. In New Orleans the boy gave me great concern, since he simply did not improve any at all. In fact in the first few weeks on shipboard he seemed visibly to be going downhill. He coughed and wheezed much, and became constantly thinner and paler. His brief seasickness really affected him. He thus gave me great concern and drove me to prayer. But behold! After about the first four weeks things turned for the better also for Constantin. In spite of the inhospitable weather, his coughing and congestion abated, and with that, his whole appearance soon improved, so that I think he hasn't been as robust for years as he is now. I am thinking of having him stay with your sister in the country if it is at all possible to arrange this, so that he can there go on a goat's milk diet and by God's blessing be strengthened by the fresh country air.

Oh my precious Emilie, let us thank the Lord fervently because He has done great things for us, and let us rejoice in Him. I am unworthy of all the mercy and steadfast love which He has shown me, this most miserable sinner. May He grant me his Holy Spirit to make me grateful. I so much want to be just that.

When I write this, you should not think that we had a trip that was physically *comfortable*. Not only was it uncomfortable to endure a number of storms as we did and to be beset day and night by bitter cold, but a journey on a sailing ship is for the most part uncomfortable. I had difficulty getting used to the relatively good but very heavy ship's fare; it was also the cause of a rather painful swelling of the finger joints, which I have not gotten rid of yet. In all that, we often wished we could eat your cooking at least once a week and be able to enjoy your tasty and wholesome dishes.

Our ship's crew and fellow passengers were certainly not the worst of people, yet to be cooped up with non-Christians for almost two months in such a tight space as the ship's cabin was certainly nothing to enjoy. How often didn't we (Stephanus, Constantin, and I) speak of you and imagine ourselves back in your midst, in order to forget about our prison. How often did we say to each other, "Now they are getting up, now they are at table, now they will still be sleeping, now they will be going to church." The most painful was our realization that we could not go to church on Sundays, and everything about us was so unlike Sunday. How much we would have given to hear a live sermon again, instead of the idle words we were compelled to hear. But, thanks be to God, we did not hear any real godless talk on the ship except at the beginning from one passenger, who later was very circumspect though and took care not to utter one godless or offensive word.

On board the *Oder* off the city of Stade, May 3, 1860

Today we finally are on the Elbe, and since it has quieted down a bit here now with the ship lying at anchor, I still continue the letter I began yesterday, so that I might, God willing, mail it in Hamburg tomorrow, lest you be burdened with all kinds of worries about our trip, since it has become unusually long, if the news of the successful conclusion of our sea journey were to reach you even later.

Our plan is to stay over in Hamburg tomorrow (Friday before Cantate Sunday) to visit the sainted Professor Biewend's brother and to visit the used bookstores. The day after tomorrow we want to leave for Zwickau, in order to visit Aunt Zschenderlein there. From there we will proceed to Lugau, where Robert Engel is pastor. After that we go to Chursdorf to my sister Constantine and to Chemnitz to my sister Julie. When we are satiated in the Muldental, then with Constantin we will go on to your dear sister Emma, and as I have already remarked above, Constantin will remain there till I return from the spa.

But that is my *thinking:* God will do the *guiding.* Whether God has given His consent to my plan you will learn in the next letter. In that letter I will also enclose one for the congregation and one for one of our periodicals. For the time being, I only ask our dear Brohm to announce to my friends my safe arrival in Germany on the pages of the *Lutheraner.*

It probably goes without saying that day and night I think not only of you but also of all my American friends, especially all the brothers, sisters, friends, and benefactors in St. Louis. I am sometimes so overcome with homesickness for these precious souls that I hardly know how I can bear the long separation and how I can recuperate here in my German loneliness. If I were not convinced that it would have been better not to do anything for my health rather than to make a *halfhearted* application of the chosen remedy which is costing so much sacrifice, I would right now turn around and go home. But after so much effort has been expended for me, I consider it my *duty* to do everything possible in order to return home in as robust a state as possible. No day passes but that I pray to God from my heart that He would bless my benefactors physically and spiritually for the mercies they have shown me, and to permit them to see the fruits of their love, and to sustain their love to me. The latter two points challenge my faith every day, whereas

I do not have any doubt in my heart as to the first point. I sing in my heart already at the thought that in the person of Mr. Heinicke I will, as I hope, have an American visitor. That will be one of my more memorable days. If God sustains my health and further strengthens me, then Aug. 1 will be the latest I will start the return journey, for that is the day on which at the latest I am thinking of leaving for New York on the Hamburg steamship, which as a rule takes two weeks to New York.

At the same place, Friday, May 4, 1860

We are still at anchor. Called away by the family of the captain to make an excursion via lighter to the land, I was unable to finish my letter yesterday. Now while we are packing, and everything on the ship is thrown about helter skelter, I can barely find time and place quickly to add the last lines. In a few hours we will be in Hamburg, since the tugboat to tow us in has now arrived.

Please greet all the dear friends, brothers, and sisters in St. Louis from me individually, especially my dear colleagues with their families, the Tschirpes, Brohms, Heinickes, and Estels, Ercks, Weises, Ameises, Kampmeiers, Tirmensteins, Kalbfleisches, Augustins, Scheels, the new houseparents, Schroeters, Niedners, Schallers, both Buengers, Burkhardts, Roemers, Ahners, Uhlickes, Bischof, all the teachers in the city—but when would I finish if I would name all those whose names are indelibly written in my heart? Greet all of whom you think that they remember me in a kindly way. As far as I remember, today the annual pastoral conference meets in Altenburg. Would God that I could be among the brethren and there again have my drought-afflicted heart brought to a new greening!

One more thing I have to call to your attention, since I do not know whether I have already mentioned this to you. You are never in my absence to allow Lenchen to take part in the student's games. She is now of an age where that is no longer proper and where it could become harmful for her character as well as her reputation.

Please content yourself this time with these few lines. You may be surprised that the letters to the children are longer than yours. But do not thereby measure my love for you nor think that I prefer the children to you, my dear and faithful wife. What I have crammed into the letters to the children may be of greater significance and interest to you than to the children themselves. Stephanus sends hearty greetings. How he has fared here, you will see from my travel journal, addressed to Ferdinand.

May God bestow upon you good health as upon Sarah, good fortune as upon Esther, and grace as upon the God-fearing Elizabeth. May He give you strength to carry out, besides your motherly duties, also my duties to the dear children He has given us. May He incline their hearts to obey you in a pious attitude like dutiful children. May He constantly fill your heart with comfort and joy in your loneliness. May He help that we may see each other here again and in Him together joyfully walk the path towards our heavenly Zion. May He be a protecting wall of fire around all of you and preserve all of you like the apple of His eye.

You will see from the postmark that we have today safely arrived in Hamburg.

I am and remain till death
Your faithful spouse and intercessor before the Lord,
Carl Ferd. Wilh. Walther

TO FELLOW PASTOR J. M. BUEHLER

St. Louis, Sept. 30, 1860

My dear beloved brother in the Lord,

With great joy I received your letter of Aug. 26 the day before yesterday, and I see there that the Lord has heard our sighs and has safely brought you to your destination hale and hearty. May His faithfulness be praised always and forever! That on this trip you lost a sum of money to a thief is such a small misfortune that it is hardly worth mentioning, and certainly not worth any grieving. Don't by any means do the devil the favor of grieving over it. This evil spirit, who guided the hand of the thief, has no other objective but to make you lose heart thereby, since he notices that you are coming in faith, with the weapon of the Word of God to capture his palace. Therefore just laugh at him and show him that you have not placed your confidence on the god of mammon but in the God whom Satan nailed to the cross but who on the third day arose victorious from the dead. Joyfully sing the beautiful hymns of the cross and comfort which you find in our hymnal, also that beautiful verse of hymn number 355:

> Though all the powers of evil
> The will of God oppose,
> His purpose will not falter,
> His pleasure onward goes.

> Whate'er God's will resolveth,
> Whatever He intends,
> Will always be accomplished
> True to His aims and ends.

Consider this, that you need faith, a strong faith, to achieve anything in California. It is therefore no wonder that our dear God does everything to *exercise* you in the faith even upon your arrival. He tears away all your supports under your arms, so that you will trust only in Him, who will do His work through you. For you certainly did not go there on your own impulse. You were urgently summoned to go, after a call for help was sounded. You could have remained here in comfort, but the challenge had penetrated your conscience, so that you could not pay attention to the voice of your own flesh or anyone else's, if it had wanted to hold you back. The honor of Christ and the need of those souls gave you the first impulse. Even if the weakness of your own flesh had become intermingled in this motivation, yet the matter nonetheless remains completely the Lord's work. Do not let anyone deprive you of this insight. He who has granted you the beginning will also graciously grant you progress; He who has granted you the will, will also help you to the conclusion.

Indeed things in California look dreadful—abominable, as you describe it. But I really did not expect anything else. That should not discourage us, but rather must encourage us. If the people there were pious, your services there would not be required. The sadder the conditions are, the more your call there is certain. When the apostles came to the cities of Rome, Corinth, Ephesus, etc., where a truly Sodomite atmosphere prevailed, how disheartened they no doubt were! They were also made of flesh, and it undoubtedly gave them trouble enough. But they began their work in the name of the Lord, and behold, in that mass of humanity which looked like a heap of profligates, soon a number of elect became evident. Now thus follow the holy apostles and you will see the glory of the Lord (John 11:40).

As to your question about the Freemasons, I am of the strong opinion that you should not begin with polemics against Freemasonry. If among them one individual should become evident who learns to love God's Word, do not burden that one immediately with the condition that he dissolve his connections. That you have to reserve for a later time and you have to bear the false fellowship for a time as a weakness. But don't say or preach anything which could be construed as condoning it. Just *be quiet* about it and preach in general that "friendship with the world is enmity with God" (James 4:4).

Above all things be careful not to arrange for the celebration of the Lord's Supper too quickly. Hold those who desire the Lord's Supper off for a while, till you see that you have a small congregation, that there really is a communion there. At first also do not preach about the difference between Lutheran, Reformed, and the United Church, etc., but only about the difference between Christians and non-Christians. Seek to work on the hearts of your hearers and to depict with lively colors the sad condition of those who have no Savior and thus have no hope of eternal life, and at the same time portray the blessedness of those who can say: "Now I have found the firm foundation."

Do not let either a feeling of your own weakness or the seeming lack of results of your work beat you down, but steadfastly pursue your calling. Also consider that there are many who pray for you, which certainly will be heard in due time. Just wait for the help of the Lord. "If He does not help on every occasion, He will help when it is necessary. And even when He delays, He has not abandoned you." And do not be afraid that we are going to let you sit there and force you for the sake of attaining a livelihood to surrender some of the truth and seek paying members at any cost. A neat little sum of money has come in again for you, which I will exchange into a draft and send to you in San Francisco one of these days.

We must outstrip Satan. Pray diligently and strengthen and encourage yourself with the Psalms. Picture to yourself the glorious reward of grace which awaits you if you remain faithful. Even though it may look disheartening, you can say with David: "This is my infirmity, but I will remember the years of the right hand of the Most High." And just consider all the beautiful psalms of comfort. He is coming, before we even know it, and will permit much good to come too.

As often as you may write, please designate what and how much of your news I may publicize, since I am not familiar with your conditions there and do not know whether any of this information could become harmful for you if it would find its way back to California. But in any case write diligently, and I will also diligently answer. In the *Lutheraner* I have also challenged your friends to write to you faithfully, and therefore have published your present address. I arrived here Aug. 28 almost completely healed of my bodily weakness. It was no small joy for me, when I heard on my arrival that you had already left. I bless you in my heart and am constantly of the joyful hope that the Lord will prepare your path for you and will not permit your labors to be in vain, according to His promise (Isaiah 55:10-11).

All the brothers and sisters here send the most sincere greetings to you. They remember you in the innermost love. Our whole Concordia is at your side in spirit and salutes you.

Please content yourself with these few lines. Soon I shall write more.

May the Lord take you under His wings of grace and stand mightily at your side, give you rich comfort in all your need, fill you with joy and peace, aid your hand in your labors, and give you the victory over flesh, world, and devil.

Yours in unchangeable love
C. F. W. Walther

HARRIET BEECHER STOWE (1811-1896)

Harriet Beecher was a member of a distinguished theological family. Her father, Lyman Beecher, was a noted clergyman in both New England and Cincinnati; her brothers, Henry Ward and Edward, became acclaimed preachers; and her sister, Catherine, was a leader in women's education. Yet Harriet herself appeared destined to a domestic life when she married Calvin Ellis Stowe, a professor of theology, in 1836.

The events that changed her life dramatically began even before her marriage to Stowe. Since childhood she had dreamed of writing fiction for popular magazines. In the 1830s she began to place pieces occasionally in these publications, and she continued such writing for the better part of two decades. When her husband accepted a teaching position at Maine's Bowdoin College in 1850, Harriet Beecher Stowe was returning to her native New England after eighteen years in Cincinnati. Because she had spent so many years just across the river from Kentucky, a slave state, she was keenly aware of the suffering that followed in slavery's wake. Inspired by what she claimed to be a divine vision of an innocent man suffering unjustly, she set to work on an antislavery novel.

The result was *Uncle Tom's Cabin,* which first appeared in serial form. It was a phenomenal success; when brought out as a book in 1852, it sold 350,000 copies within a year. The work came to have political as well as literary impact. The evangelical zeal of its story inspired many to work against slavery in the years leading up to the Civil War. The novel's picture of a triumphant, Christian love was immensely appealing to Northern readers.

Stowe published several other novels in the next three decades, including *The Pearl of Orr's Island* (1862) and *Oldtown Folks* (1869). But none of her other books had the widespread appeal of *Uncle Tom's Cabin.*

The chapter that follows, entitled "The Martyr," comes near the conclusion of the novel. In it Tom's vicious master, Simon Legree, mortally assaults Tom because of his refusal to reveal the whereabouts of two runaway slaves, Cassy and Emmeline, who are actually hiding in a house nearby. Stowe clearly intended Tom to serve as an image of Christ, the sacrificial Lamb who gave his life so that others might live.

The Martyr

"Deem not the just by Heaven forgot!
Though life its common gifts deny,—
Though, with a crushed and bleeding heart,
And spurned of man, he goes to die!
For God hath marked each sorrowing day,
And numbered every bitter tear;
And heaven's long years of bliss shall pay
For all his children suffer her[e]."

Bryant

The longest way must have its close,—the gloomiest night will wear on to a morning. An eternal, inexorable lapse of moments is ever hurrying the day of the evil to an eternal night, and the night of the just to an eternal day. We have walked with our humble friend thus far in the valley of slavery; first through flowery fields of ease and indulgence, then through heart-breaking separations from all that man holds dear. Again, we have waited with him in a sunny island, where generous hands concealed his chains with flowers; and, lastly, we have followed him when the last ray of earthly hope went out in night, and seen how, in the blackness of earthly darkness, the firmament of the unseen has blazed with stars of new and significant lustre.

The morning-star now stands over the tops of the mountains, and gales and breezes, not of earth, show that the gates of day are unclosing.

The escape of Cassy and Emmeline irritated the before surly temper of Legree to the last degree; and his fury, as was to be expected, fell upon the defenceless head of Tom. When he hurriedly announced the tidings among his hands, there was a sudden light in Tom's eye, a sudden upraising of his hands, that did not escape him. He saw that he did not join the muster of the pursuers. He thought of forcing him to do it, but, having had, of old, experience of his inflexibility when commanded to take part in any deed of inhumanity, he would not, in his hurry, stop to enter into any conflict with him.

Tom, therefore, remained behind, with a few who had learned of him to pray, and offered up prayers for the escape of the fugitives.

When Legree returned, baffled and disappointed, all the long-working hatred of his soul towards his slave began to gather in a deadly and desperate form. Had not this man braved him,—steadily, powerfully, resistlessly,—ever since he bought him? Was there not a spirit in him which, silent as it was, burned on him like the fires of perdition?

"I *hate* him!" said Legree, that night, as he sat up in his bed; "I *hate* him! And isn't he MINE? Can't I do what I like with him? Who's to hinder, I wonder?" And Legree clenched his fist, and shook it, as if he had something in his hand that he could rend in pieces.

But, then, Tom was a faithful, valuable servant; and, although Legree hated him the more for that, yet the consideration was still somewhat of a restraint to him.

The next morning, he determined to say nothing, as yet; to assemble a party, from some neighboring plantations, with dogs and guns; to surround the swamp, and go about the hunt systematically. If it succeeded, well and good; if not, he would summon Tom before him, and—his teeth clenched and his blood boiled—*then* he would break the fellow down, or—there was a dire inward whisper, to which his soul assented.

Ye say that the *interest* of the master is a sufficient safeguard for the slave. In the fury of man's mad will, he will wittingly, and with open eye, sell his own soul to the devil to gain his ends; and will he be more careful of his neighbor's body?

"Well," said Cassy, the next day, from the garret, as she reconnoitred through the knot-hole, "the hunt's going to begin again, to-day!"

Three or four mounted horsemen were curvetting about, on the space front of the house, and one or two leashes of strange dogs were struggling with the negroes who held them, baying and barking at each other.

The men are, two of them, overseers of plantations in the vicinity; and others were some of Legree's associates at the tavern-bar of the neighboring city, who had come for the interest of the sport. A more hard-favored set, perhaps, could not be imagined. Legree was serving brandy, profusely, round among them, as also among the negroes, who had been detailed from the various plantations for this service; for it was an object to make every service of this kind, among the negroes, as much of a holiday as possible.

Cassy placed her ear at the knot-hole; and, as the morning air blew directly towards the house, she could overhear a good deal of the conversation. A grave sneer overcast the dark, severe gravity of her face, as she listened, and heard them divide out the ground, discuss the rival merits of the dogs, give orders about firing, and the treatment of each, in case of capture.

Cassy drew back; and, clasping her hands, looked upward, and said, "O, great Almighty God! we are *all* sinners; but what have *we* done, more than all the rest of the world, that we should be treated so?"

There was a terrible earnestness in her face and voice, as she spoke.

"If it wasn't for *you*, child," she said, looking at Emmeline, "I'd *go* out to them; and I'd thank any one of them that *would* shoot me down, for what use will freedom be to me? Can it give me back my children, or make me what I used to be?"

Emmeline, in her child-like simplicity, was half afraid of the dark moods of Cassy. She looked perplexed, but made no answer. She only took her hand, with a gentle, caressing movement.

"Don't!" said Cassy, trying to draw it away; "you'll get me to loving you; and I never mean to love anything, again!"

"Poor Cassy!" said Emmeline, "don't feel so! If the Lord gives us liberty, perhaps he'll give you back your daughter; at any rate, I'll be like a daughter to you. I know I'll never see my poor old mother again! I shall love you, Cassy, whether you love me or not!"

The gentle, child-like spirit conquered. Cassy sat down by her, put her arm round her neck, stroked her soft, brown hair; and Emmeline then wondered at the beauty of her magnificent eyes, now soft with tears. .

"O, Em!" said Cassy, "I've hungered for my children, and thirsted for them, and my eyes fail with longing for them! Here! here!" she said, striking her breast, "it's all desolate, all empty! If God would give me back my children, then I could pray."

"You must trust him, Cassy," said Emmeline; "he is our Father!"

"His wrath is upon us," said Cassy; "he has turned away in anger."

"No, Cassy! He will be good to us! Let us hope in Him," said Emmeline,— "I always have had hope."

The hunt was long, animated, and thorough, but unsuccessful; and, with grave, ironic exultation, Cassy looked down on Legree, as, weary and dispirited, he alighted from his horse.

"Now, Quimbo," said Legree, as he stretched himself down in the sitting-room, "you jest go and walk that Tom up here, right away! The old cuss is at the bottom of this yer whole matter; and I'll have it out of his old black hide, or I'll know the reason why!"

Sambo and Quimbo, both, though hating each other, were joined in one mind by a no less cordial hatred of Tom. Legree had told them, at first, that he had bought him for a general overseer, in his absence; and this had begun an ill will, on their part, which had increased, in their debased and servile natures, as they saw him becoming obnoxious to their master's displeasure. Quimbo, therefore, departed, with a will, to execute his orders.

Tom heard the message with a forewarning heart; for he knew all the plan of the fugitives' escape, and the place of their present concealment;—he knew the deadly character of the man he had to deal with, and his despotic power. But he felt strong in God to meet death, rather than betray the helpless.

He sat his basket down by the row, and looking up, said, "Into thy hands I commend my spirit! Thou has redeemed me, oh Lord God of truth!" and then quietly yielded himself to the rough, brutal grasp with which Quimbo seized him.

"Ay, ay!" said the giant, as he dragged him along; "ye'll cotch it, now! I'll boun' Mas'r's back's up *high!* No sneaking out, now! Tell ye, ye'll get it, and no mistake! See how ye'll look, now, helpin' Mas'r's niggers to run away! See what ye'll get!"

The savage words none of them reached that ear!—a higher voice there was saying, "Fear not them that kill the body, and, after that, have no more that they can do." Nerve and bone of that poor man's body vibrated to those words, as if touched by the finger of God; and he felt the strength of a thousand souls in one. As he passed along, the trees and bushes, the huts of his servitude, the whole scene of his degradation, seemed to whirl by him as the landscape by the rushing car. His soul throbbed,—his home was in sight,—and the hour of release seemed at hand.

"Well, Tom!" said Legree, walking up, and seizing him grimly by the collar of his coat, and speaking through his teeth, in a paroxysm of determined rage, "do you know I've made up my mind to KILL you?"

"It's very likely, Mas'r," said Tom, calmly.

"I *have,*" said Legree, with grim, terrible calmness, "*done—just—that—thing,* Tom, unless you'll tell me what you know about these yer gals!"

Tom stood silent.

"D' ye hear?" said Legree, stamping, with a roar like that of an incensed lion. "Speak!"

'*I han't got nothing to tell, Mas'r,* " said Tom, with a slow, firm, deliberate utterance.

"Do you dare to tell me, ye old black Christian, ye don't *know?*" said Legree.

Tom was silent.

"Speak!" thundered Legree, striking him furiously. "Do you know anything?"

"I know, Mas'r; but I can't tell anything. *I can die!*"

Legree drew in a long breath; and, suppressing his rage, took Tom by the arm, and, approaching his face almost to his, said, in a terrible voice, "Hark 'e, Tom!—ye think, 'cause I've let you off before, I don't mean what I say; but, this time, I've *made up my mind,* and counted the cost. You've always stood it out agin' me: now, I'll *conquer ye; or kill ye!*—one or t' other. I'll count every drop of blood there is in you, and take 'em, one by one, till ye give up!"

Tom looked up to his master, and answered, "Mas'r, if you was sick, or in trouble, or dying, and I could save ye, I'd *give* ye my heart's blood; and, if taking every drop of blood in this poor old body would save your precious soul, I'd give 'em freely, as the Lord gave his for me. O, Mas'r! don't bring this great sin on your soul! It will hurt you more than 't will me! Do the worst you can, my troubles'll be over soon; but, if ye don't repent, yours won't *never* end!"

Like a strange snatch of heavenly music, heard in the lull of a tempest, this burst of feeling made a moment's blank pause. Legree stood aghast, and looked at Tom; and there was such a silence, that the tick of the old clock could be heard, measuring, with silent touch, the last moments of mercy and probation to that hardened heart.

It was but a moment. There was one hesitating pause,—one irresolute, relenting thrill,—and the spirit of evil came back, with seven-fold vehemence; and Legree, foaming with rage, smote his victim to the ground.

Scenes of blood and cruelty are shocking to our ear and heart. What man has nerve to do, man has not nerve to hear. What brother-man and brother-Christian must suffer, cannot be told us, even in our secret chamber, it so harrows up the soul! And yet, oh my country! these things are done under the shadow of thy laws! O, Christ! thy church sees them, almost in silence!

But, of old, there was One whose suffering changed an instrument of torture, degradation and shame, into a symbol of glory, honor, and immortal life; and, where His spirit is, neither degrading stripes, nor blood, nor insults, can make the Christian's last struggle less than glorious.

Was he alone, that long night, whose brave, loving spirit was bearing up, in that old shed, against buffeting and brutal stripes?

Nay! There stood by him ONE,—seen by him alone,—"like unto the Son of God."

The tempter stood by him, too,—blinded by furious, despotic will,—every moment pressing him to shun that agony by the betrayal of the innocent. But the brave, true heart was firm on the Eternal Rock. Like his Master, he knew that, if he saved others, himself he could not save; nor could utmost extremity wring from him words, save of prayers and holy trust.

"He's most gone, Mas'r," said Sambo, touched, in spite of himself, by the patience of his victim.

"Pay away, till he gives up! Give it to him!—give it to him!" shouted Legree. "I'll take every drop of blood he has, unless he confesses!"

Tom opened his eyes, and looked upon his master. "Ye poor miserable critter!" he said, "there ain't no more ye can do! I forgive ye, with all my soul!" and he fainted entirely away.

"I b'lieve, my soul, he's done for, finally," said Legree, stepping forward, to look at him. "Yes, he is! Well, his mouth's shut up, at last,—that's one comfort!"

Yes, Legree, but who shall shut up that voice in thy soul? that soul, past repentance, past prayer, past hope, in whom the fire that never shall be quenched is already burning!

Yet Tom was not quite gone. His wondrous words and pious prayers had struck upon the hearts of the imbruted blacks, who had been the instruments of cruelty upon him; and, the instant Legree withdrew, they took him down, and, in their ignorance, sought to call him back to life,—as if *that* were any favor to him.

"Sartin, we's been doin' a drefful wicked thing!" said Sambo; "hopes Mas'r 'll have to 'count for it, and not we."

They washed his wounds,—they provided a rude bed, of some refuse cotton, for him to lie down on; and one of them, stealing up to the house, begged a drink of brandy of Legree, pretending that he was tired, and wanted it for himself. He brought it back, and poured it down Tom's throat.

"O, Tom!" said Quimbo, "we's been awful wicked to ye!"

"I forgive ye, with all my heart!" said Tom, faintly.

"O, Tom! do tell us who is *Jesus*, anyhow?" said Sambo;—"Jesus, that's been a standin' by you so, all this night!—Who is he?"

The word roused the failing, fainting spirit. He poured forth a few energetic sentences of that wondrous One,—his life, his death, his everlasting presence, and power to save.

They wept,—both the two savage men.

"Why didn't I never hear this before?" said Sambo; "but I do believe!—I can't help it! Lord Jesus, have mercy on us."

"Poor critters!" said Tom, "I'd be willing to bar' all I have, if it'll only bring ye to Christ! O, Lord! give me these two more souls, I pray!"

That prayer was answered!

FREDERICK DOUGLASS (1817?-1895)

Indignation at the behavior of Christians has always had a place in American piety. Revivalists like George Whitefield and Charles Finney railed at their hearers to become Christian in deed as well as in word. Countless social reformers have done the same by asking believers to live up to the ideals of their faith. None have had better reason for such an appeal than the American slaves who besought their Christian masters to set them free. Among blacks, few have made this appeal with greater force than Frederick Douglass.

Douglass was born in Maryland as Frederick Augustus Washington Bailey, the son of an unknown white father and a slave mother. After a childhood of neglect and cruelty, he was eventually taken to Baltimore to serve as a house slave. There he learned to read and write. When he was sent back to the country to work in the fields, he plotted a flight to freedom that did not succeed. Soon, however, his master sent him back to Baltimore to work as a ship's caulker, and while pursuing that trade he managed to escape on September 3, 1838. Shortly thereafter he changed his name to Frederick Douglass, and married and established a home in New Bedford, Massachusetts. His native ability as a speaker soon brought him to the attention of the Massachusetts Anti-Slavery Society, which hired him as an agent.

Traveling in the North to speak against slavery opened Douglass's eyes about conditions for blacks in that region, for he was beaten, abused, and regularly denied accommodations as he attempted to tell Northerners about the horrors of slavery. When skeptics claimed that such a well-spoken, well-educated person could not possibly have been a slave, Douglass wrote a narrative describing his life through the time of his escape. Fearing recapture as a fugitive after this public disclosure, he fled to Great Britain, where he remained until 1847. Then he returned to the United States, established the abolitionist periodical *North Star,* and continued a multitude of activities aimed at ending slavery. His lot was not easy until after the end of the Civil War, when he became a respected figure in the North. During that war he helped recruit blacks to fight for the Union; afterward he served in several government positions, including that of minister to Haiti.

During his life as a slave and his early years of freedom, Douglass had encountered the Christian faith in several forms. He worked for Christian slaveowners who treated him brutally, non-Christian masters who acted with some humanity, and genteel urban Christians who seemed not to have considered the moral dimensions of slavery at all. In the North he met abolitionists of many religious varieties and was also opposed by Christians who rejected the abolitionist message. In his narrative Douglass commented at several points on the inconsistencies involved in a "Christian country" upholding slavery, comments that he expanded into an appendix to the book. In this appendix Douglass countered the suggestion that since he had condemned the actions of Christians, he was an enemy of the faith. Just the opposite was the case, he argued. He was urging Christians to see the hypocrisy of their actions. True Christianity, "the pure, peaceable, and impartial Christianity of Christ," should move people to oppose such a system.

Seven years after the publication of his narrative, Douglass addressed the Ladies' Anti-Slavery Society of Rochester, New York, where he again returned to the question of Christian support of slavery: "You profess to believe," he said, " 'that, of one blood, God made all nations of men to dwell on the face of the earth' [Acts 17:26], and hath commanded all men, everywhere, to love one another; yet you notoriously hate (and glory in your hatred) all men whose skins are not colored like your own." Following is the appendix to his narrative, reprinted below, in which he expressed this contradiction in even stronger terms.

Appendix

I find, since reading over the foregoing Narrative, that I have, in several instances, spoken in such a tone and manner, respecting religion, as may possibly lead those unacquainted with my religious views to suppose me an opponent of all religion. To remove the liability of such misapprehension, I deem it proper to append the following brief explanation. What I have said respecting and against religion, I mean strictly to apply to the *slaveholding religion* of this land, and with no possible reference to Christianity proper; for, between the Christianity of this land, and the Christianity of Christ, I recognize the widest possible difference—so wide, that to receive the one as good, pure, and holy, is of necessity to reject the other as bad, corrupt, and wicked. To be the friend of the one, is of necessity to be the enemy of the other. I love the pure, peaceable, and impartial Christianity of Christ: I therefore hate the corrupt, slaveholding, women-whipping, cradle-plunder-

---

Source: *Narrative of the Life of Frederick Douglass an American Slave. Written by Himself,* originally published in 1845 in Boston by the Anti-Slavery Society there.

ing, partial and hypocritical Christianity of this land. Indeed, I can see no reason, but the most deceitful one, for calling the religion of this land Christianity. I look upon it as the climax of all misnomers, the boldest of all frauds, and the grossest of all libels. Never was there a clearer case of "stealing the livery of the court of heaven to serve the devil in." I am filled with unutterable loathing when I contemplate the religious pomp and show, together with the horrible inconsistencies, which every where surround me. We have men-stealers for ministers, women-whippers for missionaries, and cradle-plunderers for church members. The man who wields the blood-clotted cowskin during the week fills the pulpit on Sunday, and claims to be a minister of the meek and lowly Jesus. The man who robs me of my earnings at the end of each week meets me as a class-leader on Sunday morning, to show me the way of life, and the path of salvation. He who sells my sister, for purposes of prostitution, stands forth as the pious advocate of purity. He who proclaims it a religious duty to read the Bible denies me the right of learning to read the name of the God who made me. He who is the religious advocate of marriage robs whole millions of its sacred influence, and leaves them to the ravages of wholesale pollution. The warm defender of the sacredness of the family relation is the same that scatters whole families,— sundering husbands and wives, parents and children, sisters and brothers,— leaving the hut vacant, and the hearth desolate. We see the thief preaching against theft, and the adulterer against adultery. We have men sold to build churches, women sold to support the gospel, and babes sold to purchase Bibles for the *poor heathen! all for the glory of God and the good of souls!* The slave auctioneer's bell and the church-going bell chime in with each other, and the bitter cries of the heart-broken slave are drowned in the religious shouts of his pious master. Revivals of religion and revivals in the slave-trade go hand in hand together. The slave prison and the church stand near each other. The clanking of fetters and the rattling of chains in prison, and the pious psalm and solemn prayer in the church, may be heard at the same time. The dealers in the bodies and souls of men erect their stand in the presence of the pulpit, and they mutually help each other. The dealer gives his blood-stained gold to support the pulpit, and the pulpit, in return, covers his infernal business with the garb of Christianity. Here we have religion and robbery the allies of each other—devils dressed in angels' robes, and hell presenting the semblance of paradise.

> "Just God! and these are they,
>   Who minister at thine altar, God of right!
> Men who their hands, with prayer and blessing, lay
>   On Israel's ark of light.
>
> "What! preach, and kidnap men?

Give thanks, and rob thy own afflicted poor?
Talk of thy glorious liberty, and then
    Bolt hard the captive's door?

"What! servants of thy own
    Merciful Son, who came to seek and save
The homeless and the outcast, fettering down
    The tasked and plundered slave!

"Pilate and Herod friends!
    Chief priests and rulers, as of old, combine!
Just God and holy! is that church which lends
    Strength to the spoiler thine?"

The Christianity of America is a Christianity, of whose votaries it may be as truly said, as it was of the ancient scribes and Pharisees, "They bind heavy burdens, and grievous to be borne, and lay them on men's shoulders, but they themselves will not move them with one of their fingers. All their works they do for to be seen of men.—They love the uppermost rooms at feasts, and the chief seats in the synagogues, . . . and to be called of men, Rabbi, Rabbi.—But woe unto you, scribes and Pharisees, hypocrites! for ye shut up the kingdom of heaven against men; for ye neither go in yourselves, neither suffer ye them that are entering to go in. Ye devour widows' houses, and for a pretence make long prayers; therefore ye shall receive the greater damnation. Ye compass sea and land to make one proselyte, and when he is made, ye make him twofold more the child of hell than yourselves.—Woe unto you, scribes and Pharisees, hypocrites! for ye pay tithe of mint, and anise, and cumin, and have omitted the weightier matters of the law, judgment, mercy, and faith; these ought ye to have done, and not to leave the other undone. Ye blind guides! which strain at a gnat, and swallow a camel. Woe unto you, scribes and Pharisees, hypocrites! for ye make clean the outside of the cup and of the platter; but within, they are full of extortion and excess.—Woe unto you, scribes and Pharisees, hypocrites! for ye are like unto whited sepulchres, which indeed appear beautiful outward, but are within full of dead men's bones, and of all uncleanness. Even so ye also outwardly appear righteous unto men, but within ye are full of hypocrisy and iniquity."

Dark and terrible as is this picture, I hold it to be strictly true of the overwhelming mass of professed Christians in America. They strain at a gnat, and swallow a camel. Could any thing be more true of our churches? They would be shocked at the proposition of fellowshipping a *sheep*-stealer; and at the same time they hug to their communion a *man*-stealer, and brand me with being an infidel, if I find fault with them for it. They attend with Pharisaical strictness to the outward forms of religion, and at the same time neglect the weightier matters of the law, judgment, mercy, and faith. They are always ready to sacrifice, but seldom to show mercy. They are they who are represented as professing to love God whom they have not seen, whilst they hate their brother whom they have seen. They love the heathen on the other side of the globe. They can pray for him, pay money to have the Bible put into his hand, and missionaries to instruct him; while they despise and totally neglect the heathen at their own doors.

Such is, very briefly, my view of the religion of this land; and to avoid any misunderstanding, growing out of the use of general terms, I mean, by the religion of this land, that which is revealed in the words, deeds, and actions, of those bodies, north and south, calling themselves Christian churches, and yet in union with slaveholders. It is against religion, as presented by these bodies, that I have felt it my duty to testify.

I conclude these remarks by copying the following portrait of the religon of the south, (which is, by communion and fellowship, the religion of the north,) which I soberly affirm is "true to the life," and without caricature or the slightest exaggeration. It is said to have been drawn, several years before the present anti-slavery agitation began, by a nothern Methodist preacher, who, while residing at the south, had an opportunity to see slaveholding morals, manners, and piety, with his own eyes. "Shall I not visit for these things? saith the Lord. Shall not my soul be avenged on such a nation as this?"

A Parody

"Come, saints and sinners, hear me tell
How pious priest whip Jack and Nell,
And women buy and children sell,
And preach all sinners down to hell,
    And sing of heavenly union.

"They'll bleat and baa, dona like goats,
Gorge down black sheep, and strain at motes,
Array their backs in fine black coats,
Then seize their negroes by their throats,
    And choke, for heavenly union.

"They'll church you if you sip a dram,
And damn you if you steal a lamb;
Yet rob old Tony, Doll, and Sam,
Of human rights, and bread and ham;
    Kidnapper's heavenly union.

"They'll loudly talk of Christ's reward,
And bind his image with a cord,
And scold, and swing the lash abhorred,
And sell their brother in the Lord
    To handcuffed heavenly union.

"They'll read and sing a sacred song,
And make a prayer both loud and long,
And teach the right and do the wrong,
Hailing the brother, sister throng,
    With words of heavenly union.

"We wonder how such saints can sing,
Or praise the Lord upon the wing,
Who roar, and scold, and whip, and sting,
And to their slaves and mammon cling,
    In guilty conscience union.

"They'll raise tobacco, corn, and rye,
And drive, and thieve, and cheat, and lie,
And lay up treasures in the sky,
By making switch and cowskin fly,
    In hope of heavenly union.

"They'll crack old Tony on the skull,
And preach and roar like Bashan bull,
Or braying ass, of mischief full,
Then seize old Jacob by the wool,
    And pull for heavenly union.

"A roaring, ranting, sleek man-thief,
Who lived on mutton, veal, and beef,
Yet never would afford relief
To needy, sable sons of grief,
    Was big with heavenly union.

"'Love not the world,' the preacher said,
And winked his eye, and shook his head;
He seized on Tom, and Dick, and Ned,
Cut short their meat, and clothes, and bread,
    Yet still loved heavenly union.

"Another preacher whining spoke
Of One whose heart for sinners broke:
He tied old Nanny to an oak,
And drew the blood at every stroke,
    And prayed for heavenly union.

"Two others oped their iron jaws,
And waved their children-stealing paws;
There sat their children in gewgaws;
By stinting negroes' backs and maws,
   They kept up heavenly union.

"All good from Jack another takes,
And entertains their flirts and rakes,
Who dress as sleek as glossy snakes,
And cram their mouths with sweetened cakes;
   And this goes down for union."

Sincerely and earnestly hoping that this little book may do something toward throwing light on the American slave system, and hastening the glad day of deliverance to the millions of my brethren in bonds—faithfully relying upon the power of truth, love, and justice, for success in my humble efforts— and solemnly pledging my self anew to the sacred cause,—I subscribe myself,

FREDERICK DOUGLASS
LYNN, MASS., APRIL 28, 1845.

HERMAN MELVILLE (1819-1891)

In its first thirty-six years in print, Herman Melville's novel *Moby Dick* sold a total of only 3,797 copies. An English reviewer took it sharply to task for its "huge dose of hyperbolical slang, maudlin sentimentalism, and tragic-comic bubble and squeak." Only long after Melville died did the public rediscover this book, which now is universally recognized as one of the great American novels, perhaps the greatest.

One of the reasons for the novel's lack of popularity when it was published in 1851 was its sober picture of human destiny. The ferocious Captain Ahab, driven by some unknown demon in pursuit of the great white whale, is not a comfortable character. Ishmael, the narrator, is a rootless young man who carefully observes the world that flows by him on the ships that sail the deep, but who shows little resolution, little of that American get-up-and-go so much admired in that day and since. The most appealing figures in the book are the foreigners, like Ishmael's friend, the pagan harpooner Queequeg of the South Sea Islands. None of the characters are masters of their fate; none are captains of their souls. All seem caught up in an undefined cosmic drama even as they toil to catch the whales.

Melville was descended on both sides of his family from heroes of the Revolutionary War. His own father was a prosperous businessman in New York City who went bankrupt in the Panic of 1830 and then died shortly thereafter. Melville and his seven brothers and sisters were left to fend for themselves. He tried a string of jobs—teaching, clerking, surveying—before going to sea at age nineteen. Little more than two years later he embarked from New Bedford, Massachusetts, on the whaler *Acushnet* on a voyage that would not end for over three years. During that time Melville served on various whaling ships, was cast adrift on Tahiti, visited several of the Islands as well as Hawaii, and served for fourteen months as a common seaman of the United States Navy. He also accumulated the stories and the observations of human nature that would fuel the nine novels and fifteen short stories he would write when he returned. *Moby Dick* was the last and greatest of these.

Before Melville sailed on that memorable voyage, he visited the seamen's chapel in New Bedford, where he may have heard something like the sermon that he wrote for *Moby Dick*. Father Mapple, the character who preaches that sermon, may also have resembled sea chaplains of Melville's acquaintance. In any event, Father Mapple's address is one of the most affecting expositions of Scripture in American literature.

Melville was not a conventional religious believer. But he was always one who, like his contemporary Abraham Lincoln, showed the profoundest respect for divine providence and its mysteries. Unlike some representatives of the more respectable religion of his age, Melville understood the predicament of humans who, try as they will, cannot escape God or the elemental forces of the world.

The following is Chapter Nine of *Moby Dick*, entitled simply "The Sermon." In the preceding chapter, "The Pulpit," Ishmael describes Father Mapple as "a very great favorite" of the whalers, "a sailor and a harpooner in his youth, [who] for many years past had dedicated his life to the ministry. At the time I now write of, Father Mapple was in the hardy winter of a healthy old age; that sort of old age which seems merging into a second flowering youth, for among all the fissures of his wrinkles, there shone certain mild gleams of a newly developing bloom." The pulpit in the seamen's chapel was carved in the shape of a ship's prow. "Its panelled front was in the likeness of a ship's bluff bows, and the Holy Bible rested on a projecting piece of scroll work, fashioned after a ship's fiddle-headed beak." From that striking setting come the no less striking words of Father Mapple as recorded by the wandering Ishmael.

The Sermon

FATHER MAPPLE rose, and in a mild voice of unassuming authority ordered the scattered people to condense. "Starboard gangway, there! side away to larboard—larboard gangway, to starboard! Midships! midships!"

There was a low rumbling of heavy sea-boots among the benches, and a still slighter shuffling of women's shoes, and all was quiet again, and every eye on the preacher.

He paused a little; then kneeling in the pulpit's bows, folded his large brown hands across his chest, uplifted his closed eyes, and offered a prayer so deeply devout that he seemed kneeling and praying at the bottom of the sea.

This ended, in prolonged solemn tones, like the continual tolling of a bell in a ship that is foundering at sea in a fog—in such tones he commenced reading the following hymn; but changing his manner towards the concluding stanzas, burst forth with a pealing exultation and joy—

> "The ribs and terrors in the whale,
> Arched over me a dismal gloom,

While all God's sun-lit waves rolled by,
And left me deepening down to doom.

"I saw the opening maw of hell,
With endless pains and sorrows there;
Which none but they that feel can tell—
Oh, I was plunging to despair.

"In black distress, I called my God,
When I could scarce believe him mine,
He bowed his ear to my complaints—
No more the whale did me confine.

"With speed he flew to my relief,
As on a radiant dolphin borne;
Awful, yet bright, as lightning shone
The face of my Deliverer God.

"My song for ever shall record
That terrible, that joyful hour;
I give the glory to my God,
His all the mercy and the power."

Nearly all joined in singing this hymn, which swelled high above the howling of the storm. A brief pause ensued; the preacher slowly turned over the leaves of the Bible, and at last, folding his hand down upon the proper page, said: "Beloved shipmates, clinch the last verse of the first chapter of Jonah—'And God had prepared a great fish to swallow up Jonah.'

"Shipmates, this book, containing only four chapters—four yarns—is one of the smallest strands in the mighty cable of the Scriptures. Yet what depths of the soul does Jonah's deep sea-line sound! what a pregnant lesson to us is this prophet! What a noble thing is that canticle in the fish's belly! How billow-like and boisterously grand! We feel the floods surging over us; we sound with him to the kelpy bottom of the waters; sea-weed and all the slime of the sea is about us! But *what* is this lesson that the book of Jonah teaches? Shipmates, it is a two-stranded lesson; a lesson to us all as sinful men, and a lesson to me as a pilot of the living God. As sinful men, it is a lesson to us all, because it is a story of the sin, hard-heartedness, suddenly awakened fears, the swift punishment, repentance, prayers and finally the deliverance and joy of Jonah. As with all sinners among men, the sin of this son of Amittai was in his wilful disobedience of the command of God—never mind now what that command was, or how conveyed—which he found a hard command. But all the things that God would have us do are hard for us to do—remember that—and hence, he oftener commands us than endeavors to persuade. And if we obey God, we must disobey ourselves; and it is in this disobeying ourselves, wherein the hardness of obeying God consists.

"With this sin of disobedience in him, Jonah still further flouts at God, by seeking to flee from Him. He thinks that a ship made by men, will carry him into countries where God does not reign, but only the Captains of this earth. He skulks about the wharves of Joppa, and seeks a ship that's bound for Tarshish. There lurks, perhaps, a hitherto unheeded meaning here. By all accounts Tarshish could have been no other city than the modern Cadiz. That's the opinion of learned men. And where is Cadiz, shipmates? Cadiz is in Spain; as far by water, from Joppa, as Jonah could possibly have sailed in those ancient days, when the Atlantic was an almost unknown sea. Because Joppa, the modern Jaffa, shipmates, is on the most easterly coast of the Mediterranean, the Syrian; and Tarshish or Cadiz more than two thousand miles to the westward from that, just outside the Straits of Gibraltar. See ye not then, shipmates, that Jonah sought to flee world-wide from God? Miserable man! Oh! most contemptible and worthy of all scorn; with slouched hat and guilty eye, skulking from his God; prowling among the shipping like a vile burglar hastening to cross the seas. So disordered, self-condemning is his look, that had there been policemen in those days, Jonah, on the mere suspicion of something wrong, had been arrested ere he touched a deck. How plainly he's a fugitive! no baggage, not a hat-box, valise, or carpet-bag,—no friends accompany him to the wharf with their adieux. At last, after much dodging search, he finds the Tarshish ship receiving the last items of her cargo; and he steps on board to see its Captain in the cabin, all the sailors for the moment desist from hoisting in the goods, to mark the stranger's evil eye. Jonah sees this; but in vain he tries to look all ease and confidence; in vain essays his wretched smile. Strong intuitions of the man assure the mariners he can be no innocent. In their gamesome but still serious way, one whispers to the other—'Jack, he's robbed a widow;' or, 'Joe, do you mark him; he's a bigamist;' or, 'Harry lad, I guess he's the adulterer that broke jail in old Gomorrah, or belike, one of the missing murderers from Sodom.' Another runs to read the bill that's stuck against the spile upon the wharf to which the ship is moored, offering five hundred gold coins for the apprehension of a parricide, and containing a description of his person. He reads, and looks from Jonah to the bill; while all his sympathetic shipmates now crowd around Jonah, prepared to lay their hands upon him. Frighted Jonah trembles, and summoning all his boldness to his face, only looks so much the more a coward. He will not confess himself suspected; but that itself is strong suspicion. So he makes the best of it; and when the sailors find him not to be the man that is advertised, they let him pass, and he descends into the cabin.

" 'Who's there?' cries the Captain at his busy desk, hurriedly making out his papers for the Customs—'Who's there?' Oh! how that harmless question mangles Jonah! For the instant he almost turns to flee again. But he rallies. 'I seek a passage in this ship to Tarshish; how soon sail ye, sir?' Thus far the busy Captain had not looked up to Jonah, though the man now stands before him; but no sooner does he hear that hollow voice, than he darts a scrutinizing glance. 'We sail with the next coming tide,' at last he slowly answered, still intently eyeing him. 'No sooner, sir?'—'Soon enough for any honest man that goes a passenger.' Ha! Jonah, that's another stab. But he swiftly calls away the Captain from that scent. 'I'll sail with ye,'—he says,— 'the passage money, how much is that?—I'll pay now.' For it is particularly written, shipmates, as if it were a thing not be overlooked in this history, 'that he paid the fare thereof' ere the craft did sail. And taken with the context, this is full of meaning.

"Now Jonah's Captain, shipmates, was one whose discernment detects crime in any, but whose cupidity exposes it only in the penniless. In this world, shipmates, sin that pays its way can travel freely, and without a passport; whereas Virtue, if a pauper, is stopped at all frontiers. So Jonah's Captain prepares to test the length of Jonah's purse, ere he judge him openly. He charges him thrice the usual sum; and it's assented to. Then the Captain knows that Jonah is a fugitive; but at the same time resolves to help a flight that paves its rear with gold. Yet when Jonah fairly takes out his purse, prudent suspicions still molest the Captain. He rings every coin to find a counterfeit. Not a forger, any way, he mutters; and Jonah is put down for his passage. 'Point out my state-room, Sir,' says Jonah now, 'I'm travel-weary; I need sleep.' 'Thou look'st like it,' says the Captain, 'there's thy room.' Jonah enters, and would lock the door, but the lock contains no key. Hearing him foolishly fumbling there, the Captain laughs lowly to himself, and mutters something about the doors of convicts' cells being never allowed to be locked within. All dressed and dusty as he is, Jonah throws himself into his berth, and finds the little state-room ceiling almost resting on his forehead. The air is close, and Jonah gasps. Then, in that contracted hole, sunk, too, beneath the ship's water-line, Jonah feels the heralding presentiment of that stifling hour, when the whale shall hold him in the smallest of his bowel's wards.

"Screwed at its axis against the side, a swinging lamp slightly oscillates in Jonah's room; and the ship, heeling over towards the wharf with the weight of the last bales received, the lamp, flame and all, though in slight motion, still maintains a permanent obliquity with reference to the room; though, in truth, infallibly straight itself, it but made obvious the false, lying levels among which it hung. The lamp alarms and frightens Jonah; as lying in his berth his tormented eyes roll round the place, and this thus far successful fugitive finds no refuge for his restless glance. But that contradiction in the lamp more and more appals him. The floor, the ceiling, and the side, are all awry. 'Oh! so my conscience hangs in me!' he groans, 'straight upward, so it burns; but the chambers of my soul are all in crookedness!'

"Like one who after a night of drunken revelry hies to his bed, still reeling, but with conscience yet pricking him, as the plungings of the Roman race-horse but so much the more strike his steel tags into him; as one who in that miserable plight still turns and turns in giddy anguish, praying God for annihilation until the fit be passed; and at last amid the whirl of woe he feels, a deep stupor steals over him, as over the man who bleeds to death, for conscience is the wound, and there's naught to staunch it; so, after sore wrestlings in his berth, Jonah's prodigy of ponderous misery drags him drowning down to sleep.

"And now the time of tide has come; the ship casts off her cables; and from the deserted wharf the uncheered ship for Tarshish, all careening, glides to sea. That ship, my friends, was the first of recorded smugglers! the contra-band was Jonah. But the sea rebels; he will not bear the wicked burden. A dreadful storm comes on, the ship is like to break. But now when the boatswain calls all hands to lighten her; when boxes, bales, and jars are clattering overboard; when the wind is shrieking, and the men are yelling, and every plank thunders with trampling feet right over Jonah's head; in all this raging tumult, Jonah sleeps his hideous sleep. He sees no black sky and raging sea, feels not the reeling timbers, and little hears he or heeds he the far rush of the mighty whale, which even now with open mouth is cleaving the seas after him. Aye, shipmates, Jonah was gone down into the sides of the ship—a berth in the cabin as I have taken it, and was fast asleep. But the frightened master comes to him, and shrieks in his dead ear, 'What meanest thou, O sleeper! arise!' Startled from his lethargy by that direful cry, Jonah staggers to his feet, and stumbling to the deck, grasps a shroud, to look out upon the sea. But at that moment he is sprung upon by a panther billow leaping over the bulwarks. Wave after wave thus leaps into the ship, and finding no speedy vent runs roaring fore and aft, till the mariners come nigh to drowning while yet afloat. And ever, as the white moon shows her af-frighted face from the steep gullies in the blackness overhead, aghast Jonah sees the rearing bowsprit pointing high upward, but soon beat downward again towards the tormented deep.

"Terrors upon terrors run shouting through his soul. In all his cringing attitudes, the God-fugitive is now too plainly known. The sailors mark him; more and more certain grow their suspicions of him, and at last, fully to test the truth, by referring the whole matter to high Heaven, they fall to casting lots, to see for whose cause this great tempest was upon them. The lot is Jonah's; that discovered, then how furiously they mob him with their ques-tions. 'What is thine occupation? Whence comest thou? Thy country? What people?' But mark now, my shipmates, the behavior of poor Jonah. The eager mariners but ask him who he is, and where from; whereas, they not only receive an answer to those questions, but likewise another answer to a question not put by them, but the unsolicited answer is forced from Jonah by the hard hand of God that is upon him.

"'I am a Hebrew,' he cries—and then—'I fear the Lord the God of Heaven who hath made the sea and the dry land!' Fear him, O Jonah? Aye, well mightest thou fear the Lord God *then*! Straightaway, he now goes onto make a full confession; whereupon the mariners became more and more appalled, but still are pitiful. For when Jonah, not yet supplicating God for mercy, since he but too well knew the darkness of his deserts,—when wretched Jonah cries out to them to take him and cast him forth into the sea, for he knew that for *his* sake this great tempest was upon them; they mercifully turn from him, and seek by other means to save the ship. But all in vain; the indignant gale howls louder; then, with one hand raised invokingly to God, with the other they not unreluctantly lay hold of Jonah.

"And now behold Jonah taken up as an anchor and dropped into the sea; when instantly an oily calmness floats out from the east, and the sea is still, as Jonah carries down the gale with him, leaving smooth water behind. He goes down in the whirling heart of such a masterless commotion that he scarce heeds the moment when he drops seething into the yawning jaws awaiting him; and the whale shoots-to all his ivory teeth, like so many white bolts, upon his prison. Then Jonah prayed unto the Lord out of the fish's belly. But observe his prayer, and learn a weighty lesson. For sinful as he is, Jonah does not weep and wail for direct deliverance. He feels that his dreadful punishment is just. He leaves all his deliverance to God, contenting himself with this, that spite of all his pains and pangs, he will still look towards His holy temple. And here, shipmates, is true and faithful repentance; not clamorous for pardon, but grateful for punishment. And how pleasing to God was this conduct in Jonah, is shown in the eventual deliverance of him from the sea and the whale. Shipmates, I do not place Jonah before you to be copied for his sin but I do place him before you as a model for repentance. Sin not; but if you do, take heed to repent of it like Jonah."

While he was speaking these words, the howling of the shrieking, slanting storm without seemed to add new power to the preacher, who, when describing Jonah's sea-storm, seemed tossed by a storm himself. His deep chest heaved as with a ground-swell; his tossed arms seemed the warring elements at work; and the thunders that rolled away from off his swarthy brow, and the light leaping from his eye, made all his simple hearers look on him with a quick fear that was strange to them.

There now came a lull in his look, as he silently turned over the leaves of the Book once more; and, at last, standing motionless, with closed eyes, for the moment seemed communing with God and himself.

But again he leaned over towards the people, and bowing his head lowly, with an aspect of the deepest yet manliest humility, he spake these words:

"Shipmates, God has laid but one hand upon you; both his hands press upon me. I have read ye by what murky light may be mine the lesson that Jonah teaches to all sinners; and therefore to ye, and still more to me, for I am a greater sinner than ye. And now how gladly would I come down from this mast-head and sit on the hatches there where you sit, and listen as you listen, while some one of you reads *me* that other and more awful lesson which Jonah teaches to *me,* as a pilot of the living God. How being an anointed pilot-prophet, or speaker of true things, and bidden by the Lord to sound those unwelcome truths in the ears of a wicked Nineveh, Jonah, appalled at the hostility he should raise, fled from his mission, and sought to escape his duty and his God by taking ship at Joppa. But God is everywhere; Tarshish he never reached. As we have seen, God came upon him in the whale, and swallowed him down to living gulfs of doom, and with swift slantings tore him along 'into the midst of the seas,' where the eddying depths wrapped about him ten thousand fathoms down, and 'the weeds were wrapped about his head,' and all the watery world of woe bowled over him. Yet even then beyond the reach of any plummet—'out of the belly of hell'—when the whale grounded upon the ocean's utmost bones, even then, God heard the engulphed, repenting prophet when he cried. Then God spake unto the fish; and from the shuddering cold and blackness of the sea, the whale came breeching up towards the warm and pleasant sun, and all the delights of air and earth; and 'vomited out Jonah upon the dry land;' when the word of the Lord came a second time; and Jonah, bruised and beaten—his ears, like two sea-shells, still multitudinously murmuring of the ocean—Jonah did the Almighty's bidding. And what was that, shipmates? To preach the Truth to the face of Falsehood! That was it!

"This, shipmates, this is that other lesson; and woe to that pilot of the living God who slights it. Woe to him whom this world charms from Gospel duty! Woe to him who seeks to pour oil upon the waters when God has brewed them into a gale! Woe to him who seeks to please rather than to appal! Woe to him whose good name is more to him than goodness! Woe to him who, in this world, courts not dishonor! Woe to him who would not be true, even though to be false were salvation! Yea, woe to him who, as the great Pilot Paul has it, while preaching to others is himself a castaway!"

He drooped and fell away from himself for a moment; then lifting his face to them again, showed a deep joy in his eyes, as he cried out with a heavenly enthusiasm,—"But oh! shipmates! on the starboard hand of every woe, there is a sure delight; and higher the top of that delight, than the bottom of the woe is deep. Is not the main-truck higher than the kelson is low? Delight is to him—a far, far upward, and inward delight—who against the proud gods and commodores of this earth, ever stands forth his own inexorable self. Delight is to him whose strong arms yet support him, when the ship of this base treacherous world has gone down beneath him. Delight is to him, who gives no quarter in the truth, and kills, burns, and destroys all sin though he pluck it out from under the robes of Senators and Judges. Delight,—top-gallant delight is to him, who acknowledges no law or lord, but the Lord his God, and is only a patriot to heaven. Delight is to him, whom all the waves of the billows of the seas of the boisterous mob can never shake from this sure Keel of the Ages. And eternal delight and deliciousness will be his, who coming to lay him down, can say with his final breath—O Father! chiefly known to me by Thy rod—mortal or immortal, here I die. I have striven to be Thine, more than to be this world's or mine own. Yet this is nothing; I leave eternity to Thee; for what is man that he should live out the lifetime of his God?"

He said no more, but slowly waving a benediction, covered his face with his hands, and so remained kneeling, till all the people had departed, and he was left alone in the place.

EMILY DICKINSON (1830-1886)

Few writers embody the tensions of American culture more fully than Emily Dickinson. In her poetry, Puritan Calvinism and Romantic optimism were constantly at war with one another. Dickinson was raised in the Connecticut River Valley within miles of the church in Northampton, Massachusetts, where Jonathan Edwards had served for more than twenty years. During her lifetime the area was still a bastion of orthodoxy, and as a young girl, Emily received a typical evangelical upbringing. What drew her away from Calvinist orthodoxy was the very Boston liberalism against which her family and neighbors had striven for generations. At an early age Dickinson was attracted to the English Romantic poets. When she was an adult, the American Romantic essayist Ralph Waldo Emerson was perhaps the single greatest influence upon her writing. In his work she found a captivating celebration of the power of the imaginative self, and his glorification of the poet greatly appealed to her.

Yet despite her attraction to Romanticism, Dickinson maintained a Puritan view of human limitations, suffering, and death. The critic Albert Gelpi, for instance, has described the "awareness of human aspirations and human limitations at cross-purposes" in her poetry. In Dickinson's poems the intense desires of the human heart regularly find themselves shipwrecked upon the shoals of hard realities. "This World is not Conclusion. / A Species stands beyond—," one of her poems begins. But Dickinson knows little of the nature of that world:

> Faith slips—and laughs, and rallies—
> Blushes, if any see—
> Plucks at a twig of Evidence—
> And asks a Vane, the way—

The piety of Emily Dickinson is a piety of the restless spirit. It is not only skeptical about the public relevance of piety but uncertain about its private possibilities as well. In his *Confessions* Augustine wrote that "we are forever restless, Lord, until we find our rest in thee." In the world of Emily Dickinson's poetry, there is neither a definite place nor a sure time for rest. Hers is a piety of homeless devotion:

> Of course—I prayed—And did God care?
> He cared as much as on the Air
> A Bird—had stamped her foot—And cried

"Give Me"—My Reason—Life—
I had not had—but for Yourself—
'Twere better Charity
To leave Me in the Atom's Tomb—
Merry, and Nought, and gay, and numb—
Than this smart misery.

The intense and contradictory feelings of this poem also shape the poems that follow. At times Dickinson appears ready to submit to a God who is greater than herself, only to step back from that commitment to proclaim that the self, especially the creative poetic self, has within it all the resources of the ancient world's Jehovah.

Safe in their Alabaster Chambers—
Untouched by Morning—
And untouched by Noon—
Lie the meek members of the Resurrection—
Rafter of Satin—and Roof of Stone!
Grand go the Years—in the Crescent—above them—
Worlds scoop their Arcs—
And Firmaments—row—
Diadems—drop—and Doges—surrender—
Soundless as dots—on a Disc of Snow—

*   *   *   *   *

I reckon—when I count at all—
First—Poets—Then the Sun—
Then Summer—Then the Heaven of God—
And then—the List is done—

But, looking back—the First so seems
To Comprehend the Whole—
The Others look a needless Show—
So I write—Poets—All—

Their Summer—lasts a Solid Year—
They can afford a Sun
The East—would deem extravagant—
And if the Further Heaven—

Source: *The Complete Poems of Emily Dickinson*, ed. Thomas Johnson (Boston: Little, Brown & Company, 1960), pp. 100, 243, 277, 312-13, 353-54, 644, 646.

Be Beautiful as they prepare
For Those who worship Them—
It is too difficult a Grace—
To justify the Dream—

*   *   *   *   *

The Brain—is wider than the Sky—
For—put them side by side—
The one the other will contain
With ease—and You—beside—

The Brain is deeper than the sea—
For—hold them—Blue to Blue—
The one the other will absorb—
As Sponges—Buckets—do—

The Brain is just the weight of God—
For—Heft them—Pound for Pound—
And they will differ—if they do—
As Syllable from Sound—

*   *   *   *   *

Behind Me—dips Eternity—
Before Me—Immortality—
Myself—the Term between—
Death but the Drift of Eastern Gray,
Dissolving into Dawn away,
Before the West begin—

'Tis Kingdoms—afterward—they say—
In perfect—pauseless Monarchy—
Whose Prince—is Son of None—
Himself—His Dateless Dynasty—
Himself—Himself diversify—
In Duplicate divine—

'Tis Miracle before Me—then—
'Tis Miracle behind—between—
A Crescent in the Sea—
With Midnight to the North of Her—
And Midnight to the South of Her—
And Maelstrom—in the Sky—

This World is not Conclusion.
A Species stands beyond—
Invisible, as Music—
But positive, as Sound—
It beckons, and it baffles—
Philosophy—dont know—
And through a Riddle, at the last—
Sagacity, must go—
To guess it, puzzles scholars—
To gain it, Men have borne
Contempt of Generations
And Crucifixion, shown—
Faith slips—and laughs, and rallies—
Blushes, if any see—
Plucks at a twig of Evidence—
And asks a Vane, the way—
Much Gesture, from the Pulpit—
Strong Hallelujahs roll—
Narcotics cannot still the Tooth
That nibbles at the soul—

  * * * * *

The Bible is an antique Volume—
Written by faded Men
At the suggestion of Holy Spectres—
Subjects—Bethlehem—
Eden—the ancient Homestead—
Satan—the Brigadier—
Judas—the Great Defaulter—
David—the Troubadour—
Sin—a distinguished Precipice
Others must resist—
Boys that "believe" are very lonesome—
Other Boys are "lost"—
Had but the Tale a warbling Teller—
All the Boys would come—
Orpheus' Sermon captivated—
It did not condemn—

DWIGHT L. MOODY (1837-1899)

Dwight Lyman Moody was the leading professional evangelist and one of the most beloved Americans during the second half of the nineteenth century. After moving from his native New England to Chicago shortly before the Civil War, he took an active part in the work of the Young Men's Christian Association. He was also an energetic helper in efforts to found Sunday schools, distribute Christian literature, and bring a general Christian influence to the burgeoning metropolis on Lake Michigan. Moody and a song-leader friend, Ira Sankey, embarked on a modestly conceived preaching tour of Great Britain in 1873 that changed the course of their lives. The meetings they held proved unexpectedly successful, and the two Americans remained abroad for two full years. When Moody returned to the States, he was everywhere in demand.

Moody's manner as a preacher nicely fit the character of his age. He was not as intense as Charles Finney, his famous predecessor, nor did he engage in the theatrical antics of Billy Sunday, his best-known successor. Rather, Moody tried to talk sense to his audiences about God and their need for a Savior. He dressed like a conventional businessman, and spoke calmly and plainly. Moody's message was a basic Christian one, which he summarized as the "Three R's": Ruin by Sin, Redemption by Christ, and Regeneration by the Holy Ghost. Increasingly his concerns turned away from the effort to bring about thoroughgoing social reform. He saw himself first and foremost as a winner of souls. In the most famous statement he made about his work, Moody said, "I look upon this world as a wrecked vessel. God has given me a lifeboat and said to me, 'Moody, save all you can.'"

Moody's personal influence was extended through his founding of important institutions. These included a Bible training center for lay workers in Chicago (later the Moody Bible Institute) and the summer missions conferences held near his home in Northfield, Massachusetts. From these meetings came the founding, in 1876, of the Student Volunteer Movement, a great effort that encouraged thousands of students to seek "the evangelization of the world in this generation."

The secret of Moody's success as a preacher was his ability to communicate to a very broad audience. One of the tools that he used most effectively was the anecdote, as the following examples illustrate. His stories not only illustrated the major points of his message but also provided down-to-earth points of contact with people from every level of society.

Selected Stories

SHOULD NOT BE POSTPONED

In 1871 I preached a series of sermons on the life of Christ in old Farwell hall, Chicago, for five nights. I took Him from the cradle and followed Him up to the judgment hall, and on that occasion I consider I made as great a blunder as ever I made in my life. It was upon that memorable night in October, and the court-house bell was sounding an alarm of fire, but I paid no attention to it. You know we were accustomed to hear the fire-bell often, and it didn't disturb us much when it sounded. I finished the sermon upon "What Shall I Do with Jesus?" and said to the audience:

"Now, I want you to take the question with you and think it over, and next Sunday I want you to come back and tell me what you are going to do with Him."

What a mistake! It seems now as if Satan was in my mind when I said this. Since then I never have dared give an audience a week to think of their salvation. If they were lost, they might rise up in judgment against me. "Now is the accepted time."

I remember Mr. Sankey singing, and how his voice rang when he came to that pleading verse:

"Today the Savior calls,
For refuge fly!
The storm of Justice falls,
And death is nigh!"

After the meeting we went home. I remember going down La Salle street with a young man, and saw the glare of flames. I said to the young man: "This means ruin to Chicago."

About one o'clock Farwell hall was burned; soon the church in which I had preached went down, and everything was scattered. I never saw that audience again.

My friends, we don't know what may happen to-morrow, but there is one thing I do know, and that is, if you take the gift of God you are saved. If you have eternal life you need not fear fire, death, or sickness. Let disease or death come, you can shout triumphantly over the grave if you have Christ. My friends, what are you going to do with Him? Will you not decide now?

Source: *Moody's Stories: Being a Second Volume of Anecdotes, Incidents and Illustrations* (New York: Fleming H. Revell, 1899), pp. 10-11, 19, 24-25, 28-29, 36-37, 53-54, 72-73, 78, 80, 86-87, 88-89, 91, 104-5, 120-21.

A FATHER'S NEGLECT

A story has gone the round of the American press that made a great impression upon me as a father. A father took his little child out into the field one Sabbath, and, it being a hot day, he lay down under a beautiful shady tree. The little child ran about gathering wild flowers and little blades of grass, and coming to its father and saying:

"Pretty! pretty!"

At last the father fell asleep, and while he was sleeping the little child wandered away. When he awoke, his first thought was:

"Where is my child?"

He looked all around, but he could not see him. He shouted at the top of his voice, but all he heard was the echo. Running to a little hill, he looked around and shouted again. No response! Then going to a precipice at some distance, he looked down, and there, upon the rocks and briars, he saw the mangled form of his loved child. He rushed to the spot, took the lifeless corpse, and hugged it to his bosom, and accused himself of being the murderer of his child. While he was sleeping his child had wandered over the precipice.

I thought as I read that, what a picture of the church of God! How many fathers and mothers, how many Christian men and women, are sleeping now while their children wander over the terrible precipice right into the bottomless pit! Father, mother, where is your boy tonight?

ALL THINGS WORK FOR GOOD

There is one passage of Scripture which has always been a great comfort to me. In the eighth chapter of Romans Paul says: "All things work together for good to them that love God." Some years ago a child of mine had scarlet fever. I went to the druggist's to get the medicine which the doctor had ordered, and told him to be sure and be very careful in making up the prescription. The druggist took down one bottle after another, in any one of which there might be what would be rank poison for my child; but he stirred them together and mixed them up, and made just the medicine which my child needed. And so God gives us a little adversity here, a little prosperity there, and all works for our good.

NOT TROUBLED WITH DOUBTS

One of the happiest men I ever knew was a man in Dundee, Scotland, who had fallen and broken his back when he was a boy of fifteen. He had lain on his bed for about forty years, and could not be moved without a good deal of pain. Probably not a day had passed in all those years without acute suffering. But day after day the grace of God had been granted to him, and when I was in his chamber it seemed as if I was as near heaven as I could get on earth. I can imagine that when the angels passed over Dundee, they had to stop there to get refreshed.

When I saw him, I thought he must be beyond the reach of the tempter, and I asked him: "Doesn't Satan ever tempt you to doubt God, and to think that He is a hard Master?"

"Oh, yes," he said, "he does try to tempt me. I lie here and see my old schoolmates driving along in their carriages, and Satan says: 'If God is so good, why does He keep you here all these years? You might have been a rich man, riding in your own carriage.' Then I see a man who was young when I was walk by in perfect health, and Satan whispers: 'If God loved you, couldn't He have kept you from breaking your back?'"

"What do you do when Satan tempts you?"

"Ah, I just take him to Calvary, and I show him Christ, and I point out those wounds in His hands and feet and side, and say, 'Doesn't He love me?' and the fact is, he got such a scare there eighteen hundred years ago that he cannot stand it; he leaves me every time."

That bedridden saint had not much trouble with doubts; he was too full of the grace of God.

WILLIE AND THE BEARS

I said to my little family, one morning, a few weeks before the Chicago fire, "I am coming home this afternoon to give you a ride."

My little boy clapped his hands. "Oh, papa, will you take me to see the bears in Lincoln Park?"

"Yes."

I had not been gone long when my little boy said, "Mamma, I wish you would get me ready."

"Oh," she said, "it will be a long time before papa comes."

"But I want to get ready, mamma."

At last he was ready to have the ride, face washed, and clothes all nice and clean.

"Now, you must take good care, and not get yourself dirty again," said mamma.

Of course, he was going to take care; he wasn't going to get dirty! So off he ran to watch for me. However, it was a long time yet until the afternoon, and after a little he began to play. When I got home, I found him outside, with his face all covered with dirt.

"I can't take you to the park that way, Willie."

"Why, papa? you said you would take me."

"Ah, but I can't; you're all over mud. I couldn't be seen with such a dirty little boy."

"Why, I'se clean, papa; mamma washed me."

"Well, you've got dirty again."

But he began to cry, and I could not convince him that he was dirty.

"I'se clean; mamma washed me!" he cried.

Do you think I argued with him? No. I just took him up in my arms, and carried him into the house, and showed him his face in the looking-glass. He had not a word to say. He would not take my word for it; but one look at the glass was enough; he saw for himself. He didn't say he wasn't dirty after that!

Now, the looking-glass showed him that his face was dirty—*but I did not take the looking-glass to wash it;* of course not. Yet that is just what thousands of people do. The Law is the looking-glass to see ourselves in, to show us how vile and worthless we are in the sight of God; but they take the Law and try to *wash* themselves with it, instead of being washed in the blood of the Lamb.

STEER CLEAR

A steamboat was stranded in the Mississippi River, and the captain could not get her off. Eventually a hard-looking fellow came on board, and said:

"Captain, I understand you want a pilot to take you out of this difficulty?"

The captain said, "Are you a pilot?"

"Well, they call me one."

"Do you know where the snags and sand-bars are?"

"No, sir."

"Well, how do you expect to take me out of here if you don't know where the snags and sand-bars are?"

"I know where they ain't!" was the reply.

Beware of temptations. "Lead us not into temptation," our Lord taught us to pray; and again He said, "Watch and pray, lest ye enter into temptation." We are weak and sinful by nature, and it is a good deal better for us to pray for deliverance rather than to run into temptation and then pray for strength to resist.

THE USUAL WAY

I used at one time to read so many chapters of the Bible a day, and if I did not get through my usual quantity, I thought I was getting cold and backsliding. But, mind you, if a man had asked me two hours afterward what I had read, I could not tell him; I had forgotten it nearly all.

When I was a boy I used, among other things, to hoe corn on the farm; and

I used to hoe it so badly, in order to get over so much ground, that at night I had to put down a stick in the ground, so as to know next morning where I had left off.

That was somewhat in the same fashion as running through so many chapters every day. A man will say, "Wife, did I read that chapter?"

"Well," says she, "I don't remember."

And neither of them can recollect. And perhaps he reads the same chapter over and over again; and they call that "studying the Bible." I do not think there is a book in the world we neglect so much as the Bible.

CONVERTED THE REGULAR WAY

I never yet knew a man converted just in the time and manner he expected to be. I have heard people say, "Well, if ever I am converted, it won't be in a Methodist church; you won't catch me there." I never knew a man say that but, at last, if converted at all, it was in a Methodist church.

In Scotland a man was converted at one of our meetings—an employer. He was very anxious that all his employees should be reached, and he used to send them one by one to the meetings. But there was one employee that wouldn't come. We are all more or less troubled with stubbornness; and the moment this man found that his employer wanted him to go to the meetings, he made up his mind he wouldn't go. If he was going to be converted, he said, he was going to be converted by some ordained minister; he was not going to any meeting that was conducted by unordained Americans. He believed in conversion, but he was going to be converted the regular way. He believed in the regular Presbyterian Church of Scotland, and that was the place for him to be converted.

The employer tried every way he could to get him to attend the meetings, but he wouldn't come.

After we left that town and went away up to Inverness, the employer had some business up there, and he sent this employee to attend to it, in the hope that he would attend some of our meetings.

One night, as I was preaching on the bank of a river, I happened to take for my text the words of Naaman: "I thought; I thought." I was trying to take men's thoughts up and to show the difference between their thoughts and God's thoughts. This man happened to be walking along the bank of the river. He saw a great crowd, and heard some one talking, and he wondered to himself what that man was talking about. He didn't know who was there, so he drew up to the crowd, and listened. He heard the sermon, and became convicted and converted right there. Then he inquired who was the preacher, and he found out it was the very man that he said he would not hear—the man he disliked. The very man he had been talking against was the very man God used to convert him.

THE TRUE SHEEP KNOWS

I tell you the true sheep know a true shepherd. I got up in Scotland once and quoted a passage of Scripture a little different from what it was in the Bible, and an old woman crept up and said:

"Mr. Moody, you said—."

I might make forty misquotations in an ordinary audience, and no one would tell me about them. Like two lawyers: one said in court the other didn't know the Lord's Prayer. The other said he did:

"Now I lay me down to sleep."

"Well," the first said, "I give it up. I did not think you knew it."

Didn't either one of them know it, you see.

KNOWN BY NAME

A friend of mine was in Syria, and he found a shepherd that kept up the old custom of naming his sheep. My friend said he wouldn't believe that the sheep knew him when he called them by name. So he said to the shepherd:

"I wish you would just call one or two."

The shepherd said, "Carl."

The sheep stopped eating and looked up.

The shepherd called out, "Come here."

The sheep came, and stood looking up into his face.

He called another, and another, and there they stood looking up at the shepherd.

"How can you tell them apart?"

"Oh, there are no two alike. See, that sheep toes in a little; this sheep is a little bit squint-eyed; that sheep has a black spot on its nose."

My friend found that he knew every one of his sheep by their failings. He didn't have a perfect one in his flock.

I suppose that is the way the Lord knows you and me. There is a man that is covetous; he wants to grasp the whole world. He wants a shepherd to keep down that spirit. There is a woman down there who has an awful tongue; she keeps the whole neighborhood stirred up. There is a woman over there who is deceitful, terribly so. She needs the care of a shepherd to keep her from deceit, for she will ruin all her children; they will all turn out just like their mother. There is a father over there who wouldn't swear for all the world before his children, but sometimes he gets provoked in his business and swears before he knows it. Doesn't he need a shepherd's care? I would like to know if there is a man or woman on earth who doesn't need the care of a shepherd. Haven't we all got failings? If you really want to know what your failings are, you can find some one who can point them out. God would never have sent Christ into the world if we didn't need His care. We are as weak and foolish as sheep.

THE INVITATION TO A SALOON OPENING

They were going to have a great celebration at the opening of a saloon and
billiard hall in Chicago, in the northern part of the city, where I lived. It was
to be a gateway to death and to hell, one of the worst places in Chicago. As a
joke they sent me an invitation to go to the opening. I took the invitation, and
went down and saw the two men who had the saloon, and I said:

"Is that a genuine invitation?"

They said it was.

"Thank you," I said; "I will be around, and if there is anything here I don't
like I may have something to say about it."

They said, "You are not going to *preach*, are you?"

"I may."

"We don't want you. We won't let you in."

"How are you going to keep me out?" I asked. "There is the invitation."

"We will put a policeman at the door."

"What is the policeman going to do with that invitation?"

"We won't let you in."

"Well," I said, "I will be there."

I gave them a good scare, and then I said, "I will compromise the matter; if
you two men will get down here and let me pray with you, I will let you off."

I got those two rum-sellers down on their knees, one on one side of me and
the other on the other side, and I prayed God to save their souls and smite
their business. One of them had a Christian mother, and he seemed to have
some conscience left. After I had prayed, I said:

"How can you do business? How can you throw this place open to ruin
the young men of Chicago?"

Within three months the whole thing smashed up, and one of them was
converted shortly after. I have never been invited to a saloon since.

JOHN JOSEPH KEANE (1839-1918)

After the Civil War, the American Catholic Church entered a new era. By the 1860s it had become the largest denomination in the country, and as the century wore on, considerable numbers of Catholic immigrants continued to make their way from Europe across the Atlantic. The Catholic Church enjoyed more than just mere numbers, however, as it emerged from its earlier status as a "foreign" denomination often distrusted by American Protestants. A significant group of capable leaders also appeared on the scene to mark the beginning of a new day for Catholics in America. These leaders included converts like Orestes Brownson, a former Transcendentalist, and Isaac Hecker, founder of the Paulist order. But they included members of the immigrant communities as well. One of these was John Joseph Keane, an energetic administrator and pastor. Keane was born in County Donegal, Ireland, in 1839. With his family, he migrated to New Brunswick, Canada, in 1846, and then to Baltimore two years later. He showed an early aptitude for church work, and after being educated at local institutions, he was ordained a priest in 1866. Keane then served twelve years as a pastor and an administrator in Washington, D.C., before being named the bishop of Richmond. He is best known for his work in founding the Catholic University of America, which he served as rector from 1889 to 1896. But Keane was also perpetually busy with other tasks. He helped to organize several temperance societies, spent time evangelizing among blacks, and spoke widely to Protestant as well as Catholic groups.

Keane stood with those Catholic leaders in the New World who felt that American values had something positive to contribute to the Catholic faith. Such opinions, however, did not always sit well with conservatives in Europe, who in the 1890s mounted a campaign to purge the church of "Americanist" elements. Keane's leadership of the Catholic University was terminated as a result of this controversy, but he went on to serve faithfully in Rome, and in his last years he was archbishop of Dubuque. There he followed his earlier interests by working for the support of yet another institution of higher learning, Loras College.

Keane's activism did not blind him to the need for inner spiritual strength. In fact, he was a leader in promoting special devotional exercises to worship the Holy Spirit. While bishop of Richmond, he organized a "Confraternity of the Servants of the Holy Ghost" and wrote a short book to assist his parishioners in their worship of the third person of the Trinity. It was called *A Sodality Manual for the Use of the Servants of the Holy Ghost*. The association (or confraternity, sodality) that Keane founded eventually included well over a thousand people who pledged themselves to pray regularly to the Holy Spirit and to meet at certain times throughout the year to celebrate special services in the Spirit's honor.

Included in the *Sodality Manual* is "The Little Office of the Holy Ghost," a pattern of worship for public or private use that is organized according to the seven canonical "hours" of daily prayer that had come into existence during the Middle Ages. The "Little Office" is made up of hymns, biblical readings, and prayers. It centers on the seven gifts of the Holy Spirit: wisdom, understanding, counsel, fortitude, knowledge, piety, and the fear of the Lord. It reflects a distinctly Catholic spirit and employs the Catholic translation of the Scriptures. But it also testifies to the broad range of common beliefs and aspirations that American Catholics have always shared with Protestant Americans. The reading that follows contains three of the canonical "hours"—the first (Matins and Lauds) and the last two (Vespers and Compline).

From "The Little Office of the Holy Ghost"

The Opening Prayer

Open, O Lord, our mouths to bless Thy holy name; cleanse our hearts from all vain, bad, and distracting thoughts; enlighten our understanding, inflame our will, that we may worthily, attentively and devoutly recite this holy Office, and may deserve to be heard in the presence of Thy Divine Majesty. Through Christ Our Lord. Amen.

O Lord, in union with that divine intention with which Thou, whilst on earth, didst render homage to God, we offer these prayers to Thee.

Our Father. Hail Mary.

The Spirit of the Lord shall rest upon Him; the Spirit of Wisdom and of Understanding, the Spirit of Counsel and of Fortitude, the Spirit of Knowledge and of Piety, and He shall be filled with the Spirit of the Fear of the Lord. (*Isaias* xi, 2, 3.)

Source: The *Sodality Manual* was published in 1880 by John Murphy and Company in Baltimore. An excellent modern introduction to Keane and a complete text of this "Little Office" may be found in *Devotion to the Holy Spirit in American Catholicism*, ed. Joseph P. Chinnici, O.F.M. (Mahwah, N.J.: Paulist Press, 1985). This selection omits some of Keane's original directions for the public presentation of the office.

MATINS AND LAUDS

The Gift of Wisdom

*(Wisdom is the Gift of the Holy Ghost by which we know and bear in mind
the end for which God created us, and use all things as means for its
attainment.)*

Come, O Holy Ghost, fill the hearts of Thy faithful;
And kindle in them the fire of Thy love.
Send forth Thy Spirit, and they shall be created;
And Thou wilt renew the face of the earth.
Glory be to the Father, &c.

Hymn

O Holy Ghost, we Thee adore,
Thou Breath and Bliss and Life of God,
Thou glorious Bond of Love, in Whom
The Father and the Son are one.

Thou brooded'st o'er creation's dawn,
Awaiting Thy abode in man;
That, made for Love, his soul should seek
No other end save Love Divine.

O grant us Wisdom for our guide
That our life-journey may not err,
That nought of earth may lead astray,
But all things help us up to God. Amen.

Psalm VIII

[1.] O Lord, our Lord, how admirable is Thy name in the whole earth!

2. For Thy magnificence is elevated: above the heavens.

3. For I will behold Thy heavens, the works of Thy fingers: the moon and
the stars which Thou has set.

4. What is man that Thou art mindful of him? or the son of man that Thou
visitest him?

5. Thou hast made him a little less than the Angels, Thou hast crowned
him with glory and honor, and hast set him over the works of Thy hands.

6. Thou hast put all things under his feet: all sheep and oxen, yea, and all
the beasts of the field.

7. O Lord, our Lord, how admirable is Thy name in all the earth!
Glory be to the Father, and to the Son and to the Holy Ghost.

As it was in the beginning, is now, and ever shall be, world without end. Amen.

Psalm CXVI

O praise the Lord, all ye nations, praise Him, all ye people.

For His mercy is confirmed upon us: and the truth of the Lord endureth for ever.

Glory be to the Father, &c.

The Voice of the Holy Ghost Concerning the Gift of Wisdom.

The Lord hath made all things for Himself. (*Prov.* xvi, 4.)

Wisdom reacheth from end to end mightily, and ordereth all things sweetly. (*Wis.* viii, 1.)

Wisdom is an infinite treasure to men, which they that use become the friends of God, being commended for the gifts of discipline. (*Wis.* vii, 14.)

If any one want Wisdom, let him ask of God, who giveth to all abundantly, and upbraideth not, and it shall be given him. (*James* i, 5.)

Hath not God made void the wisdom of this world? . . . For we preach Christ crucified: unto the Jews indeed a stumbling block, and unto the gentiles foolishness; but unto them that are called, Christ the Power of God and the Wisdom of God. (*I Cor.* i, 20-24.)

And do Thou, O Lord, have mercy on us.

Thanks be to God.

Blessed are the peace makers;

For they shall be called the children of God.

Let us Pray.

O Holy Ghost, adorable Spirit of Wisdom, we beseech Thee, make us truly wise. Make us ever bear in mind that God alone is our First Beginning and our Last End, and that all things must be used as means to bring us to Him. Save us from the concupiscence that would lead us astray after earthly ends; and grant that we may at last reach safely the bosom of our Eternal Father. Through Christ Our Lord. Amen.

VESPERS

The Gift of Piety

(*Piety is the gift of the Holy Ghost by which we know and bear in mind the end for which God created us, and use all things as means for its attainment.*)

Come, O Holy Ghost, &c., *as at Matins.*

Hymn

O Holy Ghost, we Thee adore,
Thou Fount of Love in Jesus' Heart,
Poured forth in ours, that we, made sons,
May with Him, "Abba, Father," cry.

When Jesus the baptismal flood
For our regeneration blessed,
Thou, Spirit Dove, wast there to teach
Our souls to wing their way to God.

O grant that Piety may melt
The ice from round our frozen hearts;
That, winged with love, our souls may soar,
In Jesus' Heart to find their rests. Amen.

Psalm XLI

1. As the hart panteth after the water-springs so panteth my soul after Thee, O God.

2. My soul hath thirsted after the strong living God; when shall I come, and appear before the face of God?

3. My tears have been my bread day and night; whilst it is said to me daily, Where is thy God?

4. These things I remembered, and I poured out my soul in me: for I shall go over into the place of the wonderful tabernacle, even unto the house of God.

5. With the voice of joy and praise: the noise of one feasting.

6. Why art thou sad, O my soul? and why dost thou disquiet me?

7. Hope thou in God, for I will yet praise Him. *He is* the salvation of my countenance, and my God.

Glory be to the Father, &c.

The Voice of the Holy Ghost Concerning the Gift of Piety.

God sent his Son . . . that we might receive the adoption of sons. And because we are sons, God hath sent the Spirit of His Son into our hearts, crying: Abba, Father. (*Gal.* iv, 4-6.)

We have known and have believed the charity which God hath to us. God is charity; and he that abideth in charity abideth in God, and God in him. Let us therefore love God, because God first hath loved us. (*I John* iv, 16, 19.)

I am come to cast fire on the earth, saith the Lord, and what will I but that it be enkindled. (*Luke* xii, 49.)

He that hath my commandments and keepth them, he it is that loveth me.

If any one love me, he will keep my word, and my Father will love him, and we will come to him, and will make our abode with him. (*John* xiv, 21, 23.)

To them that love God, all things work together unto good. (*Rom.* viii, 28.)

And do Thou, O Lord, have mercy on us.

Thanks be to God.

Blessed are the meek;

For they shall possess the land.

Let Us Pray.

O Holy Ghost, adorable Spirit of Piety, we beseech Thee, inflame our hearts with that blessed Fire which Jesus came to cast on the earth, and which He so ardently desires to see enkindled. Thou seest, alas! how our souls are chilled by this cold world in which we have to live. Save us from not loving God, and save us from serving Him with lukewarmness. And since we are made the children of God, through Thee, the Spirit of His Son, O grant that our hearts may ever share in that filial love with which the Heart of Jesus burns for His Father and our Father. Through the same Christ our Lord. Amen.

COMPLINE

The Gift of the Fear of the Lord

(The Fear of the Lord is the Gift of the Holy Ghost which restrains us from evil by a salutary dread of our own weakness, the heinousness of sin, and the judgments of God.)

Come, O Holy Ghost, &c., *as at Matins.*

Hymn

O Holy Ghost, we thee adore,
Thou awful Holiness of God,
Whose Majesty, with trembling song,
Celestial choirs adoring praise,

On Thabor, in the shining Cloud
That veiled our radiant Saviour's brow,
Thou show'st how dread th' Omnipotence
That deigns our puny love to crave.

O may Thy Fear surround our lives
With ramparts 'gainst the wiles of sin,
And spur our lagging steps to where
We'll praise Thy name for evermore. Amen.

Psalm XXXIII

1. I will bless the Lord at all times, His praise shall be always in my mouth.

2. My soul shall glory in the Lord: let the meek hear and rejoice.

3. I sought the Lord, and He heard me: and He delivered me from all my troubles.

4. The angel of the Lord shall encamp round about them that fear Him: and shall deliver them.

5. O taste, and see that the Lord is sweet: blessed is the man that hopeth in Him.

6. Fear the Lord, all ye His saints: for there is no want to them that fear Him.

7. The Lord is nigh unto them that are of a contrite heart: and He will save the humble of spirit.

Glory be to the Father, &c.

The Voice of the Holy Ghost Concerning the Gift of the Fear of the Lord.

The Fear of the Lord is the beginning of Wisdom. (*Eccl.* i, 16.)

Be not afraid of them who kill the body, and after that have no more that they can do. But I will show you whom ye shall fear: fear ye Him, who after He hath killed, hath power to cast into hell; yea, I say to you, fear Him. (*Luke* xii, 4-5.)

His mercy is from generation unto generations, to them that fear Him. (*Luke* i, 50.)

With fear and trembling work out your salvation. (*Phil.* ii, 12.)

He that thinketh himself to stand, let him take heed lest he fall. (*I Cor.* x, 12.)

Grieve not the Holy Spirit of God, whereby you are sealed unto the day of redemption. (*Eph.* iv, 30.)

The fear of the Lord is honor, and glory, and gladness, and a crown of joy. With him that feareth the Lord it shall go well in the latter end, and in the day of his death he shall be blessed. (*Eccli.* i, 11, 13.)

And do Thou, O Lord, have mercy on us.

Thanks be to God.

Blessed are the poor in spirit:
For theirs is the kingdom of heaven.

Let Us Pray.

O Holy Ghost, adorable Spirit of the Fear of the Lord, we beseech Thee, keep ever Thy salutary restraint on our wayward inclinations. Make us fear sin above all evils, and the loss of God above all calamities. Save us from the folly of presumption, the snares of self-deceit, and the blindness of false security. Guide us through the safe paths of Thy holy Fear to that blessed end of our journey, where all fear will be cast out by perfect love, and Thy Seven Gifts will be transformed into the plenitude of eternal bliss. Through Christ our Lord. Amen.

WOODROW WILSON (1856-1924)

After Woodrow Wilson was elected the Democratic governor of New Jersey in 1910, organizations from all around the country wanted to see him in person. Wilson had already earned a reputation as a public speaker during his years as president of Princeton University, and now his entrance into the political lime-light—and the chance that this reforming governor might become presidential timber—greatly increased the number of those who wanted to hear from him. Despite the fact that Wilson found himself in new circumstances, traveling to more and more places and speaking before more and more people, he nonetheless retained the central convictions that had inspired his entire career. He believed that the institutions of American government provided an unprecedented opportunity for the enjoyment of human liberty, that many difficulties remained to be overcome at home and around the world if the potential of American ideals was to be realized, and that the course of American destiny was intimately related to the will of God. When Wilson came to Denver in early May of 1911, he talked about these convictions before 12,000 eager listeners at the Denver Auditorium. In that notable speech, reproduced below, he spoke directly about the Bible and its relationship to the ideals of America.

Woodrow Wilson was born in Staunton, Virginia, the son of a Presbyterian minister. He was educated at private schools, Davidson College, Princeton, and the law school of the University of Virginia. He practiced law briefly but then entered Johns Hopkins University to study for a Ph.D. in political science. He spent nearly two decades as a teacher of government and history, mostly at Princeton, where he enjoyed a reputation for brilliance. In 1902 he became president of that venerable institution. By that time he was widely known because of his advanced studies on American government as well as his more popular works, like his biography of George Washington. His transition to practical politics in 1910 was a successful one and did indeed lead to the White House.

As president, Wilson instituted several significant domestic reforms and led the country through World War I. Through all of this his great ambition was to construct a system of international cooperation that would forever make a great armed struggle like World War I unnecessary. Wilson hoped that his creation, the League of Nations, would insure this result, but opposition in the United States Senate prevented the participation of his own country in that international body. Wilson suffered a serious stroke in 1919, which made the last years of his presidency extremely difficult. He died in Washington on February 3, 1924.

Wilson's vision for America had a distinctly religious character, just as his ideal for religion always manifested a political quality. A man of great personal integrity, Wilson was also a man of genuine piety. He was a lifelong Christian who never questioned the principles he learned from his father. But his was a civil piety. He believed that spirituality had public effects, and that public policy had spiritual consequences. In Wilson we see some of the sharp edges of Puritan religion rubbed smooth. Yet he retained a full measure of the Puritan belief that faith was as important for life in the world as it was for the private life of the individual.

Wilson, who never abandoned his practice of reading the Scriptures regularly even as he moved further and further up the political ladder, was well qualified to deliver the following speech on the Bible.

An Address on the Bible

The thought that entered my mind first as I came into this great room this evening framed itself in a question—Why should this great body of people have come together upon this solemn night? There is nothing here to be seen. There is nothing delectable here to be heard. Why should you run together in a great host when all that is to be spoken of is the history of a familiar book?

But as I have sat and looked upon this great body of people I have thought of the very suitable circumstance that here upon the platform sat a little group of ministers of the gospel lost in this great throng.

I say the "suitable circumstance," for I come here to-night to speak of the Bible as the book of the people, not the book of the minister of the gospel, not the special book of the priest from which to set forth some occult, unknown doctrine withheld from the common understanding of men, but a great book of revelation—the people's book of revelation. For it seems to me that the Bible has revealed the people to themselves. I wonder how many persons in this great audience realize the significance for English-speaking peoples of the translation of the Bible into the English tongue. Up to the time of the translation of the Bible into English, it was a book for long ages withheld from the perusal of the peoples of other languages and of other tongues, and not a little of the history of liberty lies in the circumstance that the moving

Source: The Trenton *True American*, May 17, 1911; a modern critical edition is found in *The Papers of Woodrow Wilson*, vol. 23: *1911-1912*, ed. Arthur S. Link (Princeton: Princeton University Press, 1977), pp. 12-20.

sentences of this book were made familiar to the ears and the understanding of those peoples who have led mankind in exhibiting the forms of government and the impulses of reform which have made for freedom and for self-government among mankind.

For this is a book which reveals men unto themselves, not as creatures in bondage, not as men under human authority, not as those bidden to take counsel and command of any human source. It reveals every man to himself as a distinct moral agent, responsible not to men, not even to those men whom he has put over him in authority, but responsible through his own conscience to his Lord and Maker. Whenever a man sees this vision he stands up a free man, whatever may be the government under which he lives, if he sees beyond the circumstances of his own life.

I heard a very eloquent sermon to-day from an honored gentleman who is with us to-night [Rev. Dr. Robert Francis Coyle, pastor of the Central Presbyterian Church of Denver]. He was speaking upon the effect of a knowledge of the future life upon our conduct in this life. And it seemed to me as I listened to him I saw the flames of those fires rekindled at which the martyrs died—died forgetful of their pain, with praise and thanksgiving upon their lips, that they had the opportunity to render their testimony that this was not the life for which they had lived, but that there was a house builded in the heavens not built of men but built of God, to the vision of which they had lifted their eyes as they passed through the world, which gave them courage to fear no man but to serve God. And I thought that all the records of heroism of the great things that had illustrated human life were summed up in the power of men to see that vision.

Our present life, ladies and gentlemen, is a very imperfect and disappointing thing. We do not judge our own conduct in the privacy of our own closets by the standard of expediency by which we are daily and hourly governed. We know that there is a standard set for us in the heavens, a standard revealed to us in this book which is the fixed and eternal standard by which we judge ourselves, and as we read this book it seems to us that the pages of our own hearts are laid open before us for our own perusal. This is the people's book of revelation, revelation of themselves not alone, but revelation of life and of peace. You know that human life is a constant struggle. For a man who has lost the sense of struggle, life has ceased.

I believe that my confidence in the judgment of the people in matters political is based upon my knowledge that the men who are struggling are the men who know; that the men who are in the midst of the great effort to keep themselves steady in the pressure and rush of life are the men who know the significance of the pressure and the rush of life, and that they, the men on the make, are the men to whom to go for your judgments of what life is and what its problems are. And in this book there is peace simply because we read here the object of the struggle. No man is satisfied with himself as the object of the struggle.

There is a very interesting phrase that constantly comes to our lips which we perhaps do not often enough interpret in its true meaning. We see many a young man start out in life with apparently only this object in view—to make name and fame and power for himself, and there comes a time of maturity and reflection when we say of him, "He has come to himself." When may I say that I have come to myself? Only when I have come to recognize my true relations with the rest of the world. We speak of a man losing himself in a desert. If you reflect a moment you will see that is the only thing he has not lost. He himself is there. What he means when he says that he has lost himself is that he has lost all the rest of the world. He has nothing to steer by. He does not know where any beaten path and highway is. If he could establish his relationship with anything else in the world he would have found himself. Let it serve as a picture.

A man has found himself when he has found his relation to the rest of the universe, and here is the book in which those relations are set forth. And so when you see a man going along the highways of life with his gaze lifted above the road, lifted to the sloping ways in front of him, then be careful of that man and get out of his way. He knows the kingdom for which he is bound. He has seen the revelation of himself and of his relations to mankind. He has seen the revelations of his relation to God and his Maker and therefore he has seen his responsibility in the world. This is the revelation of life and of peace. I do not know that peace lies in constant accommodation. I was once asked if I would take part in a great peace conference, and I said, "Yes, if I may speak in favor of war"—not the war which we seek to avoid, not the senseless and useless and passionate shedding of human blood, but the only war that brings peace, the war with human passions and the war with human wrong—the war which is that untiring and unending process of reform from which no man can refrain and get peace.

No man can sit down and withhold his hands from the warfare against wrong and get peace out of his acquiescence. The most solid and satisfying peace is that which comes from this constant spiritual warfare, and there are times in the history of nations when they must take up the crude instruments of bloodshed in order to vindicate spiritual conceptions. For liberty is a spiritual conception, and when men take up arms to set other men free, there is something sacred and holy in the warfare. I will not cry "Peace" so long as there is sin and wrong in the world. And this great book does not teach any doctrine of peace so long as there is sin to be combated and overcome in one's own heart and in the great moving force of human society.

And so it seems to me that we must look upon the Bible as the great charter of the human soul—as the "Magna Charta" of the human soul. You know the interesting curcumstances which gave rise to the Magna Charta. You know the moving scene that was enacted upon the heath at Runnymede. You know how the barons of England, representing the people of England—for they consciously represented the people of England—met upon that historic spot and parleyed with John, the king. They said: "We will come to terms with you here." They said: "There are certain inalienable rights of English-speaking men which you must observe. They are not given by you, they cannot be taken away by you. Sign your name here to this parchment upon which these rights are written and we are your subjects. Refuse to put your name to this document and we are sworn enemies. Here are our swords to prove it."

The franchise of human liberty made the basis of a bargain with a king! There are kings upon the pages of Scripture, but do you think of any king in Scripture as anything else than a mere man? There was the great king David, of a line blessed because [it was] the line from which should spring our Lord and Savior, a man marked in the history of mankind as the chosen instrument of God to do justice and exalt righteousness in the people.

But what does this Bible do for David? Does it utter eulogies upon him? Does it conceal his faults and magnify his virtues? Does it set him up as a great statesman would be set up in a modern biography? No, the book in which his annals are written strips the mask from David, strips every shred of counterfeit and concealment from him and shows him as, indeed, an instrument of God, but a sinful and selfish man, and the verdict of the Bible is that David, like other men, was one day to stand naked before the judgment seat of God and be judged not as a king, but as a man. Isn't this the book of the people? Is there any man in this Holy Scripture who is exempted from the common standard and judgment? How these pages teem with the masses of mankind! Are these the annals of the great? These are the annals of the people—of the common run of men.

The New Testament is the history of the life and the testimony of common men who rallied to the fellowship of Jesus Christ and who by their faith and preaching remade a world that was under the thrall of the Roman army. This is the history of the triumph of the human spirit, in the persons of humble men. And how many sorts of men march across the pages, how infinite is the variety of human circumstance and of human dealings and of human heroism and love! Is this a picture of extraordinary things? This is a picture of the common life of mankind. It is a mirror held up for men's hearts, and it is in this mirror that we marvel to see ourselves portrayed.

How like to the Scripture is all great literature! What is it that entrances us when we read or witness a play of Shakespeare? It is the consciousness that this man, this all-observing mind, saw men of every cast and kind as they were in their habits as they lived. And as passage succeeds passage we seem to see the characters of ourselves and our friends portrayed by this ancient writer, and a play of Shakespeare is just as modern to-day as upon the day it was penned and first enacted. And the Bible is without age or date or time. It is a picture of the human heart displayed for all ages and for all sorts and conditions of men. Moreover, the Bible does what is so invaluable in human life—it classifies moral values. It apprises us that men are not judged according to their wits, but according to their characters, that the test of every man's reputation is his truthfulness, his squaring his conduct with the standards that he knew to be the standards of purity and rectitude.

How many a man we appraise, ladies and gentlemen, as great to-day, whom we do not admire as noble! A man may have great power and small character. And the sweet praise of mankind lies not in their admiration of the smartness with which the thing was accomplished, but in that lingering love which apprises men that one of their fellows has gone out of life to his own reckoning, where he is sure of the blessed verdict, "Well done, good and faithful servant."

Did you ever look about you in any great city, in any great capital, at the statues which have been erected in it? To whom are these statues erected? Are they erected to the men who have piled fortunes about them? I do not know of any such statue anywhere unless after he had accumulated his fortune the man bestowed it in beneficence upon his fellowmen and alongside of him will stand a statue of another meaning, for it is easy to give money away. I heard a friend of mine say that the standard of generosity was not the amount you gave away, but the amount you had left. It is easy to give away of your abundance, but look at the next statue, the next statue and the next in the marketplace of great cities and whom will you see? You will see here a soldier who gave his life to serve, not his own ends, but the interests and the purposes of his country.

I would be the last, ladies and gentlemen, to disparage any of the ordinary occupations of life, but I want to ask you this question: Did you ever see anybody who had lost a son hang up his yardstick over the mantel-piece? Have you not seen many families who had lost their sons hang up their muskets and their swords over the mantel-piece? What is the difference between the yardstick and the musket? There is nothing but perfect honor in the use of the yardstick, but the yardstick was used for the man's own interest, for his own self-support. It was used merely to fulfil the necessary exigencies of life, whereas the musket was used to serve no possible purpose of his own. He took every risk without any possibility of profit. The musket is the symbol of self-sacrifice and the yardstick is not. A man will instinctively elevate the one as the symbol of honor and never dream of using the other as a symbol of distinction.

Doesn't that cut pretty deep, and don't you know why the soldier has his monument as against the civilian? The civilian may have served his State—he also—and here and there you may see a statesman's statue, but the civilian has generally served his country—has often served his country, at any rate— with some idea of promoting his own interests, whereas the soldier has everything to lose and nothing but the gratitude of his fellowmen to win.

Let every man pray that he may in some true sense be a soldier of fortune, that he may have the good fortune to spend his energies and his life in the service of his fellowmen in order that he may die to be recorded upon the rolls of those who have not thought of themselves but have thought of those whom they served. Isn't this the lesson of our Lord and Savior Jesus Christ? Am I not reminding you of these common judgments of our life, simply expounding to you this book of revelation, this book which reveals the common man to himself, which strips life of its disguises and its pretences and elevates those standards by which alone true greatness and true strength and true valor are assessed?

Do you wonder, therefore, that when I was asked what my theme this evening would be I said it would be "The Bible *and* Progress"? We do not judge progress by material standards. America is not ahead of the other nations of the world because she is rich. Nothing makes America great except her thoughts, except her ideals, except her acceptance of those standards of judgment which are written large upon these pages of revelation. America has all along claimed the distinction of setting this example to the civilized world—that men were to think of one another, that governments were to be set up for the service of the people, that men were to be judged by these moral standards which pay no regard to rank or birth or conditions, but which assess every man according to his single and individual value. That is the meaning of this charter of the human soul. This is the standard by which men and nations have more and more come to be judged. And so, reform has consisted in nothing more nor less than this—in trying to conform actual conditions, in trying to square laws with the right judgments of human conduct and human liberty.

That is the reason that the Bible has stood at the back of progress. That is the reason that reform has come, not from the top but from the bottom. If you are ever tempted to let a government reform itself, I ask you to look back in the pages of history and find me a government that reformed itself. If you are ever tempted to let a party attempt to reform itself I ask you to find a party that ever reformed itself.

A tree is nourished by its bloom and by its fruit. It is nourished by its roots, which are down deep in the common and hidden soil, and every process of purification and rectification comes from the bottom—not from the top. It comes from the masses of struggling human beings. It comes from the instinctive efforts of millions of human hearts trying to beat their way up into the light and into the hope of the future.

Parties are reformed and governments are corrected by the impulses coming out of the hearts of those who never exercised authority and never organized parties. Those are the sources of strength, and I pray God that these sources may never cease to be spiritualized by the immortal subjections of these words of inspiration of the Bible.

If any statesman sunk in the practices which debase a nation will but read this single book he will go to his prayers abashed. Do you not realize, ladies and gentlemen, that there is a whole literature in the Bible? It is not one book, but a score of books. Do you realize what literature is? I am sometimes sorry to see the great classics of our English literature used in the schools as textbooks, because I am afraid that little children may gain the impression that these are formal lessons to be learned. There is no great book in any language, ladies and gentlemen, that is not the spontaneous outpouring of some great mind or the cry of some great heart. And the reason that poetry moves us more than prose does is that it is the rhythmic and passionate voice of some great spirit that has seen more than his fellowmen can see.

I have found more true politics in the poets of the English-speaking race than I have ever found in all the formal treatises on political science. There is more of the spirit of our own institutions in a few lines of Tennyson than in all the text-books on governments put together:

> "A nation still, the rulers and the ruled,
> Some sense of duty, something of a faith,
> Some reverence for the laws ourselves have made,
> Some patient force to change them when we will,
> Some civic manhood firm against the crowd."

Can you find summed up the manly self-helping spirit of Saxon liberty anywhere better than in those few lines? Men afraid of nobody, afraid of nothing but their own passions, on guard against being caught unaware by their own sudden impulses and so getting their grapple upon life in firm-set institutions, some reverence for the laws they themselves have made, some patience, not passionate force, to change them when they will, some civic manhood firm against the crowd. Literature, ladies and gentlemen, is a revelation of the human spirit, and within the covers of this one book is a whole lot of literature, prose and poetry, history and rhapsody, the sober narration and the ecstasy of human excitement—things that ring in one's ears like songs never to be forgotten. And so I say, let us never forget that these deep sources, these wells of inspiration, must always be our sources of refreshment and of renewal. Then no man can put unjust power upon us. We shall live in that chartered liberty in which a man sees the things unseen, in which he knows that he is bound for a country in which there are no questions mooted any longer of right or wrong.

Can you imagine a man who did not believe these words, who did not believe in the future life, standing up and doing what has been the heart and center of liberty always—standing up before the king himself and saying, "Sir, you have sinned and done wrong in the sight of God and I am his messenger of judgment to pronounce upon you the condemnation of Almighty God. You may silence me, you may send me to my reckoning with my Maker, but you cannot silence or reverse the judgment." That is what a man feels whose faith is rooted in the Bible. And the man whose faith is rooted in the Bible knows that reform can not be stayed, that the finger of God that moves upon the face of the nations is against every man that plots the nation's downfall or the people's deceit; that these men are simply groping and staggering in their ignorance to a fearful day of judgment and that whether one generation witnesses it or not, the glad day of revelation and of freedom will come in which men will sing by the host of the coming of the Lord in His glory, and all of those will be forgotten, those little, scheming, contemptible creatures that forgot the image of God and tried to frame men according to the image of the Evil One.

You may remember that allegorical narrative in the Old Testament of those who searched through one cavern after another, cutting the holes in the walls and going into the secret places where all sorts of noisome things were worshipped. Men do not dare to let the sun shine in upon such things and upon such occupations and worships. And so I say there will be no halt to the great movement of the armies of reform until men forget their God, until they forget this charter of their liberty. Let no man suppose that progress can be divorced from religion, or that there is any other platform for the ministers of reform than the platform written in the utterances of our Lord and Savior.

America was born a Christian nation. America was born to exemplify that devotion to the elements of righteousness which are derived from the revelations of the Holy Scripture.

Ladies and gentlemen, I have a very simple thing to ask of you. I ask of every man and woman in this audience that from this night on they will realize that part of the destiny of America lies in their daily perusal of this great book of revelations—that if they would see America free and pure they will make their own spirits free and pure by this baptism of the Holy Scripture.

WALTER RAUSCHENBUSCH (1861-1918)

Walter Rauschenbusch came to be known as "the father of the Social Gospel" because of his conviction that the Christian faith needed to speak to the specific material crises of the modern world. Rauschenbusch was led to this belief by his experience as pastor of the Second German Baptist Church in New York's Lower East Side from 1886 to 1897. Rauschenbusch had been born in upstate New York, where his father was a professor in the German Department of the Rochester Baptist Theological Seminary. The younger Rauschenbusch was educated first in Rochester and then in his father's ancestral home, Germany. What Rauschenbusch found when he returned to the United States and came to New York's "Hell's Kitchen" as a twenty-five-year-old minister moved him profoundly. The sordid living conditions of the immigrants, labor exploitation by industrial giants, and governmental indifference to the suffering of the poor led him to rethink his religion. It also led him to look afresh at Scripture and to examine the views of social critics who were calling for wholesale reform of American economic and political life.

The result was Rauschenbusch's formulation of a Christian message for the modern industrialized world. In his first major book, *Christianity and the Social Crisis* (1907), he urged his contemporaries to hear again the social concerns of the Old Testament prophets and to follow the social communalism of the New Testament church. In later books he spelled out the need for believers to examine their social assumptions in the light of the Bible and of modern analyses of economic life. And he appealed for public policy based on principles of justice and mercy rather than on exploitation and self-gratification. Rauschenbusch called himself a Christian socialist, but he also took care to separate his positions from Marxist views on economics and the state.

As he worked to articulate programs for large-scale public reform, Rauschenbusch did not forsake his early grounding in Christian experience. Although he did modify some traditional Christian doctrines, he also continued to hold that humans were sinners who desperately needed the grace given in Christ. This conviction in turn led him to seek ways for encouraging a piety alive to both personal needs and social realities. One of the products of this search was the book *Prayers of the Social Awakening*, published in 1910.

According to Winthrop Hudson, a recent editor of Rauschenbusch's works, Rauschenbusch had come to feel that "traditional prayers were too individualistic, too general, [and] too archaic in language, and too infrequently voiced contemporary needs and aspirations." So he set about composing prayers more in tune with the needs of the twentieth century. The first of these were published in *American Magazine*. They generated so much interest that Rauschenbusch wrote more until he had the makings of a small book. These prayers are like many of the other selections in this volume. They offer a window into the spirituality of a particular time and a specific person, but they also may serve as a call to a deeper piety in our time and place.

From *Prayers of the Social Awakening*

PREFACE

The new social purpose, which has laid its masterful grasp on modern life and thought, is enlarging and transforming our whole conception of the meaning of Christianity. The Bible and all past history speak a new and living language. The life of men about us stands out with an open-air color and vividness which it never had in the dusky solemnity of the older theological views about humanity. All the older tasks of church life have taken on a new significance, and vastly larger tasks are emerging as from the mists of a new morning.

Many ideas that used to seem fundamental and satisfying seem strangely narrow and trivial in this greater world of God. Some of the old religious appeals have utterly lost their power over us. But there are others, unknown to our fathers, which kindle religious passions of wonderful intensity and purity. The wrongs and sufferings of the people and the vision of a righteous and brotherly social life awaken an almost painful compassion and longing, and these feelings are more essentially Christian than most of the fears and desires of religion in the past. Social Christianity is adding to the variety of religious experience, and is creating a new type of Christian man who bears a striking family likeness to Jesus of Galilee.

These new religious emotions ought to find conscious and social expression. But the church, which has brought down so rich an equipment from the past for the culture of individual religion, is poverty-stricken in face of this

---

Source: A generous selection from the 1910 edition as well as solid commentary on this important religious thinker may be found in *Walter Rauschenbusch: Selected Writings*, ed. Winthrop S. Hudson, Sources of American Spirituality Series, ed. John Farina (New York: Paulist Press, 1984).

new need. The ordinary church hymnal rarely contains more than two or three hymns in which the triumphant chords of the social hope are struck. Our liturgies and devotional manuals offer very little that is fit to enrich and purify the social thoughts and feelings.

Even men who have absorbed the social ideals are apt to move within the traditional round in public prayer. The language of prayer always clings to the antique for the sake of dignity, and plain reference to modern facts and contrivances jars the ear. So we are inclined to follow the broad avenues beaten by the feet of many generations when we approach God. We need to blaze new paths to God for the feet of modern men.

* * *

PRAYERS FOR THE DAILY ROUND

Morning Prayers

Oh God, we thank thee for the sweet refreshment of sleep and for the glory and vigor of the new day. As we set our faces once more toward our daily work, we pray thee for the strength sufficient for our tasks. May Christ's spirit of duty and service ennoble all we do. Uphold us by the consciousness that our work is useful work and a blessing to all. If there has been anything in our work harmful to others and dishonorable to ourselves, reveal it to our inner eye with such clearness that we shall hate it and put it away, though it be at a loss to ourselves. When we work with others, help us to regard them, not as servants to our will, but as brothers equal to us in human dignity, and equally worthy of their full reward. May there be nothing in this day's work of which we shall be ashamed when the sun has set, nor in the eventide of our life when our task is done and we go to our long home to meet thy face.

Once more a new day lies before us, our Father. As we go out among men to do our work, touching the hands and lives of our fellows, make us, we pray thee, friends of all the world. Save us from blighting the fresh flower of any heart by the flare of sudden anger or secret hate. May we not bruise the rightful self-respect of any by contempt or malice. Help us to cheer the suffering by our sympathy, to freshen the drooping by our hopefulness, and to strengthen in all the wholesome sense of worth and the joy of life. Save us from the deadly poison of class-pride. Grant that we may look all men in the face with the eyes of a brother. If any one needs us, make us ready to yield our help ungrudgingly, unless higher duties claim us, and may we rejoice that we have it in us to be helpful to our fellowmen.

O God, we beseech thee to save us this day from the distractions of vanity and the false lure of inordinate desires. Grant us the grace of a quiet and humble mind, and may we learn of Jesus to be meek and lowly of heart. May we not join the throng of those who seek after things that never satisfy and who draw others after them in the fever of covetousness. Save us from adding our influence to the drag of temptation. If the fierce tide of greed beats against the breakwaters of our soul, may we rest at peace in thy higher contentment. In the press of life may we pass from duty to duty in tranquillity of heart and spread thy quietness to all who come near.

O Thou great Companion of our souls, do thou go with us today and comfort us by the sense of thy presence in the hours of spiritual isolation. Give us a single eye for duty. Guide us by the voice within. May we take heed of all the judgments of men and gather patiently whatever truth they hold, but teach us still to test them by the words and the spirit of the one who alone is our Master. May we not be so wholly of one mind with the life that now is that the world can fully approve us, but may we speak the higher truth and live the purer righteousness which thou hast revealed to us. If men speak well of us, may we not be puffed up; if they slight us, may we not be cast down; remembering the words of our Master who bade us rejoice when men speak evil against us and tremble if all speak well, that so we may have evidence that we are still soldiers of God.

O God, we who are bound together in the tender ties of love pray thee for a day of unclouded love. May no passing irritation rob us of our joy in one another. Forgive us if we have often been keen to see the human failings, and slow to feel the preciousness of those who are still the dearest comfort of our life. May there be no sharp words that wound and scar, and no rift that may grow into estrangement. Suffer us not to grieve those whom thou hast sent to us as the sweet ministries of love. May our eyes not be so holden by selfishness that we know thine angels only when they spread their wings to return to thee.

O Lord, we lift our hearts to thee in the pure light of morning and pray that they be kept clean of evil passion by the power of forgiving love. If any slight or wrong still rankles in our souls, help us to pluck it out and to be healed of thee. Suffer us not to turn in anger on him who has wronged us, seeking his hurt, lest we increase the sorrows of the world and taint our own souls with the poisoned sweetness of revenge. Grant that by the insight of love we may understand our brother in his wrong, and if his soul is sick, to bear with him in pity and to save him in the gentle spirit of our Master. Make us determined to love even at cost to our pride, that so we may be soldiers of thy peace on earth.

Evening Prayers

O Lord, we praise thee for our sister the Night, who folds all the tired folk of the earth in her comfortable robe of darkness and gives them sleep. Release now the strained limbs of toil and smooth the brow of care. Grant us the refreshing draught of forgetfulness that we may rise in the morning with a smile on our face. Comfort and ease those who toss wakeful on a bed of pain, or whose aching nerves crave sleep and find it not. Save them from evil or despondent thoughts in the long darkness, and teach them so to lean on thy all-pervading life and love, that their souls may grow tranquil and their bodies, too, may rest. And now through thee we send Good Night to all our brothers and sisters near and far, and pray for peace upon all the earth.

Our Father, as we turn to the comfort of our rest, we remember those who must wake that we may sleep. Bless the guardians of peace who protect us against men of evil, the watchers who save us from the terrors of fire, and all the many who carry on through the hours of the night the restless commerce of men on sea and land. We thank thee for their faithfulness and sense of duty. We pray for thy pardon if our covetousness or luxury makes their nightly toil necessary. Grant that we may realize how dependent the safety of our loved ones and the comforts of our life are on these our brothers, that so we may think of them with love and gratitude and help to make their burden lighter.

Accept the work of this day, O Lord, as we lay it at thy feet. Thou knowest its imperfections, and we know. Of the brave purposes of the morning only a few have found their fulfillment. We bless thee that thou art no hard taskmaster, watching grimly the stint of work we bring, but the father and teacher of men who rejoices with us as we learn to work. We have naught to boast before thee, but we do not fear thy face. Thou knowest all things and thou art love. Accept every right intention however brokenly fulfilled, but grant that ere our life is done we may under thy tuition become true master workmen, who know the art of a just and valiant life.

Our Master, as this day closes and passes from our control, the sense of our shortcomings is quick within us and we seek thy pardon. But since we daily crave thy mercy on our weakness, help us now to show mercy to those who have this day grieved or angered us and to forgive them utterly. Suffer us not to cherish dark thoughts of resentment or revenge. So fill us with thy abounding love and peace that no ill-will may be left in our hearts as we turn to our rest. And if we remember that any brother justly hath aught against us through this day's work, fix in us this moment the firm resolve to make good the wrong and to win again the love of our brother. Suffer us not to darken thy world by lovelessness, but give us the power of the sons of God to bring in the reign of love among men.

Our Father, we thank thee for all the friendly folk who have come into our life this day, gladdening us by their human kindness, and we send them now our parting thoughts of love through thee. We bless thee that we are set amidst this rich brotherhood of kindred life with its mysterious power to quicken and uplift. Make us eager to pay the due price for what we get by putting forth our own life in wholesome good will and by bearing cheerily the troubles that go with all joys. Above all we thank thee for those who share our higher life, the comrades of our better self, in whose companionship we break the mystic bread of life and feel the glow of thy wonderful presence. Into thy keeping we commit our friends, and pray that we may never lose their love by losing thee.

O God, in whom is neither near nor far, through thee we yearn for those who belong to us and who are not here with us. We would fain be near them to shield them from harm and to touch them with the tenderness of love. We cast our cares for them on thee in this evening hour, and pray thee to do better for them than we could do. May no distance have power to wean their hearts from us and no sloth of ours cause us to lag behind the even pace of growth. In due time restore them to us and gladden our souls with their sweet sight. We remember too the loved ones into whose dear eyes we cannot look again. O God, in whom are both the living and the dead, thou art still their life and light as thou art ours. Wherever they be, lay thy hand tenderly upon them and grant that some day we may meet again and hear once more their broken words of love.

Grace Before Meat

Our Father, thou art the final source of all our comforts and to thee we render thanks for this food. But we also remember in gratitude the many men and women whose labor was necessary to produce it, and who gathered it from the land and afar from the sea for our sustenance. Grant that they too may enjoy the fruit of their labor without want, and may be bound up with us in a fellowship of thankful hearts.

O God, we thank thee for the abundance of our blessings, but we pray that our plenty may not involve want for others. Do thou satisfy the desire of every child of thine. Grant that the strength which we shall draw from this food may be put forth again for the common good, and that our life may return to humanity a full equivalent in useful work for the nourishment which we receive from the common store.

Our Father, we thank thee for the food of our body, and for the human love which is the food of our hearts. Bless our family circle, and make this meal a sacrament of love to all who are gathered at this table. But bless thou too that great family of humanity of which we are but a little part. Give to all thy children daily bread, and let our family not enjoy its comforts in selfish isolation.

O Lord, we pray for thy presence at this meal. Hallow all our joys, and if there is anything wanton or unholy in them, open our eyes that we may see. If we have ever gained our bread by injustice, or eaten it in heartlessness, cleanse our life and give us a spirit of humility and love, that we may be worthy to sit at the common table of humanity in the great house of our Father.

For a Family Reunion

O Lord, our hearts are full of gratitude and praise, for after the long days of separation thou has brought us together again to look into the dear faces and read their love as of old. As the happy memories of the years when we were young together rise up to cheer us, may we feel anew how closely our lives were wrought into one another in their early making, and what a treasure we have had in our home. Whatever new friendships we may form, grant that the old loves may abide to the end and grow ever sweeter with the ripening years.

For a Guest

Our Father, we rejoice in the guest who sits at meat with us, for our food is the more welcome because he shares it, and our home the dearer because it shelters him. Grant that in the happy exchange of thought and affection we may realize anew that all our gladness comes from the simple fellowship of our human kind, and that we are rich as long as we are loved.

Before a Parting

O God, as we break bread once more before we part, we turn to thee with the burden of our desires. Go with him who leaves us and hold him safe. May he feel that we shall not forget him and that his place can never be filled till he returns. Make this meal a sacrament of human love to us, and may our hearts divine the thoughts too tender to be spoken.

In Time of Trouble

O Lord, thou knowest that we are sore stricken and heavy of heart. We beseech thee to uphold us by thy comfort. Thou wert the God of our fathers, and in all these years thine arm has never failed us, for our strength has ever been as our days. May this food come to us as an assurance of thy love and care and a promise of thy sustenance and relief.

Morituri te salutant

O Thou Eternal One, we who are doomed to die lift up our souls to thee for strength, for Death has passed us in the throng of men and touched us, and we know that at some turn of our pathway he stands waiting to take us by the hand and lead us—we know not whither. We praise thee that to us he is no more an enemy but thy great angel and our friend, who alone can open for some of us the prison-house of pain and misery and set our feet in the roomy spaces of a larger life. Yet we are but children, afraid of the dark and the unknown, and we dread the parting from the life that is so sweet and from the loved ones who are so dear.

Grant us of thy mercy a valiant heart, that we may tread the road with head uplifted and a smiling face. May we do our work to the last with a wholesome joy, and love our loves with an added tenderness because the days of love are short. On thee we cast the heaviest burden that numbs our soul, the gnawing fear for those we love, whom we must leave unsheltered in a selfish world. We trust in thee, for through all our years thou hast been our stay. O thou Father of the fatherless, put thy arm about our little ones! And ere we go, we pray that the days may come when the dying may die unafraid, because men have ceased to prey on the weak, and the great family of the nation enfolds all with its strength and care.

We thank thee that we have tasted the rich life of humanity. We bless thee for every hour of life, for all our share in the joys and strivings of our brothers, for the wisdom gained which will be part of us forever. If soon we must go, yet through thee we have lived and our life flows on in the race. By thy grace we too have helped to shape the future and bring in the better day.

If our spirit droops in loneliness, uphold us by thy companionship. When all the voices of love grow faint and drift away, thy everlasting arms will still be there. Thou art the father of our spirits; from thee we have come; to thee we go. We rejoice that in the hours of our purer vision, when the pulse-throb of thine eternity is strong within us, we know that no pang of mortality can reach our unconquerable soul, and that for those who abide in thee death is but the gateway to life eternal. Into thy hands we commend our spirit.

* * *

THE AUTHOR'S PRAYER

O thou who are the light of my soul, I thank thee for the incomparable joy of listening to thy voice within, and I know that no word of thine shall return void, however brokenly uttered. If aught in this book was said through lack of knowledge, or through weakness of faith in thee or of love for men, I pray thee to over-rule my sin and turn aside its force before it harm thy cause. Pardon the frailty of thy servant, and look upon him only as he sinks his life in Jesus, his Master and Saviour. Amen.

OLE RÖLVAAG (1876-1931)

Immigration and religion are tightly bound in the history of America. The succeeding waves of men and women on the move who have ventured into this land have often been people of faith. Sometimes the belief nurtured in the Old Country has flourished in the environment of the new land. At other times immigrants have forgotten religious precepts they learned in another country and with another tongue. But most often life in the New World has altered, extended, distorted, refined, or in some other way carried further the earlier faith. The God of our fathers does not die when we cross over the Atlantic or the Pacific, but neither does he look exactly the same.

Ole Rölvaag, who was born in 1876 on Norway's Dönna Island, just south of the Arctic Circle, and who came to the United States as a twenty-year-old, captured the tensions of immigrant religious experience as powerfully as any other twentieth-century writer. He was an educator who spent most of his life teaching Norwegian language and culture at St. Olaf College in Minnesota. Rölvaag steadfastly maintained that when immigrants retained the speech, the faith, and the culture of their homeland, they gained a proper sense of themselves even as they added to the richness of their new national home.

Rölvaag's greatest contribution to understanding the immigrant experience was his series of novels: *Giants in the Earth* (1927), *Peder Victorious* (1929), and *Their Fathers' God* (1931), which told the story of two generations of Norwegian settlers struggling to establish a new life on the vast Dakota prairies. Rölvaag wrote these books, as he did almost all of his published work, in Norwegian, and then worked closely with translators in preparing editions for an American audience.

Giants in the Earth: A Saga of the Prairie takes its title from Genesis 6:4 ("There were giants in the earth in those days; and also after that, when the sons of God came in unto the daughters of men, and they bare children to them, the same became mighty men which were of old, men of renown"). It is probably the most effective of Rölvaag's novels, and certainly one of the most revealing books ever written about the religious dimension of immigrant life. It tells the story of Per Hansa, a vigorous pioneer who moves fearlessly and energetically into his new life on the Dakota prairie. But it is also the story of Per Hansa's wife, Beret, for whom the move from familiar home, family, and religion is traumatic. Beret's inner turmoil, her deep longing for home, possesses a deeply religious significance, for she feels that somehow she has abandoned the God of her youth. The drama of the novel, at once morbid and exhilarating, turns on the relationship of Per Hansa and Beret, and that hinges in large measure on Beret's sense of destiny under God. Through their life together, Beret, Per Hansa, and the rest of the tiny band of immigrants huddled in huts on the vast Dakota plain find unexpected vitality in the words, the rites, the values, and the spirit of an old-world faith.

The following, from a section entitled "The Heart That Dared Not Let in the Sun," is the last part of the novel's First Book. (It was published in 1927 by Harper.) Rölvaag regularly employed ellipsis points in his writing; the two sections deleted by the editors are indicated by asterisks.

From "The Heart That Dared Not Let in the Sun"

The days wore on . . . sunny days . . . bleak, gloomy days, with cold that congealed all life.

There was one who heeded not the light of the day, whether it might be grey or golden. Beret stared at the earthen floor of the hut and saw only night round about her.

Yes . . . she faced only darkness. She tried hard, but she could not let in the sun.

Ever since she had come out here a grim conviction had been taking stronger and stronger hold on her.

This was her retribution!

Now had fallen the punishment which the Lord God had meted out to her; at last His visitation had found her out and she must drink the cup of His wrath. Far away she had fled, from the rising of the sun to the going down thereof . . . so it had seemed to her . . . but the arm of His might had reached farther still. No, she could not escape—this was her retribution!

The stillness out here had given her full opportunity for reflection; all the fall she had done nothing but brood and remember. . . . Alas! she had much to remember!

She had accepted the hand of Per Hansa because she must—although no law had compelled her; she and he were the only people who had willed it thus. She had been gotten with child by him out of wedlock; nevertheless, no one had compelled her to marry him—neither father, nor mother, nor anyone in authority. It had been wholly her own doing. Her parents, in fact, had set themselves against the marriage with all their might, even after the child, Ole, had come.

. . . It had mattered nothing at all what they had said, nor what anyone else had said; for her there had been no other person in the world but Per Hansa! Whenever she had been with him she had forgotten the admonitions and prayers of her father and mother. . . . He had been life itself to her; without him there had been nothing. . . . Therefore she had given herself to him, although she had known it was a sin—had continued to give herself freely, in a spirit of abandoned joy.

Now she found plenty of time to remember how her parents had begged and threatened her to break with him; she recalled all that they had said, turning it over in her mind and examining it minutely. . . . Per Hansa was a shiftless fellow, they had told her; he drank; he fought; he was wild and reckless; he got himself tangled up in all sorts of brawls; no honourable woman could be happy with such a man. He probably had affairs with other women, too, whenever he had a chance. . . . All the other accusations she knew to be true; but not the last—no, not the last! She alone among women held his heart. The certainty of this fact had been the very sweetness of life to her. . . . What did she care for the rest of it! All was as nothing compared with this great certainty. . . . Ah, no—she knew it well enough: for him she was the only princess!

But now she understood clearly all that her parents had done to end it between them, and all the sacrifices they had been willing to make; she had not realized it at the time. . . . Oh, those kind-hearted parents on whom she had turned her back in order that she might cleave to him: how they must have suffered! The life which she and he had begotten in common guilt they had offered to take as their own, give it their name and their inheritance, and bring it up as their very child. They had freely offered to use their hard-earned savings to send her away from the scene of her shame . . . *so* precious had she been to them! But she had only said no, and no, and *no,* to all their offers of sacrifice and love! . . . Had there ever been a transgression so grievous as hers!

. . . Yet how could she ever have broken with him? Where Per Hansa was, there dwelt high summer and there it bloomed for her. How can a human forsake his very life? . . . Whenever she heard of one of his desperately reckless cruises through rough and stormy seas, on which he had played with the lives of his comrades as well as his own, her cheeks would glow and her heart would flame. This was the man her heart had chosen—this was he, and he alone! a voice would sing within her. Or when she sat among the heather on the mountain side in the fair summer night, and he came to her and laid his head in her lap—the tousled head that only she could lull to sleep—then

she felt that now she was crossing the very threshold of paradise! . . .
Though she had had a thousand lives, she would have thrown them all away
for one such moment—and would have been glad of the bargain! . . .
. . . Yes, she remembered all that had happened in those days; it was so
still out here . . . so easy to remember!

No one had ever told her, but she knew full well who it was that had
persuaded Hans Olsa to leave the land and the ancient farm that had been in
his family for generations, and go to America. There had been only one other
person in the world whom Per Hansa loved, and that was Hans Olsa. She
had been jealous of Hans Olsa because of this; it had seemed to her that he
took something that rightfully belonged to her. She had even felt the same
way toward Sörine, who was kindness itself; on this account she had not
been able to hold her friendship as fully as she needed to, either in Norway or
here. . . .

. . . But when Per Hansa had come home from Lofoten that spring and
announced in his reckless, masterful way, that he was off for America:
would Beret come now, or wait until later? . . . Well, there hadn't been a
"no" in her mouth then! There she had sat, with three children in a nice little
home which, after the manner of simple folk, they had managed to
build. . . . But she had risen up, taken the children with her, and left it all as if
nothing mattered but him!

. . . How her mother had wept at that time! . . . How her father had
grieved when they had left! Time after time he had come begging to Per
Hansa, offering him all that he had—boat and fishing outfit, house and
farm—if only he would settle down in Norway and not take their daughter
from them forever. . . . But Per Hansa had laughed it all aside! There had
been a power in his unflinching determination which had sent hot waves
through her. She must have led a double life at that time; she had been sad
with her parents but had rejoiced with Per Hansa. He had raged like a storm
through those days, wild and reckless—and sometimes ruthless, too. . . .
No!—he had cried—they would just make that little trip across the ocean!
America—that's the country where a poor devil can get ahead! Besides, it
was only a little way; if they didn't like it, they could drift back on the first
fair western breeze! . . . So they had sold off everything that they had won
with so much toil, had left it all like a pair of worn-out shoes—parents,
home, fatherland, and people. . . . And she had done it gladly, even re-
joicingly! . . . Was there ever a sin like hers? . . .

* * *

Beret struggled with many thoughts these days.

. . . Wasn't it remarkable how ingeniously Destiny had arranged it all?
For ten long years he had cast her about like a chip on the current, and then
had finally washed her ashore here. *Here,* far off in the great stillness, where

there was nothing to hide behind—here the punishment would fall! . . .
Could a better place have been found in which to lay her low?

. . . Life was drawing to a close. One fact stood before her constantly: she
would never rise again from the bed in which she was soon to lie down. . . .
This was the end. . . . Often, now, she found herself thinking of the churchyard at home. . . . It would have been so pleasant to lie down there. . . . The
churchyard was enclosed by a massive stone wall, broad and heavy; one
couldn't imagine anything more reliable than that wall. She had sat on it
often in the years when she was still her father's little girl. . . . In the midst of
the churchyard lay the church, securely protecting everything round about.
No fear had ever dwelt in that place; she could well remember how the boys
used to jump over the graves; it had been great fun, too—at times she had
joined the game. . . . Within that wall many of her dear ones slumbered: two
brothers whom she had never seen, and a little sister that she remembered
quite clearly, though she had died long, long ago; her grandparents on both
her father's and her mother's side, also rested here, and one of her great-
grandfathers. She knew where all these graves lay. Her whole family, generation after generation, rested there—many more than she had any knowledge
of. . . . Around the churchyard stood a row of venerable trees, looking
silently down on the peace and the stillness within. . . . They gave such good
shelter, those old trees!

. . . She could not imagine where he would bury her out here. . . . Now, in
the dead of winter—the ground frozen hard! . . . How would he go about
it? . . . If he would only dig deep down . . . the wolves gave such unearthly
howls at night! No matter what he thought of it, she would have to speak to
him about the grave. . . . Well, no need to mention it just now.

One day when Beret had to go out she stayed longer than usual. Before she
finally came back to the house she went to the spot where the woodpile had
stood, visited the curious little fort which they had built of chopped wood,
and then entered the stable. . . . It worried her to know where he would find
material for a coffin. She had looked everywhere outside, but had discovered
only a few bits of plank and the box in which he had mixed the lime. . . .
Hadn't she better remind him of this at once? Then perhaps he could go to
the Trönders, east on the Sioux River, and get some lumber from them. . . .
Never mind, she wouldn't do anything about it for a few days yet.

. . . If he could only spare her the big chest! . . . Beret fell to looking at it,
and grew easier in her mind. . . . That chest had belonged to her great-
grandfather, but it must have been in the family long before this day; on it
she could make out only the words "*Anno* 16—" . . . the rest was completely worn away. Along the edges and running twice around the middle
were heavy iron bands. . . . Beret would go about looking at the chest—
would lift the lid and gaze down inside. . . . Plenty of room in there, if they

would only put something under her head and back! She felt as if she could sleep safely in that bed. She would have to talk to Sörine about all these matters. . . . One day Beret began to empty the chest; she got Per Hansa to make a small cupboard out of the mortar box, and put all the things in there; but she took great care not to do this while he was around.

She realized now the great forethought he had shown last summer in building the house and stable under one roof. They undoubtedly had the warmest house in the neighbourhood; and then she enjoyed the company of the animals as she lay awake at night; it felt so cosy and secure to lie there and listen to them. . . . She could easily distinguish each animal by its particular manner of breathing and lying down. The oxen were always the last to finish munching; Rosie was the first to go to sleep; Injun's habits were entirely different from those of the others; he moved softly, almost without noise, as if engaged in some secret business. She never could hear him, except when the howl of a wolf sounded near by; then he would snort and stamp his feet. It was probably the wild blood in him that made him so different! . . . Beret had learned to love the pony.

When she was not listening to the animals she had other things to occupy her mind. . . . As a little girl, she had often been taken into bed by her grandmother. This grandmother had been a kindly woman, sunny and always happy, in spite of her great age; each night before going to sleep she would repeat to herself pious little verses from memory. Beret could not remember them all now; but she managed to patch them together little by little, inserting new lines of her own, and repeating them over and over to herself. This she would do for hours at a time, occasionally sitting up in bed to say the verses aloud:

> "Thy heavy wrath avert
> From me, a wretched sinner;
> Thy blissful mercy grant,
> Father of love eternal!
>
> "My sins are as many
> As dust in the rays of the sun,
> And as sands on the shore of the sea—
> If by Thee requited,
> I must sink benighted.
>
> "Look with pity,
> Tender Saviour,
> At my wretched state!
> Wounds of sin are burning;
> May Thy hands, in love returning,
> Heal my stinging stripes!

"Weighed by guilt I weary wander
In the desert here below;
When I measure
My transgressions,
Breaches of Thy holy law,
I must ponder
Oft, and wonder;
Canst Thou grace on me bestow?

"Gentle Saviour,
Cast my burden
Deep into the mercy-sea!
Blessed Jesus,
Mild Redeemer,
Thou Who gav'st Thy life for me!"

The day before Christmas Eve snow fell. It fell all that night and the following forenoon. . . . Still weather, and dry, powdery snow. . . . Murk without, and leaden dusk in the huts. People sat oppressed in the sombre gloom.

. . . Things were in a bad way over at Per Hansa's now; everyone knew it and feared what might befall both Beret and him. . . . No one could help; all that could be done was to bide the time; for soon a change must come!

"Listen, folks," said Tönseten, trying to comfort them as best he could. "Beret can't keep this up forever! I think you had better go over to her again, Kjersti!"

Both neighbour women were now taking turns at staying with her, each one a day at a time. They saw clearly that Per Hansa was more in need of help than Beret; there was no helping her now, while something, at least, could be done for him and the children. Christmas would soon be here, too, and the house ought to be made comfortable and cosy!

They all felt very sorry for Per Hansa. He walked about like a ragged stray dog; his eyes burned with a hunted look. Each day, the children were sent over to Hans Olsa's to stay for a while; if they remained longer than they had been told, he made no protest; at last they formed the habit of staying the whole day. He did not realize that it was bad for Beret to be without them so much; he tried to keep the talk going himself, but she had little to say; she answered in monosyllables and had grown peculiarly quiet and distant. In the shadow of a faint smile which she occasionally gave him there lay a melancholy deeper than the dusk of the Arctic Sea on a rainy, grey fall evening.

About noon of Christmas Eve the air suddenly cleared. An invisible fan was pushed in under the thick, heavy curtain that hung trembling between the earth and heaven—made a giant sweep, and revealed the open, blue sky overhead. The sun shone down with powerful beams, and started a slight trickling from the eaves. Toward evening, it built a golden fairy castle for itself out yonder, just beyond Indian Hill.

The children were at Hans Olsa's; And-Ongen wanted to stay outside and watch the sunset. Sofie had told her that to-day was Christmas Eve, and that on every Christmas Jesus came down from heaven. The child asked many questions. . . . Would he come driving? Couldn't they lend him the pony? . . . Sofie hardly thought so—he probably would be driving an angel-pony!

Store-Hans, who was listening to them, thought this very silly and just like girls. He knew better! . . . Toward evening he suddenly wanted to go home, and was almost beside himself when his godfather said that he couldn't: all the children were to stay with Sofie to-night. They had to hold him back by force. . . . This was *Christmas Eve.* . . . He understood very well that something was about to go wrong at home. Why had his mother looked so wan and worn of late, and his father acted so queer that one couldn't talk to him?

That afternoon Beret was in childbed. . . . The grim struggle marked Per Hansa for life; he had fought his way through many a hard fight, but they had all been as nothing compared with this. He had ridden the frail keel of a capsized boat on the Lofoten seas, had seen the huge, combing waves snatch away his comrades one by one, and had rejoiced in the thought that the end would soon come for him also; but things of that sort had been mere child's play. . . . *This* was the uttermost darkness. Here was neither beginning nor end—only an awful void in which he groped alone. . . .

Sörine and Kjersti had both arrived a long time since. When they had come he had put on his coat and gone outside; but he hadn't been able to tear himself many steps away from the house.

Now it was evening; he had wandered into the stable to milk Rosie, forgetting that she had gone dry long ago; he had tended to Injun and the oxen, without knowing what he was about. . . . He listened to Beret wailing in the other room, and his heart shrivelled; thus a weak human being could not continue to suffer, and yet live. . . . And this was his own Beret!

He stood in the door of the stable, completely undone. Just then Kjersti ran out to find him; he must come in at once; Beret was asking for him! . . . Kjersti was gone in a flash. . . . He entered the house, took off his outdoor clothes, and washed his hands. . . .

. . . Beret sat half dressed on the edge of the bed. He looked at her, and thought that he had never seen such terror on any face. . . . God in heaven—this was beyond human endurance!

She was fully rational, and asked the neighbour women to leave the room for a moment, as she had something to say to her husband. She spoke with great composure; they obeyed immediately. When the door closed behind them Beret rose and came over to him, her face distorted. She laid a hand on each of his shoulders, and looked deep into his eyes, then clasped her hands behind his neck and pulled him violently toward her. Putting his arms firmly around her, he lifted her up gently and carried her to the bed; there he laid her down. He started to pull the covers over her. . . . But she held on to him; his solicitous care she heeded not at all.

When he had freed himself, she spoke brokenly, between gasps:
. . . "To-night I am leaving you. . . . Yes, I must leave you. . . . I know this is the end! The Lord has found me out because of my sins. . . . It is written, 'To fall into the hands of the living God!' . . . Oh!—it is terrible! . . . I can't see how you will get along when you are left alone . . . though I have only been a burden to you lately. . . . You had better give And-Ongen to Kjersti . . . she wants a child so badly—she is a kind woman. . . . You must take the boys with you—and *go away from here!* . . . How lonesome it will be for me . . . to lie here all alone!"

Tears came to her eyes, but she did not weep; between moans she went on strongly and collectedly:

"But promise me one thing: put me away in the big chest! . . . I have emptied it and made it ready. . . . Promise to lay me away in the big chest, Per Hansa! . . . And you must be sure to dig the grave deep! . . . You haven't heard how terribly the wolves howl at night! . . . Promise to take plenty of time and dig deep down—do you hear!"

His wife's request cut Per Hansa's heart like sharp ice; he threw himself on his knees beside the bed and wiped the cold perspiration from her face with a shaking hand.

. . . "There now, blessed Beret-girl of mine!" . . . His words sounded far off—a note of frenzy in them. . . . "Can't you understand that this will soon be over? . . . To-morrow you'll be as chipper as a lark again!"

Her terror tore her only the worse. Without heeding his words, she spoke with great force out of the clearness of her vision:

"I shall die to-night. . . . Take the big chest! . . . At first I thought of asking you not to go away when spring came . . . and leave me here alone. . . . But that would be a sin! . . . I tell you, you *must go!* . . . Leave as soon as spring comes! Human beings cannot exist here! . . . They grow into beasts. . . ."

The throes were tearing her so violently now that she could say no more. But when she saw him rise she made a great effort and sat up in bed.

. . ·. "Oh!—don't leave me!—don't go away! . . . Can't you see how sorely I need you? . . . And now I shall die! . . . Love me—oh, do love me once more, Per Hansa!" . . . She leaned her body toward him. . . . "You must go back to Norway. . . . Take the children with you . . . let them grow up there.

Ask father and mother to forgive me! . . . Tell father that I am lying in the big chest! . . . Can't you stay with me to-night . . . stay with me and love me? . . . Oh!—*there they come for me!*"

Beret gave a long shriek that rent the night. Then she sobbed violently, praying that they should not take her away from Per Hansa. . . .

Per Hansa leaped to his feet, and found his voice.

"Satan—now you shall leave her alone!" he shouted, flinging the door open and calling loudly outside. Then he vanished into the darkness.

No one thought of seeking rest that night. All the evening, lights shone from the four huts; later they were extinguished in two of them; but in the house of Hans Olsa four men sat on, grieving over the way things were going at Per Hansa's. When they could bear the suspense no longer some one proposed going over to get news.

Tönseten offered to go first. . . . When he came back little sense could be gathered from what he said. He had not been allowed inside; the women were in a frenzy; the house was completely upset; Beret was wailing so loud that it was dreadful to hear. And Per Hansa himself was nowhere to be found. . . . "We must go and look for him, boys! . . . Haven't you got a Bible or something to read from, Hans Olsa? This is an awful thing!"

. . . There they sat, each occupied with his own thoughts—but all their thoughts were of the same trend. If Beret died to-night, it would go hard with Per Hansa—indeed it would. In that case he probably wouldn't stay out here very long. . . . But if he went away, the rest of them might as well pack up and go, too!

Sam ran over to inquire; then Henry; at last it was Hans Olsa's turn. He managed to get a couple of words with his wife, who said that Beret would hardly stand it. No one had seen Per Hansa.

"Can you imagine where the man can be keeping himself?" asked Tönseten, giving voice to the fear that oppressed them all. . . . "May the Lord preserve his wits, even if He chooses to take his wife away!" . . .

Per Hansa walked to and fro outside the hut all night long; when he heard some one coming he would run away into the darkness. He could not speak to a living soul to-night. As soon as the visitor had gone he would approach the hut again, circle around it, stop, and listen. Tears were streaming down his face, though he was not aware of it. . . . Every shriek that pierced the walls of the hut drove him off as if a whip had struck him; but as soon as it had died out, something would draw him back again. At intervals he went to the door and held it ajar. . . . What did Per Hansa care for custom and decency, now that his Beret lay struggling with death! . . . Each time Sörine came to the door; each time she shook her head sadly, and told him there was no change yet; it was doubtful if Beret would be able to pull through; no person could endure this much longer; God have mercy on all of them!

That was all the comfort Sörine could give him. . . . Then he would rush off into the darkness again, to continue his endless pacing; when daylight came they found a hard path tramped into the snow around the hut.

The night was well-nigh spent when the wails in there began to weaken—then died out completely, and did not come again. Per Hansa crept up to the door, laid his ear close to it, and listened. . . . So now the end had come! His breath seemed to leave him in a great sob. The whole prairie began to whirl around with him; he staggered forward a few steps and threw himself face downward on the snow.

. . . But then suddenly things didn't seem so bad to him . . . really not so bad. . . . He saw a rope . . . a rope. . . . It was a good, strong rope that would hold any thing. . . . It hung just inside the barn door—and the crossbeam ran just *there!* . . . No trick at all to find these things. Per Hansa felt almost happy at the thought; that piece of rope was good and strong—and the crossbeam ran just *there!*

. . . A door opened somewhere; a gleam of light flashed across the snow, and vanished. Some one came out of the hut quietly—then stopped, as if searching.

"Per Hansa!" a low voice called. . . . "Per Hansa, where are you?"

. . . He rose and staggered toward Kjersti like a drunken man.

"You must come in at once!" she whispered, and hurried in before him.

The light was dim in there; nevertheless it blinded him so strongly that he could not see a thing. He stood a moment leaning against the door until his eyes had grown accustomed to it. . . . A snug, cosy warmth enveloped him; it carried with it an odd, pleasant odour. The light, the warmth, and the pleasant smell overcame him like sweet sleep that holds a person who has been aroused, but who does not care to awaken just yet.

"How is it?" he heard a man's voice ask. Then he came back to his senses. . . . Was that he himself speaking? . . .

"You'll have to ask Sörrina," Kjersti answered.

Sörine was tending something on the bed; not until now did he discover her—and wake up completely. . . . What was this? . . . the expression on her face? Wasn't it beaming with motherly goodness and kindliness?

"Yes, here's your little fellow! I have done all I know how. Come and look at him. . . . It's the greatest miracle I ever saw, Per Hansa, that you didn't lose your wife tonight, and the child too! . . . I pray the Lord I never have to suffer so!"

"Is there any hope?" was all Per Hansa could gasp—and then he clenched his teeth.

"It looks so, now—but you had better christen him at once. . . . We had to handle him roughly, let me tell you."

'*Christen him?*" Per Hansa repeated, unable to comprehend the words.

"Why, yes, of course. I wouldn't wait, if he were mine."

Per Hansa heard no more—for now Beret turned her head and a wave of
such warm joy welled up in him that all the ice melted. He found himself
crying softly, sobbing like a child. . . . He approached the bed on tiptoe, bent
over it, and gazed down into the weary, pale face. It lay there so white and
still; her hair, braided in two thick plaits, flowed over the pillow. All the
dread, all the tormenting fear that had so long disfigured her features, had
vanished completely. . . . She turned her head a little, barely opened her
eyes, and said, wearily:

"Oh, leave me in peace, Per Hansa. . . . Now I was sleeping so well."
. . . The eyelids immediately closed.

Per Hansa stood for a long time looking at his wife, hardly daring to
believe what he saw. She slept peacefully; a small bundle lay beside her, from
which peeped out a tiny, red, wrinkled face. . . . As he continued to gaze at
her he sensed clearly that this moment was making him a better man!

At last he gathered his wits sufficiently to turn to Sörine and ask:

"Tell me, what sort of a fellow is this you have brought me—a boy or a
girl?"

"Heavens! Per Hansa, how silly you talk!" . . . Kjersti and Sörine both
had to laugh as they looked at Per Hansa; such a foolish, simple expression
they had never seen on the face of a living man! . . . But Sörine immediately
grew serious once more, and said that this was no time for joking; the way
they had tugged and pulled at him during the night, you couldn't tell what
might happen; Per Hansa must get the child christened right away; if he put
it off, she refused to be responsible.

A puzzled expression came over the grinning face.

"You'd better do that christening yourself, Sörrina!"

—No!—she shook her head emphatically. That wasn't a woman's job—
he must understand! . . . "And you ought to have it done with proper de-
corum, and thank the Lord for doing so well by you!"

Without another word Per Hansa found his cap and went to the door; but
there he paused a moment to say:

"I know only one person around here who is worthy to perform such an
act; since you are unwilling, I must go and get him. . . . In the meanwhile,
you make ready what we will need; the hymn book you'll find on the shelf
over by the window. . . . I won't be long!"

                                    *   *   *

"Peace be upon this house, and a merry Christmas, folks!" he greeted them
as he entered Hans Olsa's door. . . . The room was cold; the Solum boys lay
in one bed, fully dressed; both were so sound asleep that they did not wake
up at his coming. His own children and Sofie lay in the other bed, Ole by

himself down at the foot, the other three on the pillow; Store-Hans held
And-Ongen close, as if trying to protect her. Hans Olsa and Tönseten had
moved their chairs up to the stove, and sat hunched over on either side;
Tönseten was nodding, the other was wide awake; both men jumped up
when Per Hansa came in, and stood staring at him.

Per Hansa had to laugh outright at them; they were looking at him as if
they had seen a ghost. But to the two men his laugh sounded pleasanter than
anything they had heard in many a year.

"How are things coming?" asked Tönseten, excitedly, working his
shoulders.

"Oh, it might have been worse!"

Hans Olsa grasped his hand: "Will she pull through?"

"It looks that way."

Then Tönseten suddenly seemed to realize that it was cold in the room; he
began to walk around, beating goose with his arms. . . . "I'm ready to bet
both my horses that it's a boy! I can see it in your face!" he exclaimed, still
beating.

"All signs point that way, Syvert! But he's in pretty poor condition, Sörrina tells me. . . . Now look here, Hans Olsa: it's up to you to come over and
christen the boy for me!"

Hans Olsa looked terror-stricken at his neighbour. . . . "You must be
crazy, Per Hansa!"

"Nothing of the kind, Hans Olsa. . . . You just get yourself ready. . . . It's
all written down in the hymn book—what to say, and how to go about it."

"No, no—I couldn't think of such a thing!" protested Hans Olsa, all of a
tremble with the feeling of awe that had suddenly taken possession of
him. . . . "A sinner like me!" . . .

Then Per Hansa made a remark that Tönseten thought was extremely well
put:

"How you stand with the Lord I don't know. But this I do know: that a
better man either on land or sea, He will have to look a long way to find. . . .
And it seems to me that He has got to take that, too, into His reckoning!"

But Hans Olsa only stood there in terror. . . . "You'd better ask Syvert to
do it!"

Then Tönseten grew alarmed:

"Don't stand there talking like a fool! . . . We all know that if one of us
two is to tackle this job, it must be you, Hans Olsa. . . . There is nothing for
you to do but go at once; this business won't stand any dilly-dallying, let me
tell you!"

Hans Olsa gazed straight ahead; his helplessness grew so great that he was
funny to look at; but no one thought of laughing, just the same . . . "If it
won't be blasphemy!" . . . He finally struggled into his big coat and put on

his mittens. Then he turned to Tönseten. . . . "The book says: 'In an extreme emergency a layman may perform this act'—isn't that so?"

"Yes, yes—just so! . . . Whatever else you'll need, is written there too!"

Through the frosty morning the two men walked silently across the prairie, Per Hansa in the lead. When they had covered half the distance he stopped short and said to his neighbour:

"If it had been a girl, you see, she should have been named Beret—I decided that a long while ago. . . . But seeing that it's a boy, we'll have to name him Per; you must say Peder, of course! . . . I've thought a good deal about Joseph—he was a pretty fine lad, no doubt. . . . But grandfather's name was Per, and there wasn't a braver, worthier man on that part of the coast; so it'll just have to be Per again this time. . . . But say, now—" Per Hansa paused a moment, pondering; then he looked up at his neighbour, and his eyes began to gleam. . . . "The boy must have a second name—so you'd better christen him Peder Seier [i.e., Victorious]! . . . The last is after your Sörrina. . . . She has done me a greater service this night than I can ever repay! And now the boy is to be named after her!"

Hans Olsa could think of nothing to say in answer to all this. They walked on in silence. . . .

When they came into the room, they stepped across the threshold reverently. An air of Sabbath had descended on the room. The sun shone brightly through the window, spreading a golden lustre over the white walls; only along the north wall, where the bed stood, a half shadow lingered. . . . The fire crackled in the stove; the coffeepot was boiling. The table had been spread with a white cover; upon it lay the open hymn book, with the page turned down. Beside the hymn book stood a bowl of water; beside that lay a piece of white cloth. . . . Kjersti was tending the stove, piling the wood in diligently. . . . Sörine sat in the corner, crooning over a tiny bundle; out of the bundle at intervals came faint, wheezy chirrups, like the sounds that rise from a nest of young birds.

An irresistible force drew Per Hansa to the bed. . . . She lay sound asleep. . . . Thank God, that awful look of dread had not come back! He straightened himself up and glanced around the room; never before had he seen anything that looked so beautiful. . . .

Sörine got up, went to the table, and bared a little rosy human head.

"If you are going to be the minister here," she said, turning to her husband, who had remained standing motionless at the door, "then you must hurry up and get ready. . . . First of all you must wash your hands."

The next moment they had all gathered around the table.

"Here's the book. . . . Just read it out as well as you can, and we'll do whatever the book says," Sörine encouraged her husband. She seemed to have taken charge of the ceremony, and spoke in low, reassuring tones, as if she had done nothing else all her life but attend to such duties; and it was her confidence that gave Hans Olsa the courage he needed. . . . He went up to the table, took the book, and read the ritual in a trembling voice, slowly, with many pauses. And so he christened the child Peder Victorious, pronouncing the name clearly. Whereupon he said the Lord's Prayer so beautifully, that Kjersti exclaimed she had never heard the like.

"There now!" said Kjersti with great emphasis. "I don't believe there is a thing lacking to make this christening perfectly correct! . . . Now the coffee is ready and we're all going to have a cup."

But Per Hansa was searching over in the corner; at last he produced a bottle. First he treated Sörine; then Kjersti. . . . "If ever two people have earned something good, you two are it! . . . Come on, now, have another little drop! . . . And hurry up about it, please! Hans Olsa and I feel pretty weak in the knees ourselves!"

. . . After a while both food and drink were served. . . . "It looks as if we were going to have a *real* Christmas, after all!" said Per Hansa with a laugh, as they sat around the table enjoying their coffee.

HARRY EMERSON FOSDICK (1878-1969)

According to Reinhold Niebuhr, Harry Emerson Fosdick was "the most celebrated preacher of his day." His career, another scholar has suggested, was "the biopsy of an era." This energetic, forceful personality enjoyed a series of exalted positions in the early decades of this century that gave him greater prominence than almost all of his contemporaries. Like Dwight L. Moody and Billy Graham in their eras, he was one of the country's best-known preachers.

Fosdick's career unfolded in and around New York City. He was raised in Buffalo by parents who were active in education and the Baptist Church. He attended Colgate University and New York's Union Theological Seminary, where he came under the influence of some of the most "advanced" theologians of the day. After pastoring the First Baptist Church in Montclair, New Jersey, and winning recognition as an author, he became a professor of homiletics at Union, where he served from 1908 to 1946. But Fosdick's energies were too large to be confined to the classroom. From 1919 to 1925 he served as the preaching pastor of New York's First Presbyterian Church. This congregation deeply appreciated his ministry, but Fosdick's negative comments on fundamentalism and the fundamentalists led to strife among the Presbyterians and to his resignation from this pulpit. He then became minister of the Park Avenue Baptist Church, which was transformed—after a change of location and the infusion of money from John D. Rockefeller, Jr.—into the world-renowned Riverside Church. Fosdick retired in 1946, but he lived for another twenty-four years, active almost until his death as speaker, author, and commentator on the current scene.

As an "evangelical liberal," Fosdick belonged to a rare species of American Christian. For his beliefs he earned the lasting opposition of more conservative evangelicals and fundamentalists. They objected to his undogmatic Christianity and his redefinition of classic Christian doctrines. Fosdick's faith, in the words of J. Gresham Machen, a leading conservative, was "pathetic stuff." On the other side, however, Fosdick's strong sense of human sinfulness, his lifelong attachment to the Bible, and his proclamation of the need to confront a God beyond our own imagings left him somewhat out of step with the more optimistic modernists of his day. In 1922, the same year that he made his strongest attack on the fundamentalists, Fosdick also had this to say: "Strange as it may sound to the ears of this modern age, long tickled by the amiable idiocies of evolution popularly misinterpreted, this generation's deepest need is not these dithyrambic songs about inevitable progress, but a fresh sense of personal and social sin."

Members of the urban middle and upper classes loved Fosdick because he was able to communicate a message of Christian hope in a world torn from the comfortable certainties of the past. They crowded the churches where he preached, bought millions of copies of his books, and made up a large and faithful audience once he began to broadcast over the radio. Works like *The Meaning of Prayer*, published in 1915, made faith in God understandable. This book, hailed by both conservatives and liberals, was one of several volumes that Fosdick presented as guides to daily devotion. They were comprised of devotional pieces, each usually consisting of a brief meditation, a short passage of Scripture, and a concluding prayer. Their success lay in effectively bringing piety into the rapidly changing world of the early twentieth century. The following excerpt from *The Meaning of Prayer* contains the readings for the first week of the devotional cycle; the theme is "The Naturalness of Prayer."

From *The Meaning of Prayer*

FIRST DAY, FIRST WEEK

Samuel Johnson once was asked what the strongest argument for prayer was, and he replied, "Sir, there is no argument for prayer." One need only read Johnson's own petitions, such as the one below, to see that he did not mean by this to declare prayer irrational; he meant to stress the fact that praying is first of all a native tendency. It is a practice like breathing or eating in this respect, that men engage in it because they are human, and *afterward* argue about it as best they can. As Carlyle stated it in a letter to a friend: "Prayer is and remains the native and deepest impulse of the soul of man." Consider this universal tendency to pray as revealed in "Solomon's prayer" at the dedication of the temple:

> Moreover concerning the foreigner, that is not of thy people Israel, when he shall come from a far country for thy great name's sake, and thy mighty hand, and thine outstretched arm; when they shall come and pray toward this house; then hear thou from heaven, even from thy dwelling place, and do according to all that the foreigner calleth to thee for; that all the peoples of the earth may know thy name, and fear thee, as doth thy people Israel, and that they may know that this house which I have built is called by thy name.
>
> —II Chron. 6:32, 33.

Note how this prayer takes for granted that any stranger coming from anywhere on earth is likely to be a praying man. Let us say to ourselves on this first day of our study, that in dealing with prayer we are dealing, as this Scripture suggests, with a natural function of human life.

> "All souls that struggle and aspire,
> All hearts of prayer, by thee are lit;
> And, dim or clear, thy tongues of fire
> On dusky tribes and twilight centuries sit."

> O Lord, in whose hands are life and death, by whose power I am sustained, and by whose mercy I am spared, look down upon me with pity. Forgive me that I have until now so much neglected the duty which Thou hast assigned to me, and suffered the days and hours of which I must give account to pass away without any endeavor to accomplish Thy will. Make me to remember, O God, that every day is thy gift, and ought to be used according to Thy command. Grant me, therefore, so to repent of my negligence, that I may obtain mercy from Thee, and pass the time which Thou shalt yet allow me in diligent performance of Thy commands, through Jesus Christ. Amen.
>
> —Samuel Johnson (1709-1784).

SECOND DAY, FIRST WEEK

Epictetus was a non-Christian philosopher and yet listen to him: "When thou hast shut thy door and darkened thy room, say not to thyself that thou art alone. God is in thy room." Read now Paul's appreciation of this hunger for God and this sense of his presence which are to be found among all peoples.

> Ye men of Athens, in all things I perceive that ye are very religious. For as I passed along, and observed the objects of your worship, I found also an altar with this inscription, "To an Unknown God." What therefore ye worship in ignorance, this I set forth unto you. The God that made the world and all things therein, he, being Lord of heaven and earth, dwelleth not in temples made with hands; neither is he served by men's hands, as though he needed anything, seeing he himself giveth to all life, and breath, and all things; and he made of one every nation of men to dwell on all the face of the earth, having determined their appointed seasons, and the bounds of their habitation; that they should seek God, if haply, they might feel after him and find him, though he is not far from each one of us; for in him we live, and move, and have our being; as certain even of your own poets have said, For we are also his offspring.
>
> —Acts 17:22-28.

Consider the meaning of the fact that prayer and worship are thus universal; that all peoples do "seek God, if haply, they might feel after him and find him." It is said that an ignorant African woman, after hearing her first Christian sermon, remarked to her neighbor, "There! I always told you that there ought to be a God like that." Somewhere in every man there is the capacity for worship and prayer, for the apprehension of God and the love of him. Is not this the distinctive quality of man and the noblest faculty which he possesses? How then are we treating this best of our endowments?

O Lord our God, grant us grace to desire Thee with our whole heart; that so desiring we may seek and find Thee; and so finding Thee may love Thee; and loving Thee, may hate those sins from which Thou hast redeemed us. Amen.

—Anselm (1033-1109).

THIRD DAY, FIRST WEEK

Prayer has been greatly discredited in the minds of many by its use during war. Men have felt the absurdity of praying on opposite sides of a battle, of making God a tribal leader in heaven, to give victory, as Zeus and Apollo used to do, to their favorites. Let us grant all the narrow, bitter, irrational elements that thus appear in prayer during a war, but let us not be blind to the meaning of this momentous fact: *whenever in national life a time of great stress comes, men, however sceptical, feel the impulse to pray.* How natural is Hezekiah's cry in the siege of Jerusalem!

O Jehovah, the God of Israel, that sittest above the cherubim, thou art the God, even thou alone, of all the kingdoms of the earth; thou hast made heaven and earth. Incline thine ear, O Jehovah, and hear; open thine eyes, O Jehovah, and see; and hear the words of Sennacherib, wherewith he hath sent him to defy the living God. Of a truth, Jehovah, the kings of Assyria have laid waste the nations and their lands, and have cast their gods into the fire; for they were no gods but the work of men's hands, wood and stone; therefore they have destroyed them. Now therefore, O Jehovah our God, save thou us, I beseech thee, out of his hand, that all the kingdoms of the earth may know that thou Jehovah art God alone.

—II Kings 19:15-19.

Consider now the same tendency to pray in a crisis, which appears in the European war. Here is a passage from a Scotchman's letter, describing the infidel in his town, who never went to church, but who now sits in the kirk, and is moved to tears when he hears the minister pray for the king's forces, and for the bereaved at home: "It was then that my friend stifled a sob. There was Something after all, Something greater than cosmic forces, greater than law—with an eye to pity and an arm to save. There was God. My friend's son was with the famous regiment that was swaying to and fro, grappling with destiny. He was helpless—and there was only God to appeal to. There comes an hour in life when the heart realizes that instinct is mightier far than logic. With us in the parish churches of Scotland the great thing is the sermon. But today it is different; the great thing now is prayer." So always a crisis shakes loose the tendency to pray.

O Lord God of Hosts, grant to those who have gone forth to fight our battles by land or sea, protection in danger, patience in suffering, and moderation in victory. Look with compassion on the sick, the wounded, and the captives; sanctify to them their trials, and turn their hearts unto Thee. For Thy dear Son's sake, O Lord, pardon and receive the dying; have mercy upon the widow and fatherless, and comfort all who mourn. O gracious Father, who makest wars to cease in all the world, restore to us, Thy people, speedily the blessing of peace, and grant that our present troubles may be overruled to Thy glory, in the extension of the Redeemer's Kingdom, and the union of all nations in Thy faith, fear, and love. Hear, O Lord, and answer us; for Jesus Christ's sake. Amen.

—E. Hawkins (1789-1882).

FOURTH DAY, FIRST WEEK

H. Clay Trumbull tells us that a soldier in the Civil War, wounded in a terrific battle at Fort Wagner, was asked by an army chaplain, "Do you ever pray?" "Sometimes," was the answer; "I prayed last Saturday night, when we were in that fight at Wagner. I guess everbody prayed *there*." Consider how inevitably the impulse to pray asserts itself whenever critical danger comes suddenly upon any life. In view of this, read the Psalmist's description of a storm at sea:

They that go down to the sea in ships,
That do business in great waters;
These see the works of Jehovah,
And his wonders in the deep.
For he commandeth, and raiseth the stormy wind,
Which lifteth up the waves thereof.
They mount up to the heavens, they go down again to the depths:
Their soul melteth away because of trouble.
They reel to and fro, and stagger like a drunken man,
And are at their wits' end.
Then they cry unto Jehovah in their trouble.

—Psalm 107:23-28.

Remember those times in your experience of observation when either you or some one else has been thrown back by an emergency upon this natural tendency to pray in a crisis. Consider what it means that this impulse to pray is not simply age-long and universal; that it also is exhibited in every one of us—at least occasionally. How natural as well as how noble is this prayer of Bishop Ridley during the imprisonment that preceded his burning at the stake!

> O Heavenly Father, the Father of all wisdom, understanding, and true strength, I beseech Thee, for Thy only Son our Savior Christ's sake, look mercifully upon me, wretched creature, and send Thine Holy Spirit into my breast; that not only I may understand according to Thy wisdom, how this temptation is to be borne off, and with what answer it is to be beaten back; but also, when I must join to fight in the field for the glory of Thy name, that then I, being strengthened with the defence of Thy right hand, may manfully stand in the confession of Thy faith, and of Thy truth, and may continue in the same unto the end of my life, through the same our Lord Jesus Christ. Amen.
>
> —Bishop Ridley (1500-1555).

FIFTH DAY, FIRST WEEK

The instinctive turning of the heart to a "Power not ourselves" is often felt, not alone in crisis of peril, but in the presence of great *responsibility,* for which a man unaided feels inadequate. Despite Solomon's shallowness of life, there were times when something finer and deeper was revealed in him than his deeds would have suggested. When he first realized that the new responsibility of kingship was upon him, how elevated the spirit of his impulsive prayer!

> And now, O Jehovah my God, thou hast made thy servant king instead of David my father: and I am but a little child; I know not how to go out or come in. And thy servant is in the midst of thy people which thou hast chosen, a great people, that cannot be numbered nor counted for multitude. Give thy servant therefore an understanding heart to judge thy people, that I may discern between good and evil; for who is able to judge this thy great people?
>
> —I Kings 3:7-9.

As a companionpiece with this cry of Solomon, see Lincoln's revealing words: "I have been driven many times to my knees by the overwhelming conviction that I had nowhere else to go; my own wisdom and that of all around me seemed insufficient for the day." Whenever a man faces tasks for which he feels inadequate and upon whose accomplishment much depends, he naturally turns to prayer. Let us imagine ourselves in Luther's place, burdened with new and crushing responsibilities, and facing powerful enemies, when he cried:

O Thou, my God! Do Thou, my God, stand by me, against all the world's
wisdom and reason. Oh, do it! Thou must do it! Yea, Thou alone must do
it! Not mine, but Thine, is the cause. For my own self, I have nothing to do
with these great and earthly lords. I would prefer to have peaceful days, and
to be out of this turmoil. But Thine, O Lord, is this cause; it is righteous and
eternal. Stand by me, Thou true Eternal God! In no man do I trust. All that
is of the flesh and savours of the flesh is here of no account. God, O God!
dost Thou not hear me, O my God? Art Thou dead? No. Thou canst not
die; Thou art only hiding Thyself. Hast Thou chosen me for this work? I ask
Thee how I may be sure of this, if it be Thy will; for I would never have
thought, in all my life, of undertaking aught against such great lords. Stand
by me, O God, in the Name of Thy dear Son, Jesus Christ, who shall be my
Defence and Shelter, yea, my Mighty Fortress, through the might and
strength of Thy Holy Spirit. God help me. Amen.

—Martin Luther (1483-1546).

SIXTH DAY, FIRST WEEK

And when Daniel knew that the writing was signed, he went into his house
(now his windows were open in his chamber toward Jerusalem); and he
kneeled upon his knees three times a day, and prayed, and gave thanks
before his God, as he did aforetime.

—Daniel 6:10.

We are evidently dealing here with a new element in prayer, not apparent
in our previous discussion. *Prayer, to Daniel, was not simply an impulsive
cry of need, wrung from him by sudden crises or by overwhelming responsibilities.* Daniel had done with the impulse to pray what all wise people do
with the impulse to eat. They do not neglect it until special work absolutely
forces them to it. They rather recognize eating as a normal need of human
beings, to be met regularly. So Daniel not only prayed in emergencies of peril
and responsibility; he prayed three times a day. How many of us leave the
instinct of prayer dormant until a crisis calls it into activity! "Jehovah, in
trouble have they visited thee; they poured out a prayer *when thy chastening
was upon them*" (Isaiah 26:16). Consider how inadequate such a use of
prayer is.

I am forced, good Father, to seek Thee daily, and Thou offerest Thyself
daily to be found: whensoever I seek, I find Thee, in my house, in the fields,
in the temple, and in the highway. Whatsoever I do, Thou art with me;
whether I eat or drink, whether I write or work, go to ride, read, meditate,
or pray, Thou art ever near me; wheresoever I am, or whatsoever I do, I feel
some measure of Thy mercies and love. If I be oppressed, Thou defendest
me: if I be envied, Thou guardest me; if I hunger, Thou feedest me; what-

soever I want Thou givest me. O continue this Thy loving-kindness towards me for ever, that all the world may see Thy power, Thy mercy, and Thy love, wherein Thou hast not failed me, and even my enemies shall see that Thy mercies endure forever.

—J. Norden (1548-1625).

SEVENTH DAY, FIRST WEEK

For this cause I bow my knees unto the Father, from whom every family in heaven and on earth is named, that he would grant you, according to the riches of his glory, that ye may be strengthened with power through his Spirit in the inward man; that Christ may dwell in your hearts through faith; to the end that ye, being rooted and grounded in love, may be strong to apprehend with all the saints what is the breadth and length and height and depth, and to know the love of Christ which passeth knowledge, that ye may be filled unto all the fulness of God.

—Eph. 3:14-19.

Compare praying like this with the spasmodic cry of occasional need and see how great the difference is. Here prayer has risen into an elevated demand on life, unselfish and constant. It gathers up the powers of the soul in a constraining desire for God's blessing on the one who prays and on all men. What starts in the pagan as an unregulated and fitful impulse has become in Paul an intelligent, persevering, and well-directed habit. As power of thought confused and weak in an Australian aboriginal, becomes in a Newton capable of grasping laws that hold the stars together, so prayer may begin in the race or in the individual as an erratic and ineffective impulse, but may grow to be a dependable and saving power. Consider how much you understand this latent force in your own life and how effectively you are using it.

O God, Thou art Life, Wisdom, Truth, Bounty, and Blessedness, the Eternal, the only true Good! My God and my Lord, Thou art my hope and my heart's joy. I confess, with thanksgiving, that Thou hast made me in Thine image, that I may direct all my thoughts to Thee, and love Thee. Lord, make me to know Thee aright, that I may more and more love, and enjoy, and possess Thee. And since, in the life here below, I cannot fully attain this blessedness, let it at least grow in me day by day, until it all be fulfilled at last in the life to come. Here be the knowledge of Thee increased, and there let it ripen; that my joy being here great in hope, may there in fruition be made perfect. Amen.

—Anselm (1033-1109).

WILLIAM FAULKNER (1897-1962)

In a series of novels that took him several decades to write and that tell the story of a single region—the fictional Yoknapatawpha County in northern Mississippi—William Faulkner created perhaps the most richly imagined and morally significant body of fiction in American literature. In book after book about the Compsons, the Sutpens, the McCaslins, the Snopeses, and countless others, Faulkner told what he called the story of the heart's struggle against itself.

In relative obscurity, Faulkner labored in his native region and produced a series of stunning books: *The Sound and the Fury* (1929), *As I Lay Dying* (1930), *Light in August* (1932), *Absalom, Absalom!* (1936), *The Hamlet* (1940), and *Go Down, Moses* (1942). Fame did eventually come to him, and in 1949 he received the Nobel Prize for Literature. But it is for the work that he did between 1929 and 1942 that he will be remembered. It is doubtful that any other American writer has had a decade as startlingly productive as this.

What gives a lasting quality to Faulkner's fiction—in addition to its sheer technical virtuosity—is its moral seriousness. Having grown up under the long shadow of the defeat of the Confederacy, Faulkner was obsessed with the presence of the past. Unlike their northern counterparts, who seem poised to leap from glory to glory in a saga of endless progress, Faulkner's characters must struggle with the awful and yet somehow rich burden of the past. Like Shakespeare and Dickens before him, Faulkner at his best is both a great comic writer and a man of profoundly tragic vision.

The following selection gives us intriguing insight into Faulkner's view of the Christian faith. The passage, which is from the final section of *The Sound and the Fury*, describes a church experience on Easter Sunday. Its central characters are Dilsey, a black servant of the Compson family, and Benjy, the thirty-three-year-old idiot who is a Compson child. Reverend Shegog's vision of the resurrected Lamb is an inspiration for the beleaguered Dilsey. In the midst of the decaying fortunes of the Compson household, she clings to the vision of "de first en de last." With faith in God's creation and hope in final deliverance, Dilsey struggles to hold together a fragmenting family, and she ministers, however sternly, to a discarded child. Though he did not share the fullness of Dilsey's beliefs, Faulkner did look with amazed admiration at this woman of faith. It is clear from the novel itself and from Faulkner's later comments about it that Dilsey is one of his most treasured characters. Lacking a similar commitment, Faulkner could nonetheless imagine and admire a deeply rooted piety that issued in acts of genuine compassion.

Reverend Shegog's Sermon

The road rose again, to a scene like a painted backdrop. Notched into a cut of red clay crowned with oaks the road appeared to stop short off, like a cut ribbon. Beside it a weathered church lifted its crazy steeple like a painted church, and the whole scene was as flat and without perspective as a painted cardboard set upon the ultimate edge of the flat earth, against the windy sunlight of space and April and a midmorning filled with bells. Toward the church they thronged with slow sabbath deliberation. The women and children went on in, the men stopped outside and talked in quiet groups until the bell ceased ringing. Then they too entered.

The church had been decorated, with sparse flowers from kitchen gardens and hedgegrows, and with streamers of coloured crepe paper. Above the pulpit hung a battered Christmas bell, the accordian sort that collapses. The pulpit was empty, though the choir was already in place, fanning themselves although it was not warm.

Most of the women were gathered on one side of the room. They were talking. Then the bell struck one time and they dispersed to their seats and the congregation sat for an instant, expectant. The bell struck again one time. The choir rose and began to sing and the congregation turned its head as one, as six small children—four girls with tight pigtails bound with small scraps of cloth like butterflies, and two boys with close napped heads,— entered and marched up the aisle, strung together in a harness and white ribbons and flowers, and followed by two men in single file. The second man was huge, of a light coffee colour, imposing in a frock coat and white tie. His head was magisterial and profound, his neck rolled above his collar in rich folds. But he was familiar to them, and so the heads were still reverted when he had passed, and it was not until the choir ceased singing that they realised that the visiting clergyman had already entered, and when they saw the man who had preceded their minister enter the pulpit still ahead of him an indescribable sound went up, a sigh, a sound of astonishment and disappointment.

The visitor was undersized, in a shabby alpaca coat. He had a wizened

Source: *The Sound and The Fury* (New York: Vintage Books, 1954), pp. 364-71.

black face like a small, aged monkey. And all the while that the choir sang
again and while the six children rose and sang in thin, frightened, tuneless
whispers, they watched the insignificant looking man sitting dwarfed and
countrified by the minister's imposing bulk, with something like consternation. They were still looking with consternation and unbelief when the
minister rose and introduced him in rich, rolling tones whose very unction
served to increase the visitor's insignificance.

"En dey brung dat all de way fum Saint Looey," Frony whispered.

"I've knowed de Lawd to use cuiser tools dan dat," Dilsey said. "Hush,
now," she said to Ben, "Dey fixin to sing again in a minute."

When the visitor rose to speak he sounded like a white man. His voice was
level and cold. It sounded too big to have come from him and they listened at
first through curiosity, as they would have to a monkey talking. They began
to watch him as they would a man on a tight rope. They even forgot his
insignifi[c]ant appearance in the virtuosity with which he ran and posed and
swooped upon the cold inflectionless wire of his voice, so that at last, when
with a sort of swooping glide he came to rest again beside the reading desk
with one arm resting upon it at shoulder height and his monkey body as reft
of all motion as a mummy or an emptied vessel, the congregation sighed as if
it waked from a collective dream and moved a little in its seats. Behind the
pulpit the choir fanned steadily. Dilsey whispered, "Hush, now. Dey fixin to
sing in a minute."

Then a voice said, "Brethren."

The preacher had not moved. His arm lay yet across the desk, and he still
held that pose while the voice died in sonorous echoes between the walls. It
was as different as day and dark from his former tone, with a sad, timbrous
quality like an alto horn, sinking into their hearts and speaking there again
when it had ceased in fading and cumulate echoes.

"Brethren and sisteren," it said again. The preacher removed his arm and
he began to walk back and forth before the desk, his hands clasped behind
him, a meagre figure, hunched over upon itself like that of one long immured
in striving with the implacable earth, "I got the recollection and the blood of
the Lamb!" He tramped steadily back and forth beneath the twisted paper
and the Christmas bell, hunched, his hands clasped behind him. He was like
a worn small rock whelmed by the successive waves of his voice. With his
body he seemed to feed the voice that, succubus like, had fleshed its teeth in
him. And the congregation seemed to watch with its own eyes while the voice
consumed him, until he was nothing and they were nothing and there was
not even a voice but instead their hearts were speaking to one another in
chanting measures beyond the need for words, so that when he came to rest
against the reading desk, his monkey face lifted and his whole attitude that of
a serene, tortured crucifix that transcended its shabbiness and insignificance

and made it of no moment, a long moaning expulsion of breath rose from them, and a woman's single soprano: "Yes, Jesus!"

As the scudding day passed overhead the dingy windows glowed and faded in ghostly retrograde. A car passed along the road outside, labouring in the sand, died away. Dilsey sat bolt upright, her head on Ben's knee. Two tears slid down her fallen cheeks, in and out of the myriad coruscations of immolation and abnegation and time.

"Brethren," the minister said in a harsh whisper, without moving.

"Yes, Jesus!" the woman's voice said, hushed yet.

"Brethren en sistuhn!" His voice rang again, with the horns. He removed his arms and stood erect and raised his hands. "I got de ricklickshun en de blood of de Lamb!" They did not mark just when his intonation, his pronunciation, became negroid, they just sat swaying a little in their seats as the voice took them into itself.

"When de long, cold—Oh, I tells you, breddren, when de long, cold—I sees de light en I sees de word, po sinner! Dey passed away in Egypt, de swingin chariots; de generations passed away. Wus a rich man: whar he now, O breddren? Wus a po man: whar he now, O sistuhn? Oh I tells you, ef you aint got de milk en de dew of de old salvation when de long, cold years rolls away!"

"Yes, Jesus!"

"I tells you, breddren, en I tell you, sistuhn, dey'll come a time. Po sinner sayin Let me lay down wid de Lawd, lemme lay down my load. Den whut Jesus gwine say, O breddren? O sistuhn? Is you got de ricklickshun en de Blood of de Lamb? Case I aint gwine load down heaven!"

He fumbled in his coat and took out a handkerchief and mopped his face. A low concerted sound rose from the congregation: "Mmmmmmmmmmm-mmm!" The woman's voice said, "Yes, Jesus! Jesus!"

"Breddren! Look at dem little chillen settin dar. Jesus wus like dat once. He mammy suffered de glory en de pangs. Sometime maybe she helt him at de nightfall, whilst de angels singing him to sleep; maybe she look out de do' en see de Roman po-lice passin." He tramped back and forth, mopping his face. "Listen, breddren! I sees de day, Ma'y settin in de do' wid Jesus on her lap, de little Jesus. Like dem chillen dar, de little Jesus. I hears de angels singin de peaceful songs en de glory; I sees de closin eyes; sees Mary jump up, sees de sojer face: We gwine to kill! We gwine to kill! We gwine to kill yo little Jesus! I hears de weepin en de lamentation of de po mammy widout de salvation en de word of God!"

"Mmmmmmmmmmmmmmmm! Jesus! Little Jesus!" and another voice, rising:

"I sees, Oh Jesus! Oh I sees!" and still another, without words, like bubbles rising in water.

"I sees hit, breddren! I sees hit! Sees de blastin, blindin sight! I see Calvary, wid de sacred trees, sees de thief en de murderer en de last of dese; I hears de boasting en de braggin: Ef you be Jesus, lif up yo tree en walk! I hears de wailin of women en de evenin lamentations; I hears de weepin en de cryin en de turnt-away face of God: dey done kilt Jesus; they done kilt my Son!"

"Mmmmmmmmmmmmmm. Jesus! I sees, O Jesus!"

"O blind sinner! Breddren, I tells you; sistuhn, I says to you, when de Lawd did turn His mighty face, say, Aint gwine overload heaven! I can see de widowed God shet His do'; I sees de whelmin flood roll between; I sees de darkness en de death everlastin upon de generations. Den, lo! Breddren! Yes, breddren! Whut I see? Whut I see, O sinner? I sees de resurrection en de light; sees de meek Jesus saying Dey kilt Me dat ye shall live again; I died dat dem whut sees en believes shall never die. Breddren, O breddren! I sees de doom crack en hears de golden horns shoutin down de glory, en de arisen dead whus got de blood en de ricklickshun of de Lamb!"

In the midst of the voices and the hands Ben sat, rapt in his sweet blue gaze. Dilsey sat bolt upright beside, crying rigidly and quietly in the onnealment and the blood of the remembered Lamb.

As they walked through the bright noon, up the sandy road with the dispersing congregation talking easily again group to group, she continued to weep, unmindful of the talk.

"He sho a preacher, mon! He didn't look like much at first, but hush!"

"He seed de power en de glory."

"Yes, suh. He seed hit. Face to face he seed hit."

Dilsey made no sound, her face did not quiver as the tears took their sunken and devious courses, walking with her head up, making no effort to dry them away even.

"Whyn't you quit dat, mammy?" Frony said. "Wid all dese people lookin. We be passin white folks soon."

"I've seed de first en de last," Dilsey said. "Never you mind me."

"First en last whut?" Frony said.

"Never you mind," Dilsey said. "I seed de beginnin, en now I sees de endin."

REINHOLD NIEBUHR (1892-1971)

In public activity that spanned more than half a century, Reinhold Niebuhr sought to bring the truth and power of the gospel to bear upon the particular dilemmas of the twentieth century. He began his career as a parish minister in Detroit at the time of the explosive growth of the automotive industry. Throughout his life he was active as a political thinker, journalist, and scholarly writer, and he spent more than three decades as Professor of Applied Christianity at Union Theological Seminary in New York.

When Niebuhr began his work as a pastor, he was a conventional theological liberal. Believing in innate human goodness and the inevitability of progess, he went to serve in a city rife with social and economic injustice. Gradually the force of circumstances without and reflections within led him to discard bourgeois liberalism and to develop a unique American brand of neo-orthodoxy.

Though a great distance separated Niebuhr from the fundamentalist and evangelical traditions on such matters as the end of the world and the nature of the Bible's authority, he nonetheless shared with his more conservative brethren convictions about human fallibility and the limitations of human history. He was to remain forever wary of optimistic schemes and naive views of the human condition. For example, though Niebuhr served for more than a decade as a leader of the Pacifist Fellowship of Reconciliation, he eventually broke with that group because he came to see pacifism as morally irresponsible. And when the Socialist Party, of which he was also a leader, refused to abandon its pacifist stand, even in the face of Fascist aggression, Niebuhr also broke with it (in 1940).

Niebuhr's best-known work is *The Nature and Destiny of Man* (1941-43), a two-volume exploration of the human condition from a neo-orthodox perspective. This impressive work displays Niebuhr's considerable historical knowledge, his moral and spiritual sensitivity, and his astonishing ability to synthesize from many disciplines and historical periods. In this work, as well as in *Moral Man and Immoral Society* (1932) and *The Irony of American History* (1952), Niebuhr attempted to demonstrate the broad contemporary relevance of the Christian proclamation of judgment and grace. Through five decades of Christian service, he remained committed to bringing spiritual experience back into the public sphere. He was never content to have the gospel confined within the limits of private experience.

The following selections come from *Leaves from the Notebook of a Tamed Cynic*, a book in which Niebuhr speaks most revealingly of his own experience. This 1929 publication contains Niebuhr's reflections on his years in the Detroit pastorate. Though the entries may not openly display the same intensity as Puritan devotional writings or Catholic spiritual reflections, they do give evidence of an intense desire to make the gospel speak once again to all aspects of our individual and collective experience.

From *Leaves from the Notebook of a Tamed Cynic*

Whenever I exchange thoughts with H——, as I do with greater frequency and with increasing profit to myself, I have the uneasy feeling that I belong to the forces which are destroying religion in the effort to refine it. He is as critical as I am—well, perhaps not quite so critical; but in all his critical evaluations of religious forms he preserves a robust religious vitality which I seem to lack. His scholarship is of course much more extensive than mine, but it has not robbed him of religious naïveté, to use Schweitzer's phrase. He has preserved a confidence in the goodness of men and the ultimate triumph of righteousness which I do not lack, but to which I do not hold so unwaveringly. While we understand each other, we really belong to different schools of thought.

I have been profoundly impressed by the Spenglerian thesis that culture is destroyed by the spirit of sophistication and I am beginning to suspect that I belong to the forces of decadence in which this sophistication is at work. I have my eye too much upon the limitations of contemporary religious life and institutions; I always see the absurdities and irrationalities in which narrow types of religion issue. That wouldn't be so bad if I did not use the instruments of intellectualism rather than those of a higher spirituality for the critical task.

Nevertheless I hate a thoroughgoing cynic. I don't want anyone to be more cynical than I am. If I am saved from cynicism at all it is by some sense of personal loyalty to the spirit and the genius of Jesus; that and physical health. If I were physically anæmic I never would be able to escape pessimism. This very type of morbid introspection is one of the symptoms of the disease. I can't justify myself in my perilous position except by the observation that the business of being sophisticated and naïve, critical and religious, at one and the same time is as difficult as it is necessary, and only a few are able to achieve the balance. H—— says I lack a proper appreciation of the mystical values in religion. That is probably the root of the matter. Yet I can't resist another word in self-defense. The modern world is so full of bunkum that it is difficult to attempt honesty in it without an undue emphasis upon the critical faculty.

If in this civilization we cannot enter the kingdom of God because we cannot be as little children, the fault, dear Brutus, is in our stars and not in ourselves.

* * *

Out here on the Pacific coast, particularly in Los Angeles, one is forcibly impressed with the influence of environment upon religion. Every kind of cult seems to flourish in Los Angeles, and most of them are pantheistic. Every sorry oriental religious nostrum is borrowed in the vain effort to give meaning to pointless lives and to impart a thrill to vacuous existences. The pantheism is partly due, no doubt, to the salubrious nature of the southern California climate. Wherever nature is unusually benignant, men tend to identify God and the natural world and to lose all moral vigor in the process.

But that is hardly the whole explanation. There are too many retired people in Los Angeles. They left the communities where their personalities had some social significance in order to vegetate on these pleasant shores. In this sorry and monotonous existence they try to save their self-respect by grasping for some religious faith which will not disturb their ease by any too rigorous ethical demands. Of course Aimee Semple McPherson [a popular Pentecostal preacher] is more successful than the pantheistic cults. She fights the devil and gives the people a good show. She storms against the vices which flourish in this paradise without touching their roots. Furthermore she has the art of casting the glow of religious imagination over sensuality without changing its essential nature. In that art she seems to be typical rather than unique for this whole civilization. If she is unique it is only in her success.

They are always telling me that Detroit is the most typically American of our cities. Perhaps Detroit is typical of the America which works feverishly to get what it wants, while Los Angeles is typical of the America which has secured what it wants. On the whole I prefer the former to the latter. An honest enthusiasm even for inadequate ends is better than a vacuous existence from which even the charm of an imperfect ambition has departed. Of course the paganism of power is more dangerous than the paganism of pleasure, but from the perspective of a mere observer it is more interesting. Who would not prefer Napoleon to his imbecile brothers who merely luxuriated in the prosperity created by his ambition?

Only in the case of complete innocency, as that of a child's, is life more beautiful in repose than in activity. Character is created by a balance of tensions, and is more lovely even when the balance is imperfect than in a state of complete relaxation.

Of course Los Angeles has more culture than our midwestern cities. Culture flourishes in leisure and sometimes redeems it. But it will be a long time before this kind of leisure will produce more than dilettantism.

*   *   *

There is a discouraging pettiness about human nature which makes me hate myself each time I make an analysis of my inner motives and springs of action. Here I am prodding and criticizing people continually because they have made too many compromises with the necessities of life and adjusted the Christian ideal until it has completely lost its original meaning. Yet I make my own compromises all the time.

It is Christian to trust people, and my trust is carefully qualified by mistrust and caution.

It is Christian to love, and to trust in the potency of love rather than in physical coercion. Logically that means non-resistance. Yet I believe that a minimum of coercion is necessary in all social tasks, or in most of them.

It is Christian to forgive rather than to punish; yet I do little by way of experimenting in the redemptive power of forgiveness.

I am not really a Christian. In me, as in many others, "the native hue of resolution is sicklied o'er by a pale cast of thought." I am too cautious to be a Christian. I can justify my caution, but so can the other fellow who is more cautious than I am.

The whole Christian adventure is frustrated continually not so much by malice as by cowardice and reasonableness. Of course everyone must decide for himself just where he is going to put his peg; where he is going to arrive at some stable equilibrium between moral adventure and necessary caution. And perhaps everyone is justified if he tries to prove that there is a particular reasonableness about the type of compromise which he has reached. But he might well learn, better than I have learned, to be charitable with those who have made their adjustments to the right and to the left of his position. If I do not watch myself I will regard all who make their adjustments to my right as fanatics and all who make them to the left as cowards. There is a silly egotism about such an attitude. But it is difficult to be pedagogically effective if you do not hold pretty resolutely to some position.

A reasonable person adjusts his moral goal somewhere between Christ and Aristotle, between an ethic of love and an ethic of moderation. I hope there is more of Christ than of Aristotle in my position. But I would not be too sure of it.

FULTON J. SHEEN (1895-1979)

For millions of Americans in the first decades of electronic mass-communication, Fulton J. Sheen embodied the Christian message. In 1930 he became the regular speaker on the "Catholic Hour," a Sunday evening radio program presented by the National Broadcasting Company that eventually reached four million listeners a week. In 1940 he was the first individual to conduct a televised religious service. In 1951 he added a regular appearance on television to his already extensive ministry when he began the weekly series "Life Is Worth Living." In response to these broadcasts Bishop Sheen received a great deal of correspondence: once he was deluged with thirty thousand letters in a single day, and he averaged forty thousand letters per week. The bishop spread his message in other ways, too: he wrote newspaper columns for both the Catholic and the secular press, he had numerous speaking engagements in this country and abroad, and he authored nearly seventy books.

Casual observers of the American scene who equated popular preaching with a lack of formal education and a surplus of mindless emotion could not fathom Bishop Sheen or his popularity. He had been born in El Paso, Illinois, where he shouldered his share of chores on the family farm before moving with his parents and three brothers to Peoria. He excelled in the local Catholic schools there, and went on to be a stellar student at St. Viator's College (Illinois), St. Paul Seminary (Minnesota), the Catholic University of America, the Sorbonne in Paris, the University of Louvain in Belgium, and the Pollegio Angelico in Rome. He earned doctorates in philosophy and theology from Louvain and Rome, and he taught philosophy for twenty-five years at the Catholic University of America. He was an influential delegate to the Second Vatican Council, an auxiliary bishop of New York from 1951, bishop of Rochester from 1966, and titular archbishop of Newport (Wales) from 1969. He received many honors, both national and international, including an Emmy for his television work.

On radio and television as well as in person, Bishop Sheen was a compelling speaker. His habit was to speak without notes after hours of rigorous preparation, a practice that enabled him to communicate informally yet deliver a substantive message. Bishop Sheen followed time-honored missionary strategy by attempting to move his audience from the known to the unknown, from significant circumstances in everyday life to the church's message of hope in God. Tapes of his messages are still circulated and continue to draw individuals to the Christian faith.

For all his fame, however, Bishop Sheen never lost the common touch. And throughout his life, religious devotion was an anchor. Nearly every day of his adult life he set aside an hour to meditate upon Scripture and the teachings of the church. In the following account of his own priesthood, to which he was ordained on September 20, 1919, we see how securely the grand truths of the Christian faith bore him along through the many activities of his life. On October 2, 1979, in New York's St. Patrick's Cathedral (just two months before the bishop's death), Pope John Paul II embraced Fulton Sheen and said, "You have written and spoken well of the Lord Jesus. You are a loyal son of the Church."

The Gift of the Treasure

Throughout all my graduate education I was already a priest. How did that desire begin and flourish in the clay? The treasure comes from God; the clay gives the response. As our Lord told His Apostles the night of the Last Supper: "You did not choose Me; I chose you." In the Epistle to the Hebrews: "Nobody arrogates the honor (of the priesthood) to himself; he is called by God." God does not put that sacred deposit in identical human natures, nor does He do it in the same way. He varies the giving from individual to individual. The vocation may come early, it may come late; it may come as it did to St. Francis, who was riding to a knightly contest in Apulia, or it may come after a life of sin, as it did to Augustine when he heard the voice of a child making reference to the Scriptures: "Take and read."

I can never remember a time in my life when I did not want to be a priest. In the early teens my father would send us to work on one of his farms. I recall doing spring plowing, watching the young corn come up under my eyes; as I saw the rich dark soil turned over, I would say the Rosary begging for a vocation. I never mentioned my vocation to others, not even to my parents, although others often told my parents they thought that I would become a priest. Being an altar boy at the cathedral fed the fires of vocation, as did the inspiration of the priests who visited our home almost every week. Not to be omitted was the Rosary, which was said every evening by the family before retiring.

My First Communion at the age of twelve was another special appeal to the Lord to grant me the grace of priesthood. But I always had one doubt— and that was my worthiness.

Source: *Treasure in Clay: The Autobiography of Fulton J. Sheen* (Garden City, N.Y.: Doubleday, 1980), pp. 29-39.

Never once did my mother or father say a word to me about becoming a priest, nor did I speak to them about it until the day I went to the seminary. Their only response then was: "We always prayed that you might become a priest; if it is your vocation, be a good one." I often would hear relatives and friends who visited my parents talk about me, saying that I would become a priest. And my younger brother Joe said that I liked to entertain visitors with little talks that I had prepared. For myself, I do not remember that.

A vocation is so very sacred that one does not like to speak of it; I never mentioned it to anyone—my classmates, my parents, nor to the priests (except Father Kelly, a curate in the cathedral parish). Always associated with that sense of the gift of a treasure was the frailty of the earthenware pot which was to house it. I would often drive it out of my mind, only to have it come back again. For the most part, the religious vocation is rather a silent but insistent whisper, yet one that demands a response; no violent shaking of bedposts or loud noises in the night. Just "you are called to be a priest."

Neither is the vocation so imperative that it makes acceptance a necessity rather than a willing obedience. In the Old Testament story, when God spoke to young Samuel, there was no voice audible to anyone but the child. Nor was there anything to prove it was divine; that is why Samuel twice went to Eli after his name was called, believing that it was Eli who had summoned him. The experience of the aged priest, Eli, was necessary finally to convince the boy of the divinity of the speaker: "Eli perceived that the Lord had called the child." Samuel did not at first know it was the voice of the Lord. Neither do most of us, when first we are called, recognize it as such except by its persistence and the calmness and peace with which it possesses the soul.

The course of life is determined not by the trivial incidents of day to day, but by a few decisive moments. There may not be over three, four or five such moments in a human life. For many people, it would be the decision of marriage, the taking of a job or changing residence. Certainly a turning point in my life happened when I finished college. A national examination was given to college students. The prize was a three-year university scholarship. I took the examination and won one of the scholarships. I was informed sometime during the summer and immediately went up to St. Viator's College to see Father William J. Bergan, by now my dear friend. He was on the tennis court when I arrived. With great glee and delight I announced: "Father Bergan, I won the scholarship!"

He put his hands on my shoulders, looked me straight in the eyes and said: "Fulton, do you believe in God?" I replied: "You know that I do." He said: "I mean *practically*, not from a theoretical point of view." This time I was not so sure, and I said: "Well, I *hope* I do." "Then tear up the scholarship." "Father Bergan, this scholarship entitles me to three years of university training with all expenses paid. It is worth about nine or ten thousand dollars." He retorted: "You know you have a vocation; you should be going to the seminary." I countered with this proposal: "I can go to the seminary after I get my Ph.D., because there will be little chance of getting a Ph.D. after I am ordained, and I would like very much to have a good education." He repeated: "Tear up the scholarship; go to the seminary. That is what the Lord wants you to do. And if you do it, trusting in Him, you will receive a far better university education after you are ordained than before." I tore up the scholarship and went to the seminary. I have never regretted that visit and that decision.

Looking back through the years and studying vocations today, I find in my case and in many others there are three stages all illustrated in the call of the prophet Isaiah. It would seem today that many claim they have a vocation to the priesthood because they want to "work in the inner city," or "defend the political rights of prisoners," or "work for civil rights for the minorities," or "care for the handicapped," or "bring a religious mission to the political-minded in South America." No true vocation starts with "what I want" or with "a work I would like to do." If we are called by God, we may be sent to a work we do not like, and "obedience is better than sacrifice." If society calls, I can stop service; if Christ calls, I am a servant forever. If I feel my call is sociological dedication, there is no reason why I should enter a theological seminary. If I am convinced that a vocation is to be identified with the world, then I have completely forgotten Him Who warned: "I have taken you out of the world."

The first stage in vocation is a sense of the holiness of God. When Isaiah went into the temple he had a vision of the Lord seated upon His throne with angelic choirs singing:

Holy, holy, holy is the Lord of Hosts;
The whole earth is full of His glory.

Vocation begins not with "what *I* would like to do" but with God. One is confronted with a presence, not as dramatic as Paul when he was converted, but with a sense of the unworldly, the holy and the transcendent.

The second stage, which is a reaction to this, is a profound sense of unworthiness. The heart is shocked at the simultaneous vision of the clay and the treasure. God is holy, I am not. "Woe is me." God can do something with those who see what they really are and who know their need of cleansing but can do nothing with the man who feels himself worthy.

Isaiah was cleansed of his paltriness by the Seraphim who took a burning coal from the altar and touched his mouth and said: "Behold this has touched your lips, your guilt is taken away and your sin is forgiven." This purgation begins in the seminary and continues through life in the form of physical suffering, mental anguish, betrayals, scandals, false accusations—all of which summon the one called to become more worthy of the treasure.

The third stage is response. After the purging, Isaiah heard the voice of the Lord asking: "Whom shall I send?" And Isaiah answered: "Here I am, send me." That is what I said the day I was ordained.

The dialectic between the sublimity of the vocation on the one hand, and the frailty of the human clay on the other, is a kind of crucifixion. Each priest is crucified on the vertical beam of the God-given vocation and on the horizontal beam of the simple longing of the flesh and a world that so often beckons to conformity with it. The best vintage of wine is sometimes served in tin cups. To be a priest is to be called to be the happiest of men, and yet to be daily committed to the greatest of all wars—the one waged within.

But God is constantly remolding that clay, giving it a second and third, and even seventy times seven chances. The prophet Jeremiah was bidden to go to a potter's shop. Jeremiah said:

So I went down to the potter's house and found him working at the wheel. Now and then a vessel he was making out of the clay would be spoiled in his hands, and then he would start again and mold it into another vessel to his liking.

The potter may have had the original intention to make a Ming vase, but even though the clay was marred, he did not give up; he fashioned it into another vessel.

The effort of restoring love succeeds even when God's original plan is frustrated by the material with which He has to work: "Where sin did abound, grace does more abound." At the close of life, one can well see the potter's intention to make a saint. But God has not given up, so that if the vessel is not fit to hold the rose, it can at least settle for being a tin can for a geranium. The Divine Potter can change the circumstances of the human clay, maybe adding a little suffering here and there. If we refuse to be molded into the original shape meant for us, namely, holiness and perfect imitation of Christ, He molds us into useful pitchers from which He can pour out His Divine Grace. God does not make anything with the purpose of destroying it. There is no waste in life. Childhood is not a waste. It has relationship to the rest of life.

That portion of us which is tried and tested, which is subjected to many trials, is not a waste. The tears, the agonies, the frustrations, the toils are not lost. All of these, which seem to militate against life, are worked into new forms. Life may be marred into a broken thing, but God can make it into a thing of beauty. So if I were asked if I had my life to live over again, would I live the priesthood as I have, the answer is: "No, I would try to love Christ more." The only sorrow in my life, or any life, is not to have loved Him enough. For I know now:

> That nothing walks with aimless feet;
> That not one life shall be destroyed,
> Or cast as rubbish to the void,
> When God has made the pile complete.

There are many more vocations to the priesthood than those which result in Ordination, as there are more seeds planted than those which bear fruit. St. Thomas Aquinas holds that God always gives the Church a sufficient number of vocations, "provided the unworthy ones are dismissed and the worthy ones are well trained." The best vocation leaders should be the priests themselves. We may not mount pulpits to urge parents to bear children, unless we priests bear spiritual children. On the last day, God will ask us priests: "Where are your children? How many vocations have you fostered?" Though it is not given to any of us to implant the vocation, it is nonetheless within our power to widen the capacity for receptivity. We fertilize the soil by good example and encouragement.

I believe that God gives some of us an intuitive sense of seeing vocations in others. I remember preaching Midnight Mass about the year 1960 at the Shrine of the Immaculate Conception in Washington. When the Mass ended about one-thirty in the morning, several hundred people gathered around me outside to exchange greetings. I saw a black boy with his father at the edge of the crowd and I called him to me. "Young man, do you ever think of becoming a priest?" He answered in the affirmative. I said: "I believe you have a vocation." I laid my hands on his head and prayed that if God called him, he might become responsive and immediately become aware of it. The father saw me talking to his son and inquired: "What are you saying to my son?" I told him that I believed that someday he would become a priest. The father said: "Ever since that boy was born, I have prayed morning and night that God would give him a vocation." I have never heard the final issue of that meeting. It is one of the things I will learn in Heaven.

Another circumstance was more certain. I was eating alone in the main dining room of the Statler Hotel in Boston. A shoeshine boy with a D-shirt—dirty—not a T-shirt, with a shoeshine box slung over his shoulder, began swinging on the large purple curtains that framed the entrance to the dining room. As soon as the headwaiter saw this, he shouted and chased the boy from the hotel. I left my dinner and went out of the hotel to the boy and asked him where he went to school. He told me he was going to a public school. I said: "With a name like that [his name was Irish], why don't you go to a Catholic school?" He said: "I got kicked out." "Who kicked you out?" I asked. "The pastor and the Mother Superior of the school." I promised: "I will get you back in." He asked who I was but I responded that I couldn't tell him. He then remarked: "No, they said nobody could ever get me back into Catholic school; I will never be allowed to return."

I went out to see the pastor and the Mother Superior of the school and I told them: "I know of three boys who were thrown out of religious schools: one because he was constantly drawing pictures during geography class; another because he was fond of fighting; and the third because he kept revolutionary books hidden under a mattress. No one knows the valedictorians of those classes, but the first boy was Hitler, the second Mussolini and the third Stalin. I am sure that if the superiors of those schools had given those boys another chance, they might have turned out differently in the world. Maybe this boy will prove himself worthy if you take him back." They allowed him to return to the school and today he is a missionary among the Eskimos.

When I was Bishop of Rochester, while walking down the middle aisle of a parish church, I passed a young boy in a pew who struck me as being rather unusual. I stopped and asked him if he ever thought of becoming a priest. He said: "I sometimes pray for it." And I said: "I am sure you have a vocation; continue to pray to our Blessed Mother that you may be strengthened in it." Recently I received a letter from the young man that he was joining the Jesuits.

Looking back on about sixty years of my priest-victimhood, how would I answer this question before God: "Do you think you have lived the life of a good priest?" When I compare myself with missionaries who have become dry martyrs by leaving their own country and family to teach other peoples, when I think of the sufferings of my brother-priests in Eastern Europe, when I look at the saintly faces of some of my brother-priests in monasteries and in the missions, and the beautiful resignation of priests in hospitals who suffer from cancer, and when I just even look at my many brothers in Christ whom I admire so much, I say: "No, I have not been the kind of priest I should have been or would have liked to have been."

But I know there is more to the answer of this question. When you put a painting in candlelight to examine it, the imperfections do not appear; when you put it under the full glare of the sun, then you see how badly chosen are the colors and ill defined the lines. So it is when we measure ourselves by God, we fall infinitely short; and when we compare ourselves with many who have given us inspiration, we feel a deep sense of unworthiness. But behind it all, and despite all of this, there is the tremendous consciousness of the mercy of God. He did not call angels to be priests; He called men. He did not make gold the vessel for his treasure; He made clay. The motley group of Apostles that He gathered about Him became more worthy through his mercy and compassion.

I know that I am not afraid to appear before Him. And this is not because I am worthy, nor because I have loved Him with deep intensity, but because *He has loved me*. That is the only reason that any one of us is really lovable. When the Lord puts His love into us, then we become lovable.

DOROTHY DAY (1897-1980)

When Dorothy Day died in 1980, the historian David O'Brien called her "the most significant, interesting, and influential person in the history of American Catholicism." The editor of her selected writings, Robert Ellsberg, says that "such a statement is all the more extraordinary considering that it refers to someone who occupied no established position of authority, and whose views, after all, met with virtually universal rejection throughout most of her career."

For almost fifty years, Dorothy Day promoted her views as a director of the Catholic Worker movement, a lay ministry that she and fellow Catholic Peter Maurin founded in 1931. Her commitment to this cause came only several years after her conversion to Catholicism. In *From Union Square to Rome* (1938), she tells the story of her tempestuous adolescence and early adulthood, which included first an affair and an abortion, and then a common-law marriage that broke up when she converted to the faith.

In their work together in the 1930s, Day and Maurin sought to develop an alternative Catholic social philosophy in the pages of the *Catholic Worker* and a network of "Houses of Hospitality," in which Christ's acts of mercy—feeding the hungry, clothing the naked, sheltering the homeless—would be carried out by his contemporary disciples.

Day sustained her commitment to the Catholic Worker movement through the Depression, the Second World War, the Korean and Vietnam conflicts, and the civil rights upheavals of the 1950s and 1960s. Throughout those years, Day sought to retain the simple program of the movement, whose spiritual sensibility she defined as "sacrifice, worship, a sense of reverence."

Below are excerpts from her regular column in the *Catholic Worker* that give evidence of this special sensibility. They date from the final two decades of her life and bring us into contact with a special kind of piety—a spiritual devotion that encompasses both the practice of personal piety and a passionate desire to bring the message of the gospel to bear upon the suffering of the modern world.

Selected Columns

THE FEAR OF OUR ENEMIES

Last week, I stayed awake until 4 a.m. after reading too stimulating an article by Thomas Merton, "The Pasternak Affair in Perspective." In it, Merton not only analyzes the Communist concept of man, but goes on to talk of the attitudes of the West. The concluding paragraphs of the article were what caused my happy sleeplessness. Merton writes:

> [Pasternak] is just as likely to be regarded as a dangerous writer in the West as he is in the East. He is saying that political and social structures as we understand them are things of the past, and that the crisis through which we are now passing is nothing but the full and inescapable manifestation of their falsity. For twenty centuries we have called ourselves Christians, without even beginning to understand one-tenth of the Gospel. We have been taking Caesar for God and God for Caesar. Now that "charity is growing cold" and we stand facing the smoky dawn of an apocalyptic era, Pasternak reminds us that there is only one source of truth, but that it is not sufficient to know the source is there—we must go and drink from it, as he has done.
>
> Do we have the courage to do so? For obviously, if we consider what Pasternak is saying, doing, and undergoing, to read the Gospel with eyes wide open may be a perilous thing!

It was not only Merton's article but also Anne Fremantle's *Desert Calling,* her biography of Charles de Foucauld, that kept me awake. It is a wonderful book, and the more I read it, the more I get from it. How utterly and completely Brother Charles tried to follow in the footsteps of Jesus, and how little we ourselves do to rejoice in mockery and contempt and misunderstanding. As a matter of fact, how fearful most of us are! Just a few Sundays ago, Judith Gregory and I were coming from eleven o'clock Mass at our parish church, St. Patrick's old cathedral on Mott Street, and as we walked down Mulberry Street we suddenly felt objects whizzing past our ears. I thought it was snowballs thrown by the small boys, because we had had snow the week before and there was still a little in the corners of buildings. But as I turned, another missile flew past and Judith said, "Those are meant for us, all right." She went to investigate the broken mass where it had struck against a garage door, and found it to be bits of hard-boiled egg. Two had been flung at us as we passed, and I was literally afraid to turn and look, for fear some would hit me in the face. I should have been delighted, as Charles

---

Source: *By Little and By Little: The Selected Writings of Dorothy Day,* ed. Robert Ellsberg (New York: Knopf, 1983), pp. 321-23, 337-40, 346-50.

de Foucauld was when he was pelted in the streets of Nazareth, but my feeling was one of fear, just as it was when I was shot at at Koinonia. It was fear in the flesh, the fear of the flesh, and I am glad I have it because it helps me to understand the fear that is eating at the hearts of people in the world today. No one is safe. We are no longer protected by oceans separating us from the rest of the warring world. Yesterday the Russians fired a rocket 7,760 miles into the central Pacific which fell less than one and a quarter miles from its calculated target. The U.S. Defense Department confirmed the shot's accuracy.

Anywhere, at any time, we can be reached. Leaders of governments say that none but a madman would launch a war today. But there are madmen, human senses are faulty, men may think they see and hear approaching planes, bombs, rockets, and the button may be pushed to set off a counter-offensive. Everything depends on the human element.

There are all kinds of fear, and I certainly pray to be delivered from the fear of my brother, I pray to grow in the love that casts out fear. To grow in love of God and man, and to live by this charity, that is the problem. We must love our enemy, not because we fear war but because God loves him.

Mike Wallace asked me that question: Does God love murderers, does He love a Hitler, a Stalin? I could only say, "God loves all men, and all men are brothers."

There is so little time on a broadcast, in an interview, so little time to answer or to think. I could have said, "Christ loved those who crucified Him. St. Stephen loved those who stoned him to death. St. Paul was a murderer. We are all murderers."

Deane Mowrer and I knelt by the side of women who were charged with murder and who were awaiting trial, the last time we were in prison in New York, put in the corridor with those awaiting trial, because we would not give bail. There were four homicide cases on that corridor: one a very young girl, one a somber, dark Negro who, it was said, had hired someone to kill her husband, and, just opposite us, a sad Puerto Rican woman nearly forty, mother of many children, who had been beaten by a drunken husband so many times that on the last occasion as he held her choking over the kitchen table, she reached behind her for a knife and struck at him any place she could so that he would release his strangle grip upon her throat. How many of us would not do the same? Thank God for our guardian angels, thank God for all the evil we are delivered from. And oh, how close we need to be in pity and in love to such a woman, thrown into jail, separated from her children for many months.

But of course Mike Wallace was not talking of such murderers, of whom we may feel no fear. He was speaking of the Hitlers and the Stalins and of such men as those accused of putting bombs in airplanes to collect insurance.

What to do about them? I remember asking Father Roy how God could love a man who came home and beat up his wife and children in a drunken rage (there was one such in our midst), and Father Roy shook his head sadly and said, "God loves only Jesus, God sees only Jesus." A hard lesson to take, to see Jesus in another, in the prodigal son, or members of a lynch mob. Have we begun to be Christians?

February 1960

"IN PEACE IS MY BITTERNESS MOST BITTER"

It is not just Vietnam, it is South Africa, it is Nigeria, the Congo, Indonesia, all of Latin America. It is not just the pictures of all the women and children who have been burnt alive in Vietnam, or the men who have been tortured, and died. It is not just the headless victims of the war in Colombia. It is not just the words of Cardinal Spellman and Archbishop Hannan. It is the fact that whether we like it or not, we are Americans. It is indeed our country, right or wrong, as the Cardinal said in another context. We are warm and fed and secure (aside from occasional muggings and murders amongst us). We are among nations the most powerful, the most armed, and we are supplying arms and money to the rest of the world where we are not ourselves fighting. We are eating while there is famine in the world.

Scripture tells us that the picture of judgment presented to us by Jesus is of Dives sitting and feasting with his friends while Lazarus sat hungry at the gate, the dogs, the scavengers of the East, licking his sores. We are Dives. Woe to the rich! *We* are the rich. The Works of Mercy are the opposite of the works of war, feeding the hungry, sheltering the homeless, nursing the sick, visiting the prisoner. But we are destroying crops, setting fire to entire villages and to the people in them. We are not performing the Works of Mercy but the works of war. We cannot repeat this enough.

When the Apostles wanted to call down fire from heaven on the inhospitable Samaritans, the "enemies" of the Jews, Jesus said to them, "You know not of what Spirit you are." When Peter told Our Lord not to accept the way of the Cross and His own death, He said, "Get behind me, Satan. For you are not on the side of God but of men." But He also had said "Thou art Peter and upon this rock I will build my church." Peter denied Jesus three times at that time in history, but after the death on the Cross, and the Resurrection and the Descent of the Holy Spirit, Peter faced up to Church and State alike and said, "We must obey God rather than men." Deliver us, O Lord, from the fear of our enemies, which makes cowards of us all.

I can sit in the presence of the Blessed Sacrament and wrestle for that peace in the bitterness of my soul, a bitterness which many Catholics throughout the world feel, and I can find many things in Scripture to console me, to change my heart from hatred to love of enemy. "Our worst enemies are those of our own household," Jesus said. Picking up the Scriptures at random (as St. Francis used to do), I read about Peter, James, and John who went up on the Mount of Transfiguration and saw Jesus talking with Moses and Elias, transfigured before their eyes. (A hint of the life to come, Maritain said.) Jesus transfigured! He who was the despised of men, no beauty in Him, spat upon, beaten, dragged to His cruel death on the way to the Cross! A Man so much like other men that it took the kiss of a Judas to single Him out from the others when the soldiers, so closely allied to the priests, came to take Him. Reading this story of the Transfiguration, the words stood out, words foolishly babbled, about the first building project of the Church, proposed by Peter. "Lord, shall we make here three shelters, one for You, one for Moses, and one for Elias?" And the account continues, "for he did not know what to say, he was so terrified."

Maybe they are terrified, these Princes of the Church, as we are often terrified at the sight of violence, which is present every now and then in our Houses of Hospitality, and which is always a threat in the streets of the slums. I have often thought it is a brave thing to do, these Christmas visits of Cardinal Spellman to the American troops all over the world, Europe, Korea, Vietnam. But oh, God, what are all these Americans, so-called Christians, doing all over the world so far from our own shores?

But what words are those he spoke—going against even the Pope, calling for victory, total victory? Words are as strong and powerful as bombs, as napalm. How much the government counts on those words, pays for those words to exalt our own way of life, to build up fear of the enemy. Deliver us, Lord, from the fear of the enemy. That is one of the lines in the Psalms, and we are not asking God to deliver us from enemies but from the fear of them. Love casts out fear, but we have to get over the fear in order to get close enough to love them.

There is plenty to do, for each one of us, working on our own hearts, changing our own attitudes, in our own neighborhoods. If the just man falls seven times daily, we each one of us fall more than that in thought, word, and deed. Prayer and fasting, taking up our own cross daily and following Him, doing penance, these are the hard words of the Gospel.

As to the Church, where else shall we go, except to the Bride of Christ, one flesh with Christ? Though she is a harlot at times, she is our Mother. We should read the Book of Hosea, which is a picture of God's steadfast love not only for the Jews, His chosen people, but for His Church, of which we are every one of us members or potential members. Since there is no time with God, we are all one, all one body, Chinese, Russians, Vietnamese, and He has *commanded us to love one another.*

"A new commandment I give, that you love others *as I have loved you,*" not to the defending of your life, but to the laying down of your life.

A hard saying.

Love is indeed a "harsh and dreadful thing" to ask of us, of each one of us, but it is the only answer.

January 1967

MARTIN LUTHER KING

Just three weeks ago Martin Luther King was shot as he stood on the balcony of a motel in Memphis, Tennessee. I was sitting in the kitchen of one of the women's apartments on Kenmare Street watching the television when the news flash came. I sat there stunned, wondering if he was suffering a superficial wound, as James Meredith did on his Mississippi walk to overcome fear, that famous march on which the cry "Black Power" was first shouted. Martin Luther King wrote about it in his last book, *Where Do We Go From Here?*—a book which all of us should read because it makes us understand what the words "Black Power" really mean. Dr. King was a man of the deepest and most profound spiritual insights.

These were the thoughts which flashed through my mind as I waited, scarcely knowing that I was waiting, for further news. The dreaded words were spoken almost at once. "Martin Luther King is dead." The next day was Good Friday, the day commemorated by the entire Christian world as the day when Jesus Christ, true God and true Man, shed His blood.

"Unless the grain of wheat fall into the ground and die, it remains alone. But if it die it produces much fruit." Martin Luther King died daily, as St. Paul said. He faced death daily and said a number of times that he knew he would be killed for the faith that was in him. The faith that men could live together as brothers. The faith in the Gospel teaching of nonviolence. The faith that man is capable of change, of growth, of growing in love.

Cynics may say that many used nonviolence as a tactic. Many may scoff at the outcry raised at his death, saying that this is an election year and all candidates had to show honor to a fallen Black hero. But love and grief were surely in the air those days of mourning, and all that was best in the country—in the labor movement, the civil rights movement, and the peace movement—cast aside all their worldly cares and occupations to go to Memphis to march with the sanitation union men, on whose behalf, during whose strike, Martin Luther King had given himself; and to Atlanta, where half a million people gathered to walk in the funeral procession, to follow the farm cart and the two mules which drew the coffin of the dead leader.

Always, I think, I will weep when I hear the song "We Shall Overcome," and when I read the words, "Free at last, free at last, Great God Almighty, Free at last."

April 1968

PRIEST AND PROPHET

Dear Father Dan Berrigan,

I woke up thinking of you this morning with love and regret at not having been at the First Street meeting to see you. With love, and gratitude too, for all you are doing—for the way you are spending yourself. Thank God, how the young love you. You must be utterly exhausted too, yet you keep going. I feel this keenly because I've been really down and out since August, what the doctor calls a chronic cough and a "mild heart failure," and I chafe at my enforced absence because of a nervous exhaustion which I realize you must often feel, though you are a generation or more younger than I.

But thank God, you are truly bearing the Cross, giving your life for others, as Father Phil is in cramped cell and enforced idleness, away from all he must crave day and night to do, surrounded by suffering, enduring the clamor of hell itself—he too is giving his life for others.

I cannot tell you how I love you both, and see more clearly how God is using you, reaching the prisoners and reaching the young. They all call you "Dan" and "Phil," but I call you Father Dan and Father Phil because always you are to me priests and prophets.

I feel that, as in the time of the Desert Fathers, the young are fleeing the cities—wandering over the face of the land, living after a fashion in voluntary poverty and manual labor, seeming to be inactive in the "peace movement." I know they are still a part of it—just as Cesar Chavez and the Farm Workers' Movement are also part of it, committed to nonviolence, even while they resist, fighting for their lives and their families' lives.

Meanwhile, up and down on both sides of the Hudson River, religious orders own thousands of acres of land, cultivated, landscaped, but not growing food for the hungry or founding villages for families or schools for the children.

How well I understand that biblical phrase "In peace is my bitterness most bitter." How to reconcile this with Jesus' new commandment of loving others, forgiving others seventy times seven—forgiving and loving enemies of our own household? Yes, "in peace is my bitterness most bitter." Yet the bitterness subsides and the peace in my heart grows, and even a love and some understanding grows of these "enemies of our own household."

I must tell little stories, as Jesus taught us to do, in trying to teach. They call it "reminiscing," when you are old. The story is this.

We had a mean pastor once long ago who was always blasting women in his sermons for sitting around gossiping, not cleaning their houses, and spending their husband-soldiers' pay on beer and movies. It was during the Second World War. And there was a man in our House of Hospitality arrested for indecent exposure. The parish neighbor who told me this called it "insulting a child," and I had thought she said "assaulting" and nearly fainted with fear and trembling. With no one else to turn to, I went to the pastor, the rigid and cranky one, and asked him to go to the jail, visiting the prisoner being one of the Works of Mercy. With no comment at all but with the utmost kindness and the delicacy of few words, he did as I requested and even interceded for this man off the road and got him a lighter sentence of sixty days. When this happened once again some years later, another priest, a saintly, well-spoken one, was appealed to. He responded, "Too bad they don't give him a life sentence!" You can never tell!

I hope we do not lose many subscribers because of my writing so frankly about matters seldom referred to. But nowadays when there are no longer lines at the confessionals in our churches there surely is an overflowing of public confession. In our newspapers, reviews, advertisements, and novels "nothing is hidden, it seems, that has not been revealed." It is as though the fear of death and judgment has made people rush to tell all, to confess to each other, before the Dread Judge shall tell all to the universe. Poor, fearful creatures that we are, is it that in this strange perverse way of confessing we are seeking Christ, even those who deny Him? Jesus Christ is our truth. By telling the truth, or one aspect of the truth, perhaps we are clinging to the hem of His garment, seeking to touch it like the woman with the "issue of blood," so that we may be healed.

I am not wandering, in writing this way. I am meditating. I am thinking of what I have come to think of as fundamental to our search for peace, for nonviolence. A flood of water (and Christ is living water) washes out sins— all manner of filth, degradation, fear, horror. He is also the Word. And studying the New Testament, and its commentators, I have come in this my seventy-sixth year, to think of a few holy words of Jesus as the greatest comfort of my life.

"Judge not."

"Forgive us our trespasses as we forgive those who trespass against us."

"Forgive seventy times seven times."

All words of Our Lord and Savior. I "have knowledge of salvation through forgiveness of my sins," as Zacharias sang in his canticle.

And so, when it comes to divorce, birth control, abortion, I must write in this way. The teaching of Christ, the Word, must be upheld. Held up though one would think that it is completely beyond us—out of our reach, impossible to follow. I believe Christ is our Truth and is with us always. We may stretch toward it, falling short, failing seventy times seven, but forgiveness is always there. He is the kind and loving judge. And so are 99 percent of the priests in the confessional. The verdict there is always "not guilty" even though our "firm resolve with the help of His grace to confess our sins, do penance, and amend our lives" may seem a hopeless proposition.

I believe in the Sacraments. I believe Grace is conferred through the Sacraments. I believe the priest is empowered to forgive sins. Grace is defined as "participation in the divine life," so little by little we are putting off the old man and putting on the new.

Actually, "putting on Christ."

P.S. (to our readers). The day after I finished this letter I received a letter from Father Phil—a good and loving letter. He is not *dis*couraged but is strong *in courage*. He will be released on parole on December 20, so let us all pray daily, and every time we hear and see a reference to "the Berrigans" let us pray, even if it is only the briefest "God be with them"—those words so familiar in our liturgy, to which the answer is, "And with you"—and us, too.

And dear Dan, Father Dan, please excuse my wandering like this.

December 1972

ALL SOULS

This month when we celebrate the feast of All Souls it is good to write about heaven as well as death. Someone is always putting a book or article in my hands that I need just at that moment, and the other night, when we gathered for Vespers in our office-library-stencil room, Mike Kovalak handed me a little book, ninety pages long. The first paragraph of the first chapter gave me the definition of heaven I needed.

> There we shall rest and we shall see;
> We shall love and we shall praise;
> Behold what shall be in the end and shall not end.

It is St. Augustine, of course, speaking with his mother just before she died. It is Scripture also speaking to us, of a future life where we will know as we will be known. The very word "know" is used in Genesis again and again as the act of husband and wife which brings forth more life: Abraham knew Sara, and she conceived and bore a son.

An Evangelist who sends me his comments on the Bible once referred to death as a "transport," an ecstasy. And indeed we are transported, in this passover to another life.

Jacques Maritain, our beloved friend whose death this year we are also commemorating, said once that the story of the Transfiguration is a feast we should surely meditate on. Three of the Apostles, sleeping as they often do even to this day, awoke to see Jesus standing with Moses and Elias, transfigured and glorified. It is a glimpse, Maritain commented, of the future, of life after death, of the dogmas contained in the creed—in the "resurrection of the body and life everlasting."

And Peter, the rock upon which Christ said He would build His Church, was confused, as popes have been many a time since, and wanted to start to build! But let's forget about criticism of Peter and find always concordances, as Pope John, the beloved, told us to do.

I had the great privilege of standing by my mother's bed, holding her hand, as she quietly breathed her last. So often I had worried when I was traveling around the country that I would not be there with her at the time if she were suddenly taken.

And now I have seen my little four-year-old great-grandaughter worrying about me. It was just after Rita Corbin's mother's death (another member of our family to remember this month). After Carmen's death and burial in our parish cemetery, my little Tanya came and sat on my lap. It was after one of my weeks-long absences from the farm, and stroking my cheek, she said anxiously, "You're not old—you're young."

Sensing her anxiety, I could only say, "No, I'm old too, like Mrs. Ham, and someday, I don't know when, I'm going to see my mother and father and brother too." And as she was accustomed to my absences, I am sure she was comforted. How wonderful it is to have a granddaughter and her little family living with us. A House of Hospitality on the land can indeed be an "extended family."

Meanwhile, in the joys and sorrows of this life, we can pray as they do in the Russian liturgy for a death "without blame or pain." May our passing be a rejoicing.

October-November 1973

A. W. TOZER (1897-1963)

A. W. Tozer was born in Pennsylvania, reared in Ohio, and converted to the Christian faith at the age of eighteen. Soon thereafter, with the aid of his wife's family and much reading, he began a lifelong search for a deeper relationship with God. Tozer eventually became a prominent minister in the Christian and Missionary Alliance Church, a successful pastor and radio speaker in Chicago, and the longtime editor of his denomination's magazine, *The Alliance Weekly*. But his concerns were never parochial or sectarian. Rather, he pursued the disciplines of faith, the depths of belief, and the potential for knowing God.

Tozer may have been a member of the Christian and Missionary Alliance, but his spiritual kinship extended to those in the history of Christianity who had shared his burden. His teachings were familiar to Protestant evangelicals because of their similarity to the emphases of the British Keswick movement, or to domestic emphases on "the Higher Life" or "Victorious Christian Living." (Such teachings encouraged Christians to seek a more refined stage of spiritual development in which the cares of this world melted away in the face of intimate fellowship with God.) Yet Tozer himself also drew inspiration from the fathers of the early church, the medieval monastic tradition, the Catholic mystics, and theologians of spiritual experience like Fénelon, Richard Baxter, and Jonathan Edwards. Though he was a Protestant, he learned much from Roman Catholics about the heart's longing for the divine. This was a debt he freely acknowledged, both in the following selection and also in several other volumes, including *The Knowledge of the Holy* (1961) and *The Christian Book of Mystical Verse* (1963).

The kind of piety that Tozer sought has been an inspiring goal for many American Christians, especially in the last century. Tozer's search for a purer realm of the spirit was also an appeal for a fuller understanding of the Holy Spirit, a theme of his work that he developed fully in a set of meditations published as *The Pursuit of God*. Tozer called it "a modest attempt to aid God's hungry children so to find Him." In an introduction to the book, the noted missionary statesman Samuel M. Zwemer wrote,

> [Tozer is] a self-made scholar, an omnivorous reader with a remarkable library of theological and devotional books, and one who seemed to burn the midnight oil in pursuit of God. His book is the result of long meditation and much prayer. . . . The chapters could be summarized in Moses' prayer, "Show me thy glory," or Paul's exclamation, "O the depth of the

riches both of the wisdom and knowledge of God!" It is theology not of the head but of the heart.

The following is the first chapter of *The Pursuit of God*.

Following Hard after God

> My soul followeth hard after thee:
> thy right hand upholdeth me.—*Psa.* 63:8

Christian theology teaches the doctrine of prevenient grace, which briefly stated means this, that before a man can seek God, God must first have sought the man.

Before a sinful man can think a right thought of God, there must have been a work of enlightenment done within him; imperfect it may be, but a true work nonetheless, and the secret cause of all desiring and seeking and praying which may follow.

We pursue God because, and only because, He has first put an urge within us that spurs us to the pursuit. "No man can come to me," said our Lord, "except the Father which hath sent me draw him," and it is by this very prevenient *drawing* that God takes from us every vestige of credit for the act of coming. The impulse to pursue God originates with God, but the out-working of that impulse is our following hard after Him; and all the time we are pursuing Him we are already in His hand: "Thy right hand upholdeth me."

In this divine "upholding" and human "following" there is no contradiction. All is of God, for as von Hügel teaches, *God is always previous*. In practice, however, (that is, where God's previous working meets man's present response) man must pursue God. On our part there must be positive reciprocation if this secret drawing of God is to eventuate in identifiable experience of the Divine. In the warm language of personal feeling this is stated in the Forty-second Psalm: "As the hart panteth after the water brooks, so panteth my soul after thee, O God. My soul thirsteth for God, for the living God: when shall I come and appear before God?" This is deep calling unto deep, and the longing heart will understand it.

The doctrine of justification by faith—a Biblical truth, and a blessed relief

Source: *The Pursuit of God* (Camp Hill, Penn.: Christian Publications, Inc., 1948), pp. 11-20.

from sterile legalism and unavailing self-effort—has in our time fallen into evil company and been interpreted by many in such manner as actually to bar men from the knowledge of God. The whole transaction of religious conversion has been made mechanical and spiritless. Faith may now be exercised without a jar to the moral life and without embarrassment to the Adamic ego. Christ may be "received" without creating any special love for Him in the soul of the receiver. The man is "saved," but he is not hungry nor thirsty after God. In fact he is specifically taught to be satisfied and encouraged to be content with little.

The modern scientist has lost God amid the wonders of His world; we Christians are in real danger of losing God amid the wonders of His Word. We have almost forgotten that God is a Person and, as such, can be cultivated as any person can. It is inherent in personality to be able to know other personalities, but full knowledge of one personality by another cannot be achieved in one encounter. It is only after long and loving mental intercourse that the full possibilities of both can be explored.

All social intercourse between human beings is a response of personality to personality, grading upward from the most casual brush between man and man to the fullest, most intimate communion of which the human soul is capable. Religion, so far as it is genuine, is in essence the response of created personalities to the Creating Personality, God. "This is life eternal, that they might know thee the only true God, and Jesus Christ, whom thou hast sent."

God is a Person, and in the deep of His mighty nature He thinks, wills, enjoys, feels, loves, desires and suffers as any other person may. In making Himself known to us He stays by the familiar pattern of personality. He communicates with us through the avenues of our minds, our wills and our emotions. The continuous and unembarrassed interchange of love and thought between God and the soul of the redeemed man is the throbbing heart of New Testament religion.

This intercourse between God and the soul is known to us in conscious personal awareness. It is personal: that is, it does not come through the body of believers, as such, but is known to the individual, and to the body through the individuals which compose it. And it is conscious: that is, it does not stay below the threshold of consciousness and work there unknown to the soul (as, for instance, infant baptism is thought by some to do), but comes within the field of awareness where the man can "know" it as he knows any other fact of experience.

You and I are in little (our sins excepted) what God is in large. Being made in His image we have within us the capacity to know Him. In our sins we lack only the power. The moment the Spirit has quickened us to life in regeneration our whole being senses its kinship to God and leaps up in joyous recognition. That is the heavenly birth without which we cannot see the Kingdom of God. It is, however, not an end but an inception, for now begins the glorious pursuit, the heart's happy exploration of the infinite riches of the Godhead. That is where we begin, I say, but where we stop no man has yet discovered, for there is in the awful and mysterious depths of the Triune God neither limit nor end.

> Shoreless Ocean, who can sound Thee?
> Thine own eternity is round Thee,
>   Majesty divine!

To have found God and still to pursue Him is the soul's paradox of love, scorned indeed by the too-easily-satisfied religionist, but justified in happy experience by the children of the burning heart. St. Bernard stated this holy paradox in a musical quatrain that will be instantly understood by every worshipping soul:

> We taste Thee, O Thou Living Bread,
> And long to feast upon Thee still:
> We drink of Thee, the Fountainhead
> And thirst our souls from Thee to fill.

Come near to the holy men and women of the past and you will soon feel the heat of their desire after God. They mourned for Him, they prayed and wrestled and sought for Him day and night, in season and out, and when they had found Him the finding was all the sweeter for the long seeking. Moses used the fact that he knew God as an argument for knowing Him better. "Now, therefore, I pray thee, if I have found grace in thy sight, show me now thy way, that I may know thee, that I may find grace in thy sight"; and from there he rose to make the daring request, "I beseech thee, show me thy glory." God was frankly pleased by this display of ardor, and the next day called Moses into the mount, and there in solemn procession made all His glory pass before him.

David's life was a torrent of spiritual desire, and his psalms ring with the cry of the seeker and the glad shout of the finder. Paul confessed the mainspring of his life to be his burning desire after Christ. "That I may know Him," was the goal of his heart, and to this he sacrificed everything. "Yea doubtless, and I count all things but loss for the excellency of the knowledge of Christ Jesus my Lord: for whom I have suffered the loss of all things, and do count them but refuse, that I may win Christ."

Hymnody is sweet with the longing after God, the God whom, while the singer seeks, he knows he has already found. "His track I see and I'll pursue," sang our fathers only a short generation ago, but that song is heard no more in the great congregation. How tragic that we in this dark day have had our seeking done for us by our teachers. Everything is made to center upon the initial act of "accepting" Christ (a term, incidentally, which is not found in the Bible) and we are not expected thereafter to crave any further revelation of God to our souls. We have been snared in the coils of a spurious logic which insists that if we have found Him we need no more seek Him. This is set before us as the last word in orthodoxy, and it is taken for granted that no Bible-taught Christian ever believed otherwise. Thus the whole testimony of the worshipping, seeking, singing Church on that subject is crisply set aside. The experiential heart-theology of a grand army of fragrant saints is rejected in favor of a smug interpretation of Scripture which would certainly have sounded strange to an Augustine, a Rutherford or a Brainerd.

In the midst of this great chill are some, I rejoice to acknowledge, who will not be content with shallow logic. They will admit the force of the argument, and then turn away with tears to hunt some lonely place and pray, "O God, show me thy glory." They want to taste, to touch with their hearts, to see with their inner eyes the wonder that is God.

I want deliberately to encourage this mighty longing after God. The lack of it has brought us to our present low estate. The stiff and wooden quality about our religious lives is a result of our lack of holy desire. Complacency is a deadly foe of all spiritual growth. Acute desire must be present or there will be no manifestation of Christ to His people. He waits to be wanted. Too bad that with many of us He waits so long, so very long, in vain.

Every age has its own characteristics. Right now we are in an age of religious complexity. The simplicity which is in Christ is rarely found among us. In its stead are programs, methods, organizations and a world of nervous activities which occupy time and attention but can never satisfy the longing of the heart. The shallowness of our inner experience, the hollowness of our worship, and that servile imitation of the world which marks our promotional methods all testify that we, in this day, know God only imperfectly, and the peace of God scarcely at all.

If we would find God amid all the religious externals we must first determine to find Him, and then proceed in the way of simplicity. Now as always God discovers Himself to "babes" and hides Himself in thick darkness from the wise and the prudent. We must simplify our approach to Him. We must strip down to essentials (and they will be found to be blessedly few). We must put away all effort to impress, and come with the guileless candor of childhood. If we do this, without doubt God will quickly respond.

When religion has said its last word, there is little that we need other than God Himself. The evil habit of seeking *God-and* effectively prevents us from finding God in full revelation. In the "and" lies our great woe. If we omit the "and" we shall soon find God, and in Him we shall find that for which we have all our lives been secretly longing.

We need not fear that in seeking God only we may narrow our lives or restrict the motions of our expanding hearts. The opposite is true. We can well afford to make God our All, to concentrate, to sacrifice the many for the One.

The author of the quaint old English classic, *The Cloud of Unknowing,* teaches us how to do this. "Lift up thine heart unto God with a meek stirring of love; and mean Himself, and none of His goods. And thereto, look thee loath to think on aught but God Himself. So that nought work in thy wit, nor in thy will, but only God Himself. This is the work of the soul that most pleaseth God."

Again, he recommends that in prayer we practice a further stripping down of everything, even of our theology. "For it sufficeth enough, a naked intent direct unto God without any other cause than Himself." Yet underneath all his thinking lay the broad foundation of New Testament truth, for he explains that by "Himself" he means "God that made thee, and bought thee, and that graciously called thee to thy degree." And he is all for simplicity: If we would have religion "lapped and folden in one word, for that thou shouldst have better hold thereupon, take thee but a little word of one syllable: for so it is better than of two, for even the shorter it is the better it accordeth with the work of the Spirit. And such a word is this word GOD or this word LOVE."

When the Lord divided Canaan among the tribes of Israel Levi received no share of the land. God said to him simply, "I am thy part and thine inheritance," and by those words made him richer than all his brethren, richer than all the kings and rajas who have ever lived in the world. And there is a spiritual principle here, a principle still valid for every priest of the Most High God.

The man who has God for his treasure has all things in One. Many ordinary treasures may be denied him, or if he is allowed to have them, the enjoyment of them will be so tempered that they will never be necessary to his happiness. Or if he must see them go, one after one, he will scarcely feel a sense of loss, for having the Source of all things he has in One all satisfaction, all pleasure, all delight. Whatever he may lose he has actually lost nothing, for he now has it all in One, and he has it purely, legitimately and forever.

O God, I have tasted Thy goodness, and it has both satisfied me and made me thirsty for more. I am painfully conscious of my need of further grace. I am ashamed of my lack of desire. O God, the Triune God, I want to want Thee; I long to be filled with longing; I thirst to be made more thirsty still. Show me Thy glory, I pray Thee, that so I may know Thee indeed. Begin in mercy a new work of love within me. Say to my soul, "Rise up, my love, my fair one, and come away." Then give me grace to rise and follow Thee up from this misty lowland where I have wandered so long. In Jesus' Name, Amen.

ELTON TRUEBLOOD (B. 1900)

Elton Trueblood has enjoyed more than six decades of active service as a distinguished Christian educator and apologist. After brief teaching stints at Harvard University, Haverford College, and Guilford College, Trueblood served for a decade as professor and chaplain at Stanford University. In 1946, desiring to teach in "a college in which there [was] an unapologetic Christian commitment," Trueblood moved to Earlham College in Richmond, Indiana, where he taught philosophy for the next twenty years. He still resides in Richmond.

Although Trueblood served with distinction as a college professor, he established his national reputation as a writer. His earliest works were scholarly philosophical articles and occasional pieces for the Quaker journal *The Friend*. In his autobiography, *While It Is Day*, Trueblood describes how his career as an apologist for the faith began in the early 1940s: "I was beginning to read the works of C. S. Lewis, whose complete liberation from the bondage of academic jargon I much admired. Lewis dealt with the most profound questions in a style of utmost clarity. I determined to try to do in America something of what C. S. Lewis was doing in England."

Out of this effort to translate the Christian faith for a contemporary audience came such works as *The Predicament of Modern Man, The Company of the Committed, Alternative to Futility,* and *A Place to Stand*. Each of these books testified to Trueblood's conviction that "it is possible to present . . . a faith which meets the demands of rational examination."

The following selection, which is from Trueblood's autobiography, tells the story of his own deepening faith. It is written in the deliberate, understated style that has characterized all of his efforts to preach a message of abiding commitment in an age of ever-shifting loyalties.

From *While It Is Day*

In the early days of my ministry I believed in God and undoubtedly thought of myself as a Christian, but my theology was not evangelical. Though in my spoken ministry I often mentioned Christ, I did not emphasize His uniqueness. I spoke much of His compassion, of His emphasis upon love of the brethren, and of His faith in men, demonstrated by His recruitment of such unlikely specimens of humanity as the Twelve Apostles, but I tended to omit His teaching about Himself and His unique relation to the Father.

Subtly and slowly the change in my message began to appear. The influences were of course numerous, but it may have been the writings of C. S. Lewis that first shocked me out of my unexamined liberalism. In reading Lewis I could not escape the conclusion that the popular view of Christ as being a Teacher, and *only* a Teacher, has within it a self-contradiction that cannot be resolved. I saw, in short, that conventional liberalism cannot survive rigorous and rational analysis. What Lewis and a few others made me face was the hard fact that if Christ was only a Teacher, then He was a false one, since, in His teaching, He claimed to be *more*. The supposition that He taught only, or even chiefly, about loving one another is simply not true. The hard fact is that if Christ was not in a unique sense "the image of the invisible God" (Colossians 1:15), as the early Christians believed, then He was certainly the arch impostor and charlatan of history.

C. S. Lewis reached me primarily because he turned the intellectual tables. I was wholly accustomed to a world in which the sophisticates engaged in attack, while the Christians sought bravely to be on the defense, but Lewis turned this around and forced the unbeliever into a posture of defense. In the *Screwtape Letters* dated July 5, 1941, at Magdalen College, Oxford, Lewis, who up to that time had been an inconspicuous academician, inaugurated a new Christian strategy. I had already begun to sense that however vulnerable the Christian position may be, the position of the opposition is more vulnerable still. Once when a graduate student asked one of my professors whether the study of philosophy would help him in the support of the Christian faith, the professor replied, "No, it will not; but it will do something else of great importance—it will help you to see the weaknesses of the enemies of the faith."

The first of the weapons employed by Lewis as he began to establish a new style of dialogue was humor, a weapon then sorely needed. He had noted the striking advice of Martin Luther, "The best way to drive out the devil, if he

Source: *While It Is Day: An Autobiography* (New York: Harper & Row, 1974), pp. 98-103.

will not yield to texts of Scripture, is to jeer and flout him, for he cannot bear scorn." In the pre-Lewis days many supposed, uncritically, that the opponents of Christianity had a monopoly upon reason, while the Christian had nothing to rely upon except faith. Lewis, to the delight of his many readers, reversed that assumption, adopting an approach reminiscent of that initiated by G. K. Chesterton. Screwtape, the arch Devil, in advising his nephew about the handling of a person who is weakening in his atheism, and is even somewhat attracted to Christ, tells him that above all he dare not let the fellow *think*. If he thinks, says Screwtape, he will be lost to *us*.

Though Lewis helped me in many ways, he helped me most by making me face the teaching of Christ in its wholeness. If in *Screwtape* he taught me to watch for the irrationality of the opposition, it was in *The Case for Christianity* (1943) that he became unanswerable. When I first read the crucial paragraph about Christ as Teacher, it struck me with great force, partly because I had begun already to be skeptical about the conventional liberalism of my student days. In short, though I felt that something was wrong, it took a man of the intellectual straightforwardness of Lewis to make me see it definitely and clearly. What I saw in 1943, and have seen ever since, is that the Good Teacher conception is one option which Christ does not allow us to take. We can reject Him; we can accept Him on His terms; we cannot, with intellectual honesty, impose our own terms. The crucial paragraph is as follows:

A man who was merely a man and said the sort of things Jesus said would not be a great moral teacher. He would either be a lunatic—on a level with the man who says he is a poached egg—or else he would be the Devil of Hell. You must make your choice. Either this man was, and is, the Son of God: or else a madman or something worse. You can shut Him up for a fool, you can spit at Him and kill Him as a demon; or you can fall at His feet and call Him Lord and God. But let us not come with any patronizing nonsense about His being a great human teacher. He has not left that open to us. He did not intend to.

With that tremendous challenge in my consciousness I began to look at the Gospels in a new light. What *did* Christ say about Himself and His unique relation to the Father? I could of course minimize His reported teaching in John's Gospel on the hypothesis that the words reported there are a reflection of later teaching. Thus when I read "No one comes to the Father, but by me" or "He who has seen me has seen the Father" (John 14:6, 9), I could reply that those clear statements may not have been the actual utterances of Christ, but I could not employ that argument when I dealt with the Synoptics and particularly with that strand in them which, according to the best scholarship, is part of the original material on which the Synoptic authors drew.

No part of Christ's teaching has greater evidence of authenticity than that which, evidently drawn from the same source, appears in Matthew 11:27 and Luke 10:22, "All things have been delivered to me by my Father; and no one knows the Son except the Father, and no one knows the Father except the Son and any one to whom the Son chooses to reveal him."

New strength came into my ministry both public and private when I saw that either I had to reject Christ and the admiring talk, or accept Him on His own terms. As though illumined by a great light, I saw that He did not ask for admiration; He asked for commitment! To the perplexed, the confused, the distraught, he said and still says "Come to me." In all the relativities of this world there is, if Christ is right, one solid place. He offers "rest," not in the sense of passivity, but in that of a place to stand, a center of trustworthiness in the midst of the world's confusion. When I suddenly realized that my one central certainty was the trustworthiness of Christ, my preaching took on a new note of confidence, which I tried to convey to others. Thus I began to emphasize, in a new context, the concept of trustworthiness. This word had appeared in the title of my Swarthmore Lecture, given in London in May 1939 and published by Allen and Unwin as *The Trustworthiness of Religious Experience*. I kept the term, but applied it in a unique way to Jesus Christ. Without intending to do so, I had become an evangelical Christian. I found that instead of being embarrassed by them any more, as many of my associates were, I could sing with joy and full intellectual acceptance the much loved gospel hymns such as "Jesus, Lover of My Soul" and "My Faith Looks Up to Thee."

New confidence in Christ provided me with a rational answer to a number of important questions. I had of course long believed in God, and I had recognized the force of the cumulative evidence for theism, but now I had a new approach. With Christ as my center of certitude, I was driven inevitably to God because Christ believed in Him! The logic was sharp and clear: either God is, or Christ was wrong. I found that such reasoning could be made clear to "average" people who made no claims to intellectual competence.

What emerged was a new theological approach. I discovered that when I spoke of God, people were polite but unimpressed, partly because so much of the sharpness of meaning had been eroded by talk of God as an impersonal Force. It was obvious that no thoughtful person would be greatly interested in a Power so abstract as the law of gravity. At least one kind of agnosticism can be maintained with integrity, but it is something about which no one ever becomes excited. In reading Gabriel Marcel I recognized what he meant when he spoke of "the system of values ultimately bound up with the desert in which I was expected to live." If God is, but is not a Person, ours is a desert universe indeed.

The new strategy, which influenced my ministry, was to move, not from

God to Christ, but from Christ to God. Thereby we start in our epistemological pilgrimage at the point of most reasonable assurance. If Christ is trustworthy, it follows that God really and objectively *is,* for Christ prayed to Him in a completely personal way. What we experience is that which Martin Buber has taught us to call the "I-Thou" relationship. With awe and wonder I considered the tremendous significance of the prayer of Christ which appears in Matthew 11:25 and Luke 10:21, "I thank, thee, Father, Lord of heaven and earth, that thou hast hidden these things from the wise and understanding and revealed them to babes." In that one prayer I began to see an entire theology by which people can live and which is compatible with the strictest rationality.

When I found that thoughtful people would listen to a Christ-centered approach, I realized where the power of the Christian faith resides. While many churches are declining in strength, the churches which exhibit both Christ-centeredness and rationality are marked by evident vitality. A natural consequence of this fruitful combination is devotion to justice and a real concern for persons. Once a ministry accepts unapologetically the conviction of the Christlikeness of God, we have a firm launching pad from which we can operate with confidence and make a consequent difference in the world.

FRANCIS SCHAEFFER (1912-1984)

Francis Schaeffer was a leading twentieth-century apologist for the Christian faith who made a particularly strong impact on the thinking of America's fundamentalists and evangelicals. From his home in the Swiss Alps he exercised a wide-ranging ministry. The heart of that ministry was L'Abri (meaning "shelter") Fellowship, a retreat and study center in Huémoz, Switzerland, that was open to spiritual inquirers of any sort. Schaeffer's message to the many who came from all over the world was the same: the Scriptures provide an infallible guide to the character of God, the need of humans, and the salvation offered in Christ. But besides stressing these basic truths, Schaeffer also made a determined effort to reach out in love to the students who came with their doubts, perplexities, and questions. He took very seriously the despair of the modern world. Unlike most of the American Protestant conservatives of his generation, he also realized the great impact that the arts and the media have on modern life. And so at L'Abri, Schaeffer and his guests studied music, painting, and the modern writers, both with appreciation for their insight and with careful evaluation of their spiritual strengths and weaknesses.

In the last fifteen years of his life, Schaeffer became a major public figure. Many books, several film series, and well-publicized speaking tours brought him to the attention of wide audiences in the United States and significant groups in Europe. In these last years Schaeffer continued to address the personal spiritual struggles of modern life, but he also spoke out boldly on pressing social issues. However, his most effective form of ministry remained his ability to reach into the lives of troubled young people with a message combining Christian truth and loving concern.

Schaeffer was born near Philadelphia and was converted through private Bible study in 1930. He was a youthful participant in Presbyterian ecclesiastical struggles during the 1930s. First he joined the conservatives who left the northern Presbyterian church; then he continued on in a separatistic course by supporting the division that sundered the Presbyterian come-outers. For ten years he served as pastor of Bible Presbyterian congregations in the United States. In 1948 he decided to go to Europe with his family to engage in the work of child evangelism. While pursuing this new calling he experienced a crisis of faith that led him to question the wisdom of the separatistic Christianity he had embraced up until that time. Out of this struggle also came his desire to reach out in sincerity to the others who were experiencing the despair and alienation so common in the modern world. He and his wife, Edith, established the L'Abri Fellowship in 1955, and in later years founded other L'Abri centers in Europe and the United States.

The letters that follow provide Francis Schaeffer's own account of his turn from separatistic fundamentalism toward a spirituality more responsive to the modern condition. And they illustrate the seriousness with which he responded to appeals for spiritual help from those who sought shelter at L'Abri. The first two letters are to friends in America, the third to a young lady who had visited L'Abri and who later came to suffer from severe and persistent depression.

Selected Letters

November 8, 1951

Chalet Bijou
Champéry, Switzerland

My dear Jeffrey,

. . . The three and a half years since I came to Europe have been the most profitable in my life, with only one possible competitor, my three years in seminary. But certainly (with that one possible exception) no period even three times as long has marked me so.

First, the things of which I spoke above—the rectifying process of space and time—have caused my view of the Lord to grow greater, and my view of man and his works and judgments to grow proportionately smaller.

Second, for the first time since I entered college I have had a chance to think. Not that we have not been busy here; we have been, but it is a bit different from the rush of college, seminary, and then ten years in the pastorate. Gradually my thinking has changed—I have realized that in many things previously I have been mistaken.

When I first found Christ through my Bible reading He was very real to me, and I yet remember the loving wonder of His closeness. And then came the struggle against the Old [Presbyterian] Church machine, and then against Westminster, and then against the N.A.E. [National Association of Evangelicals], and gradually "the [separatist] movement" loomed larger and

---

Source: *Letters of Francis A. Schaeffer*, ed. Lane T. Dennis (Westchester, Ill.: Crossway Books, 1985), pp. 36-41, 47-50, 96-97. Dennis supplied the material in brackets and also provided pseudonyms for Schaeffer's correspondents.

larger. Do not misunderstand me: my experiences here have convinced me more than ever that each of these struggles was needed and right; but the correct perspective got mislaid in the process. And I tell you frankly, that though I realize I may be wrong, it seems to me that I was not alone in my mistake—that many are as deeply involved, or even more, than I have been. The "movement" grew in our thinking like the great bay tree until for me that wonderful closeness which I had felt to Him in previous days was lost. I wonder if that is not what happened to the Church of Ephesus in Revelation 2?

It seems to me all things became grist for the movement's mill. . . . And if things or people got in the way, they were to be blasted. The Presbyterian Church fight [in the early and mid-1930s] was a rough school of battle. First at unbelief, and then as time went on, at that which represented unbelief, the Federal Council [of Churches]. We threw everything which came to hand. And then as "the movement" grew, the N.A.E. stood in the way . . . and it seems to me we continued to throw everything we had at hand. Again, don't misunderstand me: from my experience here [in Europe] I am sure that we were correct in saying that the N.A.E. was wrong. But we could have remembered that, wrong though they are, they are for the most part brothers in Christ. . . .

But "the movement" rolls on, and now differences arise between us. Quickly the pattern repeats itself; the habit is too well learned. The movement is in jeopardy! So everything is thrown again [this time at one another within the movement]. . . . And who is wounded? We are and our Lord. . . .

I am sure "separation" is correct, but it is only one principle. There are others to be kept as well. The command to love should mean something. . . . [I am not suggesting that] I have learned to live in the light of Christ's command of love—first toward God, then the brethren, and then the lost. I know I have not. But I want to learn, and I know I must if I am to have that closeness to the Lord I wish to have, with its accompanying joy and spiritual power. . . .

God willing, I will push and politick no more. . . . The mountains are too high, history is too long, and eternity is longer. God is too great, man is too small, there are many of God's dear children, and all around there are men going to Hell. And if one man and a small group of men do not approve of where I am and what I do, does it prove I've missed success? No; only one thing will determine that—whether *this day* I'm where the Lord of lords and King of kings wants me to be. To win as many as I can, to help strengthen the hands of those who fight unbelief in the historical setting in which they are placed, to know the reality of "the Lord is my song," and to be committed to the Holy Spirit—that is what I wish I could know to be the reality of each day as it closes.

Have I learned all this? No, but I would not exchange that portion of it which I have, by God's grace, for all the hand-clapping I have had when I have been on the top of the pile. I have been a poor learner, but I'm further on than I was three years ago and I like it.

Jeffrey, I've seen the Holy Spirit work in individual lives like I have never experienced before. It reminds me of what I've heard of the revivals of yesterday. It would not be counted for much—only one's and two's—but it is as different as day and night from the way I've seen it come before. If the Lord can do it with me, with all I know is wrong with Schaeffer, with one's and two's, He can do it with hundreds too if He wishes. . . . On this last trip at one place . . . even though [I spoke] through translation, I saw them weep as I presented the wonders of our Lord. I am sure the Lord did it and not I. And whether it is one or a crowd, when that comes I am at rest.

. . . I know I've made mistakes and I know I've sinned. And where I know it, I have tried to make it right with those I have hurt, to confess it to the Lord and try to follow His way. . . . My inclination is to think that Christ meant it in a very literal way when He said to seek the lower seats. That does not mean, as I see it, that we should refuse the higher if the Lord takes us there, but He should do the taking. I regret the times in my life when this has not been the case. . . .

I am not sure as to what my future is. . . . I am not at all sure whether or not the rest of my life is meant for Europe. A new trouble has just arisen here because of the work we are doing in Champéry, and it could mean that our police permit will be lost. I guess that this will happen at least some day in this Roman Catholic canton. . . . I came to Europe because I thought I had the Lord's leading in it, and I will leave if I feel I have the same. . . .

[Through the recent difficulties I have faced], the Lord taught me more than I ever knew of the greatness of the Lord and the smallness of any man— and the corresponding importance of pleasing the Lord, and the lack of importance of pleasing any particular man. . . . [In spite of all that has happened there is no question of] personal discouragement, for I am probably less discouraged than I have ever been since those bright days when I first saw the face of the Lord, and before my feet got stuck in the problems of the prestige of man. . . .

. . . Because of our past closeness [I have written these] seventeen pages of handwriting to you. The longest letter I have written—I think—since I was courting Edith! . . .

Love from Edith to Hope, and from all of us to all of you our warmest greetings. I pray for you often and thank God for you.

In our Lord,
Francis A. Schaeffer

[The following note was added at the end of the letter:]
"Oh this self-love, this self-will! It is the Devil of Devils! Lord Jesus, may Thy blessed Spirit purge it out of all our hearts!"   Whitefield

November 12, 1954

Chalet Bijou
Champéry, Switzerland

Dear Ted,
. . . [With a very few exceptions, our movement has] produced practically no devotional literature nor serious study toward a devotional frame of mind. I include myself in this very strongly. Thinking back through the years over my own preaching, writing, and thinking, I am ashamed at this point. . . . God willing, Edith and I want to go on in these matters in which we feel we are only babes. . . .

As I see it, all devotional thinking and material largely falls under four heads:

1. *A call to God's people to the spiritual and to the supernatural.* That is, to live on the plane of a wisdom higher than, and often contrary to, the wisdom of the world; to live in the power of the Holy Spirit in the small as well as large things; to practice doing what the world would consider stupid, in faith that it will please the Lord because it is right.

2. *A call to show forth the love we should show toward God, our brothers, and all mankind*—whether saved or lost, friends or enemies. And a call to stop the hypocrisy of raising the banner of love and then forgetting it. (Let me say at once, and again very strongly, that in my preaching and in my writing in this regard, these matters speak first of all to my own heart.) However, to be worthwhile, this must be practical. For example, in the case of the separatist movement we must honestly face the question of the proper relationship between God's command for the purity of the visible church, and His equal command for an exhibition of the unity of the whole body of Christ.

3. *A call to an absolute loyalty to the headship of Christ and to the leadership of the Holy Spirit.* This cannot help but bring with it the recognition that loyalty to human leadership tends to replace this in a sinful way— i.e., loyalty to organizations and movements have always tended over time to take the place of loyalty to the person of Christ.

4. *A call to remember that the Church has one duty primarily—namely, the preaching of the gospel*—and that it should not get side-tracked into putting second things first. This cannot help but bring with it the recognition that the primary agencies (above all the church, but also home and foreign

mission boards) always tend to be reduced to being merely a means to an end in favor of other types of agencies and organizations. . . .

Through these past four years I have wrestled with this in a way that would sound dramatic if I would try to put it into words, and I have come to my conclusions. The only way that I dare to walk before God [is in accord with His leading in these matters]. I do not judge anyone else in this. I only know the message the Lord has put on my own heart, and which I must speak regardless of the cost. It has already cost me something, and may cost more. . . .

I believe most strongly . . . that our efforts in Christian service fall into three concentric circles: the outer circle is *the apologetic* and defensive. (This is an important portion of Christian activity and should never be minimized, but it is not the heart. . . .) The middle circle is inside the outer one and is more central. This is *the intellectual* statement of the doctrines of the Christian faith in a positive way. (This to me is an even more important portion of Christian activity, but if it stands alone, it still is not Christianity.)

The innermost circle is *the spiritual*—the personal relationship of the individual soul with a personal God, including all that is meant in the apostolic benediction when we say, "The communion of the Holy Spirit be with you all." It is this last, innermost circle with which the devotional deals and without which Christianity is not really Bible-believing.

To me there is no alternative but to ask for God's grace to keep these three circles in proper position in my own life—to meditate upon this and wrestle with its complete meaning and practice in my own life as I have not wrestled with anything since I wrestled as an agnostic with the claims of Christ as Savior. . . .

I would ask the three of you to be praying for us. A number of things have occurred even since leaving the States which make us feel we face certain decisions. We long to know the Lord's will, and as far as we know our own hearts we long to do His will. By His grace, may you all, and we, forever love Him more and know Him better on a personal level.

With warmest personal regards,
In the slain and risen Lamb,
Francis A. Schaeffer

July 19, 1963

Chalet les Mélèzes
Huémoz sur Ollon, Switzerland

Dear Kristina:
Thank you so much for your letter of July 2. I cannot tell you how deeply I was touched by it. I am sorry that you did not feel free to write before. You

will never know how many times I have thought of you and wondered where you were. I have kept you on a special place on my prayer list and have often really longed for you as I wondered what was happening to you. I will never forget you in the hospital when I visited you in _____. I understand too what you write about the difficulties of finding a consolation and reality. I think there are really two things to see: first, that when a person goes through the kind of difficulty you have gone through, this kind of feeling is not to be unexpected; and secondly, all men since the Fall—although in a far lesser degree and a far lesser agony than you have known—also have some such problems.

Increasingly I am so aware that just as there are no perfect people physically, so there are no perfect people psychologically. There are differences in intensity of physical problems and differences of intensity in psychological problems. But there is no such thing since man has revolted against God as people who are completely well, either physically or psychologically. Thus, as I have people come here who have problems, my own contact with them always involves a very deep realization that there may be differences of degree and kind of problem, but it is not that they are sick and I am well. I think this makes for a depth of human contact that is so lacking in much medical and psychiatric treatment. So often the doctor stands without a human contact with those who are before him. But when we come to one another on a really Christian basis, it seems to me this need not be the case; rather, we can stand together as poor people who are marked with the sorrow of a mankind who has revolted against God.

At the same time, as Christians we do not have to allow the pendulum to swing between [the extreme of] a false idealism and romantic hope, or the opposite [extreme] of despair. The infinite finished work of Christ upon Calvary's cross not only opens up the gates of Heaven to us when we accept Him as Savior; but it also provides, in the present life, for a substantial advance in the areas of psychological need.

The same thing is true in the areas of sociological need—the communication of man to man on a truly human level. There are no such things as perfect bodies, perfect psychological balance, or perfect communication between men in this world. This must wait until that glad day when Jesus comes back again and our bodies are raised from the dead. But yet, just because there is no perfect balance in the present life, this does not mean that there cannot be substantial advance. What this means will be different in different individual cases. But how thankful I am, in my own problems and in dealing with the problems of so many others, that it is possible, on the basis of the finished work of Christ, not to either have to say foolishly and falsely that all is well (when all is anything but well), or else to simply plunge into the abyss of despair.

Dear Kristina, let us find the way—each in his own way and according to his own need—[to appropriate] the meaning of the work of Christ in our present lives. I have no illusion . . . that you may not simply take this letter and throw it away, and that you could say, what does Mr. Schaeffer know about my sorrows? On the other hand, this is not absolutely so. I too have sorrows in my personal life, in my family, and in the work of L'Abri, as well as in the church at large. Thus, I say to you—let us go on and find that substantial advance which we can know even in this poor present world.

I would say again how much we love you and long to help. . . .

Please do write soon again. With love,

In the Lamb,
Francis A. Schaeffer

CATHERINE MARSHALL (1914-1983)

Catherine Marshall was born into the home of a Presbyterian minister in Tennessee. The rural upbringing she enjoyed there later became the raw material for her inspirational novel, *Christy* (1967). Before this book appeared, however, she had become widely known as the editor of her husband's sermons and the author of his biography.

When Catherine Ambrose married Peter Marshall in 1936, she entered immediately into the public eye. Peter Marshall was an eloquent Presbyterian minister and immigrant from Scotland who eventually became the minister of the New York Avenue Presbyterian Church in Washington, D.C., and, in the last years of his life, chaplain of the United States Senate.

Peter Marshall's death in 1949 was a crushing blow, but it did not undermine his wife's pluck and determination. In that same year she published a collection of her husband's sermons, *Mr. Jones, Meet the Master,* which achieved great popularity. And soon she was at work on the story of his life. The book that resulted, *A Man Called Peter: The Story of Peter Marshall,* was not an "objective" biography, but neither was it a sanitized and predictable memorial. Its lively prose and clear-sighted assessment of a preacher's life conveyed persuasively the reasons for Marshall's popularity. The book accomplished a very difficult task: showing that a pious man of God could also be a knowledgeable man of this world.

In a book filled with effective portraits, the chapter on the couple's life together is nonetheless one of the best. It comes toward the end of the book and so deals as well with Peter Marshall's last years, the time between his first heart problems and the attack that proved fatal.

The light that this chapter sheds on the life of Peter and Catherine Marshall serves also to illuminate a general truth. The way of piety, as this book has witnessed so often, is rarely solitary. It involves many kinds of relationships with other people. Often in thinking about the Christian journey, however, the most intimate of human relationships—that between wife and husband—is neglected. Catherine Marshall's account redresses this imbalance and highlights a relationship with a fundamental importance to the life of faith.

Together

The years brought many changes for Peter and me. Into our marriage came an ever-deepening fusion of heart and mind, though never a static peace. It was a harmony growing out of diversity in unity, the most melodious harmony there is.

I had successfully weathered the difficulties involved in accepting my share of responsibility for Peter's career. Even my three years in bed had contributed to our partnership. During those years, when I was necessarily shut out of the organizational work of our church, I found a more important field of service behind the scenes, at the very heart of Peter's life and ministry.

His job was constantly to pour himself out for the hungry hearts of men and women. My job was to try to feed him spiritually, to strengthen him, to supply understanding and encouragement, so that he would always have something to give to others.

We came to see this oneness between us as the open door by which the Spirit of God poured into our lives and work. When that agreement was missing, the door was closed; we were "on our own"; our work was self-managed, fruitless.

When Peter and I could stand shoulder to shoulder at the center of our congregation, the unity between us extended into the life of our church, and God's blessings rained on our flock.

It was the same invaluable lesson that the apostles had learned at Pentecost. Like those first disciples, we discovered that the results of real accord could be breathtaking, limitless.

During these years we collaborated on some writing for the Board of Christian Education of the Presbyterian Church. Together we wrote *The Mystery of the Ages,* a Bible study on Ephesians and two issues of the little devotional magazine *Today.* This collaboration not only proved to be rewarding, but was also fun. Not even our closest friends could tell where my husband's writing left off and mine began.

Increasingly we thought through and talked through Peter's projected sermons together. Frequently I did the spadework, the research, and he, the final writing.

Often he would telephone me from the church office, "Catherine, I'm working on a sermon. I'm stuck. Let me read you what I've written so far. See what you think."

Peter once confided to a friend, "You know, I think my most effective sermons have been the ones Catherine and I have worked on together; and

Source: *A Man Called Peter* (Englewood Cliffs, N.J.: McGraw-Hill, 1951), pp. 227-34.

the trips to preach away from home that have brought the greatest results are the times when I have felt no tension on leaving Catherine against her wishes. I don't see why it can't be that way all the time. *I have to accept those calls to preach.* God called me to preach; that call hasn't been revoked. If He wants me to live, He'll see to it that I do. How *can* I make Catherine see that?"

Inherent in these remarks was the greatest proof of the reality of our union. It was the pain each of us experienced when there was the least pulling apart. The one point on which we had still not achieved perfect agreement was this matter of Peter's out-of-town preaching engagements. Always we had a somewhat divergent point of view about it. Peter's heart attack drew that divergence into sharp focus. It was no longer simply a question of the advisability of this policy or that. Peter and I both knew that his life was probably at stake.

My husband's heart, the doctors told us, had been severely damaged. Nevertheless, they had promised him, after a long rest, a 90 to 95 per cent return to normal activity.

That long rest he had taken—ten weeks in the hospital, two at the Manse, three months at "Waverley." For such a vital, vigorous man, he had exhibited a disciplined patience which amazed us all.

As he resumed his ministry in September, 1946, at first my husband was cautious in deciding how much activity he would undertake. Gradually, as he did more, apparently with no ill effects to his heart, he gained confidence. His natural vitality and exuberance flowed back. He looked well; he felt well. He enjoyed life as much as ever. He had a deceitful type of heart condition. The usual hampering symptoms—shortness of breath, pain, swelling of the ankles—were entirely absent. This encouraged him to do too much; it encouraged others to demand too much of him.

The tempo of his activity steadily accelerated. A year after the heart attack, those of us close to Peter knew that he was once again treading on dangerous ground. The question was: What could we do about it? How could we stop him?

I mapped a veritable campaign in an effort to deal with the frightening juxtaposition of a seriously damaged heart and a not-to-be-contained spirit in one man.

First, I tried a direct approach—that of trying to persuade Peter to a quieter way of life. I found all my arguments and pleas unavailing. It was like reasoning with a closed door. There was in my husband a quality of iron determination to pursue his own course.

Many friends, some at my suggestion, also had long talks with him. They tried to convince him that a physically geographically limited ministry, with more time for reading, study, and prayer, could in the end be a more fruitful ministry. They got no further than I had. Peter could simply not see it that way.

My next approach was to enter into a loving conspiracy with Peter's secretary, members of his church staff, and many friends. All of us tried to shield him whenever we could, with or without his knowledge. Mostly he simply resented what he regarded as coddling.

In June of that year, the annual Sunday School picnic was held at Marshall Hall on the Potomac. To everyone's consternation their minister insisted on taking part in a baseball game.

Dr. Marshall was at bat. He swung and hit a long drive to left center.

"Dr. Marshall, let me run for you," one of the men pleaded.

"Not on your life," yelled Peter as he started for first base.

Several of the men were frightened, and actually ran the bases beside him. Peter got to third base and made it home on the next hit. He simply scoffed at the solicitude of his friends.

I saw then that Peter had tried to face up to the kind of life and ministry he would have if he decided to slow down, to protect himself as we wanted him to. He could not abide what he saw—a studied neurotic prepossession with self, a ministry geographically circumscribed, limited to Washington, an increasing curtailment of all activity. It would mean a narrow, limited life while he was still a young man at the very height of his powers. No, that was not for him, and he knew it.

Therefore, he made a bargain with his Lord. He put himself completely in God's hands. His part of the bargain was that he would continue to give his best to the ministry, leaving the result, including his health, entirely up to God. When that transaction was completed, the only unsolved problem in Peter's mind was the task of persuading me to his point of view. He knew perfectly well that I was still trying to protect him, still trying desperately to find another way out of our dilemma.

Perhaps, I reasoned, my prayers for Peter had not been answered, because I had asked God for too little. Perhaps God wanted to cure Peter's heart, so that he would not have to live a limited life.

Once again, as I had done during the crisis of Peter's first heart attack, I sought the help of prayer experts. This was done with Peter's full knowledge and cooperation. Yet those prayers were not answered in the way we hoped they would be. That door too was shut in our faces.

In the end, I did come to the relinquishment which Peter had wanted all along, but not until I had tried everything else.

Jesus said, ". . . if two of you shall agree on earth as touching anything that they shall ask, it shall be done for them of my Father which is in Heaven." (Matthew 18:19.) I began to feel that this agreement between Peter and me in relation to his health was of primary importance, and that unity could be achieved only by a giving in on my part. I knew from my own experience that the prayer of relinquishment often has great power. I hoped that in this case it would make it possible for God someway, somehow, to save Peter's life for many years. Perhaps God would have to change his temperament in order to do that, but I knew that God could do even that.

That was how it came about that in late September, 1948, I turned Peter over to God for better or for worse. We were driving to Richmond when I told Peter about it. He seemed vastly relieved. Practically speaking, this simply meant to Peter that I was saying, "Preach as often as you feel God wants you to. I'm hands off now."

So he did preach, more and more frequently, with ever-increasing power and authority.

And I stood by, loving him, alternately proud of him and desperately afraid for him, utterly helpless, with a wistful heart.

Peter's whole attitude about his own health problem can finally be understood only when viewed against the background of his attitude toward death. There was in him no fear of death.

He preached many a sermon on immortality. Yet his attitude on the subject was sometimes quite misrepresented, as when *Time* (in its February 7, 1949, issue) said of him: "Dr. Marshall . . . frequently ended services by saying, 'If I am still here, I'll be with you next week'" [*Time,* "Plain and Pertinent," Feb. 7, 1949].

I cannot remember Peter's ending any service with such a remark; nor did he who enjoyed life so much do any straining at the leash of mortality.

At the same time, Peter was exceedingly realistic and consistently Christian in his attitude toward death. In his mind, the soul and the body were two completely separate things. "You and I *are* souls," he reiterated frequently, "living *in* bodies."

One fall as we were returning home from Cape Cod, we drove over a viaduct which arched over a large New Jersey cemetery. "Nice straight plantings down there," Peter said admiringly. . . . I recoiled at such callousness, but Peter laughed . . . and refused to retract. He knew that I, up to that time, had never really faced up to the fact of death in human experience, and that *my* attitude was the unhealthy one.

Why are we so afraid to think of death? [he asked once in a sermon]
Why do we shun it so?
We try so hard to disguise the fact of death.
And we are so stupid about it.
We rouge the cheeks of the corpse, and dress it up in its best suit.
And then we say with ridiculous gravity: "How natural he looks." . . .
We, who call ourselves Christians, act in a very pagan way.
We gaze upon the lifeless, human clay . . .
We touch the cold cheek . . .
We line up to pass by the casket and "view the remains," as the stupid phrase has it,

as if we had never heard of the soul, and never understood what personality is.

If this thing that we call death were some leprous calamity that befell only a few of us . . .

If it were something that could be avoided, then we might enter into a conspiracy of silence concerning it.

But it is inevitable.

Death comes to every man—to every woman.

It is life's greatest and perhaps its only certainty.

Peter Marshall believed in immortality more surely than anyone I have ever known. As a very young preacher he had been curious about the details of the life we human beings are going to live "behind the curtain."

During the years of his Covington ministry, he ferreted out everything in the Scriptures about immortality, pored over books on spiritualism, including Sir Oliver Lodge's *Raymond* and *Phantom Walls*.

Yet, in the end, he rejected spiritualism as dangerous, unworthy of Christians, and not having the approval of Christ. Thereafter, though his curiosity remained, he left spiritualism strictly alone.

One evening at the Manse we received a telephone call telling us that a woman in our congregation had just died. She was a dear friend. She had been desperately ill for a long time, so that her death was not unexpected.

Peter came away from the telephone slowly and sank down in his favorite chair. His mind seemed far away.

"Gertrude died about ten minutes ago," he said thoughtfully. "I wonder what thrilling experience she's having at this very moment."

There was a young student at Davidson College to whom Peter Marshall was a veritable hero. This boy was killed in action in Japan in World War II.

One Sunday morning at the close of the service, the young soldier's mother spoke to Peter to tell him of her son's death.

Some time later she had occasion to tell me about Peter's reaction to the news. "Dr. Marshall gripped my hand and said, 'You'll see him again!' Of course I had believed that, but as Dr. Marshall spoke that one sentence with such depth of feeling, warm sweet comfort flowed into my lonely heart."

Ever since Peter's own brush with death at the time of his heart attack, there had been an added note of authority in his preaching that went straight to the heart of things. After that experience, Peter saw precious human life only in relation to time and eternity, which is its true perspective.

It was as if on his journey through life, Peter had mounted to the top of a plateau, where his own ultimate goal was clearly visible on the horizon. As he feverishly planned and worked on the details of the New York Avenue's building program, he seemed to have a premonition that he would not be with us when the spire of the new church rose skyward. Already, he saw himself as just another name in the long list of ministers who had served New York Avenue Presbyterian Church.

In an after-dinner talk made to those who had helped in the building campaign, he had said:

> Think of all the history these walls know . . .
> How administrations have come and gone.
> Wars have broken out in all their fury and have rumbled into silence.
> But the church goes on . . .
>   Gurley
>   Mitchell
>   Paxton
>   Bartlett
>   Radcliffe
>   Sizoo
>   Marshall
>   And those who come after us. . . .
> The church will go on.
> The church has gone on . . . not always the same, thank God, changing, adapting itself to meet new conditions, testifying in every age to the Spirit of the Living God through a new flaming forth of that spirit in new forms. No other institution has such a record, living on through the centuries, utterly dependent upon human faith and divine grace.

Nothing reveals quite so clearly Peter Marshall's own clear-eyed humility about himself as a little incident which took place soon after his heart attack. In the fall of 1946 when he had resumed work again, a minister friend from Hagerstown, Maryland, dropped in on him at the church office.

"Well, Peter," the friend asked, "I'm curious to know something. What did you learn during your illness?"

"Do you really want to know?" Peter answered promptly. "I learned that the Kingdom of God goes on without Peter Marshall."

THOMAS MERTON (1915-1968)

The story of Thomas Merton bears a number of striking parallels to that of Dorothy Day. Both had a disrupted and tumultuous adolescence and young adulthood, flirted with Communism in the years between the World Wars, and then made a deep and lasting commitment to the life of the Catholic Church.

Born in France during the First World War to a New Zealand father and an American mother, Thomas Merton divided his childhood years between Europe and America. At the age of twenty he returned to America an orphan. He enrolled in Columbia University and joined—in this time of the Great Depression, the rise of fascism in Europe, and the civil war in Spain—a young Communist group. Gradually, however, Merton began to move toward the Catholic Church, a process set in motion by his service in a Catholic settlement house in New York City. Eventually he converted to Catholicism, and several years later he joined the Trappist order.

The Seven Storey Mountain (1948) tells the tale of those early years and their many "conversions." Although this is perhaps his best-known work, Merton continued to write prolifically until his untimely death in 1968. Both of his parents had had an intense interest in art, and Merton was himself a good poet and a perceptive literary critic. He was also the author of numerous articles and books on Catholic spiritual devotion. His sensitivity to modern cultural developments and the similarity of his thought to some elements of Eastern religion have made him a thinker and writer of continuing interest.

The two selections that follow are from the manuscript of *The Seven Storey Mountain*. The first is an unpublished portion of the original manuscript describing the celebration of Christmas in Merton's monastery; this piece draws a number of parallels to the desolation of the contemporary world. The second selection is the published conclusion of *The Seven Storey Mountain*. It tells of Merton's experience in taking vows. Both passages illustrate Merton's particular sensibility, his passionate devotion to God and the holy orders of his faith, his intense sensitivity to the metaphorical possibilities of language, and his deep desire to speak the enduring Truth in terms of lively contemporaneity.

Prose Excerpts

Christ always seeks the straw of the most desolate cribs to make his Bethlehem. In all the other Christmases of my life, I had got a lot of presents and a big dinner. This Christmas I was to get no presents, and not much of a dinner: but I would have, indeed, Christ Himself, God, the Savior of the world.

You who live in the world: let me tell you that there is no comparing these two kinds of Christmas.

What an atmosphere of expectation and joy there is in a Cistercian monastery when the monks get up, not at two in the morning, but at nine in the evening. They have gone to bed at five. Now, at this unaccustomed hour, when the winter night has not yet begun to get that paralyzing desolate coldness of the small hours, the church is full of unaccustomed lights. There is the crib, all lit up with a soft glow, and in the high darkness of the sanctuary the forest of cedar branches that has grown up around the altar sparkles with tinsel here and there.

It is then that the night office begins, begins at once with a solemn and stately invitatory that nevertheless rocks the church with cadences of superlative joy; from then on it is as though the angels themselves were singing their *Gloria in Excelsis* and showering upon the earth from the near stars, the stars that seem to have become close and warm, their messages and promises of peace, peace! Peace on earth to men of good will. As the Midnight Mass begins, the whole place glows with happiness, and after that it is indescribable, building up to the climax of unworldly interior peace at Communion.

It is good that somewhere in the world there are men who realize that Christ is born. There were only a few shepherds at the first Bethlehem, and it is the same now. The ox and the ass understood more of the first Christmas than the high priests in Jerusalem. And it is the same way today.

The emptiness that had opened out within me, that had been prepared during Advent and laid open by my own silence and darkness, now became filled. And suddenly I was in a new world.

I seemed to be the same person, and I was the same person, I was still myself, I was more myself than I had ever been, and yet I was nothing. It was as if the floor had fallen out of my soul and I was free to go in and out of

Source: The first selection, part of the original manuscript of *The Seven Storey Mountain* not included in the published volume, is taken from *A Thomas Merton Reader,* ed. Thomas McDonnell, rev. ed. (Garden City, N.Y.: Doubleday-Image Books, 1974), pp. 155-58. The second selection is taken from *The Seven Storey Mountain* (San Diego, Calif.: Harcourt, Brace, 1948), pp. 421-23.

infinity. The deeps that were suddenly there could not be measured, and it was useless even to think of fathoming them. And they were not a place, not to an extent, they were a Presence. And in the midst of me they formed a citadel. And I knew at once that there was nothing that could ever penetrate into the heart of that peace, nothing from outside myself could ever get in, and there was a whole sphere of my own activity that was irrevocably excluded from it: the five senses, the imagination, the discoursing mind. I could enter in, I was free to come and go, and yet as soon as I attempted to make words or thoughts about it, I was excluded—or excluded to the extent that I attended to the words and thoughts.

Yet I could rest in this dark unfathomable peace without trouble and without worry even while the imagination and the mind itself were in some way active outside of it. They could stand and chatter at the door, in their idleness, waiting for the return of the will, their queen, upon whose orders they depended. They stood like a couple of chauffeurs at the door of a mansion which it was not their business to enter. And yet the mind was not all excluded, only in certain of its operations. But in so far as it was able to rest serene, in itself, the mind too could enter into the peace and harmony of this infinite simplicity that had come to be born within me.

But what are all these words? Shadows, illusions. The soul has not divisions into parts, into sections, into places. It merely operates this way or that, and the experience of this or that kind of operation can be translated by the imagination into terms of place and space, light and darkness: but as soon as it gets into those terms, the whole thing loses its true meaning.

Within the simplicity of that armed and walled and undivided interior peace was the sweetness of an infinite love. Yet this sweetness, as soon as it was grasped, or held, lost its savor. You must not try to reach out and possess it altogether. You must not touch it, or try to take it. You must not try to make it sweeter, or to keep it from going away. . . .

But all this is abstract. There was a far greater reality in all this, the sense of the presence of a Person; not exteriorized in space, not standing opposite one, or inside one, or outside one, not standing here or there or anywhere, but *living* in the midst. You are aware that you are alive: but where do you feel your life? Is it here? Is it here? It is inside you rather than outside you: but where? I suppose you can get to thinking it is in your heart, but it is all over you.

It is easy to realize the life of one's body, and hard to track it down, to place it. It is even easier to realize the life of your soul when it is made known to you, and even harder to track it down and place it.

And the hardest thing about it is that that life is a Person, Christ.

Vivo, jam non ego, vivit vero in me Christus [I live, yet not I, but Christ lives in me].

You know that Christ is born within you, infinite liberty: that you are free! That there are enemies which can never touch you, if this liberty loves you, and lives within you! That there are no more limitations! That you can love! That you are standing on the threshold of infinite possibilities! That the way lies open to escape from all these useless words! That the darkness has been washed out of your spiritual eyes and that you can open them and begin to see: but above all, that you can know by more perfect knowledge than vision, by the embrace of this liberty, and by the touch of infinite freedom in the midst of your spirit, and above all by rest, peace! This is the true contemplative vocation, the kernel of it, the innermost meaning of our life: *frui Deo,* heaven on earth, the love, the connatural knowledge of God: God as experience.

*　　*　　*　　*　　*

That morning when I was lying on my face on the floor in the middle of the church, with Father Abbot praying over me, I began to laugh, with my mouth in the dust, because without knowing how or why, I had actually done the right thing, and even an astounding thing. But what was astounding was not my work, but the work You worked in me.

The months have gone by, and You have not lessened any of those desires, but You have given me peace, and I am beginning to see what it is all about. I am beginning to understand.

Because You have called me here not to wear a label by which I can recognize myself and place myself in some kind of a category. You do not want me to be thinking about what I am, but about what You are. Or rather, You do not even want me to be thinking about anything much: for You would raise me above the level of thought. And if I am always trying to figure out what I am and where I am and why I am, how will that work be done?

I do not make a big drama of this business. I do not say: 'You have asked me for everything, and I have renounced all." Because I no longer desire to see anything that implies a distance between You and me: and if I stand back and consider myself and You as if something had passed between us, from me to You, I will inevitably see the gap between us and remember the distance between us.

My God, it is that gap and that distance which kill me.

That is the only reason why I desire solitude—to be lost to all created things, to die to them and to the knowledge of them, for they remind me of my distance from You. They tell me something about You: that You are far from them, even though You are in them. You have made them and Your presence sustains their being, and they hide You from me. And I would live alone, and out of them. *O beata solitudo!*

For I knew that it was only by leaving them that I could come to You: and that is why I have been so unhappy when You seemed to be condemning me to remain in them. Now my sorrow is over, and my joy is about to begin: the joy that rejoices in the deepest sorrows. For I am beginning to understand. You have taught me, and have consoled me, and I have begun again to hope and learn.

I hear You saying to me:

"I will give you what you desire. I will lead you into solitude. I will lead you by the way that you cannot possibly understand, because I want it to be the quickest way.

"Therefore all the things around you will be armed against you, to deny you, to hurt you, to give you pain, and therefore to reduce you to solitude.

"Because of their enmity, you will soon be left alone. They will cast you out and forsake you and reject you and you will be alone.

"Everything that touches you shall burn you, and you will draw your hand away in pain, until you have withdrawn yourself from all things. Then you will be all alone.

"Everything that can be desired will sear you, and brand you with a cautery, and you will fly from it in pain, to be alone. Every created joy will only come to you as pain, and you will die to all joy and be left alone. All the good things that other people love and desire and seek will come to you, but only as murderers to cut you off from the world and its occupations.

"You will be praised, and it will be like burning at the stake. You will be loved, and it will murder your heart and drive you into the desert.

"You will have gifts, and they will break you with their burden. You will have pleasures of prayer, and they will sicken you and you will fly from them.

"And when you have been praised a little and loved a little I will take away all your gifts and all your love and all your praise and you will be utterly forgotten and abandoned and you will be nothing, a dead thing, a rejection. And in that day you shall begin to possess the solitude you have so long desired. And your solitude will bear immense fruit in the souls of men you will never see on earth.

"Do not ask when it will be or where it will be or how it will be: On a mountain or in a prison, in a desert or in a concentration camp or in a hospital or at Gethsemani. It does not matter. So do not ask me, because I am not going to tell you. You will not know until you are in it.

"But you shall taste the true solitude of my anguish and my poverty and I shall lead you into the high places of my joy and you shall die in Me and find all things in My mercy which has created you for this end and brought you from Prades to Bermuda to St. Antonin to Oakham to London to Cambridge to Rome to New York to Columbia to Corpus Christi to St. Bonaventure to the Cistercian Abbey of the poor men who labor in Gethsemani:

"That you may become the brother of God and learn to know the Christ of the burnt men."

EDWARD JOHN CARNELL (1919-1967)

When he died at the relatively young age of forty-seven, Edward Carnell had already established himself as a distinguished teacher, scholar, and Christian leader. Throughout the 1950s and 1960s he was one of the few spokesmen in the fundamentalist-evangelical tradition to engage in serious dialogue with the larger Christian community. During those years, one was as likely to find an article by Carnell in the pages of *The Christian Century* as in the evangelical publications *Eternity* and *Christianity Today*.

The range of Carnell's interests is evidenced by the two doctorates he earned. One was a Th.D. from the Harvard Divinity School, where he wrote a dissertation on the work of the contemporary theologian Reinhold Niebuhr. The other was a Ph.D. from Boston University, where his dissertation concerned the thought of the nineteenth-century Danish philosopher and theologian Søren Kierkegaard. Carnell was one of the first faculty members of Fuller Theological Seminary, where he taught until 1962. That year he assumed the presidency of the Seminary, a position he filled until his death in 1967.

Carnell's writing was by turns combative and conciliatory, academic and pastoral, analytic and reflective, detached and intensely personal. The essay below is typical of much of his work. It shows him concerned to do battle with the opponents of an orthodox view of the Resurrection even as he confesses his own doubts and anxieties. From within the evangelical community, it is a particularly fine example of deep piety and intellectual rigor in harmonious union.

The Fear of Death and the Hope of the Resurrection

Illness is an evil because it saps our strength. It leaves us damaged, like a wormy apple or a chipped vase. When we are ill, we are not the self we wish to be. We cannot do the things we want, and there is so much we really want to do. . . . When we become ill, some part of our body is failing us; and when an important part fails we die, that is all. Even a headache is advance warning that death is on the way. . . .

We may delay death by prudence and circumspection. But we cannot keep death from reaching us in the end. Death's knock may be gentle at first, very deceiving, as of a friend who awaits us. But soon the knock will become rude and insistent. Then we shall have to open the door, whether by day or by night.

Some people are so afraid of death that they will not even talk about the grave. They do not avoid dying, but they think they have a better time living. They might have an even better time if they drew their wits about them and faced up to the limits God has placed on the creation. . . .

The fear of death draws many people near to God. As they sense their own weakness, they long for resources that only God can give. They believe that by surrendering themselves to God, things will work out happily in the end. God will not forsake His friends. But the fear of death also separates many from God. They are disturbed by the problem of evil.

I

In an atomic age we must learn to live with the threat of imminent death. At first glance it may seem that our predicament has no new elements in it. But this is not quite accurate. Our forefathers granted that life ends in death, but they viewed death as a *distant* foe. Now the foe is near at hand.

In the pre-atomic ages there was always the possibility—if we may compare life to an ocean voyage—that the ship might flounder on hidden reefs or be swamped by a storm or be plundered by pirates. But the voyage was reasonably safe, for the threat of imminent death was relieved by knowledge that the ship was sound, the course well plotted and the powder dry. In an atomic age we face identical perils. But we are no longer able to relieve the threat of imminent death, for we have discovered to our dismay that the ship itself is not seaworthy, that we may be sent to a watery grave at any moment.

Source: *The Case for Biblical Christianity*, ed. Ronald Nash (Grand Rapids: Eerdmans, 1969), pp. 174-82.

Thus the blue expanse which calmed our anxious souls has become an agent of terror.

Psychologists have amassed an impressive body of evidence to prove that Christians often suffer from a fear of death, and that on this particular question they in no way differ from men in general. If this is the case, with what right do Christians continue to say that God has delivered them from a fear of death?

This is no mere academic issue, nor am I dealing with cold statistics. For despite my Christian background I myself am now and then seized by feelings of consternation and alarm. Frankly, I am terrified when I am told that everything we hold dear can be reduced to atomic ashes the moment a few military men push a few buttons. This terror not only unmasks my great affection for the things of this world but makes me seriously wonder how my life differs from that of the naturalist who repudiates the idea that man is made in the image of God, and who derives no comfort from the hope of immortality.

Whenever I fall into seasons of depression a cloud of futility hovers over my soul. I keep asking myself what is the point of writing books or teaching seminary students when our very way of life is suspended over the abyss of nothingness. Nor do I feel relief when I recall that soldiers often become better men when they learn to live with the threat of imminent death; for soldiers are borne along by the consolation that after the strife of battle they will return to their homes. In the event of an atomic war we shall have no such consolation.

It is easy for self-righteous Christians to widen the gap between life and the church by boastfully contending that they transcend this whole problem. They open a copy of Scripture and read that Christ gave His life to "deliver all those who through fear of death were subject to lifelong bondage" (Heb. 2:15). Closing the sacred text and glancing up with an arrogance matching that of the doctors of the law in Christ's day, they find a certain delight in defending their own spiritual superiority. If a Christian happens to suffer from a fear of death, they imply, he is not much of a Christian.

These latter-day Pharisees conveniently overlook the manner in which Christ Himself faced the prospect of death. "When they reached a place called Gethsemane, he said to his disciples, 'Sit here while I pray.' And he took Peter and James and John with him. Horror and dismay came over him, and he said to them, 'My heart is ready to break with grief; stop here, and stay awake.' Then he went forward a little, threw himself on the ground, and prayed that, if it were possible, this hour might pass him by" (Mark 14:32-35, New English Bible). Of course, it would be easy to dismiss this passage by contending that Christ's fear was confined to His spiritual suffering as Saviour and that He had no more fear of physical death than did Socrates. But we dare not take it upon ourselves to separate the physical and spiritual elements in Christ's crucifixion. Moreover, Scripture plainly teaches that the Lord partook of flesh and blood, just as we do. And fear is an unavoidable aspect of finitude—at least in this present world.

A careful reading of the Bible shows that the feeling of depression has had a long history. The Psalmist cries: "Remember, O Lord, what the measure of life is, for what vanity thou hast created all the sons of men! What man can live and never see death? Who can deliver his soul from the power of Sheol?" (89:47-48). The author of Ecclesiastes goes so far as to claim that the dead are more fortunate than the living, and that the most fortunate one of all is he who has not been born (4:2-3). And so it goes.

Since repentance does not repeal the law of self-preservation, we should be neither surprised nor embarrassed when we find Scripture reviewing these symptoms of depression. A Christian is *nowhere* promised exemption from the law of self-preservation. If a Christian did not do his best to go on living, he might neglect his responsibility to serve as the salt of the earth. But God has checked this possibility by ordaining that the law of self-preservation should remain active unto the end. Hence we should not be disturbed when we learn that some Christians have a morbid fear of the grave. After all, we are entitled to seasons of depression if we are so inclined. God does not expect us to go about with a Cheshire-cat grin. "For he knows our frame; he remembers that we are dust" (Ps. 103:14).

It should be carefully noted, however, that after Christ poured out His soul in prayer he emerged from Gethsemane with a feeling of perfect peace. The transformation symbolizes the biblical promise that God *will* give us grace to pass through the valley and shadow of death. The experience of Samuel Johnson, whose wisdom was surpassed only by his piety, perfectly illustrates this truth. Throughout his life he suffered from a terrible fear of death. But when it came time for him to die God flooded his soul with grace. "We shall presently see," writes Boswell, "that when he approached nearer to his awful change, his mind became tranquil, and he exhibited as much fortitude as becomes a thinking man in that situation."

Thus when a Christian says he is free from the fear of death he means—or at least I think he *should* mean—that he is not afraid to meet his Maker. Having been reconciled to God through the blood of Jesus Christ, he senses a holy boldness to stand in the presence of God. "For God did not give us a spirit of timidity but a spirit of power and love and self-control" (II Tim. 1:7). If we are careful with our use of terms, we can confidently say that *no* true believer has a fear of death. Regardless of how desperately a Christian may cling to the things of this world, or of how often he may fall into depression, in his devotional self he grants that to die and be with the Lord is better.

Let us note in this connection that prison chaplains often find that inmates seek consolations which go beyond the grave and reach into the intimacies of the soul itself. "Thus conscience doth make cowards of us all," says Hamlet in his soliloquy. It is ironic, but a severely distressed person would likely be *relieved* if he could be sure that death would put an end to everything. The validity of this conjecture is illustrated by the behavior of the Nazi bigwigs at the Nuremberg trials. With the exception of the philosopher Alfred Rosenberg (who may have wept in his heart), all of them called for a priest or minister in order that they might render a good confession before going to the gallows. They could endure the agony of physical death, but they had no resources to meet God.

A hearty Yes and No may be the nearest a Christian can come to answering those who inquire whether he fears death. So long as the law of self-preservation remains active within us, we may experience times of depression similar to those recorded in Scripture. Therefore, if a Christian finds that he fears the threat of imminent death in an atomic age, he should not on that account feel guilty or unworthy. He is still a human being; he still clings to life—like everyone else. But at the same time he can forthrightly assert that he is not afraid to stand in the presence of God, for he has already made peace with God through the Lord Jesus Christ. A Christian may know little about the furniture of heaven, but he is sure of one thing, and this is all that matters: *God loves him.* "Beloved, we are God's children now; it does not yet appear what we shall be, but we know that when he appears we shall be like him, for we shall see him as he is" (I John 3:2).

Let us strive with all our might to persuade rulers and nations to enter into negotiations that will issue in a workable balance of power and a reasonable basis for peace. But if the threat of nuclear warfare continues to mount, let us remind ourselves that God is sovereign. He says to the nations, as He says to the tides of the sea: "Thus far shall you go, and no farther."

And if it is God's will that we must face apocalyptic times, let us calmly learn to say (despite the "other law" which wars against the law of the mind): "I have been crucified with Christ; it is no longer I who live, but Christ who lives in me; and the life I now live in the flesh I live by faith in the Son of God, who loved me and gave himself for me" (Gal. 2:20). As the Apostle Paul noted long ago, whether we live or die we are the Lord's. What more could the heart desire?

II

Call it folly, call it wishful thinking: the fact remains that no upright person can believe that his loved ones are only animals that perish. The intellect may accept the gloom of the grave, but the intellect is not authorized to speak for the heart. The heart draws on convictions that are foolishness to both science and philosophy. An upright person knows that if the departed do not count, then the living do not count, for the living and the departed are inseparably joined by the bond of love. . . .

When the Apostle Paul preached in Athens, his audience listened until he spoke of the resurrection. "Now when they heard of the resurrection of the dead, some mocked; but others said, 'We will hear you again about this'" (Acts 17:32). It is ironic that the Greeks were offended by the very doctrine that evokes the highest feelings of joy in Christians. Paul was so certain of his ground that he linked the very hope of mankind to the resurrection of Christ. "Now if Christ is preached as raised from the dead, how can some of you say that there is no resurrection of the dead? But if there is no resurrection of the dead, then Christ has not been raised; if Christ has not been raised, then our preaching is in vain and your faith is in vain" (I Cor. 15:12-14). Christ's resurrection is proof that the Father received the sacrifice of the Son. All who are in Christ will be raised in like manner, for Christ is the firstfruits from the dead.

The Greeks wanted eternal life, but they saw little point to the resurrection of the body. Since the real man is the rational man, the body is an extraneous element. And even worse, it is a positive hindrance to man's unclouded vision of truth. We are saved by being divested of body, not by being reunited to body. Socrates drank the hemlock on the confidence that he would soon be liberated from his corporeal prison. . . .

Martha, the sister of Lazarus, rested in the Semitic conviction that man is a vital union of body and soul. If you take away the body, you take away an essential part of man. This is why the hope of eternal life was eventually linked with the hope of the resurrection.

The Semites not only enjoyed the light of special revelation but they came at the issue by way of the convictions of the heart. Thus, when Martha tried to picture Lazarus in the kingdom of heaven, she could only picture him as she knew him in Bethany. If he did not have a body like unto the one that she remembered, he would not be the same person. . . .

Since all observable evidence supports the conclusion that man perishes at death, the resurrection of the body is as offensive to science as it is to philosophy. And when Christians speak of a *spiritual* body, critics say that the end of good sense has come.

But the Apostle Paul thought otherwise. In fact, he went to considerable pains to tell just what the resurrection body would be like. It would belong to a new order of physics. "What is sown is perishable, what is raised is imperishable. It is sown in dishonor, it is raised in glory. It is sown in weakness, it is raised in power. It is sown a physical body, it is raised a spiritual body" (I Cor. 15:42-43). But how did Paul expect cultured people to believe this? The answer is, he told them to behold the risen Lord. Jesus was raised from the dead, and His body was spiritual in substance. He not only ate fish with

His disciples, but He passed through closed doors. Therefore, as Paul saw the issue, Jesus' resurrection body proved that God not only *could* create a new order of physics, but that He actually *did*. Reality itself sets the limits to possibility.

Paul was fully convinced that Jesus was raised from the dead. The evidences were sufficient, for Jesus "appeared to Cephas, then to the twelve. Then he appeared to more than five hundred brethren at one time, most of whom are still alive, though some have fallen asleep. Then he appeared to James, then to all the apostles. Last of all, as to one untimely born, he appeared also to me" (I Cor. 15:5-8).

The Greeks groaned under the limitations that sin places on our present bodies. This is why they wanted to be emancipated. They knew that the body is subject to passions that war against the soul.

But since the Greeks did not have the light of special revelation, they did not know that the resurrection body will be divested of sin. When man is confirmed in righteousness, the conflict between soul and body will cease. The body will become a servant of the soul.

III

Scoffers dismiss the hope of heaven as an innocent but fruitless projection of wishful thinking. They grant that it would be *nice* to believe that good people have nothing to fear, but where is the evidence for this belief? Jesus has come and gone, and things continue as they were from the beginning. Nature is a conflict between regular and irregular forces, society a conflict between justice and injustice. Therefore, would it not be better, let alone more honest, to make this world a happier place in which to live, rather than selfishly dreaming about heaven?

Indeed, we *should* do all we can to make this world a happier place in which to live, for love is dedicated to the task of relieving suffering. But unless love is joined by faith and hope, it cannot complete its mission. Love is an eternal tie; it draws on consolations that reach beyond the grave. Love says to the beloved, "You have nothing to fear, now or at any other time." Hence, the hope of heaven is not a sign of selfishness. It is a sign that love is being true to its own essence.

Jesus does not distribute photographs of heaven, nor does He satisfy the standards of science and philosophy. But He does satisfy the convictions of the heart, and He satisfies them with the highest of all possible evidences. Jesus *promises* an eternal home to all who trust Him. What more could be asked?

Since the law of sin is actively at work in our members, we often promise more than we can make good. But Jesus faces no such prospect, for He is one in nature with the Father and the Holy Spirit. By His own resurrection from the grave He proved that He is Lord of the new creation. . . . Christians do not know why God was pleased to create a world into which such frightful things as illness and death should come. But they do know that God never intended to let illness and death have the last word. And they know this because God has declared Himself in the person of Jesus Christ.

When we become discouraged by the evils of the day, let us remember that Jesus gave His life with the express purpose of leading many sons into glory. As long as we are good, the evils of the day cannot harm us.

Science and philosophy will continue to boast of awesome achievements, but these achievements will neither add to nor subtract from the pleasure that a believer feels when God says, "I accept you: you count in my sight." Since our lives are hid with Christ in God, we have a reason for living and a reason for dying. "So we do not lose heart. Though our outer nature is wasting away, our inner nature is being renewed every day. For this slight momentary affliction is preparing for us an eternal weight of glory beyond all comparison" (I Cor. 4:16-17). . . .

Every beat of the heart bears witness to our finitude. We are *not* the authors of our own existence. All our striving will prove futile in the end. Death will overtake us; our bodies will become food for worms.

This is why we must set our hope on God alone. When we are joined to Christ through faith and repentance, we are justified before the law and adopted into the family of God. The Lord then tells us that death is only a chamber in which we lay aside our earthly tabernacle with its pains and hindrances.

We were alone when we entered the world, but when we leave it we shall feel the abiding presence of the Lord. As death draws near and we dread the dark journey ahead, the Lord will assure us that our lives are precious in the sight of God. He will gently say, "Child, come home." Jesus has given His word that He will never leave us nor forsake us, and his word is as firm as His character.

"Therefore, my beloved brethren, be steadfast, immovable, always abounding in the work of the Lord, knowing that in the Lord your labor is not in vain" (I Cor. 15:58).

FLANNERY O'CONNOR (1925-1964)

The spirit of this brilliant Christian writer shows forth most clearly in a verbal exchange she recorded and commented on:

> Mrs. Broadwater said when she was a child and received the Host, she thought of it as the Holy Ghost, He being the "most portable" person of the Trinity. Now she thought of it as a symbol and implied that it was a pretty good one. I then said, in a very shaky voice, "Well, if it's a symbol, to hell with it." That was all the defense I was capable of but I realize now that this is all I will ever be able to say about it . . . except that it is the center of existence for me; all the rest of life is expendable.

Here we find the passionately blunt language of a woman who was both an accomplished fiction writer and a dedicated servant of the gospel.

Flannery O'Connor received her training at Georgia State College for Women and the renowned Writers' Workshop at the University of Iowa. She quickly distinguished herself, winning a certain degree of critical acclaim and several awards and fellowships. Then, at the age of twenty-five, she was diagnosed as having lupus, a virulent disease that was to claim her life before she reached the age of forty.

In her brief career O'Connor wrote some of the most distinguished short stories to appear in America since World War II. Among her best-known works are the novels *Wise Blood* (1952) and *The Violent Bear It Away* (1960) and two collections of short stories, *A Good Man Is Hard to Find* (1955) and *Everything That Rises Must Converge* (1965). Her fiction has been acclaimed by Christian and non-Christian readers alike for its eerie truthfulness to experience, for its masterful depiction of character, and for its troubling moral implications. O'Connor set almost all of her stories in her native South. She claimed that this region was, if not Christ-centered, then at least still "Christ-haunted" in a way that the rest of the nation was not.

O'Connor's stories often deal with individuals on the fringe. Some are itinerant laborers who, though illiterate and inarticulate, act according to deeply felt reasons of the heart. Others are "respectable" people whose time has come and gone and who cling to dead patterns of belief and behavior in a frightening world. Whatever their makeup, O'Connor's main characters must confront that Truth which consumes before it consoles. Most of her stories contain a moment when a character's expectations or fortunes are shockingly overturned. It is this moment of judgment that serves also as the prelude to the Word of grace and forgiveness.

For two decades readers responded to O'Connor's stories with mystified delight, and read her occasional essays with great interest. With the publication of her letters in *The Habit of Being* (1979), from which we have chosen the following excerpts, it is possible to see more deeply into the spiritual life of this intense, accomplished writer.

Selected Letters

[To fellow writer Cecil Dawkins]   9 December 58

. . . Glibness is the great danger in answering people's questions about religion. I won't answer yours because you can answer them as well yourself but I will give you, for what it's worth, my own perspective on them. All your dissatisfaction with the Church seems to me to come from an incomplete understanding of sin. This will perhaps surprise you because you are very conscious of the sins of Catholics; however what you seem actually to demand is that the Church put the kingdom of heaven on earth right here now, that the Holy Ghost be translated at once into all flesh. The Holy Spirit very rarely shows Himself on the surface of anything. You are asking that man return at once to the state God created him in, you are leaving out the terrible radical human pride that causes death. Christ was crucified on earth and the Church is crucified in time, and the Church is crucified by all of us, by her members most particularly because she is a Church of sinners. Christ never said that the Church would be operated in a sinless or intelligent way, but that it would not teach error. This does not mean that each and every priest won't teach error but that the whole Church speaking through the Pope will not teach error in matters of faith. The Church is founded on Peter who denied Christ three times and couldn't walk on the water by himself. You are expecting his successors to walk on the water. All human nature vigorously resists grace because grace changes us and the change is painful. Priests resist it as well as others. To have the Church be what you want it to be would require the continuous miraculous meddling of God in human affairs, whereas it is our dignity that we are allowed more or less to get on with those

Source: *The Habit of Being*, ed. Sally Fitzgerald (New York: Farrar, Straus & Giroux, 1979), pp. 124-25, 307-8, 387, 419, 476-77, 516-17, 543.

graces that come through faith and the sacraments and which work through our human nature. God has chosen to operate in this manner. We can't understand this but we can't reject it without rejecting life.

Human nature is so faulty that it can resist any amount of grace and most of the time it does. The Church does well to hold her own; you are asking that she show a profit. When she shows a profit you have a saint, not necessarily a canonized one. I agree with you that you shouldn't have to go back centuries to find Catholic thought, and to be sure, you don't. But you are not going to find the highest principles of Catholicism exemplified on the surface of life nor the highest Protestant principles either. It is easy for any child to pick out the faults in the sermon on his way home from Church every Sunday. It is impossible for him to find out the hidden love that makes a man, in spite of his intellectual limitations, his neuroticism, his own lack of strength, give up his life to the service of God's people, however bumblingly he may go about it. . . .

[To close correspondent identified as "A."]   16 December 55

. . . I was once, five or six years ago, taken by some friends to have dinner with Mary McCarthy and her husband, Mr. Broadwater. (She just wrote that book, *A Charmed Life*.) She departed the Church at the age of 15 and is a Big Intellectual. We went at eight and at one, I hadn't opened my mouth once, there being nothing for me in such company to say. The people who took me were Robert Lowell and his now wife, Elizabeth Hardwick. Having me there was like having a dog present who had been trained to say a few words but overcome with inadequacy had forgotten them. Well, toward morning the conversation turned on the Eucharist, which I, being the Catholic, was obviously supposed to defend. Mrs. Broadwater said when she was a child and received the Host, she thought of it as the Holy Ghost, He being the "most portable" person of the Trinity; now she thought of it as a symbol and implied that it was a pretty good one. I then said, in a very shaky voice, "Well, if it's a symbol, to hell with it." That was all the defense I was capable of but I realize now that this is all I will ever be able to say about it, outside of a story, except that it is the center of existence for me; all the rest of life is expendable. . . .

[To a college student who had heard her lecture]   30 May 62

. . . As a freshman in college you are bombarded with new ideas, or rather pieces of ideas, new frames of reference, an activation of the intellectual life which is only beginning, but which is already running ahead of your lived experence. After a year of this, you think you cannot believe. You are just beginning to realize how difficult it is to have faith and the measure of a commitment to it, but you are too young to decide you don't have faith just because you feel you can't believe. About the only way we know whether we believe or not is by what we do, and I think from your letter that you will not take the path of least resistance in this matter and simply decide that you have lost your faith and that there is nothing you can do about it.

One result of the stimulation of your intellectual life that takes place in college is usually a shrinking of the imaginative life. This sounds like a paradox, but I have often found it to be true. Students get so bound up with difficulties such as reconciling the clashing of so many different faiths such as Buddhism, Mohammedanism, etc., that they cease to look for God in other ways. Bridges once wrote Gerard Manley Hopkins and asked him to tell him how he, Bridges, could believe. He must have expected from Hopkins a long philosophical answer. Hopkins wrote back, "Give alms." He was trying to say to Bridges that God is to be experienced in Charity (in the sense of love for the divine image in human beings). Don't get so entangled with intellectual difficulties that you fail to look for God in this way.

The intellectual difficulties have to be met, however, and you will be meeting them for the rest of your life. When you get a reasonable hold on one, another will come to take its place. At one time, the clash of the different world religions was a difficulty for me. Where you have absolute solutions, however, you have no need of faith. Faith is what you have in the absence of knowledge. The reason this clash doesn't bother me any longer is because I have got, over the years, a sense of the immense sweep of creation, of the evolutionary process in everything, of how incomprehensible God must necessarily be to be the God of heaven and earth. You can't fit the Almighty into your intellectual categories. I might suggest that you look into some of the works of Pierre Teilhard de Chardin (*The Phenomenon of Man* et al.). He was a paleontologist—helped to discover Peking man—and also a man of God. I don't suggest you go to him for answers but for different questions, for that stretching of the imagination that you need to make you a sceptic in the face of much that you are learning, much of which is new and shocking but which when boiled down becomes less so and takes its place in the general scheme of things. What kept me a sceptic in college was precisely my Christian faith. It always said: wait, don't bite on this, get a wider picture, continue to read.

If you want your faith, you have to work for it. It is a gift, but for very few is it a gift given without any demand for equal time devoted to its cultivation. For every book you read that is anti-Christian, make it your business to read one that presents the other side of the picture; if one isn't satisfactory read others. Don't think that you have to abandon reason to be a Christian. A book that might help you is *The Unity of Philosophical Experience* by Etienne Gilson. Another is Newman's *The Grammar of Assent*. To find out about faith, you have to go to the people who have it and you have to go to the most intelligent ones if you are going to stand up intellectually to agnostics and the general run of pagans that you are going to find in the majority of people around you. Much of the criticism of belief that you find today comes from people who are judging it from the standpoint of another and narrower discipline. The Biblical criticism of the 19th century, for instance, was the product of historical disciplines. It has been entirely revamped in the 20th century by applying broader criteria to it, and those people who lost their faith in the 19th century because of it, could better have hung on in blind trust.

Even in the life of a Christian, faith rises and falls like the tides of an invisible sea. It's there, even when he can't see it or feel it, if he wants it to be there. You realize, I think, that it is more valuable, more mysterious, altogether more immense than anything you can learn or decide upon in college. Learn what you can, but cultivate Christian scepticism. It will keep you free—not free to do anything you please, but free to be formed by something larger than your own intellect or the intellects of those around you.

I don't know if this is the kind of answer that can help you, but any time you care to write me, I can try to do better.

[To Dr. T. R. Spivey]   9 April 60

I don't think you are unfair to me in what you say about my stage of development etc. though I have a much less romantic view of how the Holy Spirit operates than you do. The sins of pride & selfishness and reluctance to wrestle with the Spirit are certainly mine but I have been working at them a long time and will be still doing it when I am on my deathbed. I believe that God's love for us is so great that He does not wait until we are purified to such a great extent before He allows us to receive Him. You miss a great deal of what is in my book [The Violent Bear It Away], my feeling for the old man particularly, because the Eucharist does not mean the same to you as it does to me. There are two main symbols in the book—water and the bread that Christ is. The whole action of the novel is Tarwater's selfish will against all that the little lake (the baptismal font) and the bread stand for. This book is a very minor hymn to the Eucharist.

Water is a symbol of purification and fire is another. Water, it seems to me, is a symbol of the kind of purification that God gives irrespective of our efforts or worthiness, and fire is the kind of purification we bring on ourselves—as in Purgatory. It is our evil which is naturally burnt away when it comes anywhere near God.

If you mean that all I get out of the Jung book is the fact that he misrepresents the Church, you do me an injustice, but if in his book it is not out of order for him to misrepresent the Church again and again, it is not out of order for me to defend her.

Your friend's comment about my being more interested in the way the story is told than in the story itself seems very ignorant to me, as well as untrue. Stories get to be written in different ways, of course, but this particular story was discovered in the process of finding out what I was able to make live. Even if one were filled with the Holy Ghost, the Holy Ghost would work through the given talent. You see this in Biblical inspiration, so why think that it would be different in a lesser kind of inspiration? If the Holy Ghost dictated a novel, I doubt very much that all would be flow. I doubt that the writer would be relieved of his capacity for taking pains (which is all that technique is in the end); I doubt that he would lose the habit of art. I think it would only be perfected. The greater the love, the greater the pains he would take. . . .

[To "A."]   25 November 60

I was distressed you wouldn't come and have been worrying about what could be the matter. I started to call you up and try to persuade you to change your mind and then I decided I had better mind my own business and didn't do it. Now I am sorry I didn't because I think too many people and especially me mind their own business when their real business is somebody else's business. I feel very strongly that your business is my business, even if I don't always act quick enough on the feeling. I asked B. what he thought might be the matter and he said he thought you might be depressed because you had shown something you had written to some young man who had made a lot of criticisms of it that you thought were just. Then I doubly wished that I had called up and insisted that you come and I also wished I were up there so that in the spirit of Christian charity I could knock you in the head with the nearest stick of wood.

Of course B. may be wrong and I hope he was but assuming for the moment he wasn't, I have this to say. No matter how just the criticism, any criticism at all which depresses you to the extent that you feel you cannot ever write anything worth anything is from the Devil and to subject yourself to it is for you an occasion of sin. In you, the talent is there and you are expected to use it. Whether the work itself is completely successful, or whether you ever get any worldly success out of it, is a matter of no concern to you. It is like the Japanese swordsmen who are indifferent to getting slain in the duel. I feel that you are distracted, particularly when you say, for instance, that it is B.'s writing that interests you considerably more than he does. This is certainly not so, no matter how good a writer he gets to be, or how silly he gets to be himself. The human comes before art. You do not write the best you can for the sake of art but for the sake of returning your talent increased to the invisible God to use or not use as he sees fit. Resignation to the will of God does not mean that you stop resisting evil or obstacles, it means that you leave the outcome out of your personal considerations. It is the most concern coupled with the least concern. . . .

[To Sister Mariella Gable]   4 May 63

Thank you so very much for your letter. I remember that at Marillac, you and I said we were easily defeated when it came to defending what we thought were necessary judgments about fiction in the face of people who didn't see them. I still am, and I'm much more liable to try to get out of the way as fast as possible than to struggle to make my views plain. I think though that it's the people and not the questions that defeat us.

When they ask you to make Christianity look desirable, they are asking you to describe its essence, not what you see. Ideal Christianity doesn't exist, because anything the human being touches, even Christian truth, he deforms slightly in his own image. Even the saints do this. I take it to be the effects of Original Sin, and I notice that Catholics often act as if that doctrine is always perverted and always an indication of Calvinism. They read a little corruption as total corruption. The writer has to make the corruption believable before he can make the grace meaningful.

The tendency of people who ask questions like this is always towards the abstract and therefore toward allegory, thinness, and ultimately what they are looking for is an apologetic fiction. The best of them think: make it look desirable because it is desirable. And the rest of them think: make it look desirable so I don't look like a fool for holding it. In a really Christian culture of real believers this wouldn't come up.

I know that the writer does call up the general and maybe the essential through the particular, but this general and essential is still deeply embedded in mystery. It is not answerable to any of our formulas. It doesn't rest finally in a statable kind of solution. It ought to throw you back on the living God. Our Catholic mentality is great on paraphrase, logic, formula, instant and correct answers. We judge before we experience and never trust our faith to be subjected to reality, because it is not strong enough. And maybe in this we are wise. I think this spirit is changing on account of the council but the changes will take a long time to soak through.

About the fanatics. People make a judgment of fanaticism by what they are themselves. To a lot of Protestants I know, monks and nuns are fanatics, none greater. And to a lot of the monks and nuns I know, my Protestant prophets are fanatics. For my part, I think the only difference between them is that if you are a Catholic and have this intensity of belief you join the convent and are heard from no more; whereas if you are a Protestant and have it, there is no convent for you to join and you go about in the world getting into all sorts of trouble and drawing the wrath of people who don't believe anything much at all down on your head.

This is one reason why I can write about Protestant believers better than Catholic believers—because they express their belief in diverse kinds of dramatic action which is obvious enough for me to catch. I can't write about anything subtle. Another thing, the prophet is a man apart. He is not typical of a group. Old Tarwater [in *The Violent Bear It Away*] is not typical of the Southern Baptist or the Southern Methodist. Essentially, he's a crypto-Catholic. When you leave a man alone with his Bible and the Holy Ghost inspires him, he's going to be a Catholic one way or another, even though he knows nothing about the visible church. His kind of Christianity may not be socially desirable, but it will be real in the sight of God. If I set myself to write about a socially desirable Christianity, all the life would go out of what I do. And if I set myself to write about the essence of Christianity, I would have to quit writing fiction, or become another person.

I'll be glad when Catholic critics start looking at what they've got to criticize for what it is itself, for its sort of "inscape" as Hopkins would have had it. Instead they look for some ideal intention, and criticize you for not having it.

In the gospels it was the devils who first recognized Christ and the evangelists didn't censor this information. They apparently thought it was pretty good witness. It scandalizes us when we see the same thing in modern dress only because we have this defensive attitude toward the faith. . . .

[To "A."]   26 October 63

. . . Love and understanding are one and the same only in God. Who do you think you understand? If anybody, you delude yourself. I love a lot of people, understand none of them. This is not perfect love but as much as a finite creature can be capable of. About people being stuck with those who don't love or understand them, I have read discussions of it but I can't think where at the moment. It all comes under the larger heading of what individuals have to suffer for the common good, a mystery, and part of the suffering of Christ. . . .

FREDERICK BUECHNER (B. 1926)

In a recent interview, preacher and writer Frederick Buechner explained that "in my novels I think of myself less as a defender than as a proclaimer. . . . I'm saying something like, 'Look I've got something absolutely extraordinary I want to show you.'" What Buechner has sought to show—for more than three decades, in a series of novels, sermons, autobiographical essays, and innovative theological writings—is the ineffable grace of God.

Trained at the Lawrenceville Academy and Princeton University, Buechner had already begun to establish himself as a successful novelist when he underwent conversion to the Christian faith in the mid-1950s. In *The Sacred Journey* (1982) and *Now and Then* (1983), Buechner describes that conversion and the way it transformed his life and art. He proceeded to earn a Bachelor of Divinity degree from Union Theological Seminary in New York City and was ordained as a minister-at-large in the United Presbyterian Church.

For almost three decades, Buechner has been serving the church and the gospel as a preparatory school teacher, a chaplain, and a writer. In fiction, he is perhaps best known for the four novels published in the 1970s that came to form *The Book of Bebb*. Their central character is Leo Bebb, an itinerant preacher and charlatan whose creator has described him as a "kind of oddball saint, a life-giver." Buechner has also written a number of works of nonfiction prose, several books of sermons, two disarmingly refreshing examinations of biblical characters and theological terms, and the two recent autobiographical volumes previously mentioned.

It may be naive to think that early America was a land of intense piety and uniform devotion, that the world to which Thomas Shepard, Jonathan Edwards, and Harriet Beecher Stowe spoke was united in its adherence to the Christian faith. Yet even when they could not take for granted the beliefs of their audiences, such writers could depend on their readers' familiarity with the vocabulary of spiritual devotion. Buechner, on the other hand, is aware that he writes to those for whom the language of faith is dead. "A post-Christian world is the world I know best," he explains. "Its hunger for the very God they've pretty much dismissed is particularly poignant to me."

The following excerpt from *The Sacred Journey* tells of the experiences leading up to Buechner's conversion, and it demonstrates the careful craft he employs in trying to talk to women and men who have lost the desire and ability to

speak the language of faith. In this passage Buechner refers several times to the
suicide of his father, an event that occurred when he was a young boy.

From *The Sacred Journey*

. . . Nor is it only the joy of God and the comfort of God that come at
unforeseen times. God's coming is always unforeseen, I think, and the reason, if I had to guess, is that if he gave us anything much in the way of
advance warning, more often than not we would have made ourselves scarce
long before he got there.

One evening toward the end of my five years of teaching, for instance,
what I thought was coming was just dinner with my mother. She was living
by herself in New York at the time, and it must have been some sort of
occasion, I think, because the apartment looked unusually nice, and there
were candles on the table, the best silver. It was to be just the two of us, and
we had both looked forward to it, not simply as mother and son but as two
old friends who no longer got to see each other all that much. Then, just as
we were about to sit down to eat, the telephone rang, and it was for me. It
was a friend I taught with at Lawrenceville, and he had not spoken more
than a word or two when his voice broke and I realized to my horror that he
was weeping. His mother and father and a pregnant sister had been in an
automobile accident on the West Coast, and it was uncertain whether any of
them would live. He was at the airport waiting for a flight to take him out to
them. Could I come down, he asked, and wait with him till the plane left?

There are many people in this world—I suspect they may even be in the
majority—who in face of such a cry for help as that would have seen right
away that, humanly speaking, there was no alternative but to say that they
would be at the airport as soon as a taxi would take them there. I have
known many such people in my day and can explain them only on the
grounds that they are strong, compassionate, and at least in that sense,
Christian by instinct. My instinct, on the other hand, was to be nothing so
much as afraid. I was afraid of my friend's fear and of his tears. I was afraid
of his faith that I could somehow be a comfort and help to him and afraid
that I was not friend enough to be able to be. Dating perhaps from that
November morning of my childhood when I opened the door of Jamie's and

Source: *The Sacred Journey* (New York: Harper & Row, 1982), pp. 105-12.

my bedroom on a tragic and terrifying world that I had no resources for dealing with, I was afraid of opening the door into his pain or anybody's pain. So although I knew as well as anybody that I had no choice but to say that I would come, what I said instead, Heaven help me, was that I would come if I possibly could but there were things I had to take care of first and would he phone me back in about ten minutes.

In the other room dinner was on the table and my mother was waiting, and on that placid stage there was played out a preposterous little scene that was nonetheless one of the watersheds of my life. Because when I told my mother what had happened and that I was probably going to have to leave and skip supper, her reaction caught me completely off guard. The whole thing was absurd, she said. My friend was a grown man. He had no business carrying on like a hysterical child. What earthly good could I do anyway? It was outrageous to think of spoiling an evening together that we had both been looking forward to for days. Everything she said was precisely what at some level of my being I had already been saying to myself, and that was of course what made it so appalling. It was only when I heard it on someone else's lips that I heard it for what it was, and as much out of revulsion at myself as out of pity for my friend, I resolved that as soon as he called again, I would tell him that I would come immediately.

Then, as the final absurdity, when he did call again, he said that he had gotten hold of himself and there was really no longer any need for me to come at all, and the consequence was that I did not go, and such as it was my mother and I had our evening together after all. But in the long run the consequences went much farther than that because if the result of opening that November door some seventeen years earlier was that time started for me, and my journey through time, the result of that phone call and of my response to it was the start of another kind of journey, the journey that the old monk referred to when he said I had a long way to go. My mother's apartment by candlelight was haven and home and shelter from everything in the world that seemed dangerous and a threat to my peace. And my friend's broken voice on the phone was a voice calling me out into that dangerous world not simply for his sake, as I suddenly saw it, but also for my sake. The shattering revelation of that moment was that true peace, the high and bidding peace that passeth all understanding, is to be had not in retreat from the battle, but only in the thick of the battle. To journey for the sake of saving our own lives is little by little to cease to live in any sense that really matters, even to ourselves, because it is only by journeying for the world's sake—even when the world bores and sickens and scares you half to death— that little by little we start to come alive. It was not a conclusion that I came to in time. It was a conclusion from beyond time that came to me. God knows I have never been any good at following the road it pointed me to, but at least, by grace, I glimpsed the road and saw that it is the only one worth traveling.

What followed can be quickly told although it was not so quickly lived. After five years of teaching and the publication of a second novel that fared as badly as the first one had fared well, I gave up my Lawrenceville job and in 1953 went to New York to be a full-time writer, only to discover that I could not write a word. So I decided that maybe I should try to make money instead and went to see a former partner of my uncle about the possibility of going into the advertising business; but he said that although there was plenty of money to be made there, you had to have a very tough hide to survive, and I decided that probably my hide was not tough enough. So I turned to the CIA, of all things, thinking that if there was going to be another war, I would probably stand a better chance of surviving as a spy than back in the infantry again; but when I was asked by an interviewer in Washington if I would be willing to submit a person to physical torture in order to extract information that many lives might depend on, I decided that I had no stomach for that either, and another road was barred. And somewhere in the process I fell in love again with a girl who did not fall in love with me. It all sounds like a kind of inane farce as I set it down here, with every door I tried to open slammed on my foot, and yet I suppose, too, that when you get right down to the flesh and blood of things, the pilgrimage and the farce always go hand in hand because it is a divine comedy that we are all of us involved in after all, not a divine dirge, and when Saint Paul calls us to be fools for Christ, it is not to frock coats and poke bonnets that he is calling us, but to motley and a cap with bells.

Part of the farce was that for the first time in my life that year in New York, I started going to church regularly, and what was farcical about it was not that I went but my reason for going, which was simply that on the same block where I lived there happened to be a church with a preacher I had heard of and that I had nothing all that much better to do with my lonely Sundays. The preacher was a man named George Buttrick, and Sunday after Sunday I went, and sermon after sermon I heard. It was not just his eloquence that kept me coming back, though he was wonderfully eloquent, literate, imaginative, never letting you guess what he was going to come out with next but twitching with surprises up there in the pulpit, his spectacles a-glitter in the lectern light. What drew me more was whatever it was that his sermons came from and whatever it was in me that they touched so deeply. And then there came one particular sermon with one particular phrase in it that does not even appear in a transcript of his words that somebody sent me more than twenty-five years later so I can only assume that he must have dreamed it up at the last minute and ad-libbed it—and on just such foolish, tenuous, holy threads as that, I suppose, hang the destinies of us all. Jesus

Christ refused the crown that Satan offered him in the wilderness, Buttrick said, but he is king nonetheless because again and again he is crowned in the heart of the people who believe in him. And that inward coronation takes place, Buttrick said, "among confession, and tears, and great laughter."

It was the phrase *great laughter* that did it, did whatever it was that I believe must have been hiddenly in the doing all the years of my journey up till then. It was not so much that a door opened as that I suddenly found that a door had been open all along which I had only just then stumbled upon. After church, with a great lump still in my throat, I walked up to 84th Street to have Sunday dinner with Grandma Buechner. She sat in her usual chair with the little Philco silent at her side and a glass of sherry in her hand, and when I told her something of what had happened, I could see that she was as much bemused as pleased by what I had said. I have forgotten her words, but the sense of her answer was that she was happy for me that I had found whatever it was that I had found. *Le bon Dieu.* You could never be sure what he was up to. If there was a *bon Dieu* at all. Who could say? Then old Rosa came listing in to say *Essen ist fertig, Frau Büchner,* and we went in to lunch.

Whatever it was that I had found. Whoever it was. The painting in the book. The recurring reference in those early, embarrassing poems. The name on the lips of the beery boy at the Nass. The priest trudging down the sun-drenched Bermuda lane, and the man with the beard who met all the ships when they docked and searched all the faces. The crowing of the rooster and the sound of voices I could not quite make out in another room, and the sound of my friend's voice on the phone that I could make out all too well. My father's writing on the last page of *Gone with the Wind* that he was no good, and then, because he believed that, giving his life away for what he must have thought was our good and thus in his own sad, lost way echoing with his unimaginable gift another holy gift more unimaginable still. What I found was what I had already half seen, or less than half, in many places over my twenty-seven years without ever clearly knowing what it was that I was seeing or even that I was seeing anything of great importance. Something in me recoils from using such language, but here at the end I am left with no other way of saying it than that what I found finally was Christ. Or was found. It hardly seems to matter which. There are other words for describing what happened to me—psychological words, historical words, poetic words—but in honesty as well as in faith I am reduced to the word that is his name because no other seems to account for the experience so fully.

To say that I was born again, to use that traditional phrase, is to say too much because I remained in most ways as self-centered and squeamish after the fact as I was before, and God knows remain so still. And in another way to say that I was born again is to say too little because there have been more than a few such moments since, times when from beyond time something too precious to tell has glinted in the dusk, always just out of reach, like fireflies.

I went to see Buttrick himself the week after his sermon and told him that I found myself wondering if maybe I should go to a seminary to discover more about whatever it was that seemed to have taken place and what I should do about it, and after he asked me a few questions and pointed out that there were various roads open to me, what he did was this. He was a busy man in charge of a big and busy church, but he took his hat and coat out of the closet, handed me mine, and then drove me in his car from Madison Avenue at 73rd Street to Union Theological Seminary at Broadway and 120th Street, where I eventually entered as a student the following fall.

That made a journey of forty-seven blocks all told, not counting the long crosstown blocks at the top of the park. It was a long way to go, and there is no question but that there is a vastly longer way to go still, for all of us, before we are done. And the way we have to go is full of perils, both from without and from within, and who can say for sure what we will find at the end of our journeys, or if, when that time comes, it will prove to be anything more than such a beautiful dream as Caliban dreamed. But here at the last I find myself thinking about King Rinkitink again—another king strong in his weakness and stout of heart in the face of despair—and of those three pearls that he carried with him. The blue one that conferred such strength that no one could resist it. The pink one that protected its owner from all dangers. And the pure white one that spoke wisdom.

Faith. Hope. Love. Those are their names of course, those three—as words so worn out, but as realities so rich. Our going-away presents from beyond time to carry with us through time to lighten our step as we go. And part at least of the wisdom of the third one is, as Rinkitink heard it, "Never question the truth of what you fail to understand, for the world is filled with wonders." Above all, never question the truth beyond all understanding and surpassing all other wonders that in the long run nothing, not even the world, not even ourselves, can separate us forever from that last and deepest love that glimmers in our dusk like a pearl, like a face.

ELISABETH ELLIOT (B. 1926)

The lives of missionaries have always held great fascination for Christians. These intrepid souls—who brave foreign cultures, physical and psychological hardship, and even death in order to proclaim the gospel—establish a lofty spiritual ideal for believers who remain in more familiar situations. For Protestants no less than for Catholics, missionaries are considered the elite, the specially chosen, the saints.

Elisabeth Elliot knows as much about the ideals and realities of missionary service as anyone. She was born in Brussels to missionary parents. Later her father, Philip Howard, became the longtime editor of *The Sunday School Times*. And among the wider family were many individuals who made their mark as ministers, writers on Christian themes, and missionaries. After graduating from Wheaton College in 1948 with a major in Greek, Elisabeth immediately began to prepare for missionary service in South America. She arrived there in 1952. In 1953 she married another Wheaton graduate, James Elliot, a young man of intense spirituality and undeviating purpose. Elisabeth moved from the Andes to the eastern jungles of Ecuador to assist her husband in bringing the Christian message to the Indians; soon the couple had a daughter. They helped other American missionaries plan even more adventuresome efforts to carry the gospel deep into the Ecuadorian jungle.

In January 1956 Elisabeth Elliot's world came crashing in. Her husband and four others, attempting to make initial contact with members of the Auca tribe, were brutally slain. There she was, a young widow with an infant daughter, left alone in a culture not her own, her missionary ambitions foiled. Her response, however, was not despair but work. With others she followed up on the first contacts with the Aucas and eventually was able to see many of them become Christians and embark on the life of faith. And she began to write.

The slaying of the American missionaries received major attention in the American press, and this paved the way for two powerful books by Elliot. The first, *Through Gates of Splendor* (1957), told the story of efforts to reach the Aucas. The second, *Shadow of the Almighty: The Life and Testament of Jim Elliot* (1958), was perhaps the most effective Protestant version of the life of a saint in the twentieth century. Without glossing over flaws and excesses in her husband's life, and without romanticizing missionary efforts in Ecuador, Elliot told gripping narratives that inspired many to pursue a similar vocation.

Elliot had lived with a martyr and taken part in heroic evangelistic efforts, but these experiences seemed to have made her more rather than less aware of ambiguity and complexity in the missionary task, more rather than less realistic about the effort to communicate the gospel in an alien culture. This deepening perception bore fruit in her nonfiction books, but also provided the raw material for an unusually sensitive novel, *No Graven Image*, published in 1966.

The story tells of a young missionary, Margaret Sparhawk, who, like Elliot, comes to the Andes of Ecuador to translate the Bible for the Indians. After early uncertainties, Margaret is accepted into her tribe when she successfully delivers a baby under very difficult circumstances. She is soon making steady progress in translating the Gospels with the faithful help of her native informant, Pedro. And she establishes a blossoming friendship with Pedro's wife, Rosa. But then tragedy strikes: when she gives Pedro a penicillin injection for an infection on his leg, he suffers a severe drug reaction and dies. Following are the novel's last two chapters, which detail what happens after Pedro's death.

From *No Graven Image*

It was so dark by this time I could hardly see the trail, but I must hurry. I was almost running, putting my feet down recklessly and wrenching my ankles as I tripped on the broken clods of clay. It had never seemed such a long way home. I strained toward the town, pulling it toward me, running and running, trying to push the mountain away behind, pushing the little mud hut back and back.

"Follow the Shepherd, Margaret. He knows the way."

It was too late now. My eyes strained through the dark, trying to light the lamps of the town somewhere there below me. Where was the trail? The turn onto the cobblestone road? Was it here? Hurry.

Somewhere nearby I heard the bleat of a sheep. I was out of breath and something about the feel of the road beneath my feet was not quite familiar. Every rut and rock was known to me on the usual route. I had better stop. But there isn't time. There's no time to stop. The animal look, the wild shriek, the implacable corpse—were they actually following me? No. They were back in the hut, far up the mountain now. Stop. You've lost your way.

I stood on the trail and tried to listen, but found that I was panting and my legs were trembling and it took a minute before I could hear the silence

---

Source: *No Graven Image* (New York: Harper & Row, 1966), pp. 235-44.

around me. The night was still and frigid and the stars, like fearsome watchers, hovered close above me. I should by this time have reached the turn onto my road, but somewhere I had missed it. A sheep cried again—a forsaken, human cry—and I remembered the place where the sheep lived. I was not far from my road. I knew now which way to turn. Hurry. Better start running again.

The light of the stars was not enough to enable me to see anything that I recognized, but to my right, like a jagged orange tear in the fabric of the dark, a fire glowed on the hills. It must be far away, I decided, so it must be to the east. I was going north, then, where I wanted to go. Some Indian must be burning his pasture land. The fire was like a thin dragon, trembling and creeping across the night.

I started to walk again, quickly, and in a few moments I heard a dog bark, then I saw a light, then two lights, and the trail dropped to the cobblestone road. I ran as fast as I could. Perhaps there would still be time.

Time for what? I reached my gate, jerked at the latch and fumbled with it in the dark, wanting to tear it from its screws. It came open, and I ran to the door, but my hands were shaking so that the key would not fit into the lock.

"Fear thou not; for I am with thee: be not dismayed; for I am thy God." Still with me? Still my God? No. It was too late. There. The key turned, the door opened, and I rushed into the house, turned on all the lights, and sank down by the table.

Everything was exactly as I had left it. The rag rug on the floor, the awkward chairs that had long since lost their awkwardness in my eyes, the flowered tablecloth and the teapot, the Swiss clock. But the clock had stopped. Had I forgotten to wind it, or had there actually been, as I seemed to sense, some cosmic change that marked the end of something? I picked up the clock, wound it and shook it, then listened. It was not ticking. Good, I thought, and set it down on the table. That gives me time, then. Time to begin again, slowly, carefully, to sort things out.

Surely there is a way to make it come right. This can't be it. It isn't finished yet. Go back and do it the other way this time. Do it right. For God's sake, *do it right* this time.

Was it the medicine? Would streptomycin have worked? No, no. You have to go back much farther than that. It was something else. There must have been a call that you didn't hear—or was it that you disobeyed? A dozen accusations confronted me. No. I refuse to capitulate. How could I have failed to hear the call that was meant for me? What kind of a shepherd would allow that? No one had ever listened more intently, praying, beseeching, entreating God to guide, to show the way. The call had come, the way had opened, the work had begun. Had I disobeyed? *Had* I? Where could it have been? Is God through with me now, is He saying, "Get out"? The Indians are through with me. Rosa had stabbed me with her hatred.

These four walls—they are still here. My home. My quiet place to come back to after visiting the Indians. The house is still here. They can't reach me here. Nobody can reach me here. But God can. Where is the refuge from Him? I was going to sacrifice this home for You! What of the sacrifices I have already made—did You toy with them? O ineffable, sardonic God who toys with our sacrifices and smashes to earth the humble, hopeful altars we have built for a place to put Your name! Do You mock me? Why did You let him die? Why did You let me kill him? O God! I came to bring him life—*Your* life—and I destroyed him in Your name.

A donkey clopped by on the road outside and I could hear the sound of a whip and an Indian voice. Then there was silence. I looked at the Bible on the table in front of me and started to pick it up. My hand dropped again. I could not find answers there any more. Nothing had worked for me as I had thought it would work. God had nothing to say to me now. Where was He, anyway?

The question, which in my mind was tantamount to declaring myself an atheist, found me sitting there at the table waiting for an answer. Who would answer? Who, if not God Himself? Well, I would wait for Him. Perhaps He would strike me dead. No, that is unlikely. He could hardly bother with me to that extent now. Probably He has forgotten. Or He could answer me out of the whirlwind, vindicate Himself, explain. No, I have probably gone too far astray ever to hear Him again.

What shall I do now? Make some tea. Do something. See if anything works—does water boil as before? This silence! How can things be the same? How can the house stand so smugly as it stood this morning, nothing changed, everything in its place, quiet, neat, oblivious? Only the clock has stopped.

The beginning and the end. I have come to the end of my work. God's work, I thought it was—I came here for Him. I ventured to believe He had given it to me to do, and I staked my life on it. I entered into it in faith and now . . . the end. *And omega.* God! My God!

"Señorita!" I jumped in my chair. It was Pava outside the door. "Señorita Margarita!"

I stumbled to the door and opened it. "Pava!"

"Mama says have you any candles to give us for the wake for Father?"

Candles. A wake for Father. My mind teetered to find its balance again, confronted with two specifics. Did I have any candles?

"Yes, Pava, I think I have. Come in. I will look for them." I found some candles in the kitchen cupboard and brought them out. As though my heart had been hit with a hammer, I realized that had it not been for me they would not have needed candles. Pedro would not have been dead.

"Well, good night, señorita," said Pava. "May God pay you." She turned to go.

"Good night, Pava." I opened the door for her, and saw that Romero was waiting in the dark. She would not have to go home alone. I started to close the door and Romero called, "Señorita."

"What is it, Romero?"

"Señorita—we are having a wake and Mama wanted to . . . Mama said would you come and sit with us?"

Yes, I thought. I can do that. I can go and sit with them.

If I had said no to Romero and Pava, and had not gone to their father's wake, I would probably have forsaken my place among the Indians of the highland, and perhaps my place as a missionary anywhere at all. But then I do not really know. The decision was not one which I weighed carefully. The children came and brought their request, and I went with them. It seems to me now that the decision was right, and that it was indeed the voice of God, still and small, that said, "And omega." Perhaps He would have borne with me even if I had said no, and have brought me by another way. He is indeed of great mercy. Only I know that I was glad to have been at the wake, and I am glad to be here in my house in Indi Urcu.

The sun shines today, as you know that it nearly always does in the mornings, and the great mountain Chimborazo shines with it, lifting its gleaming peak toward heaven, reminding me that the strength of the hills is His also.

The only light at the wake came from the two candles we brought. One was placed at Pedro's head, one at his feet, and Rosa bent over him in the yellow circle, her black hair falling across his face, and wailed the death wail until the cocks began to crow at dawn. People came from all over the mountain, packing themselves into the stuffy little room (the candles flickered for lack of oxygen), crying for a little while, talking, sitting stolidly in the gloom until another mourner arrived, when it was necessary briefly to renew the wailing. Rosa uncovered the face of the corpse when a relative came, and each time she did so the features looked a trifle younger and sharper, the deep tea color of his skin gradually paler. I found myself spellbound by the sight of that face, which had registered nothing when Pedro first met me, then, as time had passed, had shown shy friendliness, trust, interest, eagerness, joy—would it not change now, would not a single tiniest muscle twitch, an eyelash fall? Rosa covered the face again, more tenderly than I had seen her do anything, and then raised her arms to her head once more and rocked and chanted. And then when the cocks had crowed and darkness was driven over the far eastern hills the mourners got up one by one, straightened their ponchos and their skirts, and left the house, filing off over the cracked fields to their work. A few of the men stayed to wait for the coffin which had been sent for from the town. They put the body in it, there was another night of watching, and on the morning of the second day I saw the long file moving toward the village, four men carrying the wooden coffin on their shoulders. I went with them, too, to the Indian section of the little cemetery. The relatives had hired a few professional mourners—poor white people who knew the prayers that had to be said and possessed rosaries which they agreed to use in exchange for some corn and *chicha*.

Pava stood quietly by the open grave, a single ray of sunlight falling across her cheekbones under the wide, upturned·brim of her felt hat. As the ropes let the coffin gently into the earth I saw the glitter of tears on her lashes. When the earth was thrown onto the coffin and stamped down, she wrapped her shawl tightly around her arm, and pushed her nose into the crook of her elbow, her shoulders heaving with sobs. Rosa wept openly, as was expected of her at the grave, and when it was over she took her children home in silence, there to take up what God had left her of life.

I wonder whether I will ever live in an Indian house. Even here in Indi Urcu the people came casually, now and then, to visit me. I go to visit them and they talk as freely or they are as silent as ever. If they talk, they often speak of Pedro's death and my part in it. There is no conspiracy of silence between us on that subject. If they are silent it is not a different silence from before. Some are as hostile and suspicious as they have ever been but not, I think, more so; some are slowly losing their reticence, like Manuela, who asked me if her small relatives could join Pedro's children in the reading classes. I still have the classes. Of course they are not formal. The children come to my house now, when they feel like coming, and we spread out the books on the tiny verandah or, if the group is too large, in the fenced enclosure. Some of them make astonishing strides and then abruptly stop coming. Others, without the slightest flagging of hope and enthusiasm, learn nothing at all, though they come week after week. Perhaps the reading classes will come to an end. God knows about that. As for the translation of the Bible, of course, I cannot go ahead without an informant. God knew about that when Pedro died. I do not write prayer letters any more, for I have nothing to say about my work. It seemed, on the night of Pedro's death, as though *Finis* were written below all I had done. Now, in the clear light of day, I see that I was in part correct. God, if He was merely my accomplice, had betrayed me. If, on the other hand, He was God, He had freed me.

I find that I can no longer arrange my life in an orderly succession of projects with realizable goals and demonstrable effects. I cannot designate this activity as "useful" and that one as "useless," for often the categories are reversed and even more often I am at a loss to apply either label, for the work, in the end, as well as the labeling, is God's.

One day a few weeks ago I went down to the village graveyard again to visit Pedro's grave. The paper flowers that had been put there had faded and were laden with dust. The mound of earth had sunk a little. But at the head of the grave someone had put up a flimsy wooden cross, painted white, and had written in pencil the name PEDRO CHIMBU, and the date of his death.

Nothing else had changed. The sky was vast and blue above me, the mountains calm around me. There was no sound except that of a few sheep beyond the mud wall, and a faint piping as someone—it sounded like a child—went by on the road, playing on his panpipes.

It was as it should be. I found myself alone—Rosa was not here, but carrying out her own work at home; the MacDonalds, Lynn, my colleagues in many places had also their appointed tasks for which they would individually give account; those who prayed for me at home might at this moment be praying, and He to whom the prayers were addressed would know what answer to give. For my part, I was left alone before God—indeed, it seemed to me this morning that for the first time in my life I stood in direct relation to Him as Moses stood when he beheld the burning bush. For me, however, it was no such dramatic vision. There were before me only the dry mound of earth and the pitiful little cross with its penciled legend. What was it about that cross that cleared the way to God? I think it was this: I saw for the first time my own identity in its true perspective. Once I had envisioned Pedro, highland Indian, Christian, translator of the Bible, soldier of the Cross— because I, Margaret Sparhawk, had come. He was my project, he was the star in my crown. But here was another cross, with a name and a date, to mark where a dead man lay—because I, Margaret Sparhawk, had come.

And God? What of Him? "I am with thee," He had said. With me in *this?* He had allowed Pedro to die, or—and I could not then nor can I today deny the possibility—He had perhaps caused me to destroy him. And does He now, I asked myself there at the graveside, ask me to worship Him?

I lay down on the grass and saw that high above me a condor circled, looking down on the tops of the frosted peaks, on the lakes and the serene valley. The child went by the gate once more, piping softly.

MARTIN LUTHER KING, JR. (1929-1968)

With Martin Luther King, Jr., and the modern civil rights movement, we find again in American life a civic piety like that of the Puritans and Abraham Lincoln. Of course, much—in religion as well as in politics and society—had changed since the early days of European settlement, since the time of the Civil War. Yet something of the same energy that had inspired his predecessors inspired King. Like them, he had distinctly religious convictions that produced a social vision, an ideal of what, under God, the nation could become.

Martin Luther King, Jr., was the son of a Baptist pastor in Atlanta. He studied at Morehouse College, Crozer Theological Seminary, and Boston University. In 1955 he came to national prominence when, as the pastor of the Drexler Avenue Baptist Church in Montgomery, Alabama, he led a successful boycott of the city's buses in an effort to end racial segregation on public transportation. In 1957 he helped found the Southern Christian Leadership Conference, and from that time until his life was snuffed out by an assassin's bullet, he was the country's most visible advocate of civil rights reform. In 1964 King was awarded the Nobel Prize for Peace.

Like his predecessors, King had a dream. This "dream," as he put it so eloquently in his speech to the assembled crowd at the Lincoln Memorial on August 28, 1963, was made up of many elements. There were principles of nonviolence taken over from Gandhi. There were themes of civil disobedience from Henry David Thoreau. There were background echoes of King's academic study of modern existentialist theology and personalist philosophy. And there were emphases borrowed from the ecumenical movement. But above all, there were the convictions of Christian faith nurtured in the experience of American blacks.

These convictions are revealed in the quotations that King chose from Scripture, hymns, and spirituals. He knew the Bible well, especially those Old Testament passages calling for a practical justice aspiring to the standards of divine righteousness. And he could recite the words of Scripture as memorably as anyone in his generation. So when we hear of justice rolling down like the waters (Amos 5:24) or that every valley shall be exalted (Isa. 40:3-5), we begin to discover the source of his vision. Even more, the use of these Scriptures and of the Negro spiritual "Free at Last" reveals a deeply ingrained conviction of the black religious experience: spiritual and social problems always belong together. Love of God translates quickly into love for others and opposition to the sinful structures of society. What else could be expected from those who received the gospel under the slaver's lash, whose churches were often the one source of hope in ghettoes of discrimination?

The "I Have a Dream" speech is also a sermon. In it may be heard the echoes of countless efforts by black ministers to apply the balm of the gospel to the wounded bodies and souls of their congregations. In it may also be heard the reminder—offered on innumerable occasions in the shanty churches of the rural South, in the storefronts of the urban North, and in stately black churches throughout the country—that hope for a day of righteousness is not in vain.

I Have a Dream

A Speech by Dr. Martin Luther King, Jr.
at the Historic "March on Washington"
Lincoln Memorial, Washington, D.C., August 28, 1963

Fivescore years ago, a great American, in whose symbolic shadow we stand today, signed the Emancipation Proclamation. This momentous decree came as a great beacon light of hope to millions of Negro slaves who had been seared in the flames of withering injustice. It came as a joyous daybreak to end the long night of their captivity.

But one hundred years later, the Negro still is not free; one hundred years later, the life of the Negro is still sadly crippled by the manacles of segregation and the chains of discrimination; one hundred years later, the Negro lives on a lonely island of poverty in the midst of a vast ocean of material prosperity; one hundred years later, the Negro is still languished in the corners of American society and finds himself in exile in his own land.

So we've come here today to dramatize a shameful condition. In a sense we've come to our nation's capital to cash a check. When the architects of our republic wrote the magnificent words of the Constitution and the Declaration of Independence, they were signing a promissory note to which every American was to fall heir. This note was the promise that all men, yes, black men as well as white men, would be guaranteed the unalienable rights of life, liberty, and the pursuit of happiness.

It is obvious today that America has defaulted on this promissory note insofar as her citizens of color are concerned. Instead of honoring this sacred obligation, America has given the Negro people a bad check, a check which has come back marked "insufficient funds." But we refuse to believe that the bank of justice is bankrupt. We refuse to believe that there are insufficient funds in the great vaults of opportunity of this nation. And so we've come to cash this check, a check that will give us upon demand the riches of freedom and the security of justice.

We have also come to this hallowed spot to remind America of the fierce urgency of now. This is no time to engage in the luxury of cooling off or to take the tranquilizing drug of gradualism. Now is the time to make real the promises of democracy; now is the time to rise from the dark and desolate valley of segregation to the sunlit path of racial justice; now is the time to lift our nation from the quicksands of racial injustice to the solid rock of brotherhood; now is the time to make justice a reality for all of God's children. It would be fatal for the nation to overlook the urgency of the moment. This sweltering summer of the Negro's legitimate discontent will not pass until there is an invigorating autumn of freedom and equality.

Nineteen-sixty-three is not an end, but a beginning. And those who hope that the Negro needed to blow off steam and will now be content will have a rude awakening if the nation returns to business as usual. There will be neither rest nor tranquility in America until the Negro is granted his citizenship rights. The whirlwinds of revolt will continue to shake the foundations of our nation until the bright day of justice emerges.

But there is something that I must say to my people, who stand on the worn threshold which leads into the palace of justice. In the process of gaining our rightful place, we must not be guilty of wrongful deeds. Let us not seek to satisfy our thirst for freedom by drinking from the cup of bitterness and hatred. We must forever conduct our struggle on the high plain of dignity and discipline. We must not allow our creative protests to degenerate into physical violence. Again and again we must rise to the majestic heights of meeting physical force with soul force. The marvelous new militancy, which has engulfed the Negro community, must not lead us to a distrust of all white people. For many of our white brothers, as evidenced by their presence here today, have come to realize that their destiny is tied up with our destiny. And they have come to realize that their freedom is inextricably bound to our freedom. We cannot walk alone. And as we walk, we must make the pledge that we shall always march ahead. We cannot turn back.

There are those who are asking the devotees of civil rights, "When will you be satisfied?" We can never be satisfied as long as the Negro is the victim of the unspeakable horrors of police brutality; we can never be satisfied as long as our bodies, heavy with the fatigue of travel, cannot gain lodging in the motels of the highways and the hotels of the cities; we cannot be satisfied as long as the Negro's basic mobility is from a smaller ghetto to a larger one; we can never be satisfied as long as our children are stripped of their selfhood and robbed of their dignity by signs stating "For Whites Only"; we cannot be satisfied as long as the Negro in Mississippi cannot vote and a Negro in New York believes he has nothing for which to vote. No! No, we are not satisfied, and we will not be satisfied until "justice rolls down like waters and righteousness like a mighty stream."

I am not unmindful that some of you have come here out of great trials and tribulations. Some of you have come fresh from narrow jail cells. Some of you have come from areas where your quest for freedom left you battered by the storms of persecution and staggered by the winds of police brutality. You have been the veterans of creative suffering. Continue to work with the faith that unearned suffering is redemptive. Go back to Mississippi. Go back to Alabama. Go back to South Carolina. Go back to Georgia. Go back to Louisiana. Go back to the slums and ghettos of our northern cities, knowing that somehow this situation can and will be changed. Let us not wallow in the valley of despair.

I say to you today, my friends, [that] even though we face the difficulties of today and tomorrow, I still have a dream. It is a dream deeply rooted in the American dream. I have a dream that one day this nation will rise up and live out the true meaning of its creed, "We hold these truths to be self-evident, that all men are created equal." I have a dream that one day on the red hills of Georgia, sons of former slaves and the sons of former slave owners will be able to sit down together at the table of brotherhood. I have a dream that one day even the state of Mississippi, a state sweltering with the heat of injustice, sweltering with the heat of oppression, will be transformed into an oasis of freedom and justice. I have a dream that my four little children will one day live in a nation where they will not be judged by the color of their skin, but by the content of their character.

I have a dream today!

I have a dream that one day down in Alabama—with its vicious racists, with its governor having his lips dripping with the words of interposition and nullification—one day right there in Alabama, little black boys and black girls will be able to join hands with little white boys and white girls as sisters and brothers.

I have a dream today!

I have a dream that one day every valley shall be exalted, every hill and mountain shall be made low. The rough places will be plain and the crooked places will be made straight, "and the glory of the Lord shall be revealed, and all flesh shall see it together."

This is our hope. This is the faith that I go back to the south with. With this faith we will be able to hew out of the mountain of despair a stone of hope. With this faith we will be able to transform the jangling discords of our nation into a beautiful symphony of brotherhood. With this faith we will be able to work together, to pray together, to struggle together, to go to jail together, to stand up for freedom together, knowing that we will be free one day. And this will be the day. This will be the day when all of God's children will be able to sing with new meaning, "My country, 'tis of thee, sweet land of liberty, of thee I sing. Land where my fathers died, land of the pilgrims' pride, from every mountainside, let freedom ring." And if America is to be a great nation, this must become true.

So let freedom ring from the prodigious hilltops of New Hampshire; let freedom ring from the mighty mountains of New York; let freedom ring from the heightening Alleghenies of Pennsylvania; let freedom ring from the snow-capped Rockies of Colorado; let freedom ring from the curvaceous slopes of California. But not only that. Let freedom ring from Stone Mountain of Georgia; let freedom ring from Lookout Mountain of Tennessee; let freedom ring from every hill and molehill of Mississippi. "From every mountainside, let freedom ring."

And when this happens, and when we allow freedom to ring, when we let it ring from every village and every hamlet, from every state and every city, we will be able to speed up that day when all of God's children, black men and white men, Jews and Gentiles, Protestants and Catholics, will be able to join hands and sing in the words of the old Negro spiritual, "Free at last. Free at last. Thank God Almighty, we are free at last."

HOWARD RIENSTRA (1931-1986)

The fact that we are mortal, that each of us must die, is sobering indeed. Yet this fact also enables us to distinguish more clearly between things that are essential and things that are not. Mark Twain could joke about how the prospect of being hung concentrated the mind marvelously. Christians, more soberly, have prayed since the early days of the church for special protection "in the hour of our death."

One of the strongest resources for believers in that hour is early religious education, instruction from youth that may have been acquired quite casually but that takes on unexpected meaning during a crisis. Children who have memorized Bible verses, learned their catechism, or committed the words of hymns to heart often do not realize the treasure they have stored up for the perils of adulthood.

Howard Rienstra's account of his struggle with lymphoma is, from one angle, an ordinary story. A competent, energetic professional contracts a disease that ultimately leads to a sense of shipwreck, of life no longer under control. But from another perspective, it is not an ordinary story, for in this case the loss of control led to an existential understanding of truths communicated years before in a simple religious lesson.

Howard Rienstra was a professor of history at Calvin College in Grand Rapids, Michigan, and director of that institution's Meeter Center for Calvin Studies. Besides being committed to his academic pursuits, he was active in civic affairs: his contributions included serving as commissioner of the city of Grand Rapids. He was a lifelong member of the Christian Reformed Church.

That denomination, like several other Protestant bodies of European origin as well as the Catholic Church, continues the practice of catechizing—that is, of promoting religious instruction based on a set of officially approved questions and answers. In the case of the Christian Reformed Church, this is the Heidelberg Catechism, a statement of Reformed Protestant faith that originated in 1563 under the German Elector of the Palatinate, Frederick III. The catechism was early translated into Dutch and carried to the Netherlands, where it became the cornerstone of that nation's Reformed Church. From there it was brought by immigrants to America, where it continues to serve as a doctrinal standard for the Reformed Church in America as well as the Christian Reformed Church.

Professor Rienstra's confrontation with death in early 1985 brought him to a fresh understanding of the first question and answer of that catechism. The question reads, "What is your only comfort in life and death?" The answer is this:

> That I, with body and soul, both in life and death, am not my own, but belong unto my faithful Savior Jesus Christ; who with His precious blood has fully satisfied for all my sins, and delivered me from all the power of the devil; and so preserves me that without the will of my heavenly Father not a hair can fall from my head; yea, that all things must be subservient to my salvation, wherefore by His Holy Spirit He also assures me of eternal life, and makes me heartily willing and ready, henceforth, to live unto Him.

That is the background for the account that follows, an account of how an odd neck and early religious training became unusual means of God's grace.

Who Is in Control?

The realization that one is dying comes slowly. Six years ago I was diagnosed as having cancer. I have non-Hodgkins lymphoma. I was assured that although it was third stage, it was nonetheless treatable. It has been, and on two occasions I was in remission. At one point I lost most of my hair, and I have done an awful lot of vomiting over these years. Yet I seemed to be in control. I knew that the vomiting was only temporary, and I could feel the lymph nodes return to normal as the chemotherapy took effect. I accepted the reality of my cancer, but I denied that I had really lost control over my own life. It seemed, in fact, as if I were not yet dying.

The beginnings of a change came near midnight this past January 30. My fever had risen to 104, and Mary was driving me to the hospital for the second time this year. I said to her, "You know, don't you, that one of these times when I go to the hospital I won't return?" She quietly said, "Yes." Without using the words "death" or "dying," we came to acknowledge the reality of it and that I was losing control—however reluctant my acknowledgment remained.

Early in April, after two hospitalizations had produced no clear reasons for continuing fever and lung problems, an outpatient lung biopsy was performed. A tube was placed in my lungs through which the doctor could both visually examine the lung and take small tissue samples for analysis. At the end I returned home, but my fever flared to 103 and so I was quickly back

Source: *Reformed Journal*, Aug. 1985, pp. 13-15.

in the hospital. That first biopsy also failed to give any clear reason for my difficulties. It was decided, then, to do an open-chest biopsy. At this point the doctors were expecting to find cancer in the lung, but they were pleasantly surprised not to. The only certain thing was a mildly severe fibrosis of the lungs.

Failing to find anything specific to treat, the doctors' suspicion fell on the general condition of my cancer. I returned home, coughing and running intermittently high fevers. Mary and I recognized my worsening condition. We decided on the basis of the three hospitalizations that I would not return to the hospital again just to treat my fever and cough. I would rather die at home. We, in other words, were trying to regain control over my life, and even my death.

Later, however, because I had not received any chemotherapy since January 3, it was proposed that I begin a new kind of chemo, VP16, and on Thursday, May 2, an attempt was made. But my veins couldn't handle the chemical, and only half a dose was administered. I would have to have a Hickman catheter or a Port-a-Cath placed in my chest so that I could receive further chemo and quickly. Outpatient surgery was scheduled for the next Monday to install the Port-a-Cath.

Little did we know what would be the consequences of that decision. It seemed merely to be another decision made so I could stay in control. Dozens of such decisions had been made over the years. And this did not violate our no-hospitalization resolve, since I would walk in around noon and walk out by 4 p.m., having the procedure done with local anesthesia. Very simple. I was in control.

I was in the operating room promptly at 1 p.m., and after the usual preliminaries and administering of local anesthesia, the cutting in my neck began. The surgeon had externally seen and palpitated a vein which he thought would be appropriate. Upon exposing that vein, however, he discovered it was too small to receive the catheter tubing. He then turned to other deeper veins. Let me anticipate questions by saying that I am an oddity. The veins in my neck, as it turns out, are not positioned as in an anatomy textbook. This structural oddity would soon have profound consequences.

The surgeon eventually found a large vein which he assumed to be the external jugular vein. For most people it would have been. But as he put the catheter in that vein it could not be positioned correctly. It ran off either to my left or right arm, but it wouldn't go straight down no matter what he tried. A properly structured external jugular vein would have gone down as far as it had to for the successful operation of the Port-a-Cath. This one wouldn't.

At this point, about two hours into the surgery, some dramatic things began to happen. I began to think that I was going to die. I heard my surgeon call for another surgeon to come assist him. And the surgeons he named were the big names of Grand Rapids surgeons. At that point I began gasping for breath. In my perception I was panicking in the face of death. I said to Mary the next day, "I couldn't breathe, and they didn't know what to do about it." My whole body shook as I desperately fought for air. I asked for oxygen and was given it, but since I was breathing very shallowly, it took a while for even breathing to return and for my panic in the face of what I then thought was my imminent death to subside.

Before what finally was a four-and-a-half-hour operation was over, I went through two more similar episodes of panic and gasping for breath. I was scared to death and scared to die. I tried to pray, but couldn't. I tried to recite to myself my favorite childhood hymn, "What a Friend We Have in Jesus," but the words seemed empty. I was convinced I was dying, and I recognized more closely than ever before in my life that I was no longer in even apparent control. The loss of control came to me in the crudest of ways, as I voided my urine during each of the three episodes of panic and gasping for breath.

Meanwhile the second surgeon, an open-heart specialist, came in and, having confirmed the oddity of my vein structure, scrubbed and took over the operation. He decided to go after the internal jugular vein, which lies more deeply in the neck. It was not easy, but after about an hour he had the catheter successfully placed and the operation was then finished by the first surgeon.

I now know what had actually happened. I have been assured that I didn't really panic, but that my body was in fact seriously deprived of oxygen. Oxygen deprivation rather typically produces both the gasping for breath and the sense of panic. That is the medical explanation. I was also informed that if I had not been able to regain even breathing they would simply have given me a general anesthesia in addition to the local I was receiving. I accept these scientific explanations, and it would be very tempting to substitute them for what I had experienced. I could again think I was in control. But more lessons were to come.

After four and a half hours of surgery, I obviously was not going to walk out of the hospital that day. In fact, they kept me on 6 liters of oxygen; my fever continued to flare; and I was coughing up heavy sputum. They ran a culture on the sputum, and remarkably for the first time since January a specific infection was identified. It was pseudomonis, a rather bad infection of the lungs.

It is now being treated successfully, but it would not have been had I not stayed in the hospital. Rather I would have gone home, and the next afternoon, with the help of Tylenol, I would have attended the semi-annual meeting of the Governing Board of the Meeter Center for Calvin Studies. In fact, I could not have seen a doctor until Thursday, when the second stage of my new chemo was to be administered throught my new Port-a-Cath. Speculation is always dangerous about things that did not happen, but it could be that if the chemo had been administered, the pseudomonis would have advanced to a fatal stage. By trying to stay in control I would in fact have been committing suicide. Thus the experience of dying which I had on the operating room table was really God's way of extending my life and his clear demonstration to me that he and not I was in control.

Paradoxes are always difficult to understand. The paradox of good coming out of bad reminds me of John Milton's paradox of the "Fortunate Fall." Briefly, the fortunate fall argument is that if humankind had not fallen into sin, we would never have known the infinite love and mercy of God in Jesus Christ. In my case paradoxes abound. If when I was born I had a normal structure to my veins, I would now possibly be dying of pseudomonis without treatment. If my veins hadn't collapsed on Thursday I would not have had the Monday surgery with the same consequences. And even during the surgery, if I had not experienced the panic and gasping for breath, I would not have been willing to lose control. I had to be beaten out of my arrogant, selfish, and unbelieving sense of being in charge.

Thus the primary benefit—the real good that came out of the apparent evil—is neither physical nor psychological, but spiritual. My belief has been strengthened and my faith deepened as dying seemed so near and God so far away. Some background explanation is probably appropriate.

I have always believed, or so it seems. I have always had a sense of God's leading and directing my life. From the time of my adoption at age ten, there could be no doubt about that. Probability theory would be quite inadequate as an explanation of my life. I have had a strong faith and understanding of God's presence—but that faith and understanding were not, as I learned on the operating table, the full assurance of my salvation. To put it in terms that were popular a few years ago, *I* was still on the throne of my life rather than Christ. Intellectually I affirmed the Reformed faith without doubt and I took great delight in defending it. I have never intellectually doubted in the slightest the doctrines of the incarnation and resurrection of Christ, and I would with only slight provocation explain and defend them. And I have always known and taught the distinction between believing *that* Jesus Christ is God and believing *in* Jesus Christ. Salvation comes only from the latter.

What then went wrong? Knowing all that, teaching all that, and even trying in the practice of life to live justly, I still was trying to keep control. I refused to give myself over to Christ completely. I had to be broken for the comforting assurance of the first question and answer of the Heidelberg Catechism—that I am not my own but belong to my faithful Savior—to become a reality. It had always been real intellectually and even psychologically, but not spiritually, because I wanted to belong to myself—to stay in the driver's seat. Perhaps the best example of that is my never having prayed during these past six years for my own healing. I could pray for others, but not for myself. To pray for healing for myself would be to lose control—and God who knows the secrets of our hearts would surely not receive the prayers of one who was yet resisting him.

My brokenness began on the operating table on Monday and continued on Tuesday as I confessed my resistance in tearful prayer with Mary, and then continued the same with my minister. The assurance of salvation began to become a reality as I experienced God's pursuing grace so vividly. I am not, except in the most common biblical sense, a saint. Nor do I anticipate changes in belief or in the practice of life that will be visible to others. But I have been spiritually transformed by the grace of God coming through these paradoxical experiences. I now know more than intellectually that I am not in control, that I do not belong to myself. I have the comfort of the Heidelberg Catechism and of God's real presence.

And all this because of an odd neck.

CHARLES COLSON (B. 1931)

Significant skepticism greeted the news of Charles Colson's conversion in 1973. Here was one of Richard Nixon's top lieutenants claiming, at the height of the Watergate scandal,[1] that he had "accepted Jesus Christ." A graduate of Brown University, a veteran of the Marines, and a "special assistant to the President," Colson had developed a reputation as one of the toughest operators in the Nixon White House. As he readily admits, he was thrilled to be so close to the center of power and was willing to do almost anything necessary to hold on to power. Thus it is little wonder that many saw his conversion either as a ploy to gain sympathy or as a desperate choice made by a man facing criminal prosecution and imprisonment.

But what followed may have surprised even those who believed in Charles Colson's sincerity. Few could have gauged the depth of his convictions or charted the course of his spiritual future at the time of his conversion. Within only a few years, Colson had become a best-selling evangelical author, the founder of a ministry to convicts called Prison Fellowship, and a respected spokesman for American evangelicalism. His first book, *Born Again* (1976), tells the story of his conversion; his second book, *Life Sentence* (1979), recounts the struggles of the early years of Prison Fellowship.

In *Life Sentence,* Colson relates the events surrounding the publication of *Born Again* in February 1976. The first printing of that book, some 40,000 copies, sold out on publication day, and when Colson made the rounds of the television talk shows, he was treated like a celebrity. Because of the notoriety surrounding him and his book and because of the personal faith of Jimmy Carter, who was at that time battling for the presidency, the term "born again" became a topic of great public interest. But Colson later had second thoughts about this blaze of publicity. After a potentially harrowing interview with Barbara Walters on the "Today Show," Colson realized how shallow much of his understanding was and how much he needed to learn about the Christian faith. Unlike others who were to wave the "born again" banner in the late 1970s and early 1980s, Colson did not seem to grow weary of it, nor did he move on, as many did, to still other diversions. Instead, to his credit and the church's benefit, he continued his studied growth in the faith. He continued to develop the work in prisons and to learn about the history and mysteries of the Christian faith.

The selection that follows is Chapter 23 of *Life Sentence*. It shows the intensity of Colson's struggle to develop a piety that is both outwardly active and inwardly deep.

Inside the Walls

"Now look, Warden, we haven't lost a single prisoner yet. And no one has given us as hard a time as you have." When Paul Kramer saw me walk into the room, he rolled his eyes upward and gestured at the telephone receiver pressed against his ear.

Paul, I could tell, was in the process of lining up our next class of prisoners. Some warden was obviously being difficult about giving his permission for the release of inmates in his prison.

"Yes, Warden . . . I know, but you see . . . okay . . . but I'm not sure we could do that." Paul was clearly getting nowhere.

He hung up the phone and heaved a disgusted sigh. "That man Ralston is too much. He won't give us anyone."

The federal prison at Oxford, Wisconsin, is a tough penitentiary (average sentence more than 10 years), but Warden George Ralston is tougher. In some prisons inmates through violence or threats gain control. Not with Ralston; he runs a super-tight prison. One inmate a few months before had been furloughed out to attend our Washington seminar and turned out to be a top student. But now Ralston was adamant: he could release none of our choices because their remaining sentences were too long.

"You know what Ralston suggested?" Paul was angrily ripping off pages from a scratch pad, squeezing them into little wads and hurling them at the wastebasket across the room. "He said that if you guys are so good why don't you bring your teaching team into our prison and run your course here?"

"Stay cool, Brother," I replied. "We'll get plenty of men from other institutions."

Paul shook his head. "I'm not so sure. Ralston is a leader. If he refuses us, the others will start doing it."

Inside I feared that Paul might be correct. Ralston's stand meant that I

Source: *Life Sentence* (Lincoln, Va.: Chosen Books, 1979), pp. 252-63.

would have to go to Carlson [chief administrator of the United States prison system]. But I had just seen him about Memphis. Only so many times can an agency head be expected to overrule his subordinates.

Paul was still fuming. "Imagine telling us we should move into his prison."

"Was he serious?" I asked.

"Of course not. It was a clever ploy to get me off his back," Paul snapped.

Later the same day, Fred Rhodes, Gordon Loux and I met to map out our strategy. "What would happen if we took Ralston up on his offer?" Fred asked as a playful smile came over his face. Fred had earned the reputation of being a skilled in-fighter while running the Veteran's Administration. "Let's call his bluff," he said, slapping his hands on his knees in delight at the prospect.

"I don't know, Fred. He'd find a way to back out," I mused. "Besides, we don't have the staff to do it. Oxford is miles from the nearest town. There's a million problems and Ralston knows it."

Fred called for Paul; then Jackie Butner joined us. The verdict was unanimous: Ralston would never let us inside his prison, but Fred's suggestion was our best counter move. Then if Ralston withdrew his offer, there would be legitimate grounds to appeal to Carlson.

Paul was elected to make the call to the warden. Only minutes later he was back. Standing in the doorway he looked slightly dazed. "You won't believe this," he laughed nervously. "Ralston called our bluff. We're to go to Oxford in three weeks."

Preparations were begun at once. The next day Paul flew to Chicago, caught a feeder airline into Madison, Wisconsin, and rented a car for the two-hour drive to Oxford.

The Oxford Penitentiary had been constructed originally by the state. Before it was completed, a new governor was elected and promptly decided its location was too remote, precluding community involvement which is essential to whatever rehabilitation is achieved inside. When the state abandoned the facility, the federal government took it over and 500 men confined there were as cut off from the world as a leper colony.

From the outset, we realized that to go into the prison for a week and then leave would accomplish little, even be counter productive perhaps. Community and church involvement were essential to continue Bible studies and counseling after we left. Our first job then was to line up 20 volunteers to join us.

This was a tough order. Paul spent the first few days traveling to nearby towns, all of which were many miles from Oxford. One young couple from Madison who had been visiting the prison for us shepherded Paul from church to church.

It is a sad fact of American life that even socially conscious legislators find it politically expedient to place new prisons in the least populated areas of their state. Such small communities are generally conservative bastions of law-abiding citizens who have no use for criminals or those who "coddle" them.

Inmates, too, experience trauma when suddenly removed from familiar city surroundings and thrust into rural settings. Thus, from the standpoint of rehabilitation, our system produces the worst possible combination of city-bred prisoners amid country people.

Paul encountered the expected hostility. But in Baraboo, he found the owner of a Christian bookstore willing to join up. This man led Paul to a farmer who always had had a burden for prisoners and then to a small-town pastor who had been dreaming about working in a prison. Several house-wives from a local Bible study fellowship volunteered. Twenty-five people were recruited, though for most it meant at least a one-hour drive to be at the prison each day at daybreak.

Inside the prison, Paul discovered that Warden George Ralston was true to his word. A stern disciplinarian, he believed prison administrators had a "duty to provide a safe place where an inmate can be rehabilitated if he wants to be." Ralston's concern for security was as much to make life inside safe for the inmates as it was to keep them locked up.

"I told you I would open up this prison for you, and I will," he said. "Whether I'm for or against your approach doesn't matter. The inmates have a right to get what you can give." Ralston was the kind of person who laid all his cards face up on the table.

The arrangements began to fall into place. George Soltau was scheduled to present the one-week curriculum that included sessions from early morning through the evening. Permission was granted for us to eat meals with the inmates; the men attending the seminar would be excused from their regular jobs. Ralston even went on the prison's closed circuit TV to invite all inmates to enroll. Chaplain Steve Johnson was cooperative, turning the entire chapel area over to us. Since Paul and George were the only staff available, we persuaded a Christian counselor from California, John Jolliffe, to come and help out. Paul Kramer set up a temporary office in an $8 per night motel located at a highway truck stop a few miles from the prison.

Paul phoned reports to us in Washington each day where Gordon Loux took charge of pulling together the details. From the beginning the chief uncertainty was prisoner response. Our one seminar graduate inside was doing his best to recruit, but he reported powerful resistance. In every prison, religion is seen as "sissy stuff." To be involved is seen as a sign of weakness, or an attempt to win favor with the prison staff.

It was a suspenseful countdown during the last few days; what had begun as a lark, calling a hard-nosed warden's bluff was now deadly serious business. Other institutions, we learned, were sending observers; several chaplains, including some of our harshest critics, would be on hand. If the program worked, it might catch on throughout the prison system. If it didn't? Well, there wasn't time now to worry about that.

With only three days to go the outlook was anything but encouraging. Even Jackie Butner, whose upbeat, effervescent spirit always seemed unquenchable, was downcast.

"How's it going?" I asked, poking my head in the doorway of her cubicle office.

"Forty-six have signed up," she answered.

"Not too good, huh?" I smiled, trying to make the best of it.

"Not too good," she replied.

"Paul discouraged?"

"Yup, but we'll keep praying." There was nothing more to do.

Fred Rhodes was scheduled to open the seminar with an introductory session Sunday night during which the week's work would be outlined. Community volunteers would then mingle among the inmates with everyone assigned to small groups which would meet in between the lectures. I had speaking commitments in the far West all week and would not arrive until late Thursday.

The ringing in my ears was muffled and distant, then closer and more threatening. Suddenly, I threw the blanket off my head and fumbled for the alarm clock. The ringing continued. I rubbed my eyes and reached for the phone. The clock caught my eye, not quite 6 A.M. in Billings, Montana, where I'd flown the night before.

The voice was Fred's. "It was beautiful, just beautiful," he shouted into the phone. "Eighty-three inmates, thirty people from outside and the greatest spirit you've ever seen!"

Fred went on to report that Warden Ralston and the entire prison staff had greeted our party at the front gate. The chaplain was enthusiastic. When the men filed into the chapel, Fred could scarecely believe his eyes; it was almost double the number expected.

After the first day, Paul reported that the seminar was gaining strength. As word spread, other inmates began drifting in. By day's end 95 were in the chapel, almost 20 percent of the prison. From the questions asked and the many who were taking notes, it was obvious that the men were serious. Included were 10 Black Muslims who always gathered together at one table. They showed no emotion and stayed to themselves. But Soltau reported that they were following every word of his lectures.

On Thursday morning, John Jolliffe, a tall man in his early 30s with a commanding presence, was teaching. Midway through his lecture, he paused, put his notes down and stared around the room.

"You know we've been together all week and no one has asked you if you want to meet Jesus Christ in a personal way. It just struck me that it's time."

For several awkward moments Jolliffe looked around the room. The men stared back. Jolliffe had worked with us before and had considerable experience as staff counselor in a California prison. He knew the men would not risk ridicule in a hostile prison culture. Many had been "con" men on the outside and all of them knew the con game. They had been manipulated, first by the "system" on the street, later by the "system" in the prison. So an altar call can backfire, appear to be manipulation. We often invited those who wanted to make decisions to meet with us privately after the large meetings. Many always did.

But John Jolliffe, as he explained later, felt the moving of the Holy Spirit inside that prison and a quiet confidence came over him. "Bow your heads everyone, and if you want to receive the Lord, pray with me and raise your hands." Then in a soft voice his prayer began.

As a matter of principle, many of us, Paul included, spurn head counting. We want to labor in the fields, water and till, aware that it is God who causes the plants to grow. Totaling the harvest is God's business and He doesn't need us to keep score on Him.

There can be real hazards in head counting, I had learned, like programming the Spirit right out of evangelism altogether. The night before a big city mayor's prayer breakfast, the chairman came to my room. "Tomorrow 100 people will be won to Christ," he beamed. "I've claimed it, and I know it's true. Praise the Lord." He was a short man, so full of enthusiasm that he looked like he was bouncing all the time even when he stood still. His words were so presumptuous they made me cringe: besides, though I'm sure he never realized it, he was putting tremendous pressure on me to deliver.

Sleep that night was fitful and the man's words kept parading before me. The next day's speech was a disaster. Haunted by the "goal" of 100 I stumbled and several times lost my train of thought. I gave an invitation near the end of the speech but felt no moving of the Spirit. The harder I worked, the worse it got.

When my hosts tallied up the cards turned in by the breakfast guests, only four out of 1,500 at the breakfast had recorded decisions. "The ninety-six got away," my host told me, rubbing salt in my wounds, "because you didn't quote Scripture in your invitation."

But this day, Paul Kramer couldn't resist; he quietly drifted to the back of the room and stood against the wall. As John prayed, Paul spotted a hand go up right before him, then another, then two down front. Soon hands were popping up all over the room, so many and so fast Paul couldn't keep track. Well over 25, Paul estimated.

Gordon and I arrived that evening to join a weary but happy band of Christians at the truck stop motel where our staff was staying. Joining us was a delegation of Christian businessmen from Minneapolis, headed up by Dave Rolschau, who 18 months earlier had accompanied me to Sandstone, that isolated federal prison in Northern Minnesota.

Though the response in that prison had been as icy as the arctic winds which buffeted Dave's little green and white plane, we had prayed for God to open Sandstone. Now even as Paul was making plans for the next day's closing services at Oxford, Dave and his friends were talking enthusiastically about a week's seminar inside Sandstone. We'd wait and see, I told them.

George Ralston asked me to meet with him early the next morning. Tall, rugged as an oak and with sandy hair brushed back, Ralston looked more like a former all-American tackle turned college football coach than a warden. There was just a hint of boyish enthusiasm in his manner, as if at any moment he might say, "Okay men, let's win one for good old Oxford." Ralston was a refreshing contrast to some prison officials who seem to get squeezed into the same mold as the inmates they guard, embittered, negative and often given to vulgar language.

In Ralston's simply furnished office were pictures of the President, the attorney general, and Norman Carlson on one wall; a large, red-lettered "No Smoking" sign was on the other. He leaned across the polished desk top, empty of papers. "This has been a tremendous week. You should do this in every prison. I'll recommend it, if you want."

"We're grateful to you, Warden," I replied. "You made it possible."

"Nonsense. It's my duty to see that these men have an opportunity to better themselves. You've got something to offer, that's all."

Ralston then escorted me to the chapel where the classes were continuing. Inmates and volunteers were seated at 12-foot long folding tables lined up side by side across the front of the large open room. A lonely guard wearing a beige blazer was leaning against the wall. Many of the tough, hardened cons were wearing brightly colored stocking caps or kerchiefs around their necks, the one item of individual clothing allowed. Well dressed, middle-aged men and women volunteers were spread through their ranks. Merely walking into the room and scanning the faces, one could instantly sense that in only one week people of the most diverse backgrounds—black and white, rich and poor—had been fused together in a way that would be the envy of many churches.

My thoughts wandered while I waited for my turn to speak. How ironic that our best efforts to get men out of here were rebuffed; and so we had come here ourselves almost reluctantly. Ralston's stubbornness, and what seemed a defeat for us, was the vehicle God used to open doors for a new ministry with a far wider potential.

When I finished my short talk, two or three gave brief testimonies of what the week had meant in their lives. One young man confessed deep anger towards God, then told how the Lord had gradually softened his heart throughout the week. Early that very morning he had been awakened; a dam inside him had burst and a flood of cleansing tears poured forth. He knew that he was a new person that day.

One of the Muslims, wearing thick, horn-rimmed glasses and a heavy blue knit cap pulled down to his ears, had shown emotion several times during my talk. Slowly he stood.

"All my life," he began haltingly, "I've been looking for something." He paused, tugged at his cap and cleared his throat. "Well, I never thought I'd find it in prison, but this week I have.

"It is love," he continued. "It is the love of Jesus Christ right here." This took courage, but a few moments later everyone in the room would be put to the same test.

One of the volunteers, an older man with a camera slung around his neck, was now on his feet. "Would everyone gather on the steps for just a minute on the way to lunch so I can get a group picture?" he announced. Taking pictures inside a prison is generally forbidden, but Ralston had given permission for this one occasion.

The inmates exchanged troubled glances. At that moment the loudspeaker announced lunch and the entire prison population began streaming into the center courtyard forming lines into the mess hall. Every man in the chapel who stood for the picture would be recording his stand in front of 400 cynical onlookers.

The official prison photographer joined our volunteer in posing the seminar group on three rows of wide, concrete steps. The catcalls began, just a few at first. Then they swept across the compound in a crescendo of discordant sounds like an orchestra warming up for a performance. "Hey, man, will this get you parole?" Some waved their handkerchiefs. The men on the steps looked pained and embarrassed.

Mercifully, the photographers were soon finished. The crowd around us dissolved and the crisis passed like the evanescent fluffy clouds of the spring sky.

A communion service was held that afternoon. The inmates and volunteers arranged chairs in semicircular rows before the altar. The Muslims, who until this hour had been as inseparable as a flight of geese, were now dispersed through the crowd. True equality, I've learned, is always experienced at the foot of the cross.

When the last hymn was finished, the orderly rows suddenly turned into clusters of rejoicing people, embracing one another, reaching over chairs to shake hands. There were tears of joy and of sadness that the week was ending.

Fred's wife, Winona, having been, as she described herself, a "very proper Presbyterian," was seated next to a tall, lean black with a bushy Afro protruding in all directions above the white kerchief tied around his forehead. He had been solemn and impassive throughout communion; now he was one of the first on his feet. He spun around, leaned down and threw his long arms around Winona, who until this day used to describe the traditional Christian greeting as "that hugging foolishness." I expected her to recoil in dismay; instead she was grinning broadly.

Two somber-faced young inmates then asked if they could see Fred and me privately. We walked toward the entrance of the chaplain's office. "This is okay," one said just inside the door and out of sight of the others.

"Look, we want to make a confession and ask your forgiveness." The man speaking was short and brawny with several scars on his face and his forearms covered with tattoos.

"This morning when all you guys were getting ready for the picture . . . well, Jimmy here and me," he pointed a beefy thumb to his taller companion . . . "well, with all the guys watching . . . well, me and Jimmy took off. We didn't want the other guys to see us in this group."

Both men hung their heads, eyes fixed on my shoes.

"I understand. Don't worry. I have been here too, remember?" I put my hand on the stocky man's shoulder.

Jimmy looked Fred and then me straight in the eyes. "Mr. Rhodes, Mr. Colson, today we failed to stand up for Jesus. It will never happen again. Never again."

The words were like cold steel. They meant it.

Preparations for the week's seminar at Sandstone, Minnesota, began immediately. My concern about Sandstone was not so much its location, nearly as remote as Oxford, but its new warden, Max Mustain. The men in Minneapolis who had been visiting the prison reported that Mustain was receptive to our work, but my memories of him at Petersburg, Virginia, were of an aloof and inscrutable man who paralyzed his own staff with fear.

The seminar at Sandstone was scheduled to coincide with the Minnesota governor's prayer breakfast at which I was to speak. Sometime during the course of my talk I mentioned that I would be going to Sandstone Prison that afternoon. Afterwards out of the crowd that gathered at the head table, a tall, dark-haired man approached me. "What time are you going to Sandstone this afternoon?"

"We're flying up around 4 P.M.," I replied.

"May I join you?"

I shook my head. "Sorry, but I'm afraid it's too late to clear anyone else to visit that prison today."

He glared at me for a moment, then his facial muscles relaxed and he smiled. "I'll get in," he said, eyes twinkling.

The chairman of the breakfast, who had been silently watching the exchange, tugged at my arm. "Do you know who that was?"

"I'm sorry, but I don't."

"That was Miles Lord, senior judge of the U.S. District Court. He is probably responsible for putting away two-thirds of the inmates in Sandstone."

I gasped. What an incredible goof!

Miles Lord, former Minnesota attorney general, good friend of the late Senator Hubert Humphrey and outspoken civil libertarian, was not someone I had expected to see at the prayer breakfast. I was told that he could be a powerful ally or an implacable foe.

We learned later that Judge Lord returned to the federal courthouse after breakfast, canceled his calendar for the day, recruited a junior judge and his own pastor as companions and ordered a car for the drive to Sandstone. The officials at the prison had no idea two federal judges would be attending our seminar until they arrived at the front gate around noon.

The visit of a judge is a major event in any prison. I've heard of prisons repainted, menus changed, and regulations rewritten in anticipation of a judge's tour.

Inmates told us later that undisguised panic hit Sandstone from the minute the nearly tongued-tied guard at the front gate called the warden's office with the stunning announcement that two judges had arrived for a visit. Lord was never one to stand on formalities either, as he strode through the prison, checking little details, stopping frequently for talks with the inmates.

"Freddie, I didn't know you were still here," he exclaimed to one of the many familiar faces.

"Yes, Your Honor, but I'm ready to get out." Freddie was an older man with a long record.

"If I let you out tonight what will happen to you? Will you end up again in my court?"

Freddie's arms hung limply at his sides as he bowed his head and mumbled, "Probably so, Judge."

"Freddie, what I want you to do is go to the chapel tonight with Colson and those others and get your life straightened out. Then I'll send you home." With that the judge slapped him on the back and walked out.

We also heard that another inmate had told the judge that he had just mailed a motion to his court asking that his sentence be reduced. He tearfully pleaded for mercy, explaining that his wife was sick, a child had run away, and the bank was foreclosing his mortgage.

"Come to the chapel tonight. I'll decide there," the judge replied.

By 5:45 P.M. there was not a square foot of empty space in the chapel. Shoulders were pressed together in every pew; 250 men, it appeared, were squeezed into seats designed for 200. The aisles were so full we had difficulty getting down front. I had never seen such a crowd in any prison for any occasion.

Something else was different. I quickly realized the uniforms were spotless, many looked starched, and every inmate's face was scrubbed bright. The impact of the judge's presence was overwhelming. Nervously, I wondered how he would react to us.

I saw him in the fourth row grinning contentedly and surrounded by brown-shirted inmates. When the program started, I called on him to say a few words.

"Well, it is good to see so many old friends here tonight." His opening sentence was drowned out by laughter. "I appreciate the introduction by Mr. Colson. When he was in the White House I believed he was responsible for everything evil in the country, including *wounded knee*." (A reference to Wounded Knee, South Dakota, where a shoot-out had taken place between radical Indian groups and government forces.)

Uproarious laughter followed; the inmates were eating it up.

"I went to hear him this morning, expecting to see right through this phony. But something happened and I'm not sure what. So I decided to come and hear him again."

At this point the judge swung around and pointed menacingly at me. "Now don't try to convert me, Colson. I brought my pastor along for protection."

The judge turned back to the audience, grinning. "I could issue an order cutting all of you loose tonight." Loud applause and cheers. "But it is more important for you to be right here. All I can do is save your butts."

Then he pointed at me in a grand sweeping gesture.

"He . . ." his voice rose triumphantly. "He can save your soul."

I tried to point upward to the "Him" Judge Lord was really referring to, but in one of the most startling developments of the evening, it was the warden, Max Mustain, who did it best. At the close of the program the warden stood up before the audience. I had remembered him as hard and ruthless. Over the past year a transformation had taken place in his life. His eyes were shining, his voice was filled with emotion.

"I've been around prisoners a long time," he said, "and I've tried out a lot of programs to help these men. Let me tell you my conclusion: Only God can change a man and that's the message of this evening."

It was one of the most amazing nights I've spent in any prison. The judge said he would release the man with the personal hardships and set times for hearings on other cases as he held court informally by the speaker's rostrum.

Chaplain Norm Nissen, who indicated his legitimate doubts about us during our first visit to Sandstone, was eagerly signing up inmates for our "in-prison seminar"; there were more than we could accommodate. Nissen had become a valued friend.

Later I spotted Dave Rolschau. "Are you thinking what I'm thinking?" I called to him.

He nodded. "A year and a half ago we couldn't find one Christian in this prison. Now the place is like a church. It's unbelievable."

The timing was God-sent in my own life too, fortifying me for the toughest test yet.

HENRI NOUWEN (B. 1932)

It may appear to stretch the boundaries of this book to include a meditation by a Dutch priest concerning experiences in South America. Yet because of Henri Nouwen's great impact in North America as an author and a writer, and because his voice speaks for many who struggle to comprehend the love of an eternal Father in the very temporal realities of our world, his contribution is most appropriate.

Henri Nouwen was born and educated in the Netherlands, where he was also ordained in 1957 as a Catholic priest. His ministry to the United States began with the printed page and then was broadened through the more than ten years that he spent as a professor at the Divinity School of Yale University. Father Nouwen's many books are marked by his sensitivity to the realities of human suffering, whether that suffering arises from within, as does psychological torment, or from without, as does economic and political oppression. Even more, he has been able to restate forcefully the fundamental Christian belief that those who would bear the suffering of others must first share in that suffering themselves. In particular, his book *The Wounded Healer* (1972) demonstrates the contemporary relevance of this conviction. In other works Nouwen has tried to show how a whole range of human experiences—from merriment to meditation, from contemplating Scripture to confronting death—may lead to deeper levels of spiritual maturity.

Father Nouwen now devotes most of his time to pastoral work in Latin America. In late 1981 and early 1982 he spent six months in Bolivia and Peru, attempting to discover if it was the will of God for him to leave Yale and the instruction of North American seminarians to take up a mission in South America. During this time he studied Spanish, explored local conditions in the church, pondered the appropriate Christian response to political conflict and economic injustice, and sought advice from Catholic and Protestant missionaries in the region.

As he learned new things about Latin America and came nearer to reaching decisions about his own future, Father Nouwen also paused to reflect on the spiritual significance of his experiences. The result was *Gracias! A Latin American Journal* (1983). This book ranges widely in its commentary but rarely strays far from one central question: How does God deal with individuals in the world of the late twentieth century? Nouwen's journal shows that amid the bewildering particularities of his new experience, certain basic truths became clearer to him, including what it means to affirm the existence of God. The following meditation, dated November 21, 1981, is taken from that journal.

From *Gracias! A Latin American Journal*

God exists. When I can say this with all that I am, I have the "gnosis" (the knowledge of God) about which St. John speaks and the "Memoria Dei" (the memory of God) about which St. Basil writes. To say with all that we have, think, feel, and are: "God exists," is the most world-shattering statement that a human being can make. When we make that statement, all the distinctions between intellectual, emotional, affective, and spiritual understanding fall away and there is only one truth left to acclaim: God exists. When we say this from the heart, everything trembles in heaven and on earth. Because when God exists, all that *is* flows from him. When I want to know if I ever have come to the true knowledge, the gnosis, of God's existence, I have simply to allow myself to become aware of how I experience myself. It doesn't take much to realize that I am constantly with myself. I am aware of all of the various parts of my body, and I "know" when I am hurting and when not. I am aware of my desire for food and clothing and shelter. I am aware of my sexual urges and my need for intimacy and community. I am aware of my feelings of pity, compassion, and solidarity, my ability to be of service and my hope to give a helping hand. I am aware of my intellectual, physical, and artistic skills and my drive to use them. I am aware of my anger, my lust, my feelings of revenge and resentment, and even at times of my desire to harm. Indeed, what is central to me is: *I exist*. My own existence fills me, and wherever I turn I find myself again locked in my own self-awareness: I exist. Although experiences of hatred are different from experiences of love, and although a desire for power is different from a desire to serve, they all are the same insofar as they identify *my* existence as what *really* counts.

However, as soon as I say, "God exists," my existence no longer can remain in the center, because the essence of the knowledge of God reveals my own existence as deriving its total being from his. That is the true conversion

Source: *Gracias! A Latin American Journal* (San Francisco: Harper & Row, 1983), pp. 47-50.

experience. I no longer let the knowledge of my existence be the center from which I derive, project, deduct, or intuit the existence of God; I suddenly or slowly find my own existence revealed to me in and through the knowledge of God. Then it becomes real for me that I can love myself and my neighbor only because God has loved me first. The life-converting experience is not the discovery that I have choices to make that determine the way I live out my existence, but the awareness that my existence itself is not in the center. Once I "know" God, that is, once I experience his love and the love in which all my human experiences are anchored, I can only desire one thing: to be in that love. "Being" anywhere else, then, is shown to be illusory and eventually lethal.

All of these reflections have taken a new urgency for me, during these weeks in Bolivia. It slowly dawned on me that so much, if not most, of our energy and attention goes to the question of our own existence. We wonder how we are doing, how we feel, how we will serve in Latin America, and how we will organize our next day, weekend, year, or decade. We try hard to make responsible and moral choices that give us a sense that at least we are searching in the right direction. But all of this, the good as well as the bad, the responsible as well as the irresponsible, the acts of lust as well as the acts of service, lose their power over us when we realize that God exists, before and after, in the past and in the future, now and forever, and that in and through the knowledge of that divine existence I might get a glimpse of why there is an I and a he, she, we, and they. Then all questions have only one answer: God. What am I supposed to think about? About God, because all thoughts find their creative power in him. What am I supposed to say? His Word, because all my words are fruitful to the degree that they are a reflection of his. What am I supposed to do? His will, because his will is the loving desire that gave existence to all that is, myself included.

Is it better to be in Bolivia, in Peru, in the United States, or in Holland? Is it better to give a glass of water to a thirsty child or to work on a new world order in which children will no longer beg for water? Is it better to read a book or to walk on the street, to write a letter or bind the wounds of a dying man? Is it better to do this or that, say this or that, think about this or that? All these questions suddenly appear to me as false preoccupations, as a captivity in the illusory concern about my own existence, as an expression of my supposition that God depends on me, that his existence is derived from mine.

Nothing is real without deriving its reality from God. This was the great discovery of St. Francis when he suddenly saw the whole world in God's hands and wondered why God didn't drop it. St. Augustine, St. Teresa of Avila, St. John Vianney, and all the saints are saints precisely because for them the order of being was turned around and they saw, felt, and—above all—knew with their heart that outside God nothing is, nothing breathes, nothing moves, and nothing lives.

This makes me aware that the basis of all ministry rests not in the moral life but in the mystical life. The issue is not to live as well as we can, but to let our life be one that finds its source in the Divine Life.

God exists, and the meaning of all that I am depends totally on that knowledge. I wonder constantly if I am genuinely allowing my life to be determined by that truth. Maybe part of my reason for hesitating to embrace this truth fully is that it challenges me to give up all control over my life and to let God be God, my God, the God of my neighbor, and the God of all creation. But I also realize that as long as I do not "do" this, my life is an illusion and most of my energy is spoiled in trying to keep that illusion going.

Does all of this mean that my thoughts, plans, projects, and ideas no longer matter? That conclusion has been drawn by people who used the spiritual life as a way to manipulate others and that conclusion has led, sadly enough, to false views on asceticism, obedience, surrender to God's will, and certain forms of self-denial. The converted person does not say that nothing matters anymore, but that everything that is happens in God and that he is the dwelling place where we come to know the true order of things. Instead of saying: "Nothing matters any more, since I know that God exists," the converted person says: "All is now clothed in divine light and therefore nothing can be unimportant." The converted person sees, hears, and understands with a divine eye, a divine ear, a divine heart. The converted person knows himself or herself and all the world in God. The converted person *is* where God is, and from that place everything matters: giving water, clothing the naked, working for a new world order, saying a prayer, smiling at a child, reading a book, and sleeping in peace. All has become different while all remains the same.

Somehow I feel that all these reflections are important for me in a time during which I have to make some very concrete decisions. The "nothing matters" and the "everything matters" should never be separated in a time such as this. What brings them together is the unceasing cry coming from the heart: "God exists."

JOHN UPDIKE (B. 1932)

Considered by many to be the most talented writer of his generation, John Updike has received acclaim and numerous awards for his poetry, fiction, and nonfictional prose. He is best known, however, as a short-story writer and novelist. From his first novel, *The Poorhouse Fair* (1958), to the recent *Rabbit Is Rich* (1981), Updike has attempted, in his words, "to transcribe middleness with all its grits, bumps and anonymities, in its fullness of satisfaction and mystery."

In the early stages of his career, Updike conducted this exploration in a way that was self-consciously, and at times explicitly, Christian. (He had been raised in a Lutheran home in the small town of Shillington, Pennsylvania.) A number of his early stories dealt with crises of faith experienced by boys and young men. And his early nonfiction frequently delved into what he saw to be the glorious complexities of figures such as Søren Kierkegaard and Karl Barth.

The novels in the Rabbit series—*Rabbit, Run, Rabbit Redux,* and *Rabbit Is Rich*—chart the course of an erstwhile spiritual seeker. In the first of these novels, young Rabbit tells a minister, "Well, I don't know all about this theology, but I'll tell you, I do feel, I guess, that somewhere behind all this . . . there's something that wants me to find it." But, like so many of Updike's characters, Rabbit has precious little energy to put into a demanding search. He "has no taste for the dark, tangled, visceral aspect of Christianity, the going through quality of it, the passage into death and suffering that redeems." Unable to endure demands upon his soul, Rabbit "lacks the mindful will to walk the straight line of a paradox. His eyes turn toward the light however it glances into his retina."

The following selection is an early short story dealing with what seem to be Updike's ever-present themes of faith and lust. A young seminary student who works summers as a lifeguard is nagged by doubts and driven by spiritual and sexual desires; he is almost too conscious of himself and too aware of the demands of his glands to be wholehearted in his devotion to God. In lucid and supple prose, Updike explores the troubling possibilities of piety for an earnest young man in a decidedly post-Christian world.

Lifeguard

Beyond doubt, I am a splendid fellow. In the autumn, winter, and spring, I execute the duties of a student of divinity; in the summer I disguise myself in my skin and become a lifeguard. My slightly narrow and gingerly hirsute but not necessarily unmanly chest becomes brown. My smooth back turns the color of caramel, which, in conjunction with the whipped cream of my white pith helmet, gives me, some of my teenage satellites assure me, a delightfully edible appearance. My legs, which I myself can study, cocked as they are before me while I repose on my elevated wooden throne, are dyed a lustreless maple walnut that accentuates their articulate strength. Correspondingly, the hairs of my body are bleached blond, so that my legs have the pointed elegance of, within the flower, umber anthers dusted with pollen.

For nine months of the year, I pace my pale hands and burning eyes through immense pages of Biblical text barnacled with fudging commentary; through multivolumed apologetics couched in a falsely friendly Victorian voice and bound in subtly abrasive boards of finely ridged, prefaded red; through handbooks of liturgy and histories of dogma; through the bewildering duplicities of Tillich's divine politicking; through the suave table talk of Father D'Arcy, Etienne Gilson, Jacques Maritain, and other such moderns mistakenly put at their ease by the exquisite antique furniture and overstuffed larder of the hospitable St. Thomas; through the terrifying attempts of Kierkegaard, Berdyaev, and Barth to scourge God into being. I sway appalled on the ladder of minus signs by which theologians would surmount the void. I tiptoe like a burglar into the house of naturalism to steal the silver. An acrobat, I swing from wisp to wisp. Newman's iridescent cobwebs crush in my hands. Pascal's blackboard mathematics are erased by a passing shoulder. The cave drawings, astoundingly vital by candlelight, of those aboriginal magicians, Paul and Augustine, in daylight fade into mere anthropology. The diverting productions of literary flirts like Chesterton, Eliot, Auden, and Greene—whether they regard Christianity as a pastel forest designed for a fairyland romp or a deliciously miasmic pit from which chiaroscuro can be mined with mechanical buckets—in the end all infallibly strike, despite the comic variety of gongs and mallets, the note of the rich young man who on the coast of Judaea refused in dismay to sell all that he had.

Then, for the remaining quarter of the solar revolution, I rest my eyes on a sheet of brilliant sand printed with the runes of naked human bodies. That

Source: *Pigeon Feathers and Other Stories* (Greenwich, Conn.: Fawcett Crest, 1962).

there is no discrepancy between my studies, that the texts of the flesh complement those of the mind, is the easy burden of my sermon.

On the back rest of my lifeguard's chair is painted a cross—true, a red cross, signifying bandages, splints, spirits of ammonia, and sunburn unguents. Nevertheless, it comforts me. Each morning, as I mount into my chair, my athletic and youthfully fuzzy toes expertly gripping the slats that make a ladder, it is as if I am climbing into an immense, rigid, loosely fitting vestment.

Again, in each of my roles I sit attentively perched on the edge of an immensity. That the sea, with its multiform and mysterious hosts, its savage and senseless rages, no longer comfortably serves as a divine metaphor indicates how severely humanism has corrupted the apples of our creed. We seek God now in flowers and good deeds, and the immensities of blue that surround the little scabs of land upon which we draw our lives to their unsatisfactory conclusions are suffused by science with vacuous horror. I myself can hardly bear the thought of stars, or begin to count the mortalities of coral. But from my chair the sea, slightly distended by my higher perspective, seems a misty old gentleman stretched at his ease in an immense armchair which has for arms the arms of this bay and for an antimacassar the freshly laundered sky. Sailboats float on his surface like idle and unrelated but benevolent thoughts. The soughing of the surf is the rhythmic lifting of his ripple-stitched vest as he breathes. Consider. We enter the sea with a shock; our skin and blood shout in protest. But, that instant, that leap, past, what do we find? Ecstasy and buoyance. Swimming offers a parable. We struggle and thrash, and drown; we succumb, even in despair, and float, and are saved.

With what timidity, with what a sense of trespass, do I set forward even this obliquely a thought so official! Forgive me. I am not yet ordained; I am too disordered to deal with the main text. My competence is marginal, and I will confine myself to the gloss of flesh with which this particular margin, this one beach, is annotated each day.

Here the cinema of life is run backwards. The old are the first to arrive. They are idle, and have lost the gift of sleep. Each of our bodies is a clock that loses time. Young as I am, I can hear in myself the protein acids ticking; I wake at odd hours and in the shuddering darkness and silence feel my death rushing toward me like an express train. The older we get, and the fewer mornings left to us, the more deeply dawn stabs us awake. The old ladies wear wide straw hats and, in their hats' shadows, smiles as wide, which they bestow upon each other, upon salty shells they discover in the morning-smooth sand, and even upon me, downy-eyed from my night of dissipation. The gentlemen are often incongruous; withered white legs support brazen barrel chests, absurdly potent, bustling with white froth. How these old roosters preen on their "condition"! With what fatuous expertness they swim in the icy water—always, however, prudently parallel to the shore, at a depth no greater than their height.

Then come the middle-aged, burdened with children and aluminum chairs. The men are scarred with the marks of their vocation—the red forearms of the gasoline-station attendant, the pale X on the back of the overall-wearing mason or carpenter, the clammer's nicked ankles. The hair on their bodies has as many patterns as matted grass. The women are wrinkled but fertile, like the Iraqi rivers that cradled the seeds of our civilization. Their children are odious. From their gaunt faces leer all the vices, the greeds, the grating urgencies of the adult, unsoftened by maturity's reticence and fatigue. Except that here and there, a girl, the eldest daughter, wearing a knit suit striped horizontally with green, purple, and brown, walks slowly, carefully, puzzled by the dawn enveloping her thick smooth body, her waist not yet nipped but her throat elongated.

Finally come the young. The young matrons bring fat and fussing infants who gobble the sand like sugar, who toddle blissfully into the surf and bring me bolt upright on my throne. My whistle tweets. The mothers rouse. Many of these women are pregnant again, and sluggishly lie in their loose suits like cows tranced in a meadow. They gossip politics, and smoke incessantly, and lift their troubled eyes in wonder as a trio of flat-stomached nymphs parades past. These maidens take all our eyes. The vivacious redhead, freckled and white-footed, pushing against her boy and begging to be ducked; the solemn brunette, transporting the vase of herself with held breath; the dimpled blonde in the bib and diapers of her Bikini, the lambent fuzz of her midriff shimmering like a cat's belly. Lust stuns me like the sun.

You are offended that a divinity student lusts? What prigs the unchurched are. Are not our assaults on the supernatural lascivious, a kind of indecency? If only you knew what de Sadian degradations, what frightful psychological spelunking, our gentle transcendentalist professors set us to, as preparation for our work, which is to shine in the darkness.

I feel that my lust makes me glow; I grow cold in my chair, like a torch of ice, as I study beauty. I have studied much of it, wearing all style of bathing suit and expression, and have come to this conclusion: a woman's beauty lies, not in any exaggeration of the specialized zones, nor in any general harmony that could be worked out by means of the *sectio aurea* or a similar aesthetic superstition; but in the arabesque of the spine. The curve by which the back modulates into the buttocks. It is here that grace sits and rides a woman's body.

I watch from my white throne and pity women, deplore the demented judgment that drives them toward the braggart muscularity of the mesomorph and the prosperous complacence of the endomorph when it is we ectomorphs who pack in our scrawny sinews and exacerbated nerves the most intense gift, the most generous shelter, of love. To desire a woman is to desire to save her. Anyone who has endured intercourse that was neither predatory nor hurried knows how through it we descend, with a partner, into the grotesque and delicate shadows that until then have remained locked in the most guarded recess of our soul: into this harbor we bring her. A vague and twisted terrain becomes inhabited; each shadow, touched by the exploration, blooms, into a flower of act. As if we are an island upon which a woman, tossed by her laboring vanity and blind self-seeking, is blown, and there finds security, until, an instant before the anticlimax, Nature with a smile thumps down her trump, and the island sinks beneath the sea.

There is great truth in those motion pictures which are slandered as true neither to the Bible nor to life. They are—written though they are by demons and drunks—true to both. We are all Solomons lusting for Sheba's salvation. The God-filled man is filled with a wilderness that cries to be populated. The stony chambers need jewels, furs, tints of cloth and flesh, even though, as in Samson's case, the temple comes tumbling. Women are an alien race of pagans set down among us. Every seduction is a conversion.

Who has loved and not experienced that sense of rescue? It is not true that our biological impulses are tricked out with ribands of chivalry; rather, our chivalric impulses go clanking in encumbering biological armor. Eunuchs love. Children love. I would love.

My chief exercise, as I sit above the crowds, is to lift the whole mass into immortality. It is not a light task; the throng is so huge, and its members so individually unworthy. No *memento mori* is so clinching as a photograph of a vanished crowd. Cheering Roosevelt, celebrating the Armistice, there it is, wearing its ten thousand straw hats and stiff collars, a fearless and wooden-faced bustle of life: it is gone. A crowd dies in the street like a derelict; it leaves no heir, no trace, no name. My own persistence beyond the last rim of time is easy to imagine; indeed, the effort of imagination lies the other way— to conceive of my ceasing. But when I study the vast tangle of humanity that blackens the beach as far as the sand stretches, absurdities crowd in on me. Is it as maiden, matron, or crone that the females will be eternalized? What will they do without children to watch and gossip to exchange? What of the thousand deaths of memory and bodily change we endure—can each be redeemed at a final Adjustments Counter? The sheer numbers involved make the mind scream. The race is no longer a tiny clan of simian aristocrats lording it over an ocean of grass; mankind is a plague racing like fire across the exhausted continents. This immense clot gathered on the beach, a fraction of a fraction—can we not say that this breeding swarm is its own immortality and end the suspense? The beehive in a sense survives; and is each of us not proved to be a hive, a galaxy of cells each of whom is doubtless praying, from its pew in our thumbnail or esophagus, for personal resurrection? Indeed, to the cells themselves cancer may seem a revival of faith. No, in relation to other people oblivion is sensible and sanitary.

This sea of others exasperates and fatigues me most on Sunday mornings. I don't know why people no longer go to church—whether they have lost the ability to sing or the willingness to listen. From eight-thirty onward they crowd in from the parking lots, ants each carrying its crumb of baggage, until by noon, when the remote churches are releasing their gallant and gaily dressed minority, the sea itself is jammed with hollow heads and thrashing arms like a great bobbing backwash of rubbish. A transistor radio somewhere in the sand releases in a thin, apologetic gust the closing peal of a transcribed service. And right here, here at the very height of torpor and confusion, I slump, my eyes slit, and the blurred forms of Protestantism's errant herd seem gathered by the water's edge in impassioned poses of devotion. I seem to be lying dreaming in the infinite rock of space before Creation, and the actual scene I see is a vision of impossibility: a Paradise. For had we existed before the gesture that split the firmament, could we have conceived of our most obvious possession, our most platitudinous blessing, the moment, the single ever-present moment that we perpetually bring to our lips brimful?

So: be joyful. Be Joyful in my commandment. It is the message I read in your jiggle. Stretch your skins like pegged hides curing in the miracle of the sun's moment. Exult in your leg's scissoring, your waist's swivel. Romp; eat the froth; be children. I am here above you; I have given my youth that you may do this. I wait. The tides of time have treacherous undercurrents. You are borne continually toward the horizon. I have prepared myself; my muscles are instilled with everything that must be done. Someday my alertness will bear fruit; from near the horizon there will arise, delicious, translucent, like a green bell above the water, the call for help, the call, a call, it saddens me to confess, that I have yet to hear.

THOMAS HOWARD (B. 1935)

Thomas Howard is a member of a family with deep roots in the fundamentalist and evangelical traditions. His father, Phillip, was the editor of *The Sunday School Times;* his brother David is a prominent evangelical missions leader; and his sister Elisabeth was married to the missionary martyr Jim Elliot and is a well-known author and lecturer whose work is also represented in this book. Tom Howard is himself a noted speaker and author.

Howard came to public attention initially in 1967 with the publication of his first book, *Christ the Tiger,* an autobiographical work that vividly describes his struggle to come to terms with his fundamentalist heritage. This book struck a responsive chord in the generation of evangelical students coming to maturity in the 1960s. What they found in Howard was an articulate, inventive spokesman who captured their desire to retain the Christian faith, but a faith engaged in an aggressive dialogue with contemporary culture. Howard's early works celebrated the importance of the arts—of film and fiction, of poetry and painting—for the Christian faith. To young Christians who had been nurtured in a piety that was spiritually intense but aesthetically impoverished, Howard offered the promise of visual and verbal renewal.

Throughout the 1970s, Howard continued to write while he served as professor of English at the evangelical Gordon College in Wenham, Massachusetts. In that decade his written work concentrated increasingly on the church's sacramental experience and on the broad sweep of its doctrinal traditions. By the early 1980s Howard's frustration with the evangelical tradition was readily apparent, and in 1985 he made a widely publicized conversion to the Roman Catholic Church. Shortly thereafter he resigned his teaching position at Gordon.

The work of Thomas Howard presents a curious amalgam of several strains in the traditions of American piety. Like many before him, he has grown disenchanted with the paucity of rich symbols in the heritage of American Protestantism; he has turned to the Catholic tradition for spiritual and aesthetic sustenance. Yet even when Howard has sought to distance himself from his fundamentalist roots, he has shown clearly the imprint of his heritage, especially in seeking the intense spiritual experience that has been a hallmark of the fundamentalist tradition.

The selection that follows is from the concluding pages of *Christ the Tiger.* Its meditation upon the call to "receive Christ" captures something of the restless-

388

ness that over the course of three decades has driven Howard through a series of
theological changes and has brought him at last into the Roman Catholic
Church.

From *Christ the Tiger*

What then? Was this the announcement of pie in the sky by and by? Was it
the offer of escape from the actualities of existence into a euphoric Eden
where honeysuckle vines cut off the view of horror and terror? Was it the
invitation to join a small illuminati who would be exempted from dread and
risk and anguish? Was it a guarantee of safety and warmth and certitude and
predictability?

I could not think so.

But I could think that in the figure of Jesus we saw Immanuel, that is, God,
that is, Love. It was a figure who, appearing so inauspiciously among us,
broke up our secularist and our religious categories, and beckoned us and
judged us and damned us and saved us, and exhibited to us a kind of life that
participates in the indestructible. And it was a figure who announced the
validity of our eternal effort to discover significance and beauty beyond
inanition and horror by announcing to us the unthinkable: redemption.

It was a figure we could neither own nor manage. We claimed it as our
special possession, and exacted tribute and built shrines and established
forms in which to incarcerate it, only to discover that it had fled. It would not
be enshrined. It was the figure of a man, and a man must live and walk with
other men or die, and this man was alive. He scorned our scruple to shelter
him and to prop up his doctrine. What he spoke, he spoke loudly and freely,
and his words were their own defense. When we tried to help things by
urging sweetness and light, or by interdicting what looked threatening, or by
tithing mint, anise, and cummin, or by devising rituals and nonrituals, we
found him towering above us, scorching our efforts into clinkers, and recall-
ing us to wildness and risk and humility and love. Just at the moment when
we thought we had guaranteed our own standing in his good favor by
organizing an airtight doctrine or a flawless liturgy or an unassailable morality, he escaped us, and returned with his hammer to demolish things. Try as
we might, we could not own him. We could not protect him. We could not

---

Source: *Christ the Tiger* (Philadelphia: J. B. Lippincott, 1967), pp. 153-60.

incarcerate him. For he always emerged as our judge, exposing our cynicism and fright by the candor and boldness of his love. He tore our secularist schemes to ribbons by announcing doom and our religious schemes to tatters by announcing love.

He appeared as a man and demonstrated a kind of life wholly foreign to all of our inclinations. For he showed us what a man's life is like when it is energized by *caritas*, and in doing this, he became our judge, because we knew too well that it is that other love, *cupiditas*, that energizes us. He told us of a city, the City of God, in which *caritas* rules. He told us that all who participate in this are citizens of that city.

We experienced this announcement as both death-dealing and life-giving. It was death-dealing because we knew our own incorrigible cupidity—the energy that makes us shriek for the shovel in the sandbox, cut into the ticket line, rush for the subway seat, display our prowess, parade our clothes, and pursue delights regardless of prior considerations.

We remembered our own torrid yearning, for instance, for other bodies, and our insistence that we must seek satisfaction at all costs because this was such an ecstatic bliss. And he said to us, yes, yes, yes, you are quite right, another body *is* the most beautiful thing in the world. This kind of congress *is* ecstatic bliss, but your unexamined pursuit of this will, irony of ironies, dehumanize you, for it is a failure to ask the questions that must be asked—questions about the *imago Dei* in you and your partner, questions about sex as a form of knowledge that requires a high warrant, questions about sex as a metaphor of realities that lie at the heart of everything, and questions about the undying notion in all of us of sex as significant and binding and most holy.

And what is true here is true in all regions of experience. Your mad pursuit is for freedom and intensity and bliss. It is natural. But, by a wry irony at work in the world, the pursuit leads you into a prison where your agony is to become more and more insistent that things shall be as you wish, and less and less able to cope with denial.

But I show you a different way. It is an alien and a frightening one. It is called Love. It asks that you forswear your busy effort to collect the bits of bliss and novelty that lie about. It asks that you disavow your attempt to enlarge your own identity by diminishing that of others. It asks that you cease your effort to safeguard your own claim to well-being by assuming the inferiority of others' claims. It asks, actually, that you die.

For, paradoxically, it offers to you your own best being beyond this apparent immolation of yourself. It says that the cupidity energizing all your efforts is the principle that governs wherever hell is found, and that the dwellers in that realm are a withered host of wraiths, doomed to an eternal hunt for solidity and fulfillment among the shards that lie underfoot. This is not your best being. You were meant to find your home in the City of God, which is among you. Here duty is ecstasy. For that is what is meant by *caritas:* it is the freedom which follows upon the capacity to experience as joy what you are given to do.

But the City is not reached in a moment. It is as remote as the Towers of Trebizond, and as near as your neighbor.

And we experienced his announcement as death dealing again, because it knocked over all the little pickets and wickets that we had tapped carefully into place to guarantee the safety of our religion. He saw our masses and rosaries and prayer meetings and study groups and devotions, and he said yes, yes, yes, you are quite right to think that goodness demands rigor and vigilance and observance, but your new moons and sabbaths and bullocks and altars and vestments and Gospel teams and taboos and Bible studies are trumpery, and they nauseate me because you have elevated *them,* and I alone am the Host. Your incense is foetid, and your annotated Bibles are rubbish paper. Your meetings are a bore and your myopic exegesis is suffocating. Return, return, and think again what I have asked of you: to follow justice, and love mercy, and do your job of work, and love one another, and give me the worship of your heart—your *heart*—and be merry and thankful and lowly and not pompous and gaunt and sere.

But we experienced the announcement as life-giving because it was an announcement, appearing in a dirty barn, and heard among the dry provincial hills and then in the forum of Rome and in the halls of royal princes and in the kitchens and streets of Paris and Calcutta and Harlem and Darien, that Joy and not Havoc is the last word. It announced to us what we could not hope. It saw limitation and contingency and disparity and irrevocability and mutability and decay and death, and it said yes, yes, yes, you are quite right: terror and horror and despair are the only eventually realistic responses . . . *if* this is all there is to it. But it is not.

You have thought of a world free from such conditions. In all your imaginings, and in your myths and your mime and your songs and dances and epics—in your quest for form and significance and beauty beyond fragmentation and inanition and chaos—you have bespoken such a vision. I announce it to you. Here, from this stable, here, from this Nazareth, this stony beach, this Jerusalem, this market place, this garden, this praetorium, this Cross, this mountain, I announce it to you.

I announce to you what is guessed at in all the phenomena of your world. You see the corn of wheat shrivel and break open and die, but you expect a crop. I tell you of the Springtime of which all springtimes speak. I tell you of the world for which this world groans and toward which it strains. I tell you that beyond the awful borders imposed by time and space and contingency, there lies what you seek. I announce to you life instead of mere existence,

freedom instead of frustration, justice instead of compensation. For I announce to you redemption. Behold I make all things new. Behold I do what
cannot be done. I restore the years that the locusts and worms have eaten. I
restore the years which you have drooped away upon your crutches and in
your wheel-chair. I restore the symphonies and operas which your deaf ears
have never heard, and the snowy massif your blind eyes have never seen, and
the freedom lost to you through plunder, and the identity lost to you because
of calumny and the failure of justice; and I restore the good which your own
foolish mistakes have cheated you of. And I bring you to the Love of which
all other loves speak, the Love which is joy and beauty, and which you have
sought in a thousand streets and for which you have wept and clawed your
pillow.

So there is this, I thought, as an alternative to despair. At least it is not
meliorism or optimism. But the *peril* of staking everything on this kind of
vision . . . Incarnation. Redemption. These are far from verifiable, and this is
ridiculous in an age that insists on verification.

And *caritas*. This is impossible. How is a man to opt for a kind of life in
which he stands to lose everything? I mean, if you want to get a seat on the
subway you have to push for it. *Tant pis* for the one who has to stand. And if
you want the ecstasies, you have to go flat out to accumulate them. How can
a man be expected to opt out of everything that looks important on the
chance that there is more to it all than meets the eye? It is too great a risk.

Perhaps that is what is asked, I thought. Perhaps there is no escape from
risk. Perhaps there is no explanation offered for the staggering ambiguities,
nor any answer given to the agonizing questions. Perhaps a man is asked to
opt with all his might for authenticity. Perhaps the great thing is to respond,
with as much integrity as he can summon, to the cues. There *are* some—in his
own consciousness, in his art, in his world. And there is this great light that
has appeared in the murk, like a morning star. It is there, silent and glorious.
An odd road marker. But perhaps a man is asked to go that way on the
supposition that it is not all a ghastly cheat.

Yes. Perhaps that is what is asked.

VIRGINIA STEM OWENS (B. 1941)

Stock themes of the Christian faith are always threatened by a process of abstraction. Ministers, theologians, Sunday-school teachers, and lay people in their private religious reading regularly rehearse propositions like "the flesh is frail," "Jesus partook of human nature," "Christ suffered for us," and "we should serve our fellow humans for Jesus' sake." True as these statements are, they have little to do with actual reverence for God until they themselves become a part of human experience. In the modern world, however, the kind of elemental human experience that forms the essential context for these statements is at a premium. Our desires lead us to insulate ourselves from the tangles of life. In a society dominated by technique, it is too easy to write a check in response to human crises, to get our religion through the TV set, to hide our failures from our neighbors, or to pretend that healthy life can continue forever.

Virginia Stem Owens, a free-lance writer who has worked as a beekeeper, a houseparent for mentally retarded boys, and a library cataloguer, has paid special attention to the way in which the shape of modern life blunts the reality of the world. Her books—including *The Total Image,* which explores the incompatibility between the marketing of Jesus through television and the meaningful apprehension of the Christian faith—have argued eloquently for the necessity of face-to-face human experience. The following article makes the same point with even greater force. By paying particular attention to the wounded, Owens suggests a way for the abstractions of Christian faith to themselves take on flesh.

A Hand in the Wound

I have spent quite a few hours at the V.A. hospital this winter. Although I go there under the guise of comforting, consoling, and cheering the patients, my real reasons are almost unspeakable. I go there to see human bodies and

Source: *The Reformed Journal,* Apr. 1981, pp. 14-15.

what can happen to them. If my assigned tasks of pushing wheelchairs, conveying lab specimens, and clipping thick, yellow fingernails brings any solace to the patients, then I am glad. But those duties are only an excuse to infiltrate an area otherwise cordoned off, not from the curious, but from those who fear the flesh.

I get questions about this project of mine. "How can you do it? I couldn't stand it. I guess I'm just too sensitive." They may or may not be sensitive. I'm never sure what they mean by that. But I do know one thing: they're afraid. They do not want to touch, smell, see, or hear sickness, mutilation, or age. However much they diet, jog, bathe, or breathe deeply, they still fear to inhale the same air that is shared with amputees and wheezing old men.

I pass through the corridor that connects the medical ward to the nursing home wing. I sniff the air avidly. I want to know what age smells like when the tissue starts to break down. What aromas does it waft in warning? I know from my own children's diapers the peculiar scent of infant excreta, what signals a young rope of intestine learning to cope with digestion. I am learning to sniff out the scent of that rope, now frayed and fragile, from beneath the mask of disinfectant and deodorizer. Eskimos know twenty-three kinds of snow. Such discriminating perception we find interesting, even amusing, because it holds no danger for us. It is only flesh we are frightened of knowing so well.

Although we have no record of the Christ Child having so much as the sniffles, we do know that he ate, drank, sweated, and cried real tears. He also bled and died. The image of God, disfigured in Adam, was restored for us in Christ. But this process was not like the restoration of some chipped and broken statue. The image lived, and in life was driven to these extremities I seek to explore: suffering, distortion, exhaustion, agony, death.

Flesh is both miracle and monster. We watch National Geographic television specials agog at the translucent beauty of birth, the intricate interior traceries of blood, the shower of electricity that is intellect. At such times we are bold about the body. We are swept away by a Whitmanesque hymn to our physiologies. This is well. Flesh is a miracle. Its complex audacity ought to knock us off our feet and take our breath away; our sensibilities themselves are part of the miracle. We are fond of John's prologue: "And the Word became flesh and dwelt among us, full of grace and truth." The Incarnation hallows our humble earthen vessels. Two arms, two legs, two eyes, a mouth, our numbered hairs. Esophagus, eyelids, pancreas—all retrieved from being merely mechanisms.

All true. But that same apostolic witness whose words elevate us is also the one who describes for us wounds so deep that they swallow up the probing hand of Thomas.

Flesh is not just Olympic champions and Miss America. Flesh is also the sores of Lazarus, the Gerasene demoniac, the man with the withered arm, and the woman with the issue of blood. Or to put it in succinct biblical terms, flesh is grass. Fragile, vulnerable, even flammable. If the body of Christ had not partaken of that same frailty, if as the Docetists had it, his flesh was only a phantasm, if he had been Superman instead of Suffering Servant, able to leap tall buildings as Satan suggested and never hungry enough to be tempted, we might as well have stuck with Apollo or Hercules.

Christ's body was not made up of magic molecules, impervious to pain. He hadn't any bionic parts. Instead he was, according to his own testimony, broken.

Perhaps this is why I go to the hospital week after week. To stand and stare at the brokenness. To brush up against the limits, humanity *in extremis*. It is boundaries that give a shape to the image of God. Do the boundaries encompass the man with, literally, a hole in his head where the skull has been trepanned and the skin has sunken into the cranial crevasse? Or a human face, melted into mounds like candle wax, slick and shiny? And a hemorrhaged brain, consciously suffering its aphasia, spilling out broken cascades of phrases that do not fit together into a single stream of sense? The scabbing limbs still being eaten away, years after Viet Nam, by implacable phosphorus, the stubs of feet and legs covered decently now with red and green crocheted booties? All the ills the flesh is heir to. One has no right to speak about the Incarnation if he will not acknowledge the monstrous as well as the miraculous.

We are not so familiar with freaks as Jesus was. He daily handled as bad or worse than what I see weekly in the hospital. People coming to him for healing were maimed, mutilated, and desperate. They didn't even have on clean pajamas. It is we who have isolated ourselves from the Incarnation. Our fear of the flesh is so deep that we institutionalize death and decay wherever it breaks out. There would be little chance of Jesus meeting a leper on the road today. Any kind of freakishness, whether physical, mental, or emotional, must be put away from our midst. People on public view must be at least superficially healthy. The lame, the halt, and the blind may not have had Medicare in the first century, but neither were they incarcerated for their offense against the sensibilities of the whole.

Corrie ten Boom has told of the terror of having to strip naked before her concentration camp guards. The forced exposure of one's own flesh devastates us. Physical embarrassment has always been a cruel weapon of psychological warfare. In her humiliation she was sustained by the memory that Christ too, in his suffering, hung naked on the cross. Such close identity with the Incarnation saves not only our souls but our hide as well.

I used the word "saliva" in a church group the other night. People shifted their eyes uneasily. Yet it was spittle that Jesus used for a poultice on the blind man's eyes. Saliva and mud. Somehow we've gotten the idea salvation eliminates the efficacy of saliva.

I have a notion that our flight from flesh will end in more and more mechanical parts for the human body. It is the cleanliness of nylon and silicone we seem to desire, not sweat and saliva. If science can come up with a body that can eliminate elimination and reproduce itself in sterility, wouldn't we, as a culture, give not only our right arm, but the rest of our breakable bodies as well for such a trade? Faust sold only his soul; we're willing to throw in our corpses to boot.

Will not the shining substitutes of plastic parts begin to dampen our ardor for the Incarnation and dull our sense of the profoundity of our Lord's bodily death and resurrection? Are we not already a little secretly ashamed of the stripes that heal us, wishing instead for an unscathed savior, Jesus Superjock, borne aloft by teams of angels unwilling to let him stub his well-shod toe? The offense of the Cross began with the offense of the Incarnation. The bloody public death was foreshadowed by a bloody stable birth. Perhaps it is not in disease and disfigurement that we reach the limits of the image of God. Disease can be healed and disfigurement restored. But would the image fade with each cloned replica of the perfect physique equipped with replaceable parts?

I know the ambiguous morality of my hospital visits. Besides cultivating a morbid curiosity common to writers, I am hedging my bets. I want to know the worst that can happen to human flesh. Knowing the worst that can happen is a superstitious way of attaining power over the unpredictable future. Haunting the hospital is also a way of experiencing unmediated reality, of assuring myself of my own senses, of realizing my own incarnation. I go up and down the corridors like a guilty intruder, being careful not to puncture my patient's plastic bag gradually filling with amber wine. I do not deny the sad truth about my less than pure intentions. But by grace there is something more here too. As I struggle to insert the purple swollen foot of a diabetic into his slippers, I am also asserting my allegiance to the flesh, loved and not rejected by our Lord, who did not hesitate at the unhealthy, the flesh he clothed his own glory in, thus sanctifying it forever. It is my way, like Thomas the Doubter's, of slipping my hand in the wound.